1000 MOST OBSCURE WORDS

1000 MOST OBSCURE WORDS

Norman W. Schur

Facts On File
New York • Oxford • Sydney

Facts On File, Inc	Facts On File Limited	Facts On File Pty Ltd
460 Park Avenue South	Collins Street	Talavera & Khartoum Rds
New York NY 10016	Oxford OX4 1XJ	North Ryde NSW 2113
USA	United Kingdom	Australia

Library of Congress Cataloging-in-Publication Data

Schur, Norman W.
   1000 most obscure words / by Norman W. Schur.
   p.   cm.
   ISBN 0-8160-2014-0
   1. English language—Dictionaries. 2. English language-
  -Etymology—Dictionaries. 3. English language—Foreign elements-
  -Latin—Dictionaries. 4. English language—Foreign elements—Greek-
  -Dictionaries. I. Title. II. Title: One thousand most obscure
  words.
   PE1691.S37 1989
   423—dc19   88-11288

British and Australian CIP data available on request from Facts On File..

Facts On File books are available at special discounts when purchased in bulk
quantities for businesses, associations, institutions or sales promotions. Please
contact the Special Sales Department of our New York office at 212/683-2244
(dial 800/322-8755 except in NY, AK, or HI).

Composition by Facts On File, Inc.
Manufactured by Maple-Vail Manufacturing Group
Printed in the United States of America

10 9 8 7 6 5 4 3 2 1

This book is printed on acid-free paper.

For Marjorie, as always

Acknowledgments
(Written on my 81st birthday)

This is my fourth "1000 Word" book. In my previous works in this series (*1000 Most Important Words, 1000 Most Practical Words, 1000 Most Challenging Words*) I expressed my gratitude to kind and helpful friends. This time, I must add my thanks to three who have supported me throughout: Laurence Urdang, unarguably the best lexicographer I have had the good fortune to know; Paul S. Falla, a man of catholic knowledge, a genius in the world of words (I am deeply grateful not only for their help but for the friendships that have grown out of our common interest); and my son-in-law Eric Weber, a word expert in his own right, who many years ago urged me to enter the field. Without his help and encouragement I might have remained mute. I owe to Eric an unrepayable debt of gratitude for my enjoyment of a second career after a lifetime in the law. Thank you, Larry, Paul and Eric.

From time to time I have resorted to quotations given in various dictionaries, principally the *O.E.D.* and *Webster's Third*, as examples of the meaning and proper use of a headword. I am deeply conscious of the debt owed to those who have labored to uncover and amass those quotations, which might otherwise have been beyond the reach of one who toils alone.

Preface

I don't favor the use of complex words when simple ones will do. The main purpose of language is to communicate. Then why a book of obscure words? Mainly because they are fun and incidentally enlightening. I quote from a recent article by Joe D. Thomas, Professor Emeritus of English at Rice University: "One always refers to language as a tool; but after playing around with it for more years than there legitimately are, I tell you that it is also, in a vulgar phrase, *something else*. More precious than pearls of any price, it is a marvelous toy, a plaything of the mind."

The words in this collection are hardly ones you will run into, let alone use. But they are legitimate words, blessed by the cachet of established dictionaries that celebrate the wealth of our language, and the etymological material they evoke demonstrates our debt to the so-called dead languages, particularly those of Greece and Rome (though words from other sources appear as well). You may occasionally be surprised to find a familiar word among the entries, e.g., *aftermath, copy, dudgeon, ell, patriarch, relief, thesis*; they have been included only because they have certain unfamiliar, "obscure" applications.

I have written books that help in the expansion of vocabulary, books that aid, encourage and even challenge people to improve their verbal equipment. This book is different. It may have an incidental educational effect, but its main purpose is entertainment.

I take the liberty of quoting from the frontispiece of my *1000 Most Challenging Words*. First, the opening lines of a poem by Dryden:

> Latine is now of equal use become
> To Englishmen, as was the Greek to Rome;
> It guides our language, nothing is exprest
> Gracefull or true but by the Roman test.

Next, some lines from Samuel Butler's *Hudibras*:

> Beside, 'tis known he could speak Greek
> As naturally as pigs squeak:
> That Latin was no more difficile,
> Than to a black-bird 'tis to whistle.

(Obviously, *difficile* has to be pronounced di FIS il to conform to *whistle*.)

Finally, from the *Panegyric on Tom Coriate* by Lionel Cranfield, Earl of Middlesex:

> He Greek and Latin speaks with greater ease
> Than hogs eat acorns, and tame pigeons peas.

(Cranfield's couplet preceded Butler's *Hudibras* by a good many years. Would we could match the facility of Tom Coriate!)

That's the way it was once upon a time. Can we ever hope for a classical revival? (I am sure the reader understands that wherever the word *Greek* appears in the etymological discussion, I am referring to the Greek tongue of ancient times and that, to meet the needs of most contemporary readers, Greek words and combining forms are set forth in transliteration: the spelling of the words of one language in the more or less corresponding letters of the alphabet of another. Of the 24 letters of the Greek alphabet, only a few would be recognizable to those not versed in the classics, as the forerunners of their contemporary English equivalents.) Might a book like this spark some interest in those old, time-honored ancient tongues? If so, it would go to show that fun's not only fun but may sometimes produce unexpected results. I hope so.

Key to Abbreviations

Throughout the text abbreviations are used to refer to the following seven dictionaries:

CH	Chambers Twentieth Century Dictionary
C.O.D.	Concise Oxford Dictionary
LS	Liddell and Scott Greek English Lexicon
O.E.D.	Oxford English Dictionary
RH	Random House Dictionary, Unabridged
W II	Webster's Second New International Dictionary
W III	Webster's Third New International Dictionary

Key to Pronunciation

"a"	for "a" as in "hat"
"ay" or "a——e"	for "a" as in "hate"
"ah"	for "a" as in "bah," "o" as in gone
"air"	for "a" as in "dare," "ai" as in "air"
"a(r)"	for "a" as in "art"
"aw"	for "a" as in "awe," "ou" as in "ought"
"e" or "eh"	f or "e" as in "met"
"ee"	for "e" as in "meet"
"i" or "ih"	for "i" as in "bit"
"(e)ye" or "i——e"	for "i" as in "bite"
"o"	for "o" as in "got"
"oh" or "o——e"	for "o" as in "go" or "note"
"oo"	for "oo" as in "look"
"ooh"	for "oo" as in "boot," "u" as in "lute"
"o(r)"	for "o" as in "or"
"oy"	for "o" as in "boy" or "void"
"ou"	for "ou" as in "out"
"u" or "uh"	for "u" as in "but" and for schwa (an indefinite "uh" sound of an unaccented syllable, like the "a" in "woman," the "i" in "pencil," the "u" in "focus," etc.
"u(r)"	for "u" as in "fur"
"th"	hard, as in "thing," "thistle," or "third"
"*th*"	soft, as in "this" or "that"

1000 MOST OBSCURE WORDS

acatalectic   See **prosodion.**

acephalous   See **dolichocephal.**

acosmism, also **akosmism** (uh KOZ mis'm) *n.* From the Greek negative prefix *a-* (the *alpha privative,* equivalent to our *un-* and its variants) plus *kosmos* (cosmos, universe), the Greeks formed the term *akosmismus* to denote the theory that denies to the universe any absolute reality or any existence apart from God. It is the opposite of *pantheism* (PAN thee iz'm)—from the Greek prefix *pan-,* the combining form of *pan,* neuter of *pas* (all), plus *theos* (god)—the doctrine that identifes God with the universe or claims that God is only the combined forces of the universe as they manifest themselves. *Pantheism* has another distinct meaning—the worship of gods of various beliefs without distinction, as opposed to *theism,* belief in the existence of a god or gods, or *monotheism,* the doctrine that there is one God, the creator of mankind and the world, who transcends yet remains within the world. We are familiar with *atheism,* which opposes all the foregoing doctrines, denying the existence of any god. We must not omit mention of *polytheism*—from the Greek *polys* (many) plus *theos*—which denotes the worship of several gods, as practiced in ancient Egypt, Greece, Rome and many other early cultures. *Polytheism,* in some cultures, also involved the creation of a family relationship among these various gods through a kind of anthropomorphism, attributing quite human emotions and behavior to them, resulting in a rather cozy relationship between mankind and its pantheon. The same goes for *allotheism,* the worship of foreign, strange or unsanctioned gods, which is forbidden by the First Commandment.

acuate   See **acuminate.**

acuminate (uh KYOOH muh nuht) *adj.*; (uh KYOOH muh nate) *vb.* Note the difference in the pronunciations of the adjective and the noun. The noun *acumen* is familiar; it can be pronounced uh KYOOH muhn, a KYOOH muhn, AK yuh muhn or AK yuh men and is commonly understood to mean "keen perception" or "discernment" or "shrewdness," especially in matters of business. It has other technical meanings in botany and crustaceology, not relevant here. But *acuminate* is another matter. As an adjective, it means "pointed," and applies to anything that tapers to a fine point. As a transitive verb, it means "to sharpen"; as an intransitive verb, "to taper," i.e., "to come to a point." *Acuminous* (uh KYOOH muh nuhs) can be either the adjectival form of *acumen,* meaning "possessing (or characterized by) *acumen*" or can serve as a synonym of *acuminate* in the adjectival sense. *Acumination* (uh kyooh muh NAY shuhn) means either "sharpening" or "tapering point," depending on the context. *Acuminulate* (uh kyooh MIN yuh luht) is another adjectival form, as you might expect from the inclusion of the syllable *-ul-,* from the Latin diminutive suffix *-ulus, -a, -um,* meaning "slightly pointed" or "tapering to a minute degree."

All of these words stem from the Latin *acumen* (point), related to the verb *acuere* (to sharpen). It is well to note, too, that Latin *acus* means "needle," and *acutus*, from which we get *acute*, is the past participle of *acuere*. English also has the adjective *acuate* (AK yuh wate), meaning "sharply pointed" or "needle-shaped," derived from an assumed Middle Latin *acuatus*. *Acuity* ("acuteness," "keenness" or "sharpness," whether applying to a physical object or the mind, the understanding or the senses) is dealt with in my *1000 Most Challenging Words*, while *acumen* is fully discussed in my *1000 Most Practical Words*. They, too, go back to our old friends *acus* and *acuere*. Don't credit them, however, with *accurate*; that is from the Latin *accuratus*, the past participle of *accurare* ("to take care of," "do carefully," "prepare with care"), which is derived from the Latin prefix *ad-* (to, toward) plus *curare* (to take care of). Be acute, proceed with acumen and acuity and you'll be accurate, especially with words.

acumination   See **acuminate.**

acuminous   See **acuminate.**

acuminulate   See **acuminate.**

adscititious (ad sit ISH uhs) *adj.* Anything worthy of this impressive adjective is "added, supplemental, originating or acquired from something extrinsic, adventitious," the opposite of *inherent*. The word is derived from the Latin *adscitus* or *ascitus* (derived, foreign), the past participle of the verb *a(d)scisere* (to approve, appropriate), built of the preposition *ad-* (toward—indicating tendency or addition) plus *sciscere* (to seek, to find out). This brings up a point quite incidental to the main entry, but let's have it out now. We just mentioned *sciscere*. That word is the inchoative of *scire* (to know). But what is an *inchoative*? *Inc(h)oare* means "to begin" or "to begin to treat of" something. Its past participle is *inc(h)oatus*, and that gave us *inchoate*, which is discussed in my earlier *1000 Most Important Words* and is described as denoting "things just begun, undeveloped ..." The lengthened form, *inchoative* (in KOH uh tive), is the name given to verbs in Latin and Greek that express the concept of "beginning an action" rather than performing one. Their first person singular forms end in *-sco* in Latin and *-sko* in Greek. Thus, to swipe some examples from Fowler, in Greek, *gignosko* means "to learn," i.e., "begin to know," while in Latin, *calesco* means "to grow warm" rather than "be warm." So—at long last—*sciscere*, whose first-person singular is *scisco* (there's the *-sco* ending), means "to seek to know" rather than "to know." (Incidental moral: Seek and ye shall find.) Getting back to our headword: John Evelyn, in *Numismata; a Discourse on Medals Ancient and Modern* (1697)—*numisma* is Latin for "money, coin," from the Greek *nomisma* (custom, usage, currency, coin, akin to *nomizein*, to observe, recognize, and *numismatics* is our word for "the study of coins and medals")—writes of "... such *adscititious* Habits as may be contracted by Institution, Discipline and custom." After all this, the simplest definition of *adscititious* is "additional," in the sense of "supplemental." Forgive the anticlimax.

adytum (AD ih tuhm) *n*. The Greek word *adyton* (not to be entered), composed of the negative prefix *a-* (the "alpha privative," as in *amorphous, amoral, apolitical*, etc., meaning "not") plus *dytos*, a verbal adjective from the verb *dyein* (to enter), was Latinized to *adytum*, denoting the innermost section of a temple, the secret shrine whence oracles were uttered, and later, the chancel of a church. It acquired the figurative meaning of "sanctum." Samuel Taylor Coleridge, in *Essays on His Own Times* (1800), criticized a politician as one who carried with him "the habits of a disputing club into the *adyta* of the Cabinet." Everyone should have his own *adytum*, for solitary contemplation and search for the truth. Think of all those poor souls who don't have a roof, let alone an *adytum*!

aftermath   See **rowen.**

akratisma   See **chittering-bite.**

alieniloquy (ay lee en IL uh kwee) *n*. The *O.E.D.* quotes the definition "a talking wide from the purpose, or not to the matter at hand" from the early British lexicographer Nathan Bailey's *Universal Etymological English Dictionary* (1731 edition—first edition 1721; they preceded the publication of Samuel Johnson's *Dictionary of the English Language* (1755); the 1731 edition was published as *Dictionarium Britannicum: or a More Compleat Universal Etymological English Dictionary*; Bailey's definition was adopted by John Ash in his *New and Complete Dictionary of the English Language*, 1775, trailing Johnson by 20 years). The word is characterized as "obsolete" by the *O.E.D.*, but its Latin ancestor, *alieniloquium*, shows up in Professor Elizabeth Dipple's exhaustive study of the novels of Iris Murdoch (*Iris Murdoch, Work for the Spirit*). In a discussion of Murdoch's *The Sea, The Sea* Dipple points out that Charles Arrowby is the ostensible protagonist, "but, as in the case of the medieval idea of the *alieniloquium* (a speaking of things other than those it purports to do...) there is a sustained questioning of the spiritual life ... a profound psychic landscape whose symbolic quality very slowly, in small, subtle steps unfolds. James [Arrowby, the protagonist's brother] is its vehicle, and on him rests the deep infrastructure of the book." Dipple's definition varies somewhat from Bailey's, but the underlying meaning is the same in both. Profound stuff, in both Murdoch's novel (as in all her novels) and Dipple's analysis. In a recent letter, Professor Dipple tells me that "... *alieniloquium* seems to me a splendid way of talking about the secret agenda of many texts, and I much prefer it to coarser and more simplistic words like *allegory*." So do I.

allele (uh LEEL) *n*. This word is a shortened form of *allelomorph* (uh LEE luh morf, uh LEL uh-), a term in Mendelian genetics for any of several forms of a gene responsible for hereditary variation. The longer form, *allelomorph*, is formed from the Greek *allelo-*, the stem of *allelon* (of one another) plus *morphe* (form). Gregor Johann Mendel was an Austrian monk (1822–84) who pioneered in experimental studies of heredity, carrying out independent scientific investigations on plants, mainly garden peas, by means of controlled pollination and statistical analysis of the results, especially hybridization. Mendel's basic conclusion was that an inherited characteristic is determined by the combination of two hereditary units (now known as *genes*), one from each of the parental reproductive cells. These genes are known as *alleles* or *allelomorphs*. If you want to investigate further, see K. R. Lewis's book entitled *The Matter of Mendelian Heredity* (1964) and R. C. Olby's *Origins of Mendelism* (1966), and if they disagree with what I have said on the subject, better side with them.

allelomorph   See **allele.**

alloch(e)iria (ah loh KEYE ree uh, -KIH-) *n*. Since *allo-* is the combining form of the Greek adjective *allos*, meaning "other," and *cheiro-* the combining form of *cheir*, meaning "hand," one might jump to the (as usual, erroneous) conclusion that *alloch(e)iria* had something to do with "on the other hand," as in "on the one hand, on the other hand." Actually, *alloch(e)iria* is the name for the attribution of a sensation to the wrong part of the body. How often have you been surprised to hear from your dentist that it isn't your canine but your first premolar that has the abscess? You've been suffering not only from the abscess, my dear, but also from a case of *alloch(e)iria*. My dentist tells me it happens all the time and that the confusion can involve not just two neighboring teeth but often neck and even shoulder pains. Even with a supply of Greek combining forms at your command, be careful.

al(l)odium (ul LOH de uhm) also **al(l)od** (AL od) *n*. This word, in any of its forms, was used in feudal times to denote an estate in which the holder had absolute possession and control free of any subjection by way of rent, service or acknowledgment to a superior. The term was applied particularly in Anglo-Saxon society of the 11th century. It was the antithesis of a *feod* or *feud* (pronounced FOOHD—and this *feud* is not the Montague and Capulet type), the name then applied to an estate held of a lord or other superior on condition of the rendering of certain services by the tenant or vassal to the superior. This type of fiddlededee has long been obsolete, but if you settle down with one of those interminable historical novels set in that distant era, you'd better be acquainted with it. *Al(l)odium* is a Middle Latin term, derived from two Old High German words: *al* (all) and *od* (property).

allotheism   See **acosmism.**

alnage (OL nij) *n*. The practice of *alnage* and the office of *alnager* have long since faded from the scene, but you might bump into these terms if you were reading fact or fiction involving life in England in days of yore. *Alnage* and the office of *alnager* were introduced into English law in 1320 during the reign of Edward III. *Alnage* was the official inspection and measurement of woolen cloth by an *alnager* appointed by the court, who also declared its quality and value. The practice and office were abolished during the reign of King William III (1689–1702). *Alnage* was also the official name of the fee paid the *alnager*. Geoffrey Chaucer must have had something to do with this function since he was the comptroller of the customs on wool and hides at the port of London from 1374 to 1386. (Geoffrey held lots of important jobs and did all kinds of things besides writing *The Canterbury Tales* and other notable works that set the course of English literature.) *Alnage* and *alnager* owe their names to the fact that the measurement of the cloth was by the *ell*, which in turn got its name from Old French *aulnage*, from *aulner* (to measure by the *ell*), and which can ultimately be traced back to Latin *ulna* (elbow, and by transference, a measure of length). *Ell* has had a great diversity of meanings as a measurement, including the distance from the elbow to the wrist, from the shoulder to the wrist, from either to the fingertips—usually the middle finger—and so forth. Some Latin poets used *ulna*, for instance, to mean "as much as a man can span with both arms," others to mean "a fathom" (which is etymologically the same thing). *Ell* finally crystallized, in England, as a unit of length (chiefly for cloth) equal to 45 inches and is now no longer in use. It designated different lengths in different countries: in Holland, approximately 27 inches, in Scotland, about 37—all very confusing in earlier days, nowadays happily obsolete. It reminds one of the *cubit*, from Latin *cubitum* (elbow), which was used in olden times as a unit of length equal to the span from the elbow to the tip of the middle finger—anywhere from 18 inches to 21 or even more, based on natural variations in the length of forearms. Midgets and giants were undoubtedly omitted from consideration. Just imagine, if *ells* and *cubits* were still current in the age of basketball players. Good riddance, I say: So long to *alnage, alnagers, ells* and *cubits*!

alnager   See **alnage.**

alphonsin (al FON sin) *n*. Named after its inventor, Alphonsus Ferrier of Naples, Italy, in 1552, an *alphonsin* was a surgical instrument consisting of a forceps equipped with three elastic branches closed together by means of a ring. The purpose of this ingenious apparatus was the extraction of bullets from the body. Any follower of the Korean War television series "M.A.S.H." has watched Hawkeye and his colleagues extract bullets from wounds countless times. These excellent surgeons weren't using *alphonsins*, however. There are many different types of forceps in use these days for the extraction of foreign objects from bodies, among them the Allison and the Crile. Do not confuse *alphonsin* with the adjective *Alphonsine*, pronounced the same way but descriptive of certain astronomical tables prepared by a group of Jewish, Arabian and Christian astronomers in 1252 under the patronage of Alfonso X (the Wise), King of Castile and León. The result of such confusion in a hospital operating room would be too horrible to contemplate.

altricial   See nidicolous.

altrigenderism (al truh JEN duh riz'm) *n. Alter*, in Latin, means "other of two," as opposed to *alius*, "other of more than two." The distinction was not always maintained by the Roman writers, but that is the general rule. From *alter* we get the prefix *altri-*; from *gener-*, the stem of *genus* (class, kind—especially as applied to living beings), we get *gender*. Add the suffix *-ism* and we have *altrigenderism*, which has naught to do with change of sex but rather the happy, if often unnerving, state of development when one becomes interested in, nay, attracted to members of the opposite sex. This is an experience shared by most of us and the subject of a good deal of literature—whether poetry, short story, novel or drama. It leads to romance, elation, perplexity, suffering; but this is a book about obscure words, not psychiatry, so we'd best end the discussion right now.

alveary (AL vee uhr ee) *n.* An *alvearium*, in Latin, is a "beehive." The historian Pliny used the words *alvus* and *alveus* as synonyms of *alvearium*. *Alveary* is also the name, in anatomy, for the hollow of the external ear—a kind of pun, because that, as well as a beehive, is where wax collects. Strangely, the word has an altogether distinct meaning: an early dictionary of English, French, Greek and Latin. This is another sort of pun, as indicated by an early (1580) scholar named John Baret, who wrote: "Within a yeere, or two, they had gathered together a great volume, which (for the apt similitude between the good Scholers and diligent Bees in gathering their waxe and honie into their Hiue) I called then their Alvearie." In Latin, an *alveus* is any hollow or socket, and in English, *alveated* means "vaulted," like a beehive.

amathophobia (am uh thuh FOH bee uh) *n.* Since *amathos* is Greek for "sand," and we all know the meaning of *phobia*, one would suppose that *amathophobia* was a learned term for "fear of sand," like the dread of sandstorms that must beset denizens of desert lands. But no: It is defined by W III as "fear of *dust*," like the obsession that beset Craig's wife in the play of that name and ruined her marriage. Strangely, the word is missing from *W II* and is not to be found in any of my other dictionaries, including the *O.E.D.* and its Supplement. Lexicographers move in mysterious ways. I suppose that just about every-thing in the world is subject to somebody's phobia, even something as seem-ingly benign as health. How about hypochondriacs, who obviously suffer from *sanitaphobia*? (*Sanitas* is Latin for "health.") What about *divitiphobia* (*divitiae* is Latin for "wealth"), the fear of wealth by those devout readers of the Bible who take literally the usually misquoted statement of Paul in his First Epistle to Timothy: "The love of money is the root of all evil?" And Keats enjoined *scientiphobia* (*scientia* is Latin for "wisdom") when he wrote: "O fret not after knowledge—I have none ..." So what good does it do to go to bed early and get up early? And I beg to be forgiven for having concocted the silly hybrids *sanitaphobia, divitiphobia* and *scientiphobia*. But it does seem that *-phobia* can be attached to every noun in the dictionary.

ambidexter (am bee DEK stur) *n., adj.* As an adjective, *ambidexter* describes a person able to use both hands equally well. The word is built of the prefix *ambi-*, the combining form of Latin *ambo* (both), which is found in a number of familiar words (including *ambiguous* and *ambivalent*), and *dexter* (right), which came to mean "skillful" and gave us *dextrous* or *dexterous*. *Sinister* means "left" in Latin and by transference came to mean "wrong, unfavorable." It was taken intact into English to mean "ominous, threatening." In adjectival use, *ambidexter* is now archaic, having given way to the familiar term *ambidextrous*, and that word has been extended in meaning to denote versatility, as used, for instance, by T. S. Eliot in describing a writer equally at home in verse and prose. *Ambidexterity*, literally the ability to use both hands equally well, acquired the figurative meaning of "superior skill" generally, and, by extension, "double-dealing." It was so defined by the good Doctor Johnson in his *Dictionary* (1755) and used in that sense by Isaac D'Israeli (father of Benjamin) in *Amenities of Literature* (1841), where he wrote of " ... that intricate net of general misery, spun out of ... crafty *ambidexterity*." But, getting back to *ambidexter* in its use as an adjective, it came to mean "double-dealing" in legal parlance, of a person who takes bribes from both parties to an unlawful transaction. It's bad enough to take a bribe from either party, but *both*? And if we ever run across an ambidextrous *ambidexter*, good heavens, he'd have it four ways, wouldn't he, and that would be quadruply sinister!

ambry (AM bree), also **aumbry** (AWM bree) *n.* This word has been spelled in many different ways, including *armary, almary* and *awmry*. It came from the Latin *armarium* (cupboard, chest) and at various times has meant "repository," "a place for keeping things," "treasury," "storehouse," "safe," "locker," "press" and "cupboard," either a wall recess or a separate piece of furniture of whatever nature. It has also been applied to a pigeonhole type of compartment. In churches it has been used to designate a closed recess for keeping books, vestments, sacramental plates, consecrated oil and other ritual accessories, and in the home, a place for keeping food, a pantry, a dresser or what the British call a "meat-safe"—a compartment in which to store meat (in the days before refrigerators)—most recently made of wire gauze, but in the old days, with sides of haircloth (also known as *cilice*, itself an interesting word from Greek *kilikion* via Latin *cilicium*, so called because it was originally made of goat hair from Cilicia, an ancient country in southeast Asia Minor that became a Roman province). Additional uses of *ambry* include the following: a place for books and archives, a library, a livestock hutch. Has there ever been a more versatile word? Still another use: In Richard Stanyhurst's 1582 translation of *The Aeneid*, we see the words: "In this od hudge *ambry* [the Trojan horse] they ramd a number of hardye Tough knights." The word still showed up much later. In William Beckford's *Recollections* (1835) we read of "a press or *ambery* elaborately carved" and William Morris's poem *The Life and Death of Jason* (1867) mentions "a little *aumbrye*, with a door o'er-gilt." Anything more you'd like to know about *ambry*?

ambs-ace (AMZ ase) *n.* From the Latin *ambo asses* (both aces) comes the term *ambs-ace*, meaning "both aces" or "double ace." (*Ace* is a dice term, meaning "one," i.e., the side of the die marked with a single dot.) Two aces, in this sense, are known by the slang term "snake-eyes" and as a first throw constitute a crap. The game of dice is known as "craps"; a first throw of two ones, a one and a two, or two sixes is a crap and loses the bet, and the dice pass to an opponent. Since a throw of two aces, or *ambs-ace*, is the lowest possible throw, *ambs-ace* came to denote, figuratively, "bad luck, worthlessness, next to nothing or nothing," and the expression *within ambs ace of* was an emphatic form of *within an ace of*, i.e., on the very edge (or verge) of. *Ambs-ace* has been spelled in many different ways, one of which was *ames-ace*, a form found in *All's Well That Ends Well*, when Lafeu speaks the line: "I had rather be in this choice than throw *ames-ace* for my life." (Act II, Scene 3.) In *Among My Books*, James Russell Lowell writes of "a lucky throw of words which may come up the sices [*sixes* as a dice term] of hardy metaphor or the *ambs-ace* of conceit." An elegant turn of phrase if ever there was one!

amphiscian (am FISH ee uhn) *n., adj.* Two related words, also both nouns and adjectives, are *heteroscian* (het uh ROSH ee uhn) and *periscian* (puhr ISH ee uhn). There are endless ways of categorizing the inhabitants of this planet: by color, culture, nationality, physical traits, intellectual prowess, moral codes and so on; but did you know that there are categories based on the direction in which one's shadow is cast? And that this necessarily depends on which zone one inhabits? Let me explain: An *amphiscian* is "one who dwells in the torrid zone"; thus, his or her shadow is thrown both ways: to the north part of the year, to the south the rest of the year. Simple enough: *amphi-* is a Greek prefix meaning "on both sides," and *skia* means "shadow." *Heteroscians* are inhabitants of a temperate zone, whose noon shadows fall in one direction, either north or south. Here we have the Greek prefix *hetero-*, meaning "one or the other," plus *skia*. And finally we come to *periscian*, one who resides in a polar circle, whose shadow moves around him or her in a complete circle on those days on which the sun does not set. The Greek prefix *peri-*, meaning "around," is attached to our old friend *skia*. In this age of rapid travel from zone to zone, you should always know which of these nouns or adjectives applies. There may be more important criteria, but I can't imagine what. See also **macroscian** for more on this subject.

ampollosity   See **ampulla.**

ampulla (am POOL uh) *n.* After running into the word *ampollosity* in Browning's *The Ring and the Book* (*o* rather than *u* in *CH* as opposed to the *O.E.D.*, and the word being defined as "pretentious inanity, turgidity, bombast"), my eye leapt to *ampulla* and its plethora of definitions, of which the following are only some: "a small two-handled flask"; "a pilgrim's bottle"; "a vessel for holy oil, as at coronations"; "a cruet for the wine and water used at the altar"; "a small glass container for a hypodermic dose." These were followed by uses in biology and anatomy. To add to the confusion, variant spellings are *ampoule* and *ampul*. *Ampulla* is an irregular Latin diminutive of *amphora*—the Roman and Greek two-handled jar ubiquitous in museums of classical antiquities—a word derived from the Greek prefix *amphi-* (both, on both sides), seen in words like *amphibious,* plus *phoreus* (bearer). Derivation notes in dictionaries also credit the influence of Old English *ampulle*, Old French *ampo(u)le* and Italian *ampolla* (phial, vial). Browning's spelling must have been the result of his long romance with Italy (where the rascal was in April when he wrote "O to be in England/Now that April's there … "—a time when the weather in England is usually wet and rainy).

Amyclaean (am ih KLEE uhn) *adj.* Like the adjective **moazagotl**, which modifies only one noun, *cloud*, this adjective modifies only the noun *silence*. Just what is an *Amyclaean Silence*? *Amyclae* (uh MEYE klee) is the name of an ancient town of Laconia, the country in the southeast Peloponnesus, Greece, of which Sparta, three miles north, was the capital. At one time it was the principal city of Laconia. Again and again it was beset by false rumors of impending invasion by the Spartans, so often that the authorities issued a decree prohibiting any mention of the subject. The Spartans finally arrived, but the decree was respected and no one dared give warning. Amyclae was taken. This curious incident gave rise to the expression "more silent than Amyclae." Somehow, it brings to mind the converse legend of the boy who cried "Wolf!"

anaclitic (an uh KLIH tik) *adj.* Freud coined the German word *Anlehnungstypus,* literally, "leaning-on type," to describe one whose choice of a love object was based on dependence of the libido on another instinct, such as hunger. (This brings to mind the old vulgar, nay, repellent aphorism: "The way to a man's heart is through his stomach." Ugh!) Freud based his term on the Greek adjective *anaklitos* (reclining), from the verb *anaklinein* (to lean back, recline), built of the prefix *ana-* (back) plus *klinein* (to lean). *Anaclitic* was later extended to signify dependence on another or others generally. In Joan Riviere's translation from Freud, *S. Freud's Introductory Lectures on Psychoanalysis* (1922), she writes about " … The *anaclitic* type (*Anlehnungstypus*) in which those persons who become prized on account of the satisfactions they rendered to the primal needs of life are chosen as objects by the Libido also."

In Howard Warren's *Dictionary of Psychology* (1934), *anaclitic object-choice* is defined as "taking one's earliest attachments (to mother or nurse) as a model for the selection of the first love object." Pretty dangerous, those "earliest attachments."

anadiplosis   See **anaphora.**

anagoge (an uh GOH jee), also **anagogy** (AN uh goh jee) *n. Anagoge* or *anagogy* (the *O.E.D.* calls the latter "a better English form") is "the elevation of the mind to things celestial," "mystical interpretation," especially the interpretation of the Bible in the "fourth or mystical" sense. The "four senses" of Scripture are defined as the historical or literal, the allegorical, the moral and the *anagogical* (an uh GOJ ih kuhl). According to the *Schaff-Herzog Encyclopedia of Religious Knowledge* (Philip Schaff, 1819–93, edited the first edition of the *Realencyclopaedie* of Johann Jakob Herzog, 1805–82), "Jerusalem is *literally* a city of Palestine, *allegorically* the Church, *morally* the believing soul, *anagogically* the heavenly Jerusalem." The adjective *anagogic* (an uh GOJ ik) is applied to things pertaining to mystical interpretation and the strivings of the unconscious toward morally high ideals. The more of that the merrier!

analemma (an uh LEM uh) *n.* Although the Greek verb *lambanein* (to take) and its extended form *analambanein* (to take up—the prefix *ana-* having the force of *up*) figure in the derivation of this word, it has nothing to do with *dilemma,* the *lemma* part of which is also derived from *lambanein.* We know (all too well!) what a *dilemma* is, but how about an *analemma*? That is the Latin word for a "sundial pedestal," or the sundial itself, derived from the Greek noun *analemma* meaning "support, prop," which explains the pedestal idea. Thomas D. Nicholson, in the December 1987 issue of the magazine *Natural History,* defines the word as follows:

> The *analemma* we see on globes records how the point on the earth directly below the sun at clock noon changes during the year. The sun moves north of the equator in summer and south of the equator in winter. It is ahead of clock noon from September 1 to December 26, falls behind from December 26 to April 15, then moves ahead again until June 15, and falls behind again until September 1, alternately speeding up and slowing down with respect to clock time. It is exactly even with the clock four times a year—on December 26, April 1, June 15, and September 1.

This definition is followed by a diagram in the shape of an elongated eight, much like a child's drawing of a pussycat from the rear, missing ears and whiskers. In short, an *analemma* is a scale of the sun's daily declination drawn from tropic to tropic on artificial terrestrial globes.

anaphora (uh NAF uh ruh) *n.* This word would appear to have, among its several meanings, two that are antithetical. Thus, it is a term in rhetoric for the device of beginning successive sentences or lines with the same word or phrase for the purpose of emphasis. Example: In the 29th Psalm we read: "The voice of the Lord is upon the waters ... The voice of the Lord is powerful; the voice of the Lord is full of majesty. The voice of the Lord breaketh the cedars ... The voice of the Lord divideth the flames of fire. The voice of the Lord shaketh the wilderness ... The voice of the Lord maketh the hinds to calve ..." Another example: In Pope's *Elegy to the Memory of an Unfortunate Lady* we find these lines: "By foreign hands thy dying eyes were closed,/By foreign hands thy decent limbs composed,/By foreign hands thy humble grave adorned ..." So far so good, but *anaphora* can also mean the opposite: the avoiding of repetition of a preceding word or phrase through the use, for example, of *it* or *do*, as in : My father speaks French; I speak *it* and my mother *does* too. *Anaphora* is taken from Greek, meaning "carrying back," based on the prefix *ana-* (back) and the verb *pherein* (to carry, bear). It has a variant form, *epanaphora* (ep uh NAF uh ruh). It also denotes the central prayer sequence of the Eucharist. A related term in rhetoric is *epistrophe* (uh PIS truh fee), also known as *epiphora* (uh PIF uh ruh—which also means "involuntary weeping"!), the repetition of a word or phrase at the *end* of successive clauses or sentences. Example: Antony to the Citizens in *Julius Caesar*, Act III, Scene 2: "I should do Brutus wrong, and Cassius wrong ... I will not do them wrong ... " A further rhetorical device is *symploce* (SIM ploh see), the combining of *anaphora* and *epistrophe*. This term is derived, as so often happens, via Late Latin, from Greek *symploke* (intertwining, combination), based on the prefix *epi-* (upon) plus *strophe* (twist, turning around). A more exhaustive (and brilliant) list of obscure words having to do with rhetoric and grammar, followed by brief definitions, can be found in the Glossary/Index of Arthur Quinn's exquisite little book *Figures of Speech*, published in 1982 by Gibbs M. Smith, Inc., Salt Lake City. Included in his list and beautifully treated in the text with copious examples are the following (I omit some dealt with in my *1000 Most Challenging Words*): *anadiplosis* (repitition of an end at the next beginning); *antimetabole* (an *epanados* which is also an *antithesis*); *auxesis* (arrangement in ascending importance); *diacope* (repetition with only a word or two between); *epanados* (repetition in the opposite order); *epanalepsis* (repetition of the beginning at the end); *gradatio* (repeated *anadiplosis*); *hypozeuxis* (omission of a *zeugma*—a term dealt with in my above cited work) and *inclusio* (repetition of the beginning of a passage at its end). There will be a brief period of study before the examination.

anaptotic   See **aptote.**

anaptyxis   See **metaplasm.**

androgenesis   See **androgenous.**

androgenous (an DROJ uh nuhs) *adj.* At first glance, this word might well be mistaken as a misspelling of its homophone *androgynous*, an error confessed by the ever-entertaining William Safire in his weekly column "On Language" in the *New York Times Magazine* of January 15, 1989. The admirable Mr. Safire has always been willing to admit the error of his linguistic, if not his political, ways and is indeed the champion of the "Mea Culpa Stakes." *Androgynous* is defined in my *1000 Most Challenging Words* as "applied to man and other animals, describing specimens having the characteristics of both sexes. This can refer to sexual organs or other physical characteristics, or to personality or temperament." That word is derived from a combination of Greek *andros* (man) and *gyne* (woman). *Androgenous*, on the other hand, is differently derived, in that the *-genous* element has nothing to with the female sex but is based on the Greek suffix *-genes* (born), from the root of the verb *gignesthai* (to be born), and has the force of "generating." This word, then, means "pertaining to the production of exclusively male offspring." For those who want to go more deeply into the subject, *androgenous* is the adjectival form of *androgenesis*, which is male *parthenogenisis*, i.e., a development whereby the embryo contains only the male parent's chromosomes because of the failure of the nucleus of the ovum to participate in fertilization. As you might suspect, there is also such a thing as *gynogenesis*, and since you now know all about those Greek prefixes and suffixes, you will easily recognize that phenomenon as the situation whereby the embryo contains only the female parent's chromosomes because the sperm that activated the ovum degenerated, poor chap, before it could combine with the egg nucleus. You thought this was a book about words? Well, a little excursion into biology never hurt anyone.

aniconic (an eye KON ik) *adj.* Icon, from Greek *eikon*, in its general sense means "image" and frequently denotes—particularly in the Orthodox church and art and museum circles—a religious portrait of Christ or a saint, in oil or mosaic. In the art world, *iconic* decribes works executed in the conventional or traditional mode. Putting *an-* (the Greek prefix known as the "alpha privative," shortened to *a-* before a consonant, as in *amoral, atypical*, etc., and used to express negation) before *iconic*, we get *aniconic*: descriptive of things that are symbolic or suggestive rather than representational. For example, objects of worship or veneration in primitive religions, such as trees and rocks symbolic of gods without being images of them, can be said to be *aniconic*. The noun *aniconism* (an EYE kuhn iz'm) denotes that type of worship, and an *aniconist* (an EYE kuhn ist) is a follower of that form of religion. Animals were widely used as sacred objects in ancient religious systems. The wolf, griffon and crow represented Apollo; the stag, Diana; the heifer, Isis; the peacock and the lamb, Juno; the eagle, Jupiter; the bull, Neptune; the dove, the swan and the sparrow, Venus. How much more exciting the symbol can be than the representational image!

anicut, also **annicut** (AN uh kut) *n.* This is the name of a dam which, for irrigation purposes, is built across a river, storing up water, which in turn is drawn off into channels running in different directions to regulate and control the supply. It is an Anglo-Indian word, from Tamil *anai* (dam) and *kattu* (building); the procedure it denotes is common in southern India, primarily in Madras, as an efficient alternative to the canal system of the northern regions.

anlaut (AN lawt) *n.* There are three related terms in philology having to do with the position of a sound in a word or syllable: *anlaut*, *inlaut* (IN laut) and *auslaut* (AW slaut). They denote, respectively, the first, medial (or internal) and final sound in a word or syllable. Example: In the word *flute*, *f* is the *anlaut*, *u* is the *inlaut* and *t* is the *auslaut* (not the final letter, but the final sound). All three words are of German origin; *Laut* (pronounced lout; n.b.—all German nouns are capitalized), as a substantive, means "sound"; the prefixes *an-*, *in-* and *aus-* mean, respectively (and inter alia): "to," "to the edge or beginning of"; "in," "inside of"; "out of," "at the end of." Some philologists distinguish two types of *anlaut*: absolute, denoting the position of a sound at the beginning of a phrase, and relative, denoting a sound at the beginning of a word. None of these terms has anything to do with the more familiar *umlaut* (OOM lout), a diacritical consisting of two dots placed over a vowel. It resembles in form, but not in function, the dieresis, written over the second of two adjoining vowels to indicate that they are to be pronounced separately, not as a diphthong. In German, the *umlaut* alters the sound of the vowels *a*, *o* and *u* in ways that cannot be expressed in terms of English pronunciation and are not material to this discussion. The *um-* prefix in this word has the force of "about, around," as in "change about, change around," i.e., "convert."

anonyma (uh NON ih muh) *n.* For years, *The New Yorker* regaled us with a department headed "What Paper D'Ya Read?" juxtaposing newspaper reports on the selfsame item in (sometimes) hilariously different versions. Now, how about a "What Dictionary D'Ya Read?" We are dealing with the noun *anonyma*, and here go the dictionary definitions: *CH*: "a showy woman of easy morals"; *W III*: "the innominate artery"; and the same authority defines the innominate artery as "a large artery arising from the arch of the aorta and dividing into the right common carotid and the right subclavian arteries" and goes to great lengths to tell us all about common carotids and subclavian arteries and other anatomical doodads of interest only to medical personnel; and the impartial *O.E.D.* plays both sides of the field with: "1. A woman of the demi-monde. *Obs.* 2. *Anat.* The innominate artery." Well, if I had to choose between spending a free evening with the *Chambers* type and the *Webster*... *RH* solves the dilemma: it ignores *anonyma*.

anopisthograph   See **opisthograph**.

anthelmint(h)ic   See **helminth**.

anthropopsychism (an thruh poh SEYE kiz'm) *n. Anthropomorphism* (an thruh puh MOR fiz'm, -poh-) is a fairly familiar word. *Anthropomorphic* is defined in my *1000 Most Important Words* as descriptive of "any act or statement that ascribes human characteristics to gods, animals or objects." Obviously, *anthropomorphism* is that type of ascription. *Anthropopsychism* is a more restrictive term, denoting the ascription of spiritual faculties or traits characteristic of the human race to God or to the agencies of nature: *spiritual*, as contrasted with *physical*, to be specific. In *The Unity of Nature* (1884) the Duke of Argyll says of *anthropopsychism*: "It is not the Form of man that is in question. It is the Mind and Spirit of man—his Reason, his Intelligence, and his Will." He speaks of a "fundamental analogy ... between the Mind which is in us and the mind which is in Nature" and goes on to tell us that "the true etymological expression for this idea ... would be, not *Anthropomorphism* but *Anthropopsychism*." Consider the etymology—*psyche*, the Greek for "soul, spirit," as opposed to *morphe*, the Greek for "form, shape"—and you will more clearly understand the Duke's distinction.

antibacchius   See **bacchius.**

antilegomena (an tih leg OM ih nuh) *n. pl.* This noun is the neuter plural, used as a substantive, of the Greek adjective *antilegomenos*, the present passive participle of the verb *antilegein*, built of the prefix *anti-* (against) and the verb *legein* (to speak). The *antilegomena* were the books of the New Testament that were not at the outset accepted but were eventually admitted into the Canon (Greek word for "rule"): the books of the Bible accepted by the Christian church as having divine authority. These contested books were The Second Letter of Peter, A Letter of James, A Letter of Jude, A Letter to Hebrews, the Second and Third Letters of John and The Apocalypse (The Revelation of St. John). They are customarily contrasted with the *homolog(o)umena* (hom ol o GOO mih nuh), the books of the New Testament universally accepted as authentic in the early Church. This word, too, is a plural noun, the neuter plural of *homolog(o)umenos*, the present passive participle of the verb *homologein* (to agree), from *homologos* (agreeing), built of the prefix *homo-* (same) plus suffix *-logos*, from the same verb *legein*. The name *antilegomena*, sometimes capitalized, was first used by Eusebius of Caesarea (263?–c.340), the Christian theologian and historian who was bishop of Caesarea from c. 315 to his death. Few Christians realize that the authenticity of these books was ever disputed.

antimetabole   See **anaphora.**

antiphrasis (an TIF ruh sis) *n.* From the Greek verb *antiphrazein* (to speak the opposite), based on the preposition *anti-* (opposite of, reverse of) plus *phrasis* (speech), from *phrazein* (to speak), we get *antiphrasis*, the rhetorical device of using a word in a sense opposite to its common or literal meaning, usually for humorous or ironical purposes. Thus, when Liberace was panned by the critics after his Carnegie Hall recital, he " ... *cried* all the way to the bank." In his preface to the *Concise Oxford Dictionary*, H. W. Fowler (he of *Fowler's Modern English Usage*) said: "A dictionary-maker, unless he is a *monster* of omniscience, must deal with a great many matters of which he has no first-hand knowledge," (the older, and Latin sense of "monster" was "anything extraordinary"). Old-time jazz cognoscenti say about a great performer in that medium, "He's *bad*!" meaning "He's good." *W III* gives the example: "a *giant* of three feet, four inches." A mean-spirited acquaintance of mine can't see an unattractive man or woman go by without muttering, "I think you're *pretty*, too!" *Antiphrasis* is an effective rhetorical usage but one must make sure, by inflection or gesture, that one is not taken literally.

antiscian   See **amphiscian; macroscian.**

aphesis   See **feck; hyleg.**

apheta   See **hyleg.**

aphetic   See **feck.**

aposematic   See **epigamic.**

aptote (AP toht) *n.* This is a term in grammar for an indeclinable noun, i.e., one that does not change by virtue of its function in a sentence. The adjective describing such nouns is *aptotic* (ap TOT ik). A related adjective, *anaptotic* (an ap TOT ik), describes nouns that were once inflected but have given up inflectional modifications (case endings) as a result of what some linguists call "phonetic decay," the function of such endings being performed by rules of position in the sentence and the use of "relational words" like prepositions. *Aptote* is derived, via Latin *aptotum*, from the Greek *aptoton*, formed of initial *a-*, the "alpha privative" expressing negation, plus *ptotos* (falling), cognate with *ptosis* (case), from *piptein* (to fall); while *anaptotic* is built of the prefix *an-* (alpha privative again) plus *aptotos*, though some say it is formed of the prefix *ana-* (back) plus *ptotikos* (belonging to case). (While we're at it, *case* is simply a category in inflection; eg., nominative for the subject, possessive or genitive to indicate ownership, origin, etc.) Chinese is a language without inflection, hence *aptotic*. English is *anaptotic*, i.e., a language that has lost most of its original inflections, relying rather on *relational words*, usually prepositions, and position in the sentence. Latin, Greek, Arabic and (in a different way) Eskimo are much more highly inflected than English. In Latin, for example, we have a dative case, one that expresses "indirect object," to indicate the position of a donee or a listener. If I give something *to a boy*, or tell a story *to a man*, the Latin noun *puer* (boy) changes to *puero*, and the noun *homo* (man) to *homini*. In English, *boy* and *man* remain unchanged, and the preposition *to* does the trick. French would use the preposition à, but in German, the nouns, adjectives and articles would be inflected. English, of course, inflects for the plural of nouns (*sister, sisters*). You might well be aware of all this simple grammatical lore, but it does help to illustrate *aptote* and *anaptotic*.

aptotic   See **aptote.**

arbalest   See **matrass.**

archimandrite   See **hegumen.**

arsis   See **hemiola.**

attaccabottoni (uh TAK uh baw TOH nee) *n.* In Italian, *attaccare* can mean "to attach" or "to attack." *Bottone* means "button"; its plural is *bottoni*. *Attaccare un bottone* is literally "to attach (or attack) a button," figuratively "to button-hole." An *attaccabottoni*, then, is a "buttonholer," or in short, a bore, the type of person that more or less imprisons, or at least immobilizes, you and recounts long, pointless tales, usually relating to sad experiences that he or she well deserved. In his excellent daily column in the *Times* (London), "Word-Watching," from which I appropriated this admirable entry, Philip Howard says, "It rhymes with a lot of baloney." Pretty close, Philip! My father arrived in this country from Germany about a century ago, speaking a very correct and unidiomatic British-accented English. When met on the street and asked, "How are you?" he took the question quite literally and went to great lengths (especially on cold, windy days, or when the greeter was in a palpable hurry) to narrate just about everything that had happened to him during the previous few months. This wasn't a case of spontaneous buttonholing but one (according to my father's lights) provoked by the victim.

aumbry   See **ambry.**

auslaut   See **anlaut.**

auxesis   See **anaphora.**

axiopisty (aks ee AH pih stee) *n.* This word comes to us from the Greek *axiopistia* (trustworthiness, credibility), based on the adjective *axiopistos* (trustworthy), built from *axios* (worthy, deserving—which gave us *axiom*, in the sense of "worthy of belief"), plus *pistis* (faith, belief). *Axiopisty* means "trustworthiness, credibility," the quality that makes someone or something deserving of trust, an endowment devoutly to be wished. The American statesman Henry L. Stimson believed in trust. "The only way to make a man trustworthy," he said, "is to trust him; and the surest way to make him untrustworthy is to distrust him and show your distrust." Another saying of his: "The only deadly sin I know is cynicism." Apparently, he felt that *axiopisty* could be built by *pistis* and destroyed by *apistia* (mistrust: that little alpha privative, *a*-, rears its powerful head again!)

azyme (AY zime) *n.* From the Greek alpha privative (negating prefix *a-*) plus **zyme** (leaven, substance added to dough to produce fermentation, usually yeast) we get *azyme* (unleavened bread, bread that has not risen). This is the *matzo* (a Yiddish word, from Hebrew *massah*) that is eaten by Jews during Passover. In Exodus we read: "And the Lord spake unto Moses, saying ... (12:8) And they shall eat ... unleavened bread ... (12:15); Seven days shall ye eat unleavened bread ... (12:17); And ye shall observe the feast of unleavened bread ... (12:20); Ye shall eat nothing leavened ... (12:34); And the people took their dough before it was leavened ... (12:39); And they baked unleavened cakes of the dough which they brought forth out of Egypt, for it was not leavened; because they were thrust out of Egypt, and could not tarry ... (13:6); Seven days thou shalt eat unleavened bread ... (13:7); ... and there shall no leavened bread be seen with thee ... " The Lord was surely insistent on this matter of *azyme*, which is also consecrated by Christians of the Western Church in celebrating the Eucharist. *Azymous* (AZ ih muhs) is the adjective for "unleavened," and an *azymite* (AZ ih mite) is a member of any church that uses unleavened bread, i.e., wafers, in the Eucharist. Incidentally, *azyme* is now sold quite unceremoniously in food stores as a vehicle for transporting dips to the mouth at cocktail parties.

bacchius (buh KEYE uhs) *n.* This is a term in Greek and Latin prosody (meter), denoting a foot of two long or stressed syllables preceded by one short or unstressed one. Examples: *belabor, enticement, reluctance*. The adjective for such a foot is *bacchiac* (buh KEYE uhk). The reverse is an *antibacchius* (an tih buh KEYE uhs), a foot of two long or stressed syllables followed by a short or unstressed one; the adjective is *antibacchic* (an tih BAK uhk), as you mightn't expect. Examples: *lethargy, proofreader*. All of these terms are related to the prosody of the verse sung or recited at the festivals in honor of Bacchus (the *anti-* in *antibacchius*, *-ic* is the Greek prefix meaning "opposite to.") These festivals were known as *bacchanalia* (bak uh NAY lee uh), a term that was later applied to all drunken revels, as is *dionysiac* from Dionysus, the Greek name for Bacchus.

bahuvrihi　　See **tatpurusha.**

bambocciade (bam boh CHAHD) *n.* The Dutch painter variously known as Pieter van Laar and Peter de Laer (1592–c.1675) was known for his grotesque scenes of everyday working-class and peasant life, including realistic studies of country wakes and penny-weddings among the poor (where guests paid trifling sums to defray the expenses of the feast, with anything left over going to the newlyweds to help furnish their homes). The painter's nickname was

Bamboccio (bam BAW cho), an Italian word meaning, literally, "chubby little child" or "puppet" but used figuratively to mean "simpleton." *Bamboccio* was derived from the Italian *bambino* (baby boy) plus the intensive suffix -*occio*, giving it the sense of "big booby," and the name *bambocciade* applied to this type of rustic genre painting came, via French *bambochade* and Italian *Bambocciata*, from *bamboccio*.

banausic (buh NOS ik, -NOZ-) *adj.* This word somehow irritates me, as it runs counter to my early teachings. My wise father told me all about the laborer being worthy of his hire. "All work must be respected," he said, "provided it is honest and good. The shoemaker is worthy of your respect and appreciation, as worthy as your doctor, your professor, your famous artist, your great physicist." Well, *banausic*, derived from Greek *banausikos* (relating to artisans, from *banausos*, artisan) came to mean more or less, "practical." Wrote John Buchan (Baron Tweedsmuir, Scottish novelist, historian and governor general of Canada 1935–1940): "My approach to this literature was ... *banausic*. I wanted advice, instruction, not aids to reflection." He was using *banausic* to mean "governed by utilitarian purposes." So far so good. But the word, sadly, developed pejorative connotations: "common, dull, menial," and even "moneymaking," and "materialistic" in a disapproving, condescending, demeaning sense. I don't like that sort of elitist attitude toward the noble horny-handed sons of toil.

bebung (BAY boohng) *n.* This term in music for a maneuver on the clavichord: fluctuating the pressure of the finger on the key to produce a tremolo effect. For the benefit of those who may not be familiar with early musical instruments, a clavichord is a keyboard in a small rectangular box containing a sounding board and a set of strings. Pressure on a key causes a small metal wedge, called a *tangent*, to strike a string. The clavichord was supplanted by the piano at the end of the 18th century, but here and there specialists in ancient instruments play it at intimate recitals for the cognoscenti. The instrument makes very soft sounds and requires rapt attention: no talking (or heavy breathing). The tremolo can be performed on certain musical instruments, particularly the strings (as well as by the human voice, in which case it is known as *vibrato*), to produce an emotional effect. *Bebung* is a German word, based on the verb *beben* (to shake or quiver); it means "vibration" and in music "tremolo."

bellet(t)rist (bel LEH trist) *n. Belles-lettres* (bel LET'R), literally, in French, "fine letters," has been assimilated into English to denote elegant literature, or literature regarded as a fine art, having a purely aesthetic, as opposed to a utilitarian, function. The term embraces poetry, fiction, criticism and literary studies. The *O.E.D.* calls it a "vaguely used term ... now generally applied (when used at all) to the lighter branches of literature or the aesthetics of literary study." This term gave rise to *bellet(t)rist*, "a person devoted to *belles-*

lettres," and the adjective *belletristic* (bel let TRIS tik), describing anyone or anything in that category. Coleridge said, "I wish I could find a more familiar word than *aesthetic*, for works of taste and criticism. It is, however, in all respects better, and of more reputable origin, than *belletristic*." Matthew Arnold referred to himself as "an unlearned *belletristic* trifler." The word still bore its somewhat pejorative connotation when the English writer Mark Pattison wrote (1868), "We have risen above the mere *belletristic* treatment of classical literature."

benison   See **catmalison.**

bicorn   See **chichevache.**

biretta   See **zucchetto.**

bombus (BOM buhs) *n.* A *bombus*, in Latin, is "any hollow sound," and more specifically, "a humming, a buzzing, a booming, a trumpet blast." Its Greek antecedent, *bombos*, denoted any deep, hollow sound. Quite obviously, the word is onomatopoeic in both languages. We have taken it over in a variety of senses. As a medical term, it denotes both *tinnitus*, a humming or buzzing noise in the ears (a source of great discomfort to many people), and a rumbling of the intestines, which can be most embarrassing at dinner parties. In entomology, *bombus* is the name of the insect genus that includes the bumblebee, whose everyday name comes from *bomblen* (to boom), the Middle English descendant of *bombus*. Finally, and rather strangely, *bombus* is a term applied to an orchestral conductor's technique: the movement of the hands indicating the rhythmic flow and harmonic pattern of the buzzing of bees. This must be the only instance where an ancient source has given us a medical term, an entomological classification and the name of an orchestral conductor's technique. Dead languages indeed!

borborygmic   See **borborygmus.**

borborygmus (bawr buh RIG muhs) *n.* Taken intact from the Latin, based on Greek *borborygmos*, from the verb *borboryzein* (to have a rumbling in the bowels), we get this almost onomatopoeic word denoting the sound of flatulence in the intestines. In his *Zoonomia, or the Laws of Organic Life* (1794), Erasmus Darwin called it *borborigmi* and defined it as "rumbling of the bowels," and in 1880, Lionel S. Beale, in his book *On Slight Ailments*, used it in the plural, stating, "*Borborigmi* ... are a serious annoyance." He didn't say precisely to whom, but I would imagine the sufferers included near neighbors at a dinner party. The adjective describing one producing these unlovely sounds, and the sounds themselves, is *borborygmic* (bawr buh RIG mik), and it can be found in Vladimir Nabokov's *Ada* (1969), where we come upon this dramatic sentence: "All the toilets and waterpipes in the house had been suddenly seized with *borborygmic* convulsions." Some sentence, especially for a man writing in an acquired tongue! Seems Nabokov liked *borborygmi*. In his *Introduction to Pushkin's Poetry* (1988), he expressed his concern about the loss of the original Russian in translation. He tried to put Pushkin's lines into French, and this is what happened, in Nabokov's words:

> Even though all the words are there, I do not believe these lines [the translation] can give an idea of the ample and powerful lyricism of our poet ... [I tried] to put myself into a kind of trance so that ... the miracle of total metamorphosis might occur. At last, after several hours of these internal mutterings, of those *borborygmi* of the soul that accompany the composition of poetry, I felt the miracle had been accomplished. But ... the distance separating the Russian text from the translation ... was now evident in all its sad reality ...

So here we have *borborygmi* of the soul as well as those of the toilets! Of course, Nabokov's experience brings to mind the sad but realistic Italian pun about translation: *"Traduttore traditore"* ("Translator traitor"—and how well my poor translation from the Italian illustrates the point!).

boreen (boh REEN) *n.* When I run across a two-syllable word ending in *-een*, I sense the spirit of Ireland: *colleen, poteen* (illicitly distilled Irish whiskey), *shebeen* (an illicit liquor store). So with *boreen*, "a narrow country lane, especially in hilly country," according to *W III*, and by transference, "an opening passage through a throng." The derivation is from the Irish *bothar*, pronounced BOH uhr, plus the usual diminutive ending *-een*, from Irish *-in*. Some authorities offer the suggestion that the *bo-* element is from Old Irish *bo* (ox, cow), going back to Latin *bos* (ox, bull, cow). An especially charming term of endearment is *mavourneen* (muh VOOHR neen), "my dear one, my darling," which comes from the Irish words *mo mhurnin*. One can almost smell the peat. Both senses of *boreen* appear in Samuel and Anna Hall's *Ireland: Its Scenery, Character, etc.* (1841). At one point, we find the phrase, "At my brother's, a piece down that *boreen*," and later on, "Wheresomever he went, the people made a *boreen* for him." A sweet word, describing at first the lovely prospect of a remote narrow country road, and, by an imaginative extension, an aisle made through a crowd of people deferentially permitting the passage of a personage.

Borough-English *n.* The word *borough* has a confusing (and here irrelevant) multiplicity of meanings that depend largely on the geographical or chronological context. In all cases, it is a political subdivision of one sort or another. *Borough-English* is another matter: a custom in certain English counties (Kent, Sussex, Surrey, Somerset), abolished in 1925, whereby real estate passed to the youngest sister, and failing a sister, to the youngest brother, and so on to the youngest collateral relative of whatever degree of consanguinity. This arrangement, obviously, flew in the face of the system of primogeniture. The name was derived in a curious manner, as a partial translation of the Anglo-French *tenure en Burgh Engloys* (tenure in English borough). According to Blacksone (i.e., Sir William Blackstone, 1723–80, English jurist and author of the then-definitive *Blackstone's Commentaries*), the Normans gave it that name to distinguish this purely English custom from the universal French system of inheritance. Real estate held by those inheriting under the *Borough-English* system was occasionally known as "Cradle Land" or "Cradle Holding," an obvious reference to inheritance by the "baby" of the family. (The *O.E.D.* differs, saying that *cradle-land* means "a land in which a people dwell in their earliest times.") According to Sir Frederick Pollock, an authority on the land laws of England, in an 1882 issue of *Macmillan's Magazine*, "The custom of *borough-English* abounds in Kent, Sussex, Surrey, the neighborhood of London, and Somerset. In the midlands it is rare, and north of the Humber [the estuary between Lincolnshire and Yorkshire in the north of England] … it does not seem to occur." Another system of inheritance in Kent that went into effect after the Norman Conquest was *gavelkind*, whereby primogeniture was replaced by the division of the deceased's property equally among his sons, and the laws of inheritance by widows and widowers differed from the general customs of England. Note that all of the above relates to the case of intestacy (the absence of a will) and that changes could be effected by will.

bothros (BOTH ruhs) *n.* The only mention of *bothros* in the *O.E.D.* that I could find was a reference to "G[reek] *bothros* pit" in the etymology of a botanical term of no great interest, and in the *Supplement*, the same reference in another botanical term of little concern here; but there is no listing of *bothros* as a word. *W III* does list it, as a term in archaeology, with the definition "a hole or pit into which drink offerings to the nether gods were poured by the ancient Greeks"; and the etymological information is that it is Greek, "perhaps akin to Latin *fodere* to dig." (*W II* had listed it, characterizing it with the reference "Gr[eek] Antiq[uity]" but with no etymological material, and defining it as "a hole or pit made in the earth, esp[ecially] one in which drink offerings to the nether gods were poured." One wonders what happened in the interim before *W III* was published to cause the dropping of the "esp[ecially]" and the introduction of the etymological link to *fodere*. Obviously, the *W III* staff had come to the conclusion that the *only* function of *bothroi* [the plural form of the noun] was to receive those libations, and somebody came up with the possible kinship with *fodere*.) On the other hand, many entries or parts of entries in *W II* were dropped from *W III* for reasons of space; the new edition was confined to 5 inches in thickness for technical reasons of production. *RH* mentions Greek *bothros* in the etymology of a zoological term of no interest here but ignores it as an English word. What are we to do? All I can do is to hope that since the gods who got the libations were "nether," the Greeks didn't waste any vintage wines on them, and let it go at that.

bothy, also **bothie** (BOTH ee) *n.* The *O.E.D.* characterizes this word as Scottish, *W III* as chiefly Scottish, and *CH*, in one of its definitions, refers to Scotland but apparently accepts it as belonging to the English language. (Remember that *CH* is published in Edinburgh, and its editor is named MacDonald.) In any event, a *bothy* is "a hut, a humble abode, one-roomed and sometimes affording only temporary shelter." *CH* says it is "a barely furnished dwelling for farm-servants in the north-east of Scotland"; *W III* adds "a shepherd's or hunter's shelter" and says that the *o* can be either long or short; and *RH* says that the first two letters can be pronounced as in *thin* or *that*; the *O.E.D.* tells us that *bothies* (however pronounced) were used as collective lodgings by masons and quarrymen as well as farm laborers and makes mention of *bothies* for female servants as well. *CH* adds the information that a *bothy ballad* is a folk song, "dealing with country matters, usu[ally] bawdy" (sounds like fun), and gives us *bothyman* without bothering to define it, because the meaning is obvious. Take your choice of pronunciation and scope of function, but you get the general idea. All of these sources relate it to the noun *booth.*

bothy ballad   See **bothy.**

bothyman   See **bothy.**

brachiate (BRAKE ee ate) *adj., vb.* If you happen to remember *bracchium* (arm) from Latin 1, you would guess correctly that *bracchiate* was an adjective meaning "having arms." What you mightn't know is that as a term in botany, it describes trees that have paired branches pointing so as to form approximately right angles and crossing each other alternately. If you had had no Greek, you wouldn't know that the Romans got *bracchium* from the Greek *brachion.* It happens that *brachiate* is also a verb, describing the practice of anthropoids like apes, chimpanzees, gibbons and orangutans of swinging from branch to branch by their arms. Julian Huxley, in *Problems of Relative Growth* (1932), tells us that man "is undoubtedly descended from *brachiating* ancestors with relatively long arms." *Brachiation* is the act or practice of *brachiating* , and an anthropoid that engages in that activity is a *brachiator.* If I remember rightly, Tarzan was a pretty good *brachiator* and helped to prove Huxley's point.

brachycatalectic   See **ithyphallic.**

brachycephal   See **dolichocephal.**

breviate (BREE vee ate) *n.* At first glance, *breviate* looks like an abbreviation of *abbreviate,* but it has a life of its own as a noun meaning "brief statement, compendium, summary." It comes from *breviatum*, the neuter of the past participle of Latin *breviare* (to shorten—from which we get *breviary*), from the adjective *brevis* (short), which may be familiar from the Roman philosopher Seneca's aphorism *Vita brevis, ars longa* (Life is short, art enduring), first said three centuries earlier by the Greek physician Hippocrates (the "Father of Medicine"). One P. B. Power wrote a book entitled *Breviates: or Short Texts and their Teachings* (1862). Thomas Fuller, in *A Pisgah-sight of Palestine* (1650), wrote: "What we read in St. Luke was onely the *breviate*, sum, and abridgement of his Sermon." (*Pisgah* is the name of a mountain ridge in ancient Palestine, now in Jordan. It was from one of its peaks, Mt. Nebo, that Moses viewed the Promised Land.) Thomas Tryon used the word figuratively in *A Treatise of Dreams and Visions* (1695): "God made him [man] … a *breviate* [epitome] of the nature of all things divine and humane." *Breviate* was once used to denote a brief dispatch, a note or a lawyer's brief, but those uses are now obsolete.

bunraku (boohn RAH kooh) *n.* This term, transliterated from the Japanese, has become the generic term for the Japanese puppet theater. Originally, it was the name of a type of traditional puppet manipulation practiced by the *Bunraku-za* puppetry company in its theater. There are two schools of Japanese puppet art, the Yuki and the *Bunraki*. The former manipulates the puppets by strings, the latter by people holding the dolls. In the *Bunraku* technique, the puppets measure about three feet high and are manipulated by men who remain visible throughout the performance. The chief characters are each handled by three persons. This form of entertainment, known variously as the "puppet theater" or "doll theater," is a uniquely Japanese form requiring a high degree of expertise. Somehow, the visible manipulators seem to fade into the background so completely as to impart an uncanny realism to the puppets.

burgage   See **soc(c)age.**

ca'canny (kuh KAN ee), occasionally -**conny** *n., vb. Ca'* is a Scottish variant of *call*, and *canny* is a familiar word with some rather unfamiliar meanings, including, as an adverb, "cautiously, carefully." Put together, *ca'canny*, as a verb, means "to proceed cautiously," but in labor terms it means, "to go slow," i.e., to adopt a "go-slow policy" as an antimanagement tactic. As a noun, a *ca'canny* is "a slowdown, a deliberate slackening of the work rate or quantity produced." *Ca'canny* began as a general term for "caution" or "moderation" but soon acquired the special meaning of the labor tactic described above. As long ago as 1896, an issue of the *Westminster Gazette* described a British labor leader as the first "to reduce to a fine art the *ca'conny* policy so well known in Western America." In the same year, the *Seamen's Chronicle* discussed the subject in question-and-answer form: "What is *ca'canny*? It is a simple and handy phrase which is used to describe a new instrument or policy which may be used by the workers in place of a strike." A 1958 issue of *The Economist* contains this amusing sentence: "The teaching staff defends itself skilfully from battle to battle with cynicism and *ca'canny*." The rather awkward forms *ca'cannyism* and *ca'cannyness*, to describe the policy, or used to denote caution generally, have also been introduced. A 1963 issue of *The Economist* spoke of " ... the entrenched forces of *ca'canniness*." The use of the term may be restricted to England and Scotland—but not the practice.

cacodemon   See **evancalous.**

cacography   See **evancalous.**

cacohydrophobia   See **xenodochiophobia.**

caconym (KA kuh nim) *n. Kakos*, in Greek, means "bad" and gives us the prefix *caco-*, as in *cacophony, cacography* (bad handwriting or spelling), *cacology* (bad choice of words or incorrect pronunciation), etc. Add *-nym*, the suffix formed from *onoma* (name), as in *antonym, pseudonym*, etc., and you wind up with *caconym*, a "bad name," "bad nomenclature" or "bad terminology," especially in biology and botany. O. F. Cook, in *The American Naturalist*, states: "A name rejected for linguistic reasons [is] a *caconym*." *The National Cactus and Succulent Journal* tells us: "A name may qualify as a *caconym* in different ways. First, from sheer length. Second, from the clash of consonants making it difficult (for a European at least) to articulate." Perhaps *mesopterygium* (part of the fin in some fishes) and *mesopterygoid* (part of the pterygoid that articulates with the palatine bone of the basipterygoid process of the splenoid, or with both—bet you didn't know that!) or *blastophthoria* (the hypothetical degeneration of germ cells caused, for example, by alcoholism) or *pseudolamellabranchiate* (relating to certain mollusks such as some scallops and oysters—the definition goes on and on) might be classified as *caconyms* and candidates for rejection. Arise, a new Linnaeus!

cacorrhaphiaphobia (kah koh rahf ee uh FOH bee uh) *n.* A strange word, this, for, though the *caco-* element, from the Greek *kako-*, the combining form of *kakos* (bad), and the familiar *-phobia* suffix are straightforward enough, the central element, *rhaphia*, meaning in this context "planning, devising," is based on the verb *rhaptein*, whose literal meaning is "to sew" but which is here used metaphorically in the sense of "to plan" or "to devise." How a verb meaning "to sew" gets to be used figuratively to mean "to plan" remains something of a mystery to me. I have been unable to discover any explanation of this strange departure. Well, putting it all together, we arrive at "fear of failure" (literally, bad planning dread, from *caco-* plus *rhaphia* plus *phobia*). Fear of failure is indeed a not uncommon human experience, one that has doubtless inhibited many a promising career, but it took those Greeks to have a word for it. Shades of Zoe Akins! If you think the Germans have a genius for concocting sesquipedalian jawbreakers by stringing word elements together, just browse through a Greek dictionary when you have time on your hands. Have time on your hands? They had *two* words for that: *hesukhazein* and *skholazein*.

cacotopia   See **dystopia.**

cacuminal (ka KYOOH muhn uhl) *adj.* This is a term in phonetics. *Cacumen* is Latin for "top, tip." *Cacuminal* describes sounds produced with the tip of the tongue curled upward toward the hard palate or roof of the mouth. Synonyms, in this field, are *retroflex, inverted, cerebral* and *coronal*, all with special uses. The phonologist A. J. Ellis gave as an example of a "corona" phoneme, "The ... *d* in *do* with the tip of the tongue free from the gums, and approaching the 'crown' of the arch of the hard palate." Other examples are *l* and *n*, in the pronunciation of which the upward curl of the tongue occurs at the end of the sound, rather than the beginning, as in the case of *d*. All the adjectives mentioned above can be used alone, as substantives. A word etymologically related to *cacuminal*, but with a different meaning and application, is *cacuminous* (ka KYOOH muhn us), describing trees having pyramidal tops. In fact, in Latin, *cacumen*, by itself, can mean "treetop." Mortimer Collins, in *Pen Sketches by a Vanished Hand* (1876), wrote the lines: "Luminous books (not voluminous)/To read under beech-trees *cacuminous*." Some of the meanings of *luminous* are "clear," "lucid" and "intellectually brilliant." Lucky reader!

cacuminous   See **cacuminal.**

caduceus   See **petasus.**

caesura   See **dolichurus.**

caitiff (KAY tif) *n.* To call a man a *caitiff* is to say that he is a mean, base, despicable person. *Caitiff* can be used as an adjective as well: a *caitiff* person is mean, vile, base. Originally, the word meant "captive," a sense now obsolete but one that explains its derivation from Latin *captivus* (captive). The term took expectable forms in the Romance tongues: Old French *chaitif*, whence came modern French *chétif* (puny, pitiful, mean, worthless), Spanish *cautivo* (captive), Italian *cattivo* (bad, wicked, nasty). The word then took on a different meaning, also now obsolete: "wretched, miserable, pitiable." It is easy to see how this development came about: After all, a captive is a wretched soul, a person in a piteous situation. Eventually, *caitiff* acquired the connotation of contempt and finally, of moral disapprobation, so that it now means "villain," base, mean and despicable, totally dissociated from the "captive" sense, like *chétif* in French and *cattivo* in Italian. The same development occurred in its adjectival use. In 1501 Richard Arnolde could write, in his *Chronicle*: " ... he is kepte as a *kaytyf* in myserable seruitude," and in 1678 Samuel Butler, in *Hudibras*: "I pity'd the sad Punishment/The wretched *caitiff* underwent." Edward A. Freeman, in *The History of the Norman Conquest* (1867), described "Two *caitiffs* whose names are handed down to infamy." What a clear and interesting demonstration of the evolution of the sense of the word! There are even instances of transformation from commendatory to pejorative: *awful*, from "awe-inspiring" to "very bad"; *egregious*, from "distinguished, illustrious" to "outrageous, shocking"; *dreadful*, from "reverential, awe-inspiring" to "horrid." A case in reverse: *terrific* from "terrifying" to "excellent, (colloquially) great." As my college English professor used to say, "To be sure of the meaning, take note of the date!"

calcinate   See **phlogiston.**

calenture (KAL uhn chuhr) *n. Calere* means "to be hot" in Latin; the present participle is *calens*, of which the stem is *calent-*, and from that the Spanish took *calentar* (to be hot) and *calentura* (fever). The French turned that into *calenture*, and we took it over intact, to designate an illness affecting sailors in the tropics, causing delirium that leads the victims to believe the ocean to be green fields into which they wish to jump. The word came to mean "fever" generally, and sometimes "sunstroke." In *Robinson Crusoe*, Defoe writes: "In this voyage ... I was continually sick, being thrown into a violent *Calenture* by the excessive Heat." Swift's poem *The Bubble: a Poem (Upon the South Sea Project)* contains these dramatic lines:

> So, by a *calenture* misled,
> The mariner with rapture sees,
> On the smooth ocean's azure bed,
> Enamell'd fields and verdant trees.

The word was eventually used metaphorically to mean "burning passion, ardor." Donne wrote: "Knowledge kindles *Calentures* in some." Jeremy Taylor (*Of the Sacred Order and Offices of Episcopacy*, 1642) wrote of " ... the *Calenture* of primitive devotion." So you see, there are good and bad *calentures*, fevers that burn your body, and fevers that burn your soul.

calepin (KAL uh pin) *n.* An Augustine friar named Abrosio (no, this isn't the first line of a limerick) was born in Calepio, Italy, and thus acquired the surname Calepino, in the same way that the painter Paolo Cagliari became *Veronese* and Domenico, whose real surname we don't know, is known as *Veneziano* because of their geographical, rather than familial, associations. Ambrosio brought out a polyglot Latin dictionary in 1502. Edition after edition appeared, and it became the leading Latin dictionary of the 16th century—so much so that his geographical cognomen became generic in Italian for "dictionary," entering the French language as "calepin," in which form it was taken into English. The word then acquired the figurative meaning of "notebook, memorandum book, reference book." In earlier times people spoke of "my *Calepin*" in the same way as devotees of classical Greek have been referring to "my *Liddell & Scott*" since its appearance in 1846. Here are some lines from Donne's *Fourth Satire*:

> Whom do you prefer
> For the best linguist? And I sillily
> Said that I thought *Calepine's* Dictionary.

Calepins were highly valued in the old days, so much so that there is on record a 1569 Lancastrian will that makes one the subject matter of a specific bequest: "I wyll that Henry Marrecrofte shall have my *calapyne* ... " We must forgive the linguistically inclined testator for his fanciful spelling of*calepin*.

calotte   See **zucchetto.**

calx   See **phlogiston.**

canephor(e) (KAN uh for), also **canephora, -ros, -rus** (kan EF uh ruh, -ros, -rus) *n*. In ancient Greece, this was the name of a maiden who carried on her head a basket containing the sacred objects used at the feasts of Demeter, Dionysus (Bacchus) and Athena. In architecture, the term was applied to a sculptured figure of a young person of either sex carrying on the head a basket containing materials for the offering of sacrifices, or a caryatid (kar ee AT uhd) (a sculptured figure used as a column) supporting a basketlike member serving as a capital. According to an 1849 issue of *Fraser's Magazine*, "to be chosen *canephor* was as if 'Beautiful' were stamped on the lintel of a woman's door." Encomium indeed! Shades of the Miss America contest! The Greek noun was *kanephoros* (basket bearer), built of *kaneon* (basket) and *phoros* (bearing), akin to *pherein* (to carry).

cangue, also **cang** (KANG) *n*. This delightful object was a portable pillory consisting of a broad heavy wooden frame or board borne with the top beam supported on the shoulders by petty offenders in China in the old days. The device was 3 or 4 feet square, weighed 50 or 60 pounds and prevented any use of the hands above the shoulders, so that the poor soul had to be fed by others. It couldn't have been much fun. The related Portuguese word is *cango*, a variant of *canga*, a porter's yoke or a yoke for oxen. A letter to the Chinese embassy in Washington inquiring as to the date of the abolition of the *cangue* and the nature of its replacement in the current criminal system is awaiting an answer.

cardophagus (kar DOF uh guhs) *n*. *Kardos*, Greek for "thistle," became *carduus* in Latin. *Phagos* is Greek for "eater, glutton" and is related to *phagein* (to eat). Putting the pieces together we got *cardophagus*, which means literally "thistle-eater," and, in the bargain, "donkey." *Chardon* is French for "thistle," and the French idiom *bête à manger du chardon* (literally, silly enough to eat thistles) means "as silly as an ass," and an ass is a donkey, isn't it, so that somehow we get to *donkey* from *thistle-eater*, don't we? *Cardo* is both Italian and Spanish for "thistle"; my, how that dead Latin does persist! In Thackeray's novel *The Virginians* we read: "Kick and abuse him, you who have never brayed; but bear with him, all honest fellow-*cardophagi*." Is there a "Be Kind to Donkeys" week? In British English, *donkey's years* means "a long time." Example: "They've lived there for donkey's years," or "I haven't seen Archie for donkey's years." Some say that this picturesque expression is a pun on *donkey's ears*, which, as you know, are very long. Others say that it is an allusion to the great age to which donkeys live, based on the tradition that nobody ever sees a dead donkey. After all this, if you want to tell a friend he's silly, call him a *cardophagus* and let him think it's a compliment. Do donkeys eat thistles? I've never seen it happen, and I invite information from donkey-buffs or thistle-buffs.

catalectic   See **prosodion.**

catholicon (kuh THOL uh kuhn) *n.* At first blush, this word might appear to have some application to religious matters, but that is not the case. The derivation here has to do with the adjective *catholic* in the sense of "universal, all-encompassing," as in "catholic tastes" or "catholic interests," from which sense the ecclesiastical use derived: the Church Universal. A *catholicon* is "a panacea, a universal remedy, a cure-all." Thus, Sir Thomas Browne, in *Religio Medici* (1643), could write: "Death is the cure of all diseases. There is no *Catholicon* or universal remedy I know but this." *Catholic* comes from the Greek adjective *katholikos* (universal), and *catholicon* from *katholikon*, the neuter form of the adjective. The *O.E.D.* begins its definition with the words "An electuary supposed to be capable of evacuating all humours ... " That leads us to wonder a bit about *electuary, evacuate* and *humours*, does it not? *Electuary* (ih LEK tyooh air ee) is from the Late Latin *electuarium*, which seems to stem from the Greek verb *ekleichein* (to lick out) and is the pharmaceutical term for medicines sweetened with honey or syrup, to be licked off a spoon. *Evacuation* is used in physiology for the emptying of waste matter, especially through the bowels. *Humours* (the British spelling) were considered by the ancients to be the principal fluids of the body: blood, phlegm, choler and black bile or melancholy, the balance of which determined a person's physical and mental makeup. Would that we could find a *catholicon* for the disorders of today's world!

catholicos   See **hegumen.**

catmalison (KAT mal uh z'n, -s'n) *n.* This peculiar dialectal word is based on what is probably a misconception concerning cats. The word is constructed of *cat*, the familiar domestic pet, and *malison* (MAL uh z'n, -s'n), meaning "curse," from Old French *maleison*. A *malison* is a doublet of malediction. (*Doublet* has various meanings, one of which denotes either of a pair of words in the same language derived from the same source but divergent in meaning: e.g. one directly from Latin, the other via Old French. *RH* gives the example of *quiet* and *coy*, the former coming directly from Latin *quietus*, the latter via Old French *quei*.) *Malison* is the opposite of *benison* (BEN ih suhn), an archaic word for "blessing," which is a *doublet* of *benediction* (Latin *benedictio*, Old French *beneiçun*). But we've come a long way from *catmalison*, which means "cupboard in or near the ceiling" and therefore a "curse" to cats, for the simple reason that they can't find a way of getting into it. The misconception mentioned above is the rash underestimation of a cat's ability to get into *anything*, based on my lifetime of experience and admiration of their persistence and ingenuity. My cats, anyway!

catoptric (kat OP trik) *adj.* This adjective describes anything relating to reflection, part of the science of optics, which deals with the properties of light and vision. The word is derived from the Greek *katroptikos* (relating to a mirror), based on *katropton* (mirror), formed of the preposition *kata* (against) plus *op-* (the stem of *oran*, to see) plus *-tron* (the suffix of instrument, as in, e.g., *cyclotron*). Ansted and Latham, writing about the Channel Islands in 1862, spoke of "the light-houses each having a *catoptric* light of the first order." *Catoptrics* is the branch of optics covering reflection generally. *Catoptromancy* (kat OP troh man see) is divination by means of a mirror, the suffix *-mancy*, from Greek *manteia* (divination), being a combining form meaning "divination," as, for example, in *necromancy*. Edward Smedley, writing in 1855 about the occult sciences, described *catoptromancy* as "a species of divination by the mirror." This science didn't do Snow White's stepmother much good.

catoptromancy   See **catoptric.**

cecity (SEE sih tee) *n. Cecity* is "blindness." The word comes from the Latin *caecitas*, and like its ancestor, encompasses blindness of the mind as well as the eye. "None so blind as those that will not see," wrote Matthew Henry in *Commentaries: Jeremiah*, echoing Jer. 5:21: " … O foolish people, and without understanding; which have eyes, and see not … " Anthony Burgess (*Earthly Powers*) used the word figuratively, too: " … my love … induces a *cecity* to your inefficiency and your bad behavior." The metaphorical use appears to be more common than the literal. Incidentally, going back to the derivation of *cecity*, the ending *-ity* is our equivalent of the Latin *-itas* in abstract nouns: *capacitas, ferocitas, simplicitas* and lots more; thus, *cecity* from *caecitas*. *Cecutiency* (sih KU shun see), "tendency to blindness," is derived from *caecutiens*, the present participle of the verb *caecutire* (to be blind), and this leads me to observe that our ending *-ency* comes from the Latin *-entia*, which in turn is based on the Latin present participial endings: *dependency, emergency, exigency*, from *dependens, emergens*, etc. Disraeli wrote of "the *cecity* of superstition," and Matthew

Arnold, in *Ode to Westminster Abbey*, wrote: "After light's term, a term of *cecity*."

cenacle (SEN uh k'l) *n.* Though this word has the general meaning of "supper room," it is usually understood to refer to the room in which Christ and the apostles ate the Last Supper on the night before the crucifixion. It has also been given the meaning of a "coterie" or its meeting place. Via Late Latin *cenaculum*, the diminutive of Latin *cena* (dinner, meal), the word comes from the French *cénacle* (a guest chamber where the Lord's supper was eaten; figuratively, literary society or coterie). The scene of the Last Supper in the *cenacle* has been painted by a number of masters, the most famous by far being the one Leonardo da Vinci painted on a wall of the refectory of the convent of Santa Maria delle Grazie in Milan. In World War II, allied bombs reduced the refectory to ruins, but da Vinci's wall was practically undamaged and the painting left intact, *mirabile dictu*, though time had worn it badly. It is now, thank heaven, protected against further deterioration.

Chasid   See **Mitnagged.**

chasuble   See **phelonion.**

chernozëm (chair nuh ZYOM) *n.* Also transliterated from the Russian as *tschernozem* and *tschernosem*; but note the pronunciation of the last syllable, following the same system that requires the spelling of Gorbach*e*v, pronounced Gorbach*o*v. Why is this? Why not spell it the way it is pronounced? (Because the *e* in the last syllable is topped by a sort of umlaut and therefore takes the stress.) Be that as it may, *chernozëm* is the Russian word for "black earth," based on *cherno-* the combining form of *cherny* (black) [I must interpolate: Remember the stock Russian song *ochi chorniya*, meaning "black eyes," sung along with *The Two Guitars*, tremulously, with balalaika accompaniment, on the tiniest provocation, wherever Russians congregate? Well, here's old friend *cherny*, pronounced *chorny*, once again.]—now getting back to etymology—plus *-zem*, the combining form of Russian *zemlya* (earth). *Chernozem* is a soil extremely rich in humus and carbonates, found in cool and temperate subhumid climates, notably in central Russia and central North America. I first ran across the word in my friend Lement Harris's fascinating memoir *My Tale of Two Worlds*. In a chapter entitled "Soviet Farms and Life" (the year was 1929 and the place Egorlikskaya, near Rostov) he writes: "With the harvest completed, I spent a day driving around the countryside ... The whole region is black earth, *chernozem*, the richest soil that exists ... the black-earth band in North America runs north and south, roughly from Winnipeg, Canada, to the panhandle of Texas. The Soviet black-earth band runs east and west, from the Ukraine across the Volga River into the arid parts of Central Asia." Well, now you know about *chernozem*: what it is, where it is and why it's a blessing wherever it is.

chersonese (KUR suh neez, -nees) *n. Chersonese* means "peninsula." Whereas *peninsula* is derived from the Latin *paene* (almost) plus *insula* (island), *chersonese* comes from the Greek *chersonesos*, formed of *chersos* (dry land) plus *nesos* (island). Apparently, the Romans thought of a peninsula as "almost an island" and the Greeks as a "dry island," both rather imaginative terms. You don't see *chersonese* these days, but it was once much used in literature. In *Paradise Lost* Milton wrote: "Thence to Agra and Lahor of Great Mogul, Down to the golden *Chersonese*," and in his *Tour Through the Whole Island of Great Britain*, Defoe wrote of "this little *Chersonese*, called The Land's End." Washington Irving wrote of "that great *chersonese* or peninsula ... known by the name of Arabia." The English poet Patrick Shaw-Stewart, rereading *The Iliad* on the way to Gallipoli during World War I, according to Michael Wood in *In Search of the Trojan War* (Facts On File, New York, 1985), " ... felt a dreadful sense of *déjà vu* at the sight of ... Troy ... " and wrote a poem containing these lines:

> Achilles came to Troyland
> And I to *Chersonese*:
> He turned from wrath to battle,
> And I from three days' peace.

So *chersonese* caught the attention of writers both English and American and is therefore worthy of our attention; it is a pretty and interesting word, and, particularly in view of its derivation, right up there with *peninsula*.

chiasmus (keye AZ muhs) *n. Chi* is the 22nd letter of the Greek alphabet; its symbol is X. *Chiasmus* is a rhetorical term, taken from Greek *chiasmos*, the noun akin to the Greek verb *chiazein* (to mark with a *chi*, i.e., an X). A *chiasmus* is a device in rhetoric based on the scheme of parallelism in reverse order, i.e., a grammatical figure in which the word order in the first of two parallel clauses is reversed in the second. The word is based on the fact that a *chi*, or *X*, is a symbol of *crossing*, i.e., dividing in crossed form. Examples are given in the various dictionaries. *CH*: "Do not eat to live, but live to eat." *C.O.D.*: "To stop too fearful, and too faint to go." *W III*: "A superman in physique but in intellect a fool." The *O.E.D.* gives us one in Latin, quoting an 1871 book by A. S. Wilkins on Cicero's attack on Catiline in which Cicero, in one of the Catilinarian Orations, uses the *chiasmus*, "Frequentia sustentatur, alitur otio" (By abundance he is sustained, nourished by leisure). Wilkins comments: "This is a good instance of the ... figure called *chiasmus* ... in which the order of words in the first clause is inverted in the second." *W II* gives: "Burns with one love, with one resentment glows." These examples ought to give you a pretty good idea of what a *chiasmus* is.

chichevache (CHICH uh vash) *n. Chicheface*, a French word (*chichefache* in northern France), means literally "niggardly-face, thin face, ugly face." Chaucer changed the word to *chichevache*, meaning "lean cow, ugly cow," and used it in *The Clerk's Tale* as the name of a fabulous monster that fed only on good, patient women, and who, because there were so few of them, was always lean and hungry, all skin and bones. In the Chaucer poem, we read: "O noble wyuys ful of heigh prudence/Let noon humilytee youre tongè naille/Ne let no clerk have cause or diligence/To write of yow a storie of swich mervaille/As of Grisildis, pacient and kynde,/Lest *Chichevache* yow swelwe in hire entraille." (Freely: Noble wives, don't let anyone proclaim your virtues, comparing you to patient Griselda [the model of enduring patience and wifely obedience, heroine also of the last tale in Boccaccio's *Decameron*], lest *Chichevache* swallow you into his entrails.) That monster was the very converse of *Bicorn* or *Bycorne* (BEYE korn), a fabulous beast who was well nourished by his diet of virtuous and patient husbands. The English monk and poet John Lydgate, a younger contemporary of Chaucer, wrote a poem entitled *Chichevache and Bicorn*, in which we read: "*Chichevache* etith wymmen goode." What a pair of misogynists those English poets were; how different from their Italian contemporary!

chinook   See **moazagotl.**

chi-rho (KEE roh, KEYE-) *n.* The first two letters of the name of Christ in Greek, *kh* and *rho*, are known as *chi* and *rho* in the English language. (In the Greek alphabet they are *X* and *P*.) The monogram formed of *chi* and *rho*, *chi-rho*, also called the *Christogram*, constitutes a symbol of Christ, often embroidered on altar cloths and clerical vestments. After the conversion of the Emperor Constantine I to Christianity, he adopted a standard consisting of a purple silk banner that hung from a crosspiece on a pike, adorned with a golden crown bearing the *chi-rho*, a *P* surmounting a *X*. Known as a *labarum* (LAH buh ruhm), it became the imperial standard of the later Roman emperors, taking the form of a gilded spear bearing an eagle at its top and a cross-staff from which hung a purple streamer adorned with a fringe of gold, decorated with precious gems. *Labarum* was the Latinization of the Greek word *labaron*, of unknown origin, and came to signify any symbolic banner. It is suggested, however, that one should not apply the word to a banner bearing representations of a hammer and a sickle ...

chittering-bite (CHIT uh ring bite) *n.* *Chitter* is a British dialectal verb meaning, among other things, "to shiver with the cold," "to tremble." The *O.E.D.* calls it "a parallel form to *chatter*." What, then, is a *chittering-bite*? It is "a bit of bread (or something else that comes to hand) taken to prevent shivering or chattering of the teeth." It is also known as a *chittering-crust* or a *chittering-piece*. "The Greeks," according to a mid-19th-century writer named Charles Badham, " ... appear to have begun the day with a sort of 'chittering crust.'" The *O.E.D.* ends this observation with the Greek word *akratisma*, which is defined in my *Liddell & Scott* as "breakfast." It must have been cold early in the morning in Greece, causing enough shivering to require a chittering-bite.

chrematistics (krem uh TIS tiks) *n.* (*pl.*—treated as singular). *Chremat-* is the stem of the Greek *chrema* (thing, possession), akin to the verb *chresthai* (to use, need). From the adjective *chrematistikos* we got *chrematistics*, the "study of wealth," and *chrematistic*, "pertaining to money making." The *O.E.D.* includes in its definition "political economy" and defines *chrematist* as "political economist." In Henry Fielding's *Amelia* (1751) we find the sentences: "I am not the least versed in the *chrematistic* art ... I know not how to get a shilling, nor how to keep it in my pocket if I had it." William T. Brande's *Dictionary of Science, Literature and Art* (1842) states that the Continental writers "consider *political economy* as a term more properly applicable to the whole range of subjects which comprise the material welfare of states and citizens, and *chrematistics* ... as merely a branch of it," but William Ewart Gladstone, in *Homer* (1858), says: "The phrase ... 'political economy' cannot be defended on its merits. The name '*Chrematistic*' [sic] has been devised in its stead." You pays your money and ...

chrism (KRIZ'm) *n.*, *vb.* Late Latin took the noun *chrisma* from the Greek word for "ointment," based on the verb *chriein* (to anoint). *Chrism* is "holy or consecrated oil," usually mixed with balm and various spices, used in some churches in the administering of certain sacraments, such as baptism, confirmation, ordination and the consecration of altars and churches. The term also has the meanings of "unguent" or "ointment" generally, "sacramental anointing" and "unction." Capitalized, it is a term used in the Eastern Orthodox Church for a sacrament analogous to confirmation in the Western Church. A variant, *chrisom*, is the name of a white robe or cloth worn by a person being baptized, white being the symbol of innocence. A *chrisom child* is an "innocent child," or more specifically, one still wearing the *chrisom cloth*; or one that died in its first month, often buried in that cloth; also, more generally, any infant. Shakespeare used the form *christom* in *Henry V* (Act II, Scene 3), when the hostess of the Boar's Head Tavern, formerly Mistress Quickly, on learning from her husband Pistol that Falstaff is dead, says that he " ... made a finer end, and went away an it had been any *christom child* ... " The related word *chrismal*, besides its use as an adjective meaning "pertaining to *chrism*," means "a vessel containing *chrism*." *Chrismation* (kriz MAY shun) is a synonym of *Chrism* (uppercase *C*) in the sense mentioned above. *Chrismatory* (KRIZ muh toh ree) can mean either the "vessel containing *chrism*" or the "sacramental anointment with *chrism*." In addition to all of the above, *chrism*, as a verb, means "to anoint with *chrism*." The connection between *chrism* and *Christ* is that *Christos*, the Greek name for *Christ*, is derived from *christos* (anointed), used as a substantive, from *chriein* (to anoint—as explained above), and Christ is the Messiah, from Hebrew *messiach* (anointed), and the Lord's *Anointed*.

chrismal   See **chrism**.

chrismation   See **chrism**.

chrismatory   See **chrism.**

chrisom   See **chrism.**

christom   See **chrism.**

chunda   See **chunter.**

chunder   See **chunter.**

chunner   See **chunter.**

chunter (CHUN tur) *vb.* To *chunter* (also *chunner, chunder*) is "to murmur, mutter, grumble, complain." As to derivation, all the dictionaries I have consulted state that it is (or probably or apparently is) "imitative," or "of imitative formation," but they don't tell us what it is "imitative" of. One of the meanings of *imitative* is "onomatopoeic," and I suppose that is what the dictionaries are trying to tell us. Does *chunter* sound like the noises of murmuring, muttering, grumbling or complaining? A little, but it could evoke other images as well: huffing? puffing? panting? The variant *chunder* does sound a little like "grumbling," perhaps, but to me, despite the seeming agreement of all the lexicons, "imitative" gives the impression of groping, to avoid the dread "origin unknown." In 1863 Mrs. Toogood's *Specimens of the Yorkshire Dialect* contained the entry: "He is a *chuntering* sort of fellow, never contented." Francis K. Robinson's *A Glossary of Words Used in the Neighborhood of Whitby* [Yorkshire] (1876) defines a *chuntering bout* as "a fit of sulkiness with impertinence." But the word didn't remain confined to Yorkshire. D. H. Lawrence, in *Sea and Sardinia* (1921), speaks of "a thin old woman ... *chuntering* her head off because it was her seat," and Christopher Fry's *The Lady's Not for Burning* (1949) gives us: "You fog-blathering, chin-*chuntering*, liturgical ... base old man!" In *On the Beach* (1957) Nevil Shute writes: "The baby stirred, and started *chuntering* and making little whimpering noises." Be careful not to confuse the variant *chunder* with the Australian slang *chunder*, used as both a verb and a noun meaning "vomit." It has a variant, *chunda*. Ugly-sounding word; no "imitative" here, just plain outspoken "origin unknown." Nevil Shute used this *chunder* (and its variant *chunda*) too. In *A Town Like Alice* (1950) we read: "The way these bloody Nips go on. Makes you *chunda*." And in his *Beyond the Black Stump* (1956): "But I gets sick at the stomach. I *chundered* once today already." The London magazine *Private Eye* uses *chunder* in the Australian slang sense in two different 1970 issues. I won't quote: We've had enough of this nasty kind of *chundering* already.

Churrigeresque (chu rig ur ESK) *adj.* José Benito Churrigera (1665–1725) was a Spanish architect and sculptor renowned for his ornate *retables* (rih TAY buhlz), decorative structures raised above the backs of altars. He designed palaces, churches and cathedrals in the baroque style, and his name gave rise to this adjective as descriptive of the architectural idiom of the late 17th and early 18th centuries in Spain, notable for its extravagant design, extreme richness and exuberance. That style greatly influenced Spanish colonial architecture in both the United States and Mexico, but the work there is naive in comparison with the original because of poor workmanship. In his writings on Spain in the 1840s and 1850s, Richard Ford made frequent use of this adjective, calling one building "vile *churrigeresque*" and the ornaments of an enormous organ "*churrigeresque* and inappropriate." *Churrigeresque* has found a place in many architectural writings of the 19th and 20th centuries. I wonder, if he came back today, whether Churrigera would say, as he cried all the way to the bank, "I don't care what they say about me, as long as they spell my name right."

cicisbeo (chee cheez BAY oh, chih chiz-) *n.* Taken from the Italian, this mouthful of a word denotes a married woman's gallant, also known as a *cavalier servente* (literally, a "serving cavalier") in Italy, especially in the 18th century. There are various theories about the term's origin: It may be an inversion of *bel cece* (beautiful chick-pea, in Italian), or come from *chiche beau*—*pois chiches* are "chick-peas" in French. The modern French equivalent of *cicisbeo* is *sigisbée*, which is defined in French dictionaries as "*cicisbeo*, lover." The French are quite blunt in their definition of the relationship. *The Annual Register* of 1773 says: "The *Chichisbeo* is an appendix to matrimony." That's telling it like it is, no? But John Wesley, the English theologian and founder of Methodism (1703–91), stated flatly: "English ladies are not attended by their *cicisbys* yet; nor would any English husband suffer it." Definitions go all the way from "dangler about women" to "professed gallant" to "escort" to "gigolo" to the aforestated "appendix to matrimony" to "lover." Who knows? It might be anything from Dante's innocent long-distance adoration of Beatrice to Louis Armstrong's "(Just a) Gigolo" to the institution euphemistically known as "escort service" (by the male attendant) to hubbie's "best friend." Byron, in *Beppo*, said that *cicisbeo* had … grown vulgar and indecent … *Cavalier servente* is the [proper] phrase." I prefer *cicisbeo*.

cilice   See **ambry.**

cinquain (sing KANE) *n.* This word was taken over from the French and denotes a five-line stanza arranged as follows: two syllables in the first line, four in the second, six in the third, eight in the fourth and two again in the fifth. This eccentric form is reminiscent of the Japanese *tanka* (TAHNG kuh), also a five-line stanza but with a different arrangement: the first and third lines have five syllables and all the others seven. This brings us to another Japanese verse conformation, the *hokku* (HAW kooh or HAH kooh), with three short unrhymed lines, the first and third consisting of five syllables, the middle line of seven. The *hokku* is generally epigrammatic in content and is formed of *hok* (beginning) plus *ku* (hemistich—see **hemistich**). A 19th-century development of the *hokku* is the *haiku* (HEYE kooh), also an unrhymed three-line poem with the same syllable scheme as the *hokku*. The *haiku* refers in one way or another to one of the seasons of the year. It is a term that applies as well to a poem written in a language other than Japanese and can include some modification of the original *haiku* form. Now that we know all about *cinquains* and three different Japanese verse forms, why don't you try your hand at composing one or more of each? Here's my *haiku*:

> I love to think of
> The summer with its green leaves
> And dazzling blossoms.

Terrible poetry, and terribly easy to invent, but they say Hirohito was a master at it.

cippus (SIH puhs) *n*. This word has a variety of meanings. In Latin, it means a "post" or "stake"; in Late Latin and English, "the stocks"; in architecture, a "small low column" with or without a base or capital, usually bearing an inscription and used by the ancient Romans and Greeks as a gravestone, a landmark or the memorial of a notable event. In 1862 De Quincey wrote the following: " ... in Ceylon, a granite *cippus*, or monumental pillar, of immemorial antiquity." Baroness Frances Bunsen, in 1860, described "the inscription on the *cippus* placed over the remains of ... two children." The dictionaries include the meaning "stocks," but from the illustrations I have seen of stocks and pillories, I think "pillory" would be more appropriate, because that form of public punishment was built on a *post* or *stake* (cf. the definition above), whereas stocks consisted of a seat placed behind a frame or low wall of timber having holes for the feet, and sometimes the hands, of offenders deserving public punishment, with nothing resembling a post or stake. All this is old stuff, but these details are (or should be) of concern to lexicographers. Stocks and pillories were quite different in form, though they served the same purpose.

circadian (sur kuh DEE uhn, sur KAY dee uhn) *adj. Circa* is a Latin adverb and preposition; in the latter capacity, relating to time, it means "about." The *c, c.*, or *ca.* in dates given in encyclopedias and other works of reference—for example, the dates of the birth or death of a historical figure or the date of an event—are all abbreviations of *circa*. *Dies* is Latin for "day." From the combination of the two we get *circadian*, denoting a physiological activity or cycle repeated approximately (*circa*) every 24 hours. *Circadian* also describes the rhythm of any such activity. The term does not pretend to mean "exactly every 24 hours." Halberg says, in *Zeitschrift für Vitamin- Hormon- und Fermentforschung* (Journal of Vitamin, Hormone and Enzyme Research, 1959): "'*Circadian*' might be applied to all '24 hour' rhythms, whether or not their periods … are different from 24 hours, longer or shorter, by a few minutes or hours." This definition quite emphatically stresses the *circa*.

circumambages (sur kuhm am BAY jeez) *n. pl. Ambages*, in Latin, means "going round, winding, roundabout way," and by extension, "circumlocution, ambiguity, obscurity." In English, *ambages* is treated as a plural meaning "indirect, roundabout paths," in both literal and figurative senses, and can also, in context, mean "delays." The adjective *ambagious* is dealt with in my *1000 Most Challenging Words*, where it is defined as "circuitous." It can also mean "tortuous" and, in context, "circumlocutory." So much for *ambages* and *ambagious*. Now we come to *circumambages*, which looks a little like a case of painting the lily ("to gild the lily" is a misquotation: see Shakespeare's *King John*, Act II, Scene 2: "To gild refined gold, to paint the lily … / Is wasteful and ridiculous excess.") It isn't, however, because the use of the Latin prefix *circum-* (around) gives us a new word, which most dictionaries treat as a plural, meaning "instances of deviousness or indirectness in speech or writing," or, in a more general sense, according to the *O.E.D.*, "round-about methods," as well as "round-about modes of speech." The same dictionary lists the participial adjective *circumambaging* as meaning "using methods to get round people." The meaning "circumlocution" for *ambages* in the Latin dictionary brought to mind the wonderful bit in *Little Dorrit* where Dickens coins the term "Circumlocution Office": "Whatever was required to be done, the Circumlocution Office was beforehand with all the public departments in the art of perceiving—How not to do it," calling for the comment in *Brewer's Dictionary of Phrase and Fable*, "A term applied in ridicule … to our public offices, because each person tries to shuffle off every act to someone else; and before anything is done it has to pass through so many departments with such consequent delays that it is hardly worth having bothered about it." "*Our* [i.e., British] public offices … "? How about *universal*?

circumbendibus (sur kuhm BEN dih buhs) *n.* Jocularly formed of the Latin prefix *circum-*, the English word *bend* and the Latin ablative plural ending of certain classes of nouns, *-ibus*, a *circumbendibus* is a "roundabout method, or a roundabout expression in the nature of a circumlocution." In *The Art of Sinking*, by Alexander Pope and others (1727), we find: "The Periphrasis, which the moderns call the *circumbendibus* … " (Incidentally, *periphrasis*, in case you aren't familiar with it, is only another word for "circumlocution, roundabout way of expressing oneself." This word is fully discussed in my *1000 Most Challenging Words*.) Sir Walter Scott, in *The Waverley Novels* (1814), uses these words: "Partaking of what scholars call the periphrastic and ambagitory [Scott's version of *ambagious*: see **circumambages**], and the vulgar the *circumbendibus* … " Phony Latinization is not all that rare: e.g., *omnium gatherum*, meaning "mixture" or "open house," which I characterize in my *British English, A to Zed* as "Mock Latin," explaining that *omnium* is the genitive plural of *omnis* (all), and *gatherum* is a "phony Latinization of 'gather.'" Said to have been invented by a group of Eton boys, *floccinaucinihilipilification* is a word meaning "belit-tling," consisting of a series of genitives of four Latin nouns meaning "trifle" or "nothing," fully discussed in my *1000 Most Challenging Words*. And how about the horrible mutilation of *De gustibus non disputandum* (There is no accounting for tastes): *Disgustibus non disputandibus?* Here that tempting *-ibus* rears its ugly head twice.

circumforaneous (sur kuhm fuhr AY nee uhs) *adj.* This adjective comes from the Latin *circumforaneus*, built of the preposition *circum* (around) plus *-foraneus* (relating to the *forum*, market). The Latin adjective was used in various ways: Its general meaning was "around the forum"; modifying *aes* (literally, copper ore, bronze, but by extension, money), it meant "borrowed from the Forum bankers"; with *pharmacopola* (drug vendor, but by extension, quack), it meant "attending at markets." The English form means, literally, "wandering about from market to market"; figuratively, "wandering, vagrant, roving, vagabond" and by extension, "quack." Apparently, there is something about merchants setting up stalls from market to market that smacks of quackery and calls for *caveat emptor* in loud accents.

clapdish   See **clapperdudgeon.**

clapperdudgeon (KLAP uhr duj uhn) *n.* The *O.E.D.* says that " … the origin of the appellation is unknown" but mentions the suggestion of one Collier that the word comes from the act of knocking a *clapdish* with a *dudgeon*. A *clapper-dudgeon* is a "beggar"; a *clapdish* is a "wooden dish with a lid," once carried by lepers and beggars from the *lazar-houses* (hospitals for the diseased poor, especially lepers) which were later called *lazarets* or *lazarettos*, to announce their approach and receive alms; and *dudgeon* is the name of a type of wood used by wood turners, expecially for handles of knives, daggers and the like. *Dudgeon* is generally believed to be the root of the box shrub. This *dudgeon* hasn't a thing in the world to do with the *high dudgeon* in which irked persons walk out of rooms. Incidentally, has anybody ever walked out of a room in low dudgeon? *Clapperdudgeon* has also been used as a term of reproach or insult. George Augustus Sala, in *The Strange Adventures of Captain Dangerous* (1863), tells us that "Rogues, Thieves … and *Clapper-Dudgeons* infested the outskirts of the Old Palace," and writes of "A perfect chaos of *clapdishes* … Impostors … cripples, and gambling bullies." The word may be archaic, but the next time you want to reproach somebody, call him a *clapperdudgeon* and see whether he or she walks out of the room in you-know-what.

clerisy (KLER uh see) *n.* In German, *Klerisei* means "clergy" but is used colloquially to mean "hangers-on," a not very complimentary extension of the literal meaning. In the Middle Ages, the clergy were the only intelligentsia; hence the evolution of *clerk* from *cleric*, the dual meaning of *clerical*, etc. This *clerisy* came to signify "intelligentsia, scholars, learned men, the well-educated or academic class." This use was introduced by Samuel Taylor Coleridge, who wrote, in *Literary Remains* (1818): "After the Revolution … a learned body, or *clerisy*, as such, gradually disappeared." In *Specimens of his Table Talk* (1834) he discussed "the *clerisy* of a nation, that is, its learned men, whether poets, or philosophers, or scholars." Ralph Waldo Emerson, in *Essay on Manners* (1841), wrote of "the artist, the scholar, and in general, the *clerisy*." But it must be remembered that the term *cleric* means "clergyman," from Late Latin *clericus*, and that as late as 1858 *The Times* (London) used *clerisy* in the sense of "clericism" in writing about "the restrictions of *clerisy* and celibacy." In 1870 James Russell Lowell, in *Among My Books*, wrote of "a layman, alike indifferent to *clerisy* and heresy," a nice turn of phrase. I think, however, that nowadays, *clerisy* is used to denote the literati, the intelligentsia, and no longer refers to the church. This would seem to be borne out by the definitions given in the abridged dictionaries of Britain and America, as exemplified in both *RH* and the *C.O.D.*

cochlea (KOK lee uh) *n.* Definitions of this word vary, depending on your choice of dictionary. One is content with the anatomical meaning: the "spiral-shaped cavity forming the division of the inner ear"; the *O.E.D.* adds "spiral staircase, screw, Archimedes's water-screw [of which more later]," "spiral univalve shell, snail-shell"; *CH* goes all the way: "anything spiral-shaped" (that covers a lot of territory!), adding "snail-shell, medick-pod [*medick* is a type of clover or trefoil with spiral pods], winding stair, spiral cavity of the ear." They all agree that via Latin *coc(h)lea* (shell, screw), the word goes back to Greek *kochlias* (snail, screw). To add to the confusion, *cochlear* (KOK lee uhr) means not only "pertaining to the *cochlea* of the ear" but also "spoon" (French *cuiller*) from Latin *coc(h)leare* and *coclearium* (spoon, in the shape of a snail shell). As to the water-screw mentioned above, we have to look into the remarkable career of our old friend Archimedes (287–212 B.C.), the Greek mathematician, physicist and inventor, famous for the "Eureka!" incident and the lever with which he could "move the world." One of his many inventions was the water-screw, consisting of a cylinder containing a continuous screw the same length as the cylinder. With the lower end placed in the water, by revolving the screw, water is raised to the top. This principle is applied to drainage and irrigation machines, and the device can also handle light, loose materials like sand and grain. One must be careful with *cochleariform* (kok lee AIR uh form), which means "spoon-shaped," and *cochleiform* (ko LEE uh form) meaning "shaped like a snail shell."

cochlear   See **cochlea.**

cochleariform   See **cochlea.**

cochleiform   See **cochlea.**

cocqcigrues (KOK see groohs) *n. pl.* This is how Charles Kingsley spelled it in *The Water Babies*, when the fairy Bedonebyasyoudid said, "That is one of the seven things I am forbidden to tell you till the coming of the *Cocqcigrues.*" In French *coquecigrue,* accented on the second syllable, is a colloquialism meaning "fiddle-faddle, stuff and nonsense, idle story," and Kingsley misspelled it. *His phrase till the coming of the Cocqcigrues* was a translation from the French *à la venue des coquecigrues,* meaning "never," similar to *when the cows come home.* The *coquecigrues* were mythical animals of French legend and, since they were legendary, they'd never show up, hence the French idiom and the words Kingsley put into the mouth of Mrs. Bedonebyasyoudid.

coctile (KOK tuhl, -tile) *adj. Coquere* is Latin for "to cook, bake, boil, roast, heat," i.e., to prepare by cooking of any sort. Its past participle is *coctus,* from which the Romans formed the adjective *coctilis,* meaning "baked," used by Ovid in describing the walls of Babylon in the sense of "made of baked brick." *Coctile,* then, means "made by baking or exposure to heat," as a brick, which is hardened by fire. The related Latin noun *coctio* gave us *coction,* "boiling, cooking," which in the old days denoted the attainment of a more nearly perfect, more mature or generally more desirable state, either through natural processes or through human processes such as the application of heat, and, more specifically, the digestion of food. Another archaic meaning was "suppuration," a phase of wound healing or the development of any disease. The combining form *cocto-* has the force of "boiled" or "altered by heat," as in *coctostable* (kok toh STAY b'l—at boiling point). The verb *concoct* and the noun *concoction* are obviously products of the prefix *con-* (together) plus *coction. Concoquere* is Latin for "to boil together," with the predictable past participle and related substantive and adjectival forms. Our *concoct* and *concoction* have lost all reference to heat, now meaning simply "to devise" and "fabrication," with pejorative connotations, as in "concocting an alibi."

coction   See **coctile.**

coctostable   See **coctile.**

coenesthesia, also **cenesthesia** (see nis THEE zuh, -zee uh, sen is-); **coenesthesis,** also **cenesthesis** (see nis THEE sis), *n.* However you choose to spell it, this term denotes the totality of impressions you get from organic sensations forming the basis of your awareness of your bodily state, such as the feeling of health, vigor or apathy. Without *coenesthesia* you wouldn't be able to answer the question "How are you?" or even "How's tricks?" *Coenesthesia* is derived from two Greek words, *koino-,* the combining form of the adjective *koinos* (common), and *aisthesis* (perception), which gave us our word *esthesia* (also *aesthesia*), meaning "sensitivity, the capacity for feeling or sensation." Next time you wake up feeling just great or simply lousy, remember that you wouldn't feel anything without *coenesthesia.*

coistril   See **custrel.**

colporteur (kol POR tur) *n.* No, this is not intended as a representation of the way the French say "Cole Porter," though it must be pretty close to it. *Colporteur* was taken over intact from the French, where it means "peddler," and figuratively, "spreader of news." But in American English it means "peddler of books" and secondarily, "one employed to travel about distributing Bibles and religious tracts gratuitously or at a very low price." *Colportage* is the activity of such a person and is likewise accented on the second syllable, while in British English it can refer to peddler (they spell it *pedlar*) generally, especially one selling religious tracts and books. It all goes back to Latin *collum* (neck) and *portare* (to carry), presenting the image of one carrying a tray of books suspended from the neck and hanging in front, or more likely in back, in view of the French expression *porter à col* (to carry on one's back, though *col* means literally "neck"). Whether in front or in back, these *colporteurs* were missionary types and were generally respected as intrepid individuals. *Colportage* was a common 19th-century practice, now generally confined to the Gideons, an international association of Christian business and professional persons founded in 1899, now active in over 65 countries, distributing Bibles to hotel bedrooms and hospitals and New Testaments to schools. The name is derived from Gideon's men who overthew the Midianites (*Judges* vii).

consuetude (KON swih tyoohd) *n. Consuetude*, from Latin *consuetudo* (custom, usage, habit), is a "custom so established in human dealings as to have acquired the legal force of law." The Latin verb *consuescere* (to accustom, habituate) has an intransitive usage: "to accustom oneself." *Consuetude*, then, specifically denotes an unwritten law, never enacted by a legislature but derived from immemorial custom. If things have been done a certain way in commercial transactions over the ages, the rules governing such dealings become as fixed as though they were inscribed in black and white in the law books, and a violation of those rules and regulations cannot legally be side-stepped on the basis that they do not appear in statute form. In case of dispute, history, not enactment, governs. *Desuetude* (DEZ wih tyoohd) means "disuse" from the Latin *desuetudo*, related to the verb *desuescere* (to become unaccustomed), and its past passive participle *desuetus* (disused). When customs of long standing have passed into a state of *desuetude*, they no longer have the force of law. Before relying on *consuetude*, make sure *desuetude* has not set in. If in doubt in a commercial matter, consult the merchants as well as your lawyer.

coprophagous   See **merdivorous.**

copy   See **heriot.**

copyhold   See **heriot.**

coronal   See **cacuminal.**

corroboree (kuh ROB uh ree) *n.* You might well think that this word denotes a person who makes a statement that, needing corroboration, gets it; or, on hearing the word (note its pronunciation), that it signifies a robbery engaged in by two or more. But no: A *corroboree* is nothing more or less than a "native dance of Australian aborigines, held by moonlight or the light of a bush fire, and either festive or warlike in character." In travel accounts the word appears in a variety of forms: *caribberie, corob(b)ory, -berri,* etc. It is also used as a verb signifying the performance of the dance. It has been used, as well, as a song for such a dance or for any festive occasion among those natives. In his writings, Darwin used the form *corrobery* to describe a "great dancing party" in that part of the world. One who *corroborates* is a *corroborator,* and one who receives *corroboration* would logically be called a *corroboratee,* but there's no such word, I'm happy to say.

corsned (KORS ned) *n.* In Old English law, this was the name for "ordeal by swallowing a piece of bread or cheese." If it stuck in the throat, that proved guilt. The morsel was "consecrated by exorcism" and was known as *panis coniuratus* (sworn bread). In his *Commentaries,* the great work of early law, Sir William Blackstone wrote (1769): "*Corsned* or morsel of execration: being a piece of cheese or bread, of about an ounce in weight, which was consecrated with a form of exorcism; desiring of the Almighty that it might cause convulsions and paleness, and find no passage, if the man was really guilty; but might turn to health and nourishment, if he was innocent." *Corsned* is from the Old English *corsnaed,* formed of *coren,* the past participle of *ceosn* (to choose), plus *snaed* (piece), from *snidan* (to cut). Today we use *ordeal* in the sense of any severe test or experience. In the old days, ordeals were primitive trials to determine guilt or innocence by exposing the accused to various types of physical danger, the result being left to divine judgment, since God would defend right even by miracle if necessary. There were ordeals by battle, by fire (e.g., walking barefoot over red-hot ploughshares), boiling water (plunging the hand into boiling water), cold water (sink or swim) and the cross (the parties stood upright before a cross; the first to move was guilty). Most were abolished in favor of jury trial in the early part of the 13th century. As a practicing lawyer for more than half a century, I never cared much for juries ...

coryphaeus   See **epirrhema.**

costerdom (KOS tur duhm) *n.* The little suffix *-dom* is indeed versatile. It can indicate condition: *freedom, martyrdom, stardom;* groups having something in common: *officialdom, dogdom;* rank or office: *earldom, dukedom;* realm: *Christendom, kingdom;* and geographical area: *Anglo-Saxondom.* In *costerdom,* the suffix has the force of designating a group identifiable because of a common pursuit: *costers* or *costermongers,* those who sell fruit, vegetables, sometimes fish, etc., from barrows or pushcarts on the street. The origin of *coster* is *costard,* a large apple, indicating perhaps that at one time the wares were restricted to that commodity, and *monger*, a British word for "dealer," almost always found in combination with the particular article dealt in, as in *cheesemonger, fishmonger* or *ironmonger*. (*Monger* is found as well in other combinations of a pejorative nature, like *scandalmonger* and *warmonger*. There is a new derogatory term: *peacemonger*, for *dove*, a term of abuse in warlike quarters.) A special sector of *costerdom* is the realm of those wearing *pearlies*—costumes decorated with mother-of-pearl buttons. There are pearly kings and queens, who show up at gala occasions as buskers performing on the streets, but this, alas, like so many traditional customs, is fast disappearing from the streets of England.

cothurnus (koh THUR nuhs) *n.* From the Greek *kothornos*, this is a buskin: a thick-soled laced boot reaching halfway to the knee, worn by Greek and Roman actors in the staging of ancient tragedies. Edgeworth and Richard's *Practical Education* (1798) states: "The actor on the stage is admired whilst he is elevated by the *cothornus*." Actors on stage always seem taller than they really are, and the *cothornus* enhanced this illusion. The word eventually acquired the figurative sense of the grave, tragic and lofty style characteristic of tragedy, as evident in a passage in Frederic W. Farrar's *Life and Work of St. Paul* (1879): "St. Paul cannot always wear the majestic *cothornus*, yet his lightest words are full of dignity." Virgil used the figurative sense in describing some verses as "Sophocleo ... digna *cothurno*" (worthy of Sophoclean tragedy).

cowan (KOU uhn) *n.* It is always a disappointment, to one interested in etymology, to find the words *origin unknown* after a dictionary entry, and all too often one keeps hunting for clues and grasping at straws—to no avail. And so it is with *cowan*, which is a Scottish word for "dry-stone diker." And what is a *dry-stone diker*? In Scotland, a *dike* is a wall, and a *dry-stone* (or *dry-stane*) *dike* is one built without mortar. Thus a *dry-stone diker* is one who builds walls without the use of mortar (or nowadays, cement). But *cowan* has other meanings as well: It is a pejorative term for a person who works as a mason without having served an apprenticeship in that occupation or having been bred to it. This is made clear in these words from Robert Forsyth's *Beauties of Scotland* (1806): "The men who are employed in building walls for inclosing fields are called ... *cowans*, to distinguish them from the regular masons." Stretching the use of the word, *cowan* came to denote a person who is uninitiated into the secrets of Freemasonry, i.e., one who is not a member of that society. In a *Text-book of Freemasonry*, published in 1881, certain officials are described as "armed with a drawn sword, to keep off all *Cowans* and intruders to Masonry." They took things pretty seriously in those days. *CH* stretches the word a little further: " ... one who tries to enter a Freemason's lodge, or the like, surreptitiously." Finally, *cowan* became a slang term for any sneak, or "prying or inquisitive person," according to John C. Hotten's *Dictionary of Modern Slang, Cant, and Vulgar Words* (1859–74). John Strang's *Glasgow and its Clubs* (1856) used the word attributively to describe "outsiders," writing about a tavern "shut off from the observation and the ken of the *'cowan'* world." We have come a long way from an unapprenticed mason to a snooping outsider.

Cradle Holding   See **Borough-English.**

Cradle Land   See **Borough-English.**

cramponée   See **fylfot.**

cubit   See **alnage.**

custrel (KUS trel) *n. Custrel* was the title of a knight's attendant. The word came from the Old French *coustillier,* a soldier armed with a *coustille,* a two-edged dagger. The normal transmutation into English would have produced *custeler,* but metathesis intervened, and the *l* and *r* got switched around to form *custrel.* The term was applied as well to a knight's groom and eventually developed the secondary meaning of "knave, base fellow." This was probably the result of association with *custron,* meaning "scullion," and one in that position would have been a boy of low birth, a base-born fellow and very likely a vagabond in the bargain. A common variant of *custrel* is *coistrel* (KOY strel). The *O.E.D.* points out that "an interchange of *u* and *oi* in words from French is frequent." *Coistrel* was used for "groom" at first, but, like *custrel,* degenerated into "knave, varlet." In Scott's *The Betrothed* we read: "Nor can you fly from your standard without such infamy as even *coistrels* or grooms are unwilling to incur." We find *coistrel* (or a variant spelling) in its pejorative sense in Ben Johnson's *Every Man in his Humor:* "You whorson, bragging *Coystril?*"; and in *Twelfth Night:* "He's a Coward and a *Coystrill* that will not drinke to my Neece"; and again in *Pericles, Prince of Tyre:* "Thou'rt the damn'd doorkeeper to every *coistrel* that comes inquiring for his tib [girl—in the context of this brothel, whore]." Try to imagine an Elizabethan spelling bee!

custron   See **custrel.**

dabchick   See **didapper.**

dactyl   See **dolichurus.**

dactyliography (dak til ee AW gruh fee) *n.* In Greek, *daktylos* means "finger" and *daktylios* "finger ring." In zoology, the word *dactyl* means, inter alia, "finger" or "toe," and in classical prosody it denotes a foot of three syllables, one long and two short; in English and other modern languages, a stressed syllable followed by two unstressed ones; thus, as in the opening syllables of *The Aeneid* and *Evangeline*, respectively: *Arma vi/rumque ca; This is the/forest pri.* From *dactyl*, we get the adjective *dactylic* (dak TIL ik), and from *daktylos* a number of nouns: *dactyliography* and *dactyliology* (dak til ee AWL uh jee), both meaning "the study or lore of finger rings or engraved gems"; *dactyliomancy* (dak TIL ee uh man see), combining *dactylio-* with *manteia* (divination), "divination by means of finger rings"; *dactylogram* (dak TIL oh gram, DAK til uh gram), "fingerprint"; *dactylography* (dak tih LAW gruh fee), "the study of fingerprints"; and *dactylology* (dak tih LAW luh jee), "talking with the fingers, as with the manual language of the deaf." *Dactylion* (dak TIL ee uhn) means "tip of the middle finger," and a *dactyliotheca* (dak til ee uh THEE kuh), from Greek *daktyliotheke*, combining *daktilio-* with *theke* (box, chest), is a case for a collection of rings, gems or seals. In addition, there are a good many *dactyl-* terms in the field of biology. I may have missed one or more uses, so I'm keeping my *dactyls* crossed.

dactyliology   See **dactyliography.**

dactyliomancy   See **dactyliography.**

dactylion   See **dactyliography.**

dactyliotheca   See **dactyliography.**

dactylogram   See **dactyliography.**

dactylography   See **dactyliography.**

dactylology   See **dactyliography.**

daddock (DA duhk) *n. Daddock* means "rotten wood." The *dad-* is said to be of uncertain origin; the *-ock* is thought to be a diminutive suffix, as in *hillock* and *bullock.* An obsolete word, *doddard,* may offer a clue. It once denoted a tree that had lost its branches as a result of decay, and *dod* is an obsolete verb that meant "to lop," e.g., a tree. Whatever the etymology, Dryden, in a 1693 poem entitled *Persius,* wrote the words: " … Rots like a *doddard* oke, and piecemeal falls to ground." The participial form *dodded* is still in use in some parts of England, describing plants, trees and animals that have lost their heads, as in *dodded* trees, those that have been polled, stalks of corn that have lost their beards or awns, sheep and cattle that have lost their horns and so forth. Several old glossaries define *daddock* as "rotten wood." In *Margaret, a Tale* (1845), Sylvester Judd wrote: "The great red *daddocks* lay in the green pastures where they had lain year after year, crumbling away." A glossary of terms current in Upton-on-Severn (Worcestershire) dated 1884 defined the adjective *daddocky* as "flimsy, unsubstantial, soft with decay," indicating that the obsolescence of *daddock* didn't occur that long ago, in dialect, anyway.

daddocky   See **daddock**.

dahabeeyah, also **dahabiah** (day hah BEE ah, dah uh BEE uh) *n*. Like so many words transliterated from Arabic, this word can be spelled and pronounced in a variety of ways. It is the name given to a long shallow-draft houseboat used on the Nile, which, though lateen-rigged, is frequently propelled partly or wholly by engine. (For the benefit of landlubbers, a *lateen* sail is triangular in shape and is set on a long sloping spar. It is used commonly in the Mediterranean area.) *Dahabeeyah* has an interesting etymology, for Arabic *dhahabiyah* means "the golden one," and one might well wonder what that has to do with a Nile houseboat. Explanation: It was the name given to the golden state barge used by the Muslim rulers of Egypt. In the preface to her book *A Thousand Miles up the Nile* (1877), Amelia B. Edwards tells us: "The *Dahabeeyah* hired by the European traveller reproduces in all essential features the painted galleys represented in the tombs of the kings." As one who has looked long and enviously at the paintings of the galleys in those tombs, I can assure you that they must have afforded an extremely luxurious means of travel. The simple Nile *feluccas* (fuh LUK uhs) used nowadays are pretty crude in comparison.

dalmatic (dal MAT ik) *adj.*, *n*. As an adjective with an uppercase *D*, *Dalmatic* is a rarely used synonym of *Dalmatian*. Both refer to *Dalmatia*, a region in western Yugoslavia along the Adriatic coast. In my experience, *Dalmatian* is most commonly used as the name of a familiar breed of short-haired dog, white with irregular black (sometimes liver-colored) spots, also known as a *coach dog*, often attached to fire-engine companies (or "fire brigades," as they are known in Britain). But as a noun with a lowercase *d*, a *dalmatic* is a "vestment worn over the alb (a long-sleeved ecclesiastical linen garment) by a deacon or a bishop on certain liturgical occasions." It has a slit on either side of the skirt, wide sleeves and two stripes. A similar garment is worn by sovereigns at coronations and certain other ceremonies. An ancient Latin text tells us that the "*Dalmatica* vestis" (*Dalmatian* garment, i.e., the *dalmatic*) was first made in the province of Dalmatia and was a *tunica sacerdotalis candida cum clavis ex purpurea* (a priestly sleeved garment with purple stripes). This explains the term, which is the feminine form (modifying *vestis* understood) of Latin *Dalmaticus* (Dalmatian).

dandiprat, also **dandyprat** (DAN dih prat) *n*. This was originally the name of a small coin worth three halfpence, current in 16th-century England. In *Guevara's Familiar Epistles* (1574), by Edward Hellowes, we find this reference to the coin: " ... they aske an halfpenie for spice, a penie for candels, a *dandiprat* for an earthen pot ... " William Camden, in *Remaines of a Greater Worke*

Concerning Britaine (1605), tells us that "K. Henry the 7th stamped a small coine called *dandyprats*." Somehow the term was applied to an insignificant or contemptible fellow, or one of small physical stature, like a dwarf or a pygmy. We find in Peter A. Motteux's translation of *Cervantes' History of Don Quixote* (1733) these words: "I saw a little *Dandyprat* riding about, who, they said, was a hugeous great Lord," and in Josuah Sylvester's translation of *Du Bartas his Divine Weekes and Workes* (1606): "Am I a dog, thou Dwarfe, thou *Dandiprat?*" The word was also used of a lad or urchin, though rarely a young lass. In Scott's *Kenilworth*, we find: "It is even so, my little *dandieprat*," and in Charles S. Calverley's *The Cock and the Bull* (a parody of Browning's *The Ring and the Book*) (1875): "It's a thing I bought of a chit of a boy … 'Chop' was my snickering *dandyprat's* own term." (*Chop* was the boy's term for "exchange" or "price.") Thomas Heywood applied the term to a female, in *The Wise-Woman of Hogsdon* (1638): "Her name is Luce. With this *Dandiprat*, this pretty little Apes face, is yon blunt fellow in love." The development of *dandiprat* from the name of a coin of little worth to a contemptuous term for an insignificant person is reminiscent of the history of the word *picayune*. Originally, it was the name of a coin equal in value to half a Spanish real or six U.S. cents that circulated in Louisiana, Florida and other southern states. The name was based on *picaillon*, a copper coin of Piedmont and Savoy. It is easy, as in the case of *dandiprat*, to see how *picayune* became an adjective meaning "trifling, of little account, paltry, measly," as in *a picayune amount*, *a picayune effort*. If inflation continues at the current dizzying pace, it won't be long before *dollar* will go the way of *dandiprat* and *picayune*. "He's a pipsqueak, a *dollarish* sort of chap." Perish the thought!

dandyfunk   See **dunderfunk**.

dandyprat   See **dandiprat**.

daven (DAH vuhn, DAW-) *vb*. Taken over from Yiddish, *to daven* is "to pray," in accordance with the ritual prescribed for the daily and holiday Jewish liturgies. Orthodox Jews *daven* three times a day, adding supplementary prayers on the Sabbath, holy days and special occasions. During morning prayers, males usually wear the *tallis* (TAH luhs), "a rectangular or square shawl" with *zizis* (TSIH tsis), "tassels," attached to the four corners. The shawl, with blue or black stripes across the lower edge, is made of wool or silk and is worn over the head or around the shoulders. The congregant prays silently or barely murmers, while standing and usually swaying. In the West, he faces east, toward Israel, just as the Muslim faces Mecca wherever he or she prays. Prayers are recited in classical Hebrew (not the Hebrew of contemporary Israel), quite rapidly. Unhappily, as is sometimes the case with Catholic praying in Latin, they are often recited by rote with little understanding of the literal meaning of the words. There are many Yiddish stories about *davening*, such as the following: A devout Jew is lost in the forest. The time for evening prayer is at hand, but he has forgotten to bring along his prayer book. He tells God his memory is so poor that he can't recite the prayer by heart; he'll just recite the alphabet, and God, who knows all the prayers, will simply put the letters in proper order. God is so touched by the man's sincerity that he tells the angels: "That was the worthiest prayer I've heard all day!" Then there is the tale of the youngster who arrives, breathless, at the synagogue on Yom Kippur, the holiest day of the year. As he runs toward the door, the *shamus* (SHAH mus), or "sexton," stops him and says, "You can't go in there, dressed like a slob and without a *yarmulke!*" (YAHR m'l keh, a skullcap: the head must be covered in an Orthodox synagogue; see **zucchetto**). "But you have to let me in," cries the youth, "I have a message for Mr. Levine, my boss, and if I don't deliver it I'll lose my job!" "Go in then," says the *shamus*, "but God help you if I catch you *davening!*"

dawk-wallah (DAWK wo luh), also **dak-wallah** (DAHK wo luh) *n.* Both components, *da(w)k* and *wallah*, are Anglo-Indian terms (this does not mean "Eurasian," but pertains to the Raj, the period of British rule in India). In the old days, *dawk* was the name given in India to relays of men, on foot or horseback, used to carry mail and baggage, or people in palanquins. It was the common term for the mail system. *Wallah* was a general term for a servant or employee performing a particular service. Thus, a man in charge of the ice supply would be the *ice-wallah*, and the person who worked the punkah (the ceiling fan, made of cloth in a rectangular frame and operated by pulling a rope) was the *punkah-wallah*. (Incidentally, variants of *punkah* and *wallah* dropped the *h*.) The *dawk-wallah*, then, was a "letter carrier or mailman." We read in Edward Braddon's *Life in India* (1872): "The arrival at any village of the *dak-walla* (letter carrier) with a letter is an event to be remembered and talked of." The mail bag was known as the *dak bag*. With the independence of India and the exodus back to England, Anglo-Indian terminology was carried home, but as the years passed, it naturally died out. One hears it from the lips of old India hands, less and less, of course, and it is considered chic in some quarters to come out with a bit of the old idiom somewhat for the fun of it, but not without a twinge of nostalgia.

deblaterate   See **quisquilious.**

deblateration   See **quisquilious.**

decollate (dee KOL ate) *vb.* To *decollate* is "to behead"—it's as simple as that—and the word is derived from the Latin verb *decollare* (to behead), based on the gruesome combination of the preposition *de-* (from) and *collum* (neck). A *decollation* (dee kuh LAY shuhn) is a "beheading or decapitation," the latter synonym involving the Latin noun *caput*, whose stem, *capit-*, is seen in such words as *capital*. *Decollation* is not a case of *lallation*, also known as *pararhotacism*, the pronouncing of *r* like *l*, the converse of *rhotacism*, the pronouncing of *l* like *r*; for a discussion of these twists of pronunciation, see my *1000 Most Challenging Words*, under the entry *rhotacism*. *Decollation* means not only "beheading" but also denotes any picture of one, especially the grim painting of the head of St. John the Baptist on a *charger*—a word archaic in American English and, according to my British dictionaries, questionably not so in British English, where it denotes a flat dish capable of holding a large joint (*joint* being the British English equivalent of American English *roast*, as in *roast of beef*, according to my *British English, A to Zed*). The *decollation* of St. John at Salome's request is all too vividly related in Matt. 14:6–11.

decubitus (dih KYOOH bih tuhs) *n.* This is a medical term for one's "posture in bed"—that is, the way one lies down. It is taken from Late Latin, formed from the verb *decumbere* (to lie down), a word, built on the prefix *de-* (down) plus *-cumbere*, that is not found in classical Latin and used only in Late Latin compounds, such as *discumbere*. *Ventral decubitus* denotes lying on one's belly; *dorsal decubitus* is lying on one's side. Flint's *Principles of Medicine* (1880) warns against dorsal *decubitus*: "The dorsal *decubitus* should not be constantly maintained; changes of position are important." This advice doubtless relates to avoiding bedsores. If you ever saw Robert Benchley's hilarious short film "How to Sleep," about a constantly twisting insomniac, you would have been treated to the spectacle of whirlwind changes of *decubitus*!

decuman (DEK yuh muhn) *adj., n.* As an adjective, *decuman* means "huge, immense," or in context, "main, principal." Meaning "immense," its chief use is to modify *wave*: A *decuman* wave is a huge one. This usage is based on the popular (and baseless) notion that the tenth wave in a series is the largest and most dangerous to shipping. *Decuman* comes from the Latin *decumanus*, a variant of *decimanus* (relating to the tenth part of something), from *decimus* (tenth). On the subject of the erroneous belief as to the tenth wave, Sir Thomas Browne, in *Pseudodoxia Epidemica, or Enquiries into Very Many Received Tenets [Vulgar Errors]* (1646), included this old wives' tale in his treatment of "Vulgar Errors," and De Quincey gave it the same short shrift in *Pagan Oracles* (1862). No less an authority (?) than *Fraser's Magazine*, in an 1838 issue, declared: "The tenth, or *decuman*, is the last of the series of waves, and the most sweeping in its operation." In a wholly different context, the *Decuman Gate* was the name given to the main entrance to a Roman military camp, located on the farthest side from the enemy. It got that name because it was guarded by the *tenth* cohort (division of 300 to 600 men) of a legion. Used by itself, as a noun, a *decuman* is a great wave, one capable of wreaking great damage, but, as we have seen, it can do so not because it is tenth, but because it is big.

deipara   See **theotokion.**

dendrophilous (den DRAW fil uhs) *adj. Dendron* is Greek for "tree," and *dendro-* is its combining form. Attaching it to *-philous* (loving), we get *dendrophilous*, meaning "tree loving," and who among us isn't *dendrophilous*? (Except possibly those dreadful real estate developers who ruthlessly demolish our beautiful trees to make way for their dreadful assembly-line abodes or shoe-box commercial structures.) *Dendrophilous* has a special use in botany, to describe plants growing on or twisting around trees, like many vines, some of which are "loving" in a sense but eventually kill their hosts with too much of a good thing. We've all seen what a clinging vine like ivy can do to a tree. Combining both effects of *-philous*, and echoing Oscar Wilde's " ... each man kills the thing he loves," how fortunate that only some vines kill the trees they love!

deodand (DEE uh dand) *n. Deo* (the dative case of *deus*, Latin for "god," though in the case of *deodand* the god was the Christian God) means "to God," and *dandum* is the neuter of *dandus*, the gerundive of *dare* (to give), meaning "something that must be given." Thus, a *deodand*, in English law up to 1846, was a "thing forfeitable to God," but in practice forfeited to the crown and then put to pious uses (i.e., sold and its proceeds distributed in alms). The term was applied to a chattel (a piece of personal, as opposed to real, property) that had been the immediate cause of the death of a person, and the forfeiture to God, actually to the crown, was an expiatory offering. Here are some examples: Sir Henry Finch, in *Law, or a Discourse thereof, in Fours Bookes* (1636) wrote: "If a man being upon a Cart carrying Faggots ... fall downe by the mouuing of one of the horses in the Cart, and die of it; both that and all the other horses in the Cart, and the Cart it selfe, are forfeit ... And these are called *Deodands*." Here is a rather extreme case, from Sir William Blackstone's *Commentaries* (1765): "If a man falls from a boat or ship in fresh water, and is drowned, it hath been said, that the vessel and cargo are in strictness of law a *deodand*." Pretty sweeping judgment! What if the drownee had been drunk, or simply careless? Or someone who didn't like him pushed him overboard? And incidentally, why the restriction to "fresh water"? Okay on the bounding main?

desquamate (DES kwah mate) *vb. Squama* means "scale" in Latin (the animal kind, not the weighing or musical kind), and *desquamare* is a transitive Latin verb meaning "to scale," as a fish. From its past participle *desquamatus* we get the verb *desquamate*, which is used both transitively and intransitively. Thus, one *desquamates* a fish, or simply *desquamates*, i.e., "peels," as after a sunburn or sometimes after an attack of scarlet fever. The noun *desquamation* (des kwah MAY shuhn) covers both the transitive and intransitive uses. The adjective *desquamative* (DES kwah may tiv) can be used to describe a condition resulting in peeling or something that causes the skin to peel. Prudent people use various lotions to avoid *desquamation*, and even more prudent people stay out of the sun altogether to avoid skin cancer.

desuetude   See **consuetude**.

dharna, also **dhurna** (DUR nuh) *n.* Taken from the Hindi, *dharna* is a "method of appealing for justice, of forcing payment of an obligation or compliance with a just demand or of calling attention to an injustice, by sitting and fasting at the door of the offender until the wrong is admitted and justice done." Complainants have been known to fast even to the point of death. This procedure is known as *sitting in dharna* or *sitting dharna,* and the offending party is said to be *put in dharna.* Horace H. Wilson, in *History of British India* (1844), wrote of soldiers "detaining their commanders in the sort of arrest termed *dharna,*" and others have regarded *dharna* as a form of arrest. It must have been an effective method, putting one's case before the court of public opinion, as it were. I hardly think it would work in the western world: The party *sitting dharna* would probably be arrested for trespass.

diacope   See **anaphora.**

diastrophism (deye AS troh fiz'm) *n.* This is a general term in geology for the various processes whereby the crust of the earth is deformed. The word is based on the Greek *diastrophe* (distortion, dislocation), from *diastrephein* (to twist about, turn in different directions) and is built of the prefix *dia-* (aside) plus *strophe* (turning). The sinking and rising of regions of the earth, subsidence and upheaval, together constitute *diastrophism,* which comprises *orogeny* (oh ROJ uh nee) and *epeirogeny* (ep eye ROJ uh nee). *Orogeny* is the process of mountain formation, from *oros* (mountain) plus suffix *-geneia* (producing). *Epeirogeny* is the process of the formation of continents resulting from the deformation of the crust of the earth, which also produces ocean basins; the word is formed of the Greek *epeiros* (mainland, continent) plus the same suffix *-geneia.* All of these terms and processes are dealt with in *tectonics* (tek TON iks), the science of structural geology, dealt with briefly in my *1000 Most Challenging Words.* Since the Earth is the only planet we occupy at the moment, one ought to have at least a tiny bit of familiarity with all these geological shenanigans that shape the dear old thing.

didapper (DEYE da pur) *n.* A *didapper* is a "small diving water bird," also known as a *dabchick* or *little grebe,* which generally frequents rivers and fresh waters. The term *dive-dapper,* now obsolete but still heard in some dialects, was once used as the name of a small diving fowl, and the *di-* element in *didapper* is a relic of that *dive-,* or, as the *O.E.D.* says, a "reduced form" of it. Apart from all this ornithology, *didapper* has been applied jokingly and pejoratively to the kind of person who disappears for a while and suddenly pops up again. Alexander Pope collaborated on *The Art of Sinking* (1727), which included this satirical passage on writers: "The *didappers* are authers (sic), that keep themselves long out of sight, under water, and come up now and then, where you least expected them." Charles C. Colton, in *Lacon: or Many Things in Few Words* (1851), described a man named Wilkes as " ... one of those *didappers,* whom, if you had stripped naked, and thrown over Westminster bridge, you might have met on the very next day, with … a laced coat upon his back, and money in his pocket." Most of us have met such people; now you see them, now you don't; they vanish, they're gone forever, and whoops! here they are again, as though nothing had happened. *Didappers*, every one of them.

digamy (DIG uh mee) *n. Digamy* is a "second marriage." It rhymes with *bigamy* but is legal after a divorce, an annulment or the death of a first spouse. Dr. Johnson correctly defined it in his dictionary, but according to Boswell, when a gentleman who had been very unhappy in marriage remarried immediately after the death of his first wife, Johnson called it "the triumph of hope over experience." *Digamy* comes via Latin *digamia*, from Greek *digamia*, formed of the prefix *di-* (twice) plus *gamos* (marriage). *Trigamy*, as you might reasonably expect, is a "third marriage," and that word does exist, but even the *O.E.D.* makes no mention of the anticipatable (there is no such word as *anticipable*, which would be more euphonious) *quadrigamy, quinquigamy, sexigamy* or *septigamy* (a word to take care of the cases of Tommy Manville, Mickey Rooney and, I'm sure, others). To get back to the simpler matter of *digamy*, one who practices it is a *digamist* (DIG uh muhst), and the adjective for the resulting state is *digamous* (DIG uh muhs). You may remember a Marx Brothers film in which, on bended knee, Groucho, though already married, proposes to the surprisingly unflappable, or at least insufficiently outraged, Margaret Dumont. "But that would be bigamy!" says she. "Big o' *you*?" cries Groucho, "It would be big o' *me*!"

dimeter   See **ithyphallic.**

dioscuric (deye oh SKYOOHR ik) *adj.* This is a very fancy way of saying "twin," as in *twin brothers* or the *twin crises*, e.g., of starvation and disease after a natural catastrophe. The word arises out of Greek mythology, which is full of the complex family relationships of the gods. Leda was the wife of Tyndarus, sometimes known as Tyndareus. The wily Zeus, in the form of a swan, came upon her one day while she was bathing and seduced her. In due time she gave birth to twin sons known in Greek mythology as Castor and Polydeuces and in Roman legend as Castor and Pollux, who became demigods. Other sources tell it differently: She brought forth two eggs, from one of which Castor and Clytemnestra were hatched and from the other, Pollux and Helen of Troy. According to still other authorities, the first two were the legitimate children of Leda and her husband. Whatever the "facts" may be, the popular legend is that Castor and Pollux were the offspring of the union of Leda and Zeus, an event celebrated in a 1925 poem by William Butler Yeats. (Yeats's theme is that the "union" caused, through Helen, the war and the destruction of Troy.) They were known to the Greeks as the *Dioskouroi*, from *Dios*, the genitive of *Zeus*, plus *kouroi*, plural of *kouros* (boy, son). Thus, *dioscuric*, literally "like Castor and Pollux," came to mean "twin" generally, without reference to those two boys. When I first came across this word, I jumped to the conclusion that the *dio-* element was simply the Greek prefix *dia-*, which drops the *a* when it is attached to a word beginning with *o*, as in *diorama*, formed of *di-*, a variant of *dia-*, plus *orama* (view). In etymology, look before you jump.

dipody   See **ithyphallic.**

diptych   See **polyptych.**

dodded   See **daddock.**

dolichocephal (do li koh SEF'l) *n.* One so called is a person with a long head. *Dolichos* means "long" in Greek, and *kephale* "head." With a bit of Greek at your command, you might figure out that a *brachycephal* (brak ee SEF'l) is a person with a short head, for *brachys* means "short" in Greek, and good old *kephale* tags along. These two Greek prefixes are found in other anatomical terms relating to size. *Kephale* developed into our word element *cephalo-* as in *cephalometry* (sef'l OM eh tree), "the science of measuring the dimensions of the head." *Cephalate* (SEF uh late) or *cephalous* (SEF uh luhs) means "having a head" as opposed to *acephalous* (without a head) like, presumably, Washington Irving's famous horseman, or the queen in the old English music-hall ditty who walked the bloody tower at the midnight hour "with 'er 'ed tucked underneath 'er arm." The *a-* in *acephalous* is a prefix known as the "alpha privative," with the negating effect of *un-*, *dis-*, *-less*, etc. *Acephalous* is used figuratively to describe a nation or organization that has lost its "head" in the sense of "leader," like our country after the assassination of a president, or Monsarrat's *Tribe that Lost Its Head.*

dolichurus (dol ih KOOH ruhs) *n.* The Greek adjective *dolichouros* means "long-tailed" and is built of the prefix *dolicho-*, the combing form of the adjective *dolichos* (long), plus the noun *oura* (tail). The resulting noun is the name of a *dactylic hexameter* with a redundant syllable at the end, but that definition, in turn, may need a bit of clarification. *Dactylic hexameter* may be considered redundant, because *hexameter* alone is usually defined as "a *dactylic* line of six feet," as in Greek and Latin epic poetry (*The Iliad, The Aeneid,* etc.). The first four feet are *dactyls* (a *dactyl* is a foot of three syllables, one stressed followed by two unstressed, as in *terribly*) or *spondees* (a *spondee* is a foot of two syllables, both stressed, as in *split screen*), the fifth is a *dactyl* and the sixth is a *spondee* or a *trochee* (a *trochee* is a foot of two syllables, one stressed followed by one unstressed, as in *spinach*). A *caesura* (sih ZHOOHR uh), or "pause," usually follows the stressed syllable in the third foot. In the unlikely event that the foregoing isn't entirely clear, here is an example of a dactylic hexameter: *This is the forest primeval. The murmuring pines and the hemlocks ...* After all this, just remember that a *dolichurus* is simply a dactylic hexameter with a redundant syllable at the end, as would have been the case if Longfellow (perish the thought!) had had the bad taste to write *conifers* rather than *hemlocks*.

donzel (DON zuhl) *n.* This term, meaning a "squire, esquire, an attendant to a knight, a page," designated a young gentleman not yet knighted but an aspirant to that office. The office is obsolete; the word is included here not only because it has a nice sound but also because it illustrates that sloppiness in language is nothing new. In a delightful, hilarious little book entitled *Anguish English* by Richard Lederer, subtitled *An Anthology of Accidental Assaults Upon Our Language*, there is a final section headed "Howta Reckanize American Slurvian," bewailing the sad state of pronunciation and articulation in the United States; examples: *guvmint, hafta, "Jeetjet?"* Lederer tells us that in a 1949 *New Yorker* article, John Davenport labeled this kind of sublanguage "Slurvian." More examples: *The mill of the room; a few mince;* and so on and so on. Well, there's nothing new about Slurvian. *Donzel,* way back there, is a medieval example. Late Latin produced *domnicellus,* a diminutive of Latin *dominus* (Lord); *domnicellus* gave the Italians the Slurvian *donzello;* that gave the English the Slurvian *donzel.* People have been *slurring* their way through language for centuries. Sorry, I have no early Egyptian examples. So truzme.

dor   See **dumbledore.**

dos   See **pollicitation.**

doseh (DOH seh) *n.* This is the name of a festival that was held each year at Cairo, by the followers of the sheikh of the Sa'di dervishes, celebrating the birth of the Prophet Muhammad. The main feature was the sheikh's riding on horseback over the prostrate bodies of his devotees. Mercifully, the authorities abolished this jolly event in 1884. The name of the festival derives from the Arabic word *dowsah* meaning "treading." This brings to mind the word *juggernaut* (JUG er nawt), which has come to denote any overpowering destructive force or object, such as a giant battleship, an unbeatable football team, an overwhelming political machine or anything monstrously huge and irresistible. In England, the term has been applied to those enormous trailer trucks that have caused a great controversy about their use on country lanes and city streets, where they make a deafening noise, shake the fabric of ancient buildings and annoy the citizens no end. In my *British English, A to Zed,* I point out that "The word is related to *Jagannath,* an idol of the Hindu god Krishna, which was drawn in processions on vast carts under whose wheels fanatics threw themselves in their ecstasy, to be crushed to death."

dossil (DOS il) *n.* This little noun has a number of meanings that are only loosely related. In Late Latin, a *ducillus* was a "spigot" or "plug," and that was what *dossil* meant. Later, it came to mean a surgical dressing for wounds, also known as a "pledget," which is a kind of "plug," and which may explain this second meaning. *Pledget* (PLEJ it) also means an "oakum string for caulking ship seams," another kind of plug. *Dossil* took on still another meaning: a "cloth roll" for wiping excessive ink from engraved plates, usually of copper, of the type used in the printing process. *Dossil* is pronounced the way Americans pronounce *docile* (the British make the *o* long or short and pronounce "ile" as EYE'l), which comes from Latin *docilis* (easily taught), from *docere* (to teach), but the two words are unrelated, as are their etymologies. It might be said that the cloth roll used in printing is also a kind of "plug" in that it "stops" the flow of excessive ink, but that seems a bit farfetched. However, it must be admitted that *dossil* has a legitimate claim to versatility. As for *oakum* (OH kum), if you are not familiar with the word, it is "string or fiber obtained by untwisting and teasing or picking apart old ropes"; *picking oakum* used to be a typical convict's occupation.

doublet   See **catmalison.**

doulocracy   See **dulia.**

draegerman (DREE gur muhn) *n.* At first blush, this word looked to me like a variant or a corruption of *dragoman* (DRAY guh muhn), one of the headwords in my *1000 Most Challenging Words.* A *dragoman* is an "interpreter, sometimes also a guide," according to that learned tome. "The term is usually applied," I say in that book, "to persons who professionally interpret Near Eastern languages, particularly Arabic, Turkish, and Persian, for government offices, tour companies, and the like." But a *draegerman* doesn't interpret; he is a "member of a crew trained for underground rescue work," and his title comes from one A. B. Draeger, a German scientist who invented a certain type of breathing apparatus. The *-man* in this word is simply English for *homo,* whereas the final syllable of *dragoman* hasn't a thing in the world to do with our word *man;* it's a development from the penultimate syllable of Medieval Greek *dragomenos* that finally wound up as French *dragoman,* which we adopted. The plural of *draegerman* is *draegermen,* but the plural of *dragoman* should be *dragomans.* However, English-speaking people, assuming that the *-man* of *dragoman* was our *man,* formed the errroneous plural *dragomen,* which has now become an acceptable variant. "Insistence on *-mans,*" says Fowler, "is didacticism." The April 20, 1937 issue of of the *Ottawa Journal* speaks of the "Stellanton Draeger crew" and refers to "Stellanton's *draegermen*—a crew of rescue men trained to enter a colliery after an explosion." A little investigation in *Webster's Geographical Dictionary* revealed that there is indeed a town of Stellartown, not Stellantown, in Nova Scotia, pop. 5,575, in the heart of a coal-mining region, so it appears that the *Ottawa Journal* was guilty of a typographical error, a sin not unknown in journalistic circles. *The Times* (London) in its October 25, 1958, issue informs us that "the *draegermen* ... carry about 45 lb. of oxygen equipment on their backs." Stout fellows!

draggle (DRA g'l) *vb. Draggle* is a diminutive and frequentative (a verb expressing the frequent repetition of another verb, e.g., *drip/dribble, spark/sparkle*—fully discussed in my *1000 Most Challenging Words*) of *drag* and means "to drag or trail on the ground," as through dirt, bog or mire, and thus make limp and sodden. This is the sort of thing that used to happen when skirts were long and reached well below the ankles—a problem solved by raising hems and dramatically solved by the miniskirt. As an intransitive verb, *to draggle* means "to get dirty and wet by being trailed along damp ground." By extension, the verb has been used as a pejorative description of one shuffling along in a slovenly manner. *Draggled* is a participial adjective meaning "sodden, wet, limp and muddy." Israel Zangwill wrote of "scarecrows in battered harts or *draggled* skirts." *Draggle-tailed* took on the meaning of "sluttish, slatternly," and *draggle-tail* was used to denote a slattern. Partridge (*A Dictionary of Slang and Unconventional English*) goes further and defines a *draggle-tail* as a "nasty, dirty slut" and hence a "low prostitute." There is a couplet in John Gay's *Trivia; or the Art of Walking the Streets of London* (1717) that reads: "You'll see a *draggled* Damsel here and there/From Billingsgate her fishy Traffick bear." Unsightly image, but good, substantial John Gay! (Billingsgate, discussed in that same book of mine, was for centuries a London fish market, notorious for the foul language spoken by its vendors and porters, especially the fishwives who worked there. It gave rise to the term *billingsgate* for particularly offensive language of vituperation and vilification.)

draggle-tail   See **draggle.**

draggle-tailed   See **draggle.**

Drawcansir (draw KAN sur) *n.* This name for a swaggering, blustering, overbearing bully, based on a character of that name in *The Rehearsal*, a burlesque of which George Villiers, second duke of Buckingham (1628–87), was coauthor and producer. Villiers, a courtier of Charles II, was responsible for this satire on heroic drama, which appeared in 1671. *Drawcansir* was a parody of the character Almanzor in Dryden's *Conquest of Granada*. In the final scene of Villiers's satire, he joins in a battle and kills all the fighters on both sides. Sometimes his name is spelled *Draw-can-sir*, and that is thought to be based on "drawing a can of liquor," since his great drinking capacity is mentioned earlier in the play, in which he is described as " ... a fierce Hero, that ... does what he will, without regard to good manners, justice, or numbers." In 1880 Justin McCarthy (*A History of our Own Times*) described a politician named Layard as " ... a very *Drawcansir* of political debate, a swashbuckler, and soldado [Spanish for "soldier"] of Parliamentary Conflict." Abraham Tucker, in *The Light of Nature Pursued* (1852), referred to the original character's feat of exterminating all the combatants on both sides by describing a character as " ... such a *Drawcansir*, as to cut down both friend and foe." Given his propensity to world-class drinking, I would hardly invite a *Draw-*

cansirish acquaintance of mine to use my extra ringside ticket to a prizefight, even if he favored one of the gladiators.

drogulus (DRAW gyooh lus) *n.* Talk about obscure words! A *drogulus* is, according to the *O.E.D. Supplement A–G,* "an entity whose presence is unverifiable, because it has no physical effects." Have we finally met the man who wasn't there?

> As I was going up the stair
> I met a man who wasn't there.
> He wasn't there again today.
> I wish, I wish he'd stay away.

Had Hughes Mearns, who wrote that poem, heard about the *drogulus*? No, he came up with that bit of poesy before A.J. Ayer coined *drogulus* "on the spur of the moment" and, *A–G* hypothesizes, "perh[aps] by subconscious association with DRAGON + L[atin] *-ulus* as in DRAGUNCULUS." Ayer himself said, in 1957, "Suppose I say 'There's a *drogulus* over there,' and you say 'What?' and I say 'Drogulus,' and you say 'What's a *drogulus*?' Well I say 'I can't describe what a *drogulus* is, because it's not the sort of thing you can see or touch, it has no physical effects of any kind, but it's a disembodied being.'" Two years later, L. S. Penrose (*New Biology*) said: "I had difficulty in finding a suitable name for the activated complexes produced in ... [certain] experiments. On showing one of these to Professor A. J. Ayer, I inquired whether it might perhaps be a '*drogulus*' ... He replied that it was undoubtedly a *drogulus*." Is this obscure enough for you?

dry-stone-diker See **cowan.**

dudgeon See **clapperdudgeon.**

dulia, also **douleia** (DOOH lee uh) *n. Douleia*, in Greek, is "servitude," *doulos* "slave" and *doulosis* "enslavement." *Dulia* or *douleia* denotes the inferior or minor form of veneration, which under the code of the Roman Catholic Church is accorded to saints and angels, as opposed to *hyperdulia* (hy per DOOH lee uh), the form accorded to the Virgin Mary, and *latria* (LAH tree uh), that reserved for God alone. More *d(o)ul-* words: *Dulosis* (dooh LOH sis) denotes the type of enslavement imposed by certain ants upon, poor chaps, other ants; and *d(o)ulocracy* (dooh LOH cruh see) is "government by slaves," a word explained by Thomas Blount in his *Glossographia, or a Dictionary Interpreting Such Hard Words ... as are Now Used* (1656). "We should be the sport of chance and caprice," wrote Julius and Augustus Hare (was there a third brother named *September*?) in *Guesses at Truth* (1867), "as has ever happened to a people when fallen under a *doulocracy*." Blount explained Such Hard Words as are Now Used, whereas Schur explains Such Hard Words as are Now Not (or Hardly Ever) Used. *Useful*?

dulosis   See **dulia.**

dumbledore (DUM b'l dor) *n. Dumbledore* is the name of two different insects: the bumblebee, which the British also call *humblebee*, and the cockchafer, a large grayish-brown scarabaeoid beetle extremely destructive to forest trees and vegetation. Strange, that the same word can apply to the helpful bumblebee, so important in pollination, and the harmful cockchafer. The *hum-* of *humblebee* is undoubtedly onomatopoeic, while the *bumble-* of *bumblebee* is built on the verb *bumble*, which means "to buzz, make a humming sound" as well as "to bungle" or "muddle." As to the *-dore* in *dumbledore*, that comes from the noun *dor*, which applies to any insect that flies with a humming or buzzing sound. The *cock-* of *cockchafer* is a reference to the bird and implies size or vigor, and *chafer* is the name applied to any large, slow-moving beetle, or in Britain, to any scarabaeoid. John W. Robberds wrote *A memoir of the Life and Writings of W. Taylor of Norwhich, Containing his Correspondence with Southey* (1843), in which he quotes from Southey: "Is it not the *humble-bee*, or what we call the *'dumbledore'*, a word whose descriptive droning deserves a place in song?" Indeed, what is more melodious, on a green lawn in midsummer, than the droning of Isaac Watts's " ... little busy bee" improving "each shining hour"?

dunderfunk (DUN dur funk) *n.* This rather expressive word is the name of a ship biscuit, soaked in water, mixed with fat and molasses, then baked in a pan. An alternative name is *dandyfunk*. It sounds awful, and its origin and effect are unknown. From the sound of it, the *O.E.D.* appears to be quite right in spurning it, and it seems a good reason for avoiding the profession of seaman.

dunnage (DUHN ij) *n., vb.* To prevent cargo in the hold of a ship from moving around and to keep it dry, pieces of wood, brush, mats and other miscellaneous articles are placed under or among the cargo. The term for such material is *dunnage.* The term is applied as well to bracing installed by shippers in the hold, or in a freight car or truck, to protect goods while in the course of shipment. *Dunnage* also refers to padding in shipping containers to prevent the breakage of fragile merchandise. It is a remarkably versatile term, for it applies as well to baggage generally, personal effects and lumber of such low quality as to be unsalable. It is also a colloquial term in British English for miscellaneous baggage of any sort, and British slang for sailors' or tramps' clothes. The *C.O.D.* traces it to the Anglo-Latin word *dennagium*, of unknown derivation. (*Anglo-Latin* is the term for the Latin current in medieval England.) In addition to all this, *dunnage* is used as a verb meaning "to secure or stow with *dunnage.*" There would appear to be no connection between *dunnage* and *dun*, itself an extremely versatile little word that covers a color, variations in the color of horses, drabness, a method of curing codfish, keeping after a person to pay his debts and fortified dwellings in Ireland and Scotland protected by two or more earthen mounds enclosing deep moats.

duniwassal (DOOH nih wos'l), also **dunniwassal** (DUHN-) *n*. From Gaelic *duine* (man) and *wasal* (gentle, well-born) came the noun *duniwassal*, also *duinnie-wassal*, a "gentleman of the Scottish Highlands," particularly a younger son of a noble family. Sir Walter Scott, in *Bonny Dundee*, wrote the stirring lines: "There are wild *Duniewassals* three thousand times three/Will cry hoigh! for the bonnet o' Bonny Dundee." Bonny Dundee was John Graham of Claverhouse, Viscount Dundee, a Stuart supporter killed in 1689 at the battle of Killiecrankie. Scott wrote of these Highland gentlemen of lesser rank in the *Waverley Novels*: "His bonnet had a short feather, which indicated his claim to be treated as a *Duinhé-Wassell* [note different spelling] or sort of gentleman." *The Times* (London) in 1884 wrote of " ... *duinniewassals*, or small gentry." One had to be careful about the size of the feather in one's bonnet in those days, for the all-important matter of rank was involved.

dvandva   See **tatpurusha**.

dysgenic   See **evancalous**.

dyslogistic (dis luh JIS tik) *adj*. We are familiar with the adjective *eulogistic* and the noun *eulogy*, having to do with praise. The Greek prefix *eu-* has a positive effect and is found in such words as *eugenics*, *euphemism* and *euphonious*. In each case the *eu-* conveys the sense of "good," "well," "nice." *Eu-* is the combining form of the adjective *eus* (good), the neuter of which, *eu*, is used as an adverb meaning "well." *Dys-*, on the other hand, is a Greek prefix with the opposite sense: "bad" or "ill." Thus, we have *dyspepsia* (bad digestion), where *dys-* is joined to *pepsis* (digestion), and *dystrophy* (faulty nourishment), as in the all too familiar term *muscular dystrophy*. Here, the *dys-* is joined to the Greek noun *trophe* (nourishment). *Dysentery* is a combination of that ill-omened prefix with *enteron* (intestine). You can be sure that *eu-* something is infinitely preferable to *dys-* anything. (Don't worry about *eunuch*: that *eu-* is not a prefix but simply the first syllable of *eune*, "bed," joined to *ouchos* "keeping," a word related to the verb *echein*, "to hold," resulting in the noun *eunouchos*—eunuch, but as indicated by its formation, used by the Greeks to mean "chamberlain" or "steward," an official who kept his eye on the ladies and was carefully castrated before assuming that august office.) After all that, it would seem appropriate to inform you that *dyslogistic*, which has nothing to do with *logistics*, means quite the opposite of "laudatory": "uncomplimentary, indicating disapproval or censure" and is formed of *dys-* plus *logos* (word). A *dyslogistic* eye cast upon you can be quite *disconcerting*, but the *dis-* in that word was borrowed not from Greek but from Latin.

dysphasia   See **evancalous**.

dysphonia   See **evancalous**.

dysphoria   See **evancalous**.

dyspnea   See **evancalous.**

dysthymia   See **evancalous.**

dystocia (dih STOH shee uh, -shuh), also **dystokia** (dih STOH kee uh) *n.* Under certain headwords in this book I have discussed the Greek prefixes *eu-* and *dys-*; see, for example, **dystopia.** *Dystocia* and *eutocia* present a good example of these opposing prefixes. *Dystocia* is "slow or difficult labor or childbirth," from the Greek *dys-* (hard, bad, ill) plus *tokos* (childbirth), related to *teknon* (child). *Eutocia* (yooh TOH shee uh, -shuh) is "normal childbirth," without complications, from the Greek prefix *eu-* (good, well) plus the same *tokos.* If you happen to know the meaning of the underlying noun (in this case *tokos*), you can figure out the meanings of the compounds using these prefixes. It's as easy as that.

dystopia (dis TOH pee uh) *n.* As any dictionary will show you, there are a great many words that begin with the prefix *dys-*, taken from the Greek, where, to quote *Liddell & Scott*, it is an "insepar[able] Prefix, opp[osite] to *eu*, like our *un-* or *mis-* in *un-lucky, mis-chance*, always with a notion of *hard, bad, ill*, etc., destroying a word's good sense or increasing its bad sense." You can find a fair number of examples in my discussion of **evancalous.** *Dystopia* is a prime example, being the opposite of *Eutopia. Cacotopia* (KA ko toh pee uh)—using the Greek prefix *caco-*, from *kakos*, bad—is characterized in the *C.O.D.* as a "nonce-word" based on the mistaken notion that *Utopia*, the imaginary island described in Sir Thomas More's *Utopia* (1516) as a place blessed with perfection in law, politics, etc., was a misspelling of *Eutopia.* We must straighten this out. *Eutopia* was a play on *Utopia*, which was based on Greek *ou* plus *topos*, meaning "nowhere" (because there was no such place), while *Eutopia* was built from Greek *eu* plus *topos, eu-* being a prefix based on the adjective *eus* (good), used in its neuter form *eu* as an adverb meaning "well," so that *Eutopia* means "a place of ideal happiness and good order." If we look at *Utopia* and *Eutopia* closely, we can see that far from being synonyms, they should be used in antithesis: A region of ideal happiness and order is—nowhere! Obviously, if *cacopia* can be called a "nonce-word," so can *dystopia.* Whether or not you agree with my argument, *Dystopia* is an imaginary place where everything is as bad as possible, as imaginary as More's *Utopia*, or, with a lowercase *d*, a condition in which everything is as bad as possible. John Stuart Mill, as reported in an 1868 issue of *Hansard* (the British equivalent of our *Congressional Record*), said: "It is, perhaps, too complimentary to call them [his political opponents] *Utopians*, they ought rather to be called *dys-topians*, or *caco-topians.* What is commonly called *Utopian* is something too good to be practicable; but what they favour is too bad to be practicable." A 1967 issue of *The Listener* (the BBC radio and television journal) contained this sentence: "The modern classics— Aldous Huxley's *Brave New World* and George Orwell's *Nineteen Eighty Four*—

are *dystopias*. They describe not a world we should like to live in, but one we must be sure to avoid." Agreed!

dysuria   See **evancalous.**

ebionism   See **theandric.**

ebionite   See **theandric.**

ebionize   See **theandric.**

eccaleobion (eh kal ee oh BEYE uhn) *n*. Even if you were up on your Greek, you'd never guess what this strange word means: "egg-hatching apparatus," a contraption for hatching eggs by artificial heat instead of brood hens. It was invented circa 1839 by a man named Bucknell. Either the inventor or a scholarly friend coined the name from the Greek sentence *Ekkaleo bion*, meaning "I evoke life," a pretty fancy name for a hatchery. *Ekkaleo* is the first person singular of the verb *ekkaleisthai* (to evoke), and *bion* is the accusative of *bios* (life). In 1839 Bucknell wrote an article entitled *Eccaleobion: A Treatise on Artificial Incubation*. The term was used metaphorically in an 1880 issue of *Harper's* magazine: "Willis's *Home Journal* was at one time a very *eccaleobion* for young writers." I wonder how many readers of the magazine knew what *eccaleobion* meant. When you buy a chicken or other fowl these days, the overwhelming likelihood is that it is the product of one sort of *eccaleobion* or other. Brood hens are very much the exception.

eclosion (ih KLOH shuhn) *n*. From the Latin prefix *ex-* (out of, from) plus *clausum*, the neuter of *clausus*, itself the past participle of *claudere* (to shut) used as a noun meaning "an enclosed place," the French got *éclosion*. We took it over (without the accent) meaning "emergence from concealment," with a special meaning in entomology denoting the emergence of an imago from the puparium (the pupal case) or the emergence of a larva from an egg. (This is hardly the place to go into these entomological phenomena. There are lots of books on the subject. And remember: *etymology* is about words; *entomology* is about *ents* and other insects.) In a 1906 letter of William James, found in his *Letters*, edited by brother Henry (1920), we read: "It is queer to be assisting at the *éclosion* of a great new mental epoch, life, religion, and philosophy in one." William used the French word, not yet adopted into English.

ecmnesia (ek MNEE zhee uh, -see-) *n*. A long look at this word will find the *-mnesia* familiar from the word *amnesia*, the common word for "loss of

memory," built of the Greek negative prefix *a-* (known as the "alpha privative," as found in words like *amoral, asexual, apolitical*) plus *mnesis* (memory).
In *ecmnesia* we have, instead of *a-*, the prefix *ec-*, from the Greek *ek-* (out), and
we get a word that limits the loss of memory to the events of a particular
period, as opposed to the wiping out of the entire past. The *Billings Medical
Dictionary* defines *ecmnesia* as "a form of amnesia in which there is normal
memory of occurrences prior to a certain date, with loss of memory of what
happened for a certain time after that date." This is a common condition
following a concussion, which knocks out recollection of the accident and
subsequent events for a limited period thereafter. It may aptly describe as well
the condition of the mind on "the morning after the night before," during
which the boys had gotten together for a little serious drinking at, for instance,
a bachelor party. *Chambers's Dictionary of Psychiatry* calls the condition "amnesia with poor memory [as opposed to 'loss of memory'] for recent events,
but with relatively intact memory for events in the remote past." Perhaps the
latter definition was concocted by a lexicographer who had suffered a milder
concussion or attended a somewhat less boisterous party the night before. As
Einstein said, everything is relative.

eddish   See **rowen.**

egeria, also **aegeria**, usually capitalized (ee GEE ree uh, e-, ih-) *n.* An *egeria* is
a "female adviser." *(A)egeria* was the name of a nymph, one of the four
Camenae, the wise and prophetic fountain nymphs revered in Roman religion:
Carmentis, Egeria, Antevorta and Postvorta, later identified with the Muses.
Egeria was the nymph who advised and instructed Numa Pompilius (753–673
B.C.), second king of Rome, in his sage lawmaking, and, according to legend
was his companion and wife. From her role as adviser and instructor, her name
became generic for any female counselor. Disraeli, in *Vivian Grey*, wrote the
following lovely sentences: "It is in these moments that we gaze upon the
moon. It is in these moments that Nature becomes our *Egeria*."

electuary   See **catholicon.**

eleutherian   See **eleutherism.**

eleutherism (uh LYOOH thuh riz'm) *n.* This is the commendable emotion of
"zeal for freedom," the very opposite of the suppressive practices so painfully
evident in totalitarian regimes. *Eleutheros* is Greek for "free," and it is easy to
see how *eleutherism* was constructed. *Eleutherian* (el lyooh THEH ree uhn) was
the title of Zeus in his role of protector of political freedom, one of his more
gracious aspects. *Eleutheromania* (uh lyooh thuh roh MAY nee uh) is mad zeal
for freedom (*-mania* can be tacked onto just about anything, as in *Anglomania,
bibliomania, Beatlemania*, etc.) and can lead to anything from playing hooky to
hippyism to anarchy. One must be all out for *eleutherism*, but excessive zeal or

fanaticism is to be deplored. It was Barry Goldwater, when he campaigned for the presidency, who favored "extremism in the cause of liberty." This is a pretty good definition of *eleutheromania* and made good old conservative Barry too radical for many.

eleutheromania See **eleutherism.**

ell See **alnage.**

emblements (EM blih muhnts) *n. pl.* Dictionaries vary in their definitions of this word. Most confine its meaning to the products, and ensuing profits, from land that has been sown or planted or cultivated. Thus, *RH* provides an etymology based on Middle Latin *imbladare* (to sow with grain), built on prefix *im-*, a variant of *in-* (in) plus *blada* (grain). *W III* defines it as "the growing crop ... resulting from annual cultivation as distinguished from old roots (as pasturage) or from trees (as timber or fruit)" or the profits from a crop so sown, and attributes it to Middle French *emblaer* (to sow a field with grain). *CH* goes along with that distinction: "crops raised by the labour of the cultivator, but not tree-fruits or grass" and traces it back, via Old French *emblaer*, to Late Latin *imbladare*, from *in-* plus *bladum* (wheat). But the *O.E.D.*, after going along generally with that derivation and defining the word as "the profits of sown land" (short and sweet), tells us that "the word is sometimes used more largely for any products that arise naturally from the ground, as grass, fruit, etc.," attributing the broader definition to Tomlins's *Law Dictionary Greatly Enlarged and Improved* over that of one G. Jacobs. To play it safe, skip the grass and the fruit trees.

empolder (em POHL dur), also **impolder** *(im POHL dur) vb.* To *empolder* a piece of low-lying land is "to reclaim it from the sea by the erection of dikes." A *polder* is such a piece of land. This is a Dutch word, taken into English, and a term not generally applied outside of Holland. It was used of French land, however, in an 1894 issue of the *Westminster Gazette*: "Much of the asparagus eaten in London is grown in the *polders* reclaimed from the sea near Mont St. Michel." *Blackwell's Magazine*, in a 1922 issue, advised that some acres of low-lying land had been cleared and *"empoldered* with mud-dams." In 1951 *New Biology* reported that "an area of 100 acres ... was *empoldered* (i.e., surrounded by earth walls)." *Impoldered* showed up in an 1899 issue of the *Pall Mall Gazette*, which spoke of *"impoldering* and pumping, the raising and keeping of dykes," and in the 1929 edition of the *Encyclopedia Britannica* we find the following: "A great part of the Netherlands has now been *impoldered* ... The largest *impoldering* scheme on record has now been commenced." I discussed *polder* in my *1000 Most Challenging Words*, saying that the reclaiming of *polders* and their protection by a system of dikes is "an operation that occurs quite frequently in the Netherlands, where so much of the land is nether."

emunctory (ih MUNGK tuh ree) *n., adj.* As an adjective, *emunctory* describes anything pertaining to the conveying of waste matter from the body, especially nose blowing. As a noun, it denotes any bodily cleansing organ or canal, such as the excretory ducts, kidneys and pores. The word is derived from Late Latin *emunctorius* (excretory) and *emunctorium* (a means of cleaning through excretion; in classical Latin, a pair of nostrils). It all goes back to the Latin verb *emungere* (to clean a nose, and with the reflexive pronoun—*se emungere*—to wipe one's nose) and its past participle *emunctus*. The Latin phrase *emunctae naris* (literally, "with a clean nose") was used figuratively to mean "shrewd, discerning," and taking it a step further, as the poet Horace used it, "with a keen scent for other people's faults" ("Why beholdest thou the mote that is in thy brother's eye, but considerest not the beam that is in thine own eye?"— Matt. 7:3—or, as the *New English Bible* puts it, "Why do you look at the speck of sawdust in your brother's eye, with never a thought for the great plank in your own?"); but some say all Horace meant by *homo emunctae naris* was "a man of keen perception." You can take your choice of bibles and interpretations of Horace. In *Tristram Shandy* (1767), Laurence Sterne advises: "Blow your noses,—cleanse your *emunctories*,—sneeze, my good people."

enallage (en AL uh jee) *n.* It sounds like *analogy* (uhn AL uh jee) when you say it, but its meaning is quite different. *Enallage* is the "substitution of one grammatical form for another, the exchange of one tense, mood, case, number for another," e.g., singular for plural, present for future or past. The important aspect is that the "mistake" is intentional, at least when the author is manifestly literate. When the prizefight manager Joe Jacobs yelled, "We wuz robbed!" in 1932, it must be remembered that it was the same Joe Jacobs who said, instead of " … and may the best man win!" the immortal words: " … and may the superior gladiator emerge victorious!" Joe's *wuz* (*was*) wuz no mistake, in my opinion. And wuzn't it effective! And it is to be assumed that when the magazine *Punch* came out with "You pays your money and you takes your choice," the use of the singular verb was a conscious deviation from correct grammar. It is no secret that James Joyce was well up on his grammar, so that when he had Molly Bloom declare, "My patience are exhausted," Joyce was quite aware that his little pun involved a singular noun. For all these examples I am indebted to Professor Arthur Quinn of the University of California and his charming and learned little book *Figures of Speech*. Here's one of my own: "The old gray mare, she ain't what she used to be." Wouldn't *isn't* have made that time-honored statement insipid?

enantiomorph (en AN tee oh morf) *n., adj.* This word was first used in a German text, C. F. Naumann's *Elemente der Theoretischen Krystallographie* (1856). It is formed of the Greek *enantios* (opposite) and *morphe* (form) and means "mirror image." It gave rise to the adjectives *enantiomorphic* and *enantiomorphous* and the nouns *enantiomorphism* and *enantiomorphy*, all accented on the "MOR" syllable. In the 1885 edition of the *Encyclopedia Britannica*, A. C.

Brown provided a good example of *enantiomorphism*: " ... our two hands ... the one of which resembles in figure the mirror image of the other." *Enantiopathy* (en an tee AW puh thee), from *enantios* plus *pathos* (feeling), is the treatment of disease by an agent that is opposite to it, rather than one that is similar to it, as in the "like-cures-like" basis of homeopathy; the word is sometimes used as a synonym of *allopathy*. Another word from *enantios* is *enantiosis* (en an tee OH sis), a figure of speech using the antonym of what is meant. Remember "Oh What a Lovely War"? Among jazz musicians, *bad* means "good"; I have heard half-swooning aficionados exclaim, after a virtuoso improvisation by Louis Armstrong or Oscar Peterson, "That's *bad*, man!" You can't be more *enantiopathic* (permissible coinage?) than that. Enantiomythic?

enantiopathy   See **enantiomorph.**

enantiosis   See **enantiomorph.**

encaenia (en SEE nyah) *n.* From the Greek *enkainia* (consecration festivities), the neuter plural of *enkainios*, built of the prefix *en* (in) plus *kainos* (new), we get this word, construed as a plural, meaning "festive ceremonies commemorating the founding of a city or the consecration of a church or temple," in Jewish circles, the Temple of Jerusalem. Construed as a singular, and often capitalized, the word more specifically denotes the annual commemoration of founders and benefactors at Oxford University, held in June, a ceremony at which prize poems and essays are recited and honorary degrees conferred. This ceremony, held in the Sheldonian Theatre, concludes the academic year. The Sheldonian Theatre is the Senate House at Oxford, named after Gilbert Sheldon (1598–1677), Archbishop of Canterbury, who provided the funds for the building, which was designed by Sir Christopher Wren and opened in 1699. In my experience, it has come as a surprise to a number of Oxford men that *encaenia* ever had any meaning wider than that of the annual Oxford rite, but none of them had "read" (British English for "majored in") "Greats" (Oxford idiom for "classics").

endogamy (en DOG uh mee) *n.* We are familiar with certain *-gamy* words: *bigamy, monogamy, polygamy.* The suffix *-gamy* is derived from the Greek noun *gamos* (marriage). *Endogamy* and *exogamy* (ex OG uh mee) are antonyms also relating to marriage. *Endogamy* is "marriage between individuals of the same group as required by law or custom"; *exogamy* is "marriage to a person outside a specific group" (likewise as required by law or custom). The prefix *endo-* is the combining form of Greek *endos* (within); *exo-* that of Greek *exo* (outside of). These terms relate primarily to the social customs or regulations of primitive societies, but we all know that *outbreeding* and *inbreeding* are terms applicable to the social customs and in some cases, the religious requirements of modern times. The respective adjectives are *endogamous* (en DOG uh muhs) and *exogamous* (ex OG uh muhs). *Romeo and Juliet* demonstrates the tragic consequences of an *exogamous* union between members of groups as small as feuding families. The requirements of *endogamy* within Orthodox Jewish society have led to the gruesome custom of the recital of prayers for the dead by parents over any child of the family who marries "outside the faith." *Miscegenetic* (mis ej uh NET ik) marriages (those between members of different races; in particular, between white and black—from Latin *miscere*, to mix, plus *genus*, race) were long forbidden by many states of the American South, and even after the repeal of the restrictive laws, ostracism by both sides, blacks as well as whites, has made most of such unions unsuccessful in the United States; they are still difficult in many European societies as well. The dream of "one world" is still far from realization in ways quite apart from political considerations.

engastrimyth (en GAS truh mith) *n.* This word means "ventriloquist." What a debt we owe to the classical languages! Here we have the beautiful word *engastrimyth*, with a lovely derivation: via French *engastrimythe*, from Greek *engastrimythos*, formed of the prefix *en* (in) plus *gastri*, dative of *gaster* (belly), plus *mythos* (speech), and how do we define it? With another word of classical ancestry, *ventriloquism*, from Latin *ventri*, the combining form of *venter* (belly), plus *loqui* (to speak). We were much too "refined" to use anything as vulgar as "belly speaker," and as so often happens, preferred the nearer Latin to the more remote Greek. Somehow, belly *dancer* got through, and we were spared any such prissy and revolting concoction as *ventrisaltant* (*saltare* being Latin for "to dance," and *saltant*- the stem of its present participle).

enoplion   See **prosodion.**

enthymeme (EN thuh meem) *n.* Latin *enthymema* was taken over intact from the Greek, which derived it from the verb *enthymeisthai* (to consider, keep in mind), built of the prefix *en-* (in) plus *thymos* (mind), and we wound up with *enthymeme*. It can mean either of two things: a "syllogism in which one of the propositions, usually a premise, is understood but not stated," or in Aristotelian philosophy, a "rhetorical syllogism which, though probable and persuasive, may not be valid." You know what a *syllogism* is: "All horses have four legs; Dobbin is a horse; therefore Dobbin has four legs." "All horses have four legs" is the major premise; "Dobbin is a horse" is the minor premise; "Dobbin has four legs" is the conclusion. In an *enthymeme*, a premise is understood but missing. Example: "All horses have four legs; therefore Dobbin has four legs." The minor premise "Dobbin is a horse" is implied but not set down. The Aristotelian sense is different: The conclusion may not be justified. "The gods are all-powerful; Jove is a god; therefore Jove is all-powerful." But *are* all gods omnipotent? If not, Jove may not be. Whichever sense may be involved, the adjective is *enthymematic* (EN thee muh MAD ik). All the words in this book are obscure; therefore *enthymeme* is obscure. No longer, I hope.

eonism (EE uh niz-m) *n.* An *eon* is an indefinitely long period of time, and one might be pardoned for jumping to the conclusion that *eonism* had something to do with paleontology, archaeology or prehistory, but no. The *eon* in this word comes from the name of the Chevalier Charles d'Eon (1728–1810), a French diplomat and adventurer who wore women's clothes. *Eonism*, then, is "transvestism," especially by a male, and an *eonist* is a "transvestite." *CH* is kind to the Chevalier. It omits the "adventurer" and tells us that Charles "chose female dress as a disguise," making him appear to have been a daring Scarlet Pimpernel sort of diplomat. Havelock Ellis calls it " ... clearly a typical case of what Hirschfeld later called 'transvestism' and what I would call 'sexo-aes-thetic inversion,' or more simply '*Eonism*.' ... The *Eonist* (though sometimes emphatically of the apparent sex) sometimes shows real physical approxima-tions towards the opposite sex." The September 5, 1970, issue of *The Times* (London) had this to say: "Today we can see that the Chevalier was an a-sexual transvestite. From his name Havelock Ellis coined the term *eonism* to describe this minor deviation." Minor deviation? I suppose so: no harm done, but that does seem to have been an extraordinarily permissive view.

epanados   See **anaphora.**

epanalepsis   See **anaphora.**

epanaphora   See **anaphora.**

epeirogeny   See **diastrophism.**

epenthesis   See **metaplasm.**

epeolatry (ep ee OL uh tree) *n. Epeolatry* is "the worship of words," and is derived from the Greek nouns *epos* (word) and *latreia* (worship). A *-latry* word more familiar to us is *idolatry*, which comes from Greek *eidolatres* (idolater) based on *eidolon* (idol) and *latreuein* (to worship). *Worship* may seem to be an excessive way of describing love of words but may not be too far from one's obsessive interest in words and language generally, a condition of mind to which I have been subject since an early age. "Words," my father told me when I was about 12, "distinguish us from animals, are God-given, and we must cherish and never abuse them." Recent experiments with some species of apes demonstrate that we are not unique among the animals in knowing and using words, the distinction being more in the nature of laryngeal equipment. The writer William Gaddis (*The Recognitions*) said, explaining about his choice of unusual words: "[I] can't often comment on reasons for their selection except in some cases (as Eliot) plain homage." Worship? Idolization? Homage? Same thing.

epexegesis (ep eks uh JEE sis) *n. Exegesis* is "critical interpretation or explana-tion," especially of the Bible. It is a Greek word taken into English, meaning "explanation," formed of the prefix *ex-* (out of, from) plus *ege-*, the stem of the verb *hegeesthai* (to guide). A practitioner of *exegesis* (eks uh JEE sis) is an *exegete* (EKS ih jeet), and *exegetics* (eks uh JET iks) is the science of *exegesis*. Now when we put still another prefix, *ep-* (in the sense of *in addition*) in front of *exegesis*, we get *epexegesis*, denoting the addition of one or more words to clarify the import intended, or the specific sense intended of a preceding word, phrase or sentence, and as you might expect, there is the adjective *epexegetic* (ep ex uh JET ik), or *epexegetical*, which gives rise to the adverb *epexegetically*. I fear that *epexegesis* can be overdone. To give a homely example: My dear father arrived in this country from Germany as a lad of tender years, speaking extremely good, but not entirely idiomatic, English. He therefore took many phrases literally that weren't quite meant that way. I have been told that in his early years in Boston, when someone met him and said, "How are you?" after responding "Fine" he went on and on and *epexegetically* really told them how he was, in tremendous detail involving just about every aspect of life: health, progress on the job, marital status, plans for the future, *und so weiter und so weiter*, totally ignoring his listener's obvious straining at the leash. Daudin's plea "passons au déluge" in Racine's *Les Plaideurs* was never more appropriate. Poor dad: His eager but unwarranted *epepepexegesis* made him less popular than he deserved to be.

ephod   See **ethrog.**

epieikeia (ep ee eye KEYE uh), also **epikeia** (ep ee KEYE uh) *n. Ekipy* is an obsolete form. *Epieikeia* was taken intact from the Greek, meaning "reasonableness" or "equity," as opposed to rigid legal rules. *Equity* is the name of a branch of English and American law that overrides and supplements common or statute law and is designed to protect rights, do justice and enforce duties determined by substantive law. The Greek word is based on the adjective *epieikes* (suitable, reasonable), built of the prefix *epi-* (according to) plus *eikos* (reasonable, likely). Having got this far, what does it mean? In the Roman Catholic church, *epieikeia* is such interpretation of a canonical law as excuses compliance in a case of any hardship that violates natural and reasonable law, as when a wife, for instance, honestly presumes that she may miss Mass rather than leave the bedside of a seriously ailing husband, or in a situation where to attend, she would have to leave an infant baby alone. *Epieikeia* allows the individual to act in accordance with that type of reasonable presumption. I know that when fasting on Yom Kippur results in severe physical distress or harm, a rabbi will excuse an individual from compliance with the law. In the case of the Jewish religion, the person does not presume exoneration but takes the precaution of obtaining rabbinical permission. I am advised that there are similar procedures in other religions, and how could it be otherwise?

epigamic (ep ih GAM ik) *adj.* This adjective describes a person or animal attractive to the opposite sex. The word is derived from the Greek prefix *epi-*

(upon) plus *gamos* (marriage), which together formed the Greek adjective *epigamos* (marriageable). The term is used with respect to the mating of people and animals and the characteristics that are effective in attracting the opposite sex during courtship. In his *Essays of a Biologist* (1923), Julian Huxley writes: "The human species ... has *epigamic* characters of both kinds. Some, like voice and moustache, are different in the two sexes, others, such as colour of eyes and lips, are common to both." *Chambers's Encyclopedia* (1959) speaks of " ... display in which a sexual element is involved; aposematic or threat display, and distraction or diversionary display." *Aposematic*, a zoological term formed of the Greek prefix *apo-* (away, from, off) plus *semat-*, the combining form of *sema* (sign), is applied to markings such as colors that serve as warning signals to repel attacking enemies. Muster your *epigamic* arsenal, boys and girls; choose carefully, and you may land the mate of your dreams.

epigraphy   See **pseudepigraphy.**

epimeletic (ep ih muh LET ik) *adj.* This adjective is used to denote the care of young animals by their parents and other members of the same species. In most of those fascinating television films dealing with wildlife, a great deal of attention is paid to the extraordinary activities of parents in the gathering of food for the young, the protection of them from predators and the actual instruction given them in matters of hunting and self-protection. Of course this has to do with the instinctive concern for the preservation of the species, but it is easy to commit the "pathetic fallacy" (discussed in my *1000 Most Challenging Words*) of attributing conscious altruism to the concerned, protective and seemingly affectionate parents. The oft-repeated scenes are really touching. *CH* cites the worker bees as a conspicuous example of a group exhibiting *epimeletic* behavior. The word comes from the Greek adjective *epimeletikos* (fitted for care, management, etc.), based on the noun *epimeletes* (one who has charge of [something], a trustee, manager, overseer) and related to the verb *epimeleomai* (to take care of, have the charge or management of, pay attention to). Child abuse, so horrifyingly and inexplicably frequent in the news these days, is rare in animal society, though the fish in my pond do seem to eat lots of their young, and there are examples in some species of mothers who have to protect the kiddies from being gobbled up by dear old dad.

epinicion   See **epinikion.**

epinikion (ep i NIK ee uhn), also **epinicion** (ep ih NIS ee uhn, -NISH-) *n.* This word, taken intact from the Greek, is the name given to a song of victory, an ode written and sung to honor a victor in war or a winner in games, like those at Olympia in honor of Zeus and at Delphi in honor of Apollo. The word is built upon the prefix *epi-* (on, after) plus *nike* (victory). If you have been to the Louvre, you have seen the massive sculpture known as the *Winged Victory* (or *Nike*) *of Samothrace,* and you may remember an American guided missile that some classically oriented denizen of the Pentagon (one supposes) christened the *nike*, a public relations gesture that would have appealed, it is to be presumed, to a learned minority. Euripides wrote an *epinikion* for the Athenian politician and general Alcibiades after his victory over Sparta in the Peloponnesian War. Anyone familiar with the Book of Isaiah must rejoice with him in his sublime *epinikion*. At college football games today, the cheerleaders urge the spectators to indulge in cheers and songs, but these are only pleas for victory, not *epinikia*. *Happy Days Are Here Again*, the Democrats' paean sung at political rallies before, as well as after, victory, can turn out to have been a premature *epinikion*.

epiphonema (ep ih fuh NEE muh) *n.* The Greek verb *epiphonein* (to mention), constructed from the prefix *epi-* (upon, after) and the verb *phonein* (to speak), from *phone* (sound), was taken, via Latin, into Engligh, giving us *epiphonema*, an "exclamatory sentence, a succinct summarization of the content of a discourse, a striking, emphatic peroration." One of the most memorable *epiphonemas* of all time was that with which Cato the Elder (234–149 B.C.), the Roman statesman and senator Marcus Porcius Cato, concluded every speech he made in the Roman senate after his visit to Carthage in 157 B.C. Cato was a stern moralist who disapproved of the extravagance of Carthaginian life and saw in its revived prosperity a standing threat to Rome. His *epiphonema* was "Delenda est Carthago" ("Carthage must be destroyed"), a slogan that was instrumental in bringing on the Third Punic War in which Carthage was destroyed. This *epiphonema* became proverbial and was taken to mean that "anything standing in the way of our greatness must be removed at all costs." Patrick Henry came up with a pretty good *epiphonema* in his speech in the Virginia Convention of March 23, 1775: "Give me liberty, or give me death!" They don't come much better than that.

epiphora   See **anaphora.**

epirrhema (ep ih REE muh) *n.* This is a technical aspect of classical Greek comedy. We are somewhat familiar with classical Greek writers of tragedy— Aeschylus, Sophocles and Euripides—whose works are occasionally revived for the benefit of their woefully inadequate numbers of devotees. Less familiar are the ancient Greek writers of comedy—Aristophanes and Menander; and those who pursued that craft between the two—Cratinus and Eupolis—of whom we have only fragments. In Greek comedy, the *epirrhema* was the "address of the leader of the chorus, known as the *coryphaeus* (kor ih FEE uhs—from Greek *koryphe*, head), to the audience" after the chorus had come forward and addressed the audience on behalf of the author, a part of the program known as the *parabasis* (puh RAB uh sis). So, if anybody asks what *epirrhema* means, just tell him, no, it isn't a dread and loathsome disease like *gonorrhea*, *diarrhea* or *logorrhea*. (I suffer from only the last-named of these; and *-rrhea* is a Greek suffix meaning "flow" or "discharge" and has nothing to do with the -*rhema* of *epirrhema*, which is constructed of the prefix *epi*- "after," plus the aforesaid -*rhema*; and why the double *r*?)

epistaxis (ep ih STAK sis) *n*. This is a fancy word, taken intact from the Greek, meaning "nosebleed." The Greek word is related to the verb *epistazein* (to bleed at the nose), formed of the preposition *epi*- (upon) and the verb *stazein* (to let fall in drops). I can't quite picture a sports announcer exclaiming that the challenger in a boxing match has caused the champ to sustain an *epistaxis*, but you never know. The great radio boxing announcer Joe Humphries one evening replaced the usual "And may the best man win!" with "And may the superior gladiator emerge victorious!" Incidentally, Joe scorned the microphone, even at the old Madison Square Garden. *Stentorian* was the word for Joe. But he should have said *better* instead of *best*, since one mustn't use a superlative in comparing only two. Next time you are moved to anger by your collocutor, advise him that if he continues in that vein, you will act upon the veins inside his proboscis in such a way as to bring about an *epistaxis* and then celebrate his hasty retreat.

epistrophe   See **anaphora.**

epithumetic (ep i thooh MED ik), also **epithymetic** (ep i thim ET ik) *adj*. The form with the *u* is the preferred American spelling, the one with the *y*, the British. The 20th letter of the Greek alphabet is called *upsilon* in American English and *ypsilon* (although *upsilon* is a permissible variant) in British English. In this headword, the first form is an American dictionary listing, the second a British dictionary listing, hence the *u* and *y* in the respective variants. But let's get to the definition, which in either case is "pertaining to appetite or desire." The word is a synonym for *sensual*, as in a phrase such as *the epithumetic aspect of human nature*. The derivation is from the Greek verb *epithymein* (to long for, desire), based on the prefix *epi*- (upon) plus the noun *thymos* (desire, mind, soul). Sensual desire is something that is certainly *epi*- one's *thymos* a good deal of the time, and as usual, the Greeks had a word for it.

epithymetic   See **epithumetic.**

epopt (EP opt) *n*. Literally a "beholder, overseer, watcher," *epopt* was the name given to one initiated into the highest grade of the Eleusinian mysteries of ancient Greece. The Greek noun was *epoptes*, from the verb *epopteuein* (to look upon, observe), built from the preposition *epi*- (upon) plus *opteuein* (to see). By extension, *epopt* came to denote anyone instructed in any secret system. Mysteries, in Greek and Roman religion, were secret cults, requiring elaborate initiations that included purification rites, the observing of sacred objects and the acceptance of occult knowledge. The Eleusinian were the most important mysteries. They were taken over by the Athenians circa 600 B.C. The ritual purification in the sea took place before the procession to Eleusis, 14 miles away. The initiates were sworn to secrecy, so that we know almost nothing about the details of the ritual. In general, it celebrated the abduction of Persephone by Dis, king of the Underworld, and her return to her mother Demeter, the goddess of the fertility of the earth, identified by the Romans with Ceres, their goddess of agriculture, from whose name we got the word *cereal*. And away we go, all the way from *epopt* to Corn Flakes and Post Toasties!

ergophobia (ur goh FOH bee uh) *n*. This is a somewhat jocular word invented in 1905, as reported by the *British Medical Journal* in the February 11 issue of that year, where we read that " ... it often pays better to idle and loaf about than to work, and the consequence is that a new disease has been engendered, which I [W. D. Spanton] have termed '*ergophobia*.'" This is a rather neat concoction: the Greek noun *ergon* (work) plus the familiar suffix *-phobia*. A note in the *Daily Chronicle* a little later that year (issue of May 5/7) reads: "*Ergophobia* ... means a hatred or terror of work. It is a new disease which a medical paper has recently called attention to." The *ergon* so deftly used in inventing the name of this new "disease" was the source of the physical term *erg* adopted in 1873 for a unit of work or energy: the amount of work done when a force of one dyne (the force that produces an acceleration of one centimeter per second per second on a mass of one gram) moves its point of application one centimeter in the direction of the force. Don't worry about this technical terminology—it's inserted so that you get the general idea of the *erg-* in *ergophobia* and understand that the *o* inserted between *erg-* and *-phobia* has nothing to do with the *o* in *ergo*, meaning "therefore," and was put there purely for reasons of euphony. *Ergophobia* was defined by some wag as " ... a recognized if not a notifiable disease." Notifiable? That's a British English adjective for a disease that must be reported to public health authorities. The November 24, 1960, issue of the *Daily Mail* (London) carried the headline "*Ergophobics?*" and followed that with this definition: "Boys suffering from *ergophobia* (the dilemma of having to choose between working and stealing)." Seems a bit unkind, if one is concerned about sociological problems. Perhaps the dilemma is having to choose between working and welfare—*if* jobs are available.

estovers (es TOH vurz) *n. pl*. The usual meaning of *opus* in Latin is "work, labor." There is a special use in the phrase *opus est*, or *est opus*, literally "there is work" (for someone to do) and by transference, "there is need," "it is necessary." From *est opus* came Old French *estovoir* (to be necessary), also used as a noun (a necessary, a need), and eventually *estovers*, meaning "necessaries allowed by law," and "the right to such necessaries." The term was used especially of the wood that a tenant had the right to take from the landlord's estate as needed for the repair of his house, tools, implements, hedges, etc. It also covered the needs of a widow or a wife separated from her husband and the sustenance of an imprisoned felon for himself and his family, taken from his property during the term of his confinement. The phrase *common of estovers* denoted the right to take wood from another's estate for the use or furnishing of a house or farm. Sir William Blackstone's *Commentaries on the Laws of England* (1765), commonly referred to by lawyers as *Blackstone's Commentaries*, defined it in these terms: "a liberty of taking necessary wood." It is interesting to read of so humanitarian a system prevailing as far back as 1523 in John Fitzherbert's treatise of that date, *A ryght frutefull mater: and hath to name the boke of surueyeng* (some title!), which contains this provision: "The Lorde may giue or selle the resydewe of the sayde woodes or wastes, Except that [unless] a manne haue *commen of Estouers.*" To each according to his needs?

ethrog (EH throg), also **etrog** (ET rog) or **esrog** (ES rog) *n.* An *ethrog*, from the Hebrew *ethrogh*, is the "fruit of the *citron*," a small, shrublike citrus tree (*Citrus medica* to botanists) used by Orthodox Jews with the palm branch (known in Hebrew as the *lulab, lulal* or *lulov*, from the Hebrew *lulabh*, meaning "branch") during the festival of *Sukkoth*, or *Succoth*, the Feast of Tabernacles, a seven-day commemoration of the dwelling of the Jews in tents in the wilderness, and the celebration of harvest. Sukkoth is a festive occasion, and some Orthodox Jews erect little temporary structures festooned with palm fronds and fruits wherein food is eaten and songs are sung. This happens in the early autumn. I remember, as a child, confusing *ethrog* and *ephod*, which had nothing whatever to do with each other. An *ephod* (EH fod), in early Hebrew times, was a religious garment, an ornate apronlike vestment worn by Hebrew high priests, hanging from the shoulders and fastened with a band. By specifications ordained in Exod. 28:6, the apron was to be "of gold, of blue and purple and scarlet stuff, and of fine twined linen, skillfully worked." I remember my grandfather, who drilled me on this stuff, laughing at the thought of a high priest wearing an *ethrog*, which resembles an enormous lemon, suspended from his shoulders and topped by a palm branch. All of this is old stuff now but was taken seriously in the not-so-distant past.

eudemonia   See **evancalous.**

eupepsia   See **evancalous.**

euphuism   See **gongorism.**

eupnea   See **evancalous.**

eurybathic   See **stenobathic.**

euryhaline   See **stenobathic.**

eurythermal   See **stenobathic.**

eutocia   See **dystocia.**

Eutopia See **dystopia.**

evancalous (uh VAN kuh luhs) *adj*. *Agkalos* is Greek for "armful," related to *agkale* (the bent arm; used mostly in the plural), which in turn is based on *agke* (arm). *Eu-* is a Greek prefix meaning "good, well," the combining form of *eus* (good) or the neuter of *eus* used as an adverb (well). *Eu-* is found in many English words, imparting the concept of *good* or *well*: *eudemonia* (happiness); *eugenic* (improving offspring); *eulogy* (high praise); *eupepsia* (good digestion; the opposite of the all-too-familiar *dyspepsia*); *euphemism* (pleasant substitute to avoid a harsh word or expression); *euphonious* (pleasant-sounding); *euphoria* (a feeling of well-being, often with no basis in reality); *eupnea* (easy breathing, as opposed to *dyspnea*, labored breathing); and *eurhythmic* (characterized by pleasant rhythm). Our little *eu-* spreads a lot of happiness in the world. Away with *caco-*, from Greek *kakos* (bad: *cacodemon; cacography; cacophonous*) and *dys-* (bad: *dysentery; dysfunction; dysgenic; dyslexia; dyspepsia; dysphasia*, inability to speak or comprehend words; *dysphonia*, poor vocal function; *dysphoria*, dissatisfaction, anxiety, restlessness; *dyspnea; dysthymia*, despondency; *dystrophy*, all too familiar in *muscular dystrophy*, disorders marked by degeneration or abnormal development of muscle; and *dysuria*, difficulty and pain in urination—a great big pile of misery. Now, back to our lovely *evancalous*: with the sweet *eu-* (sometimes pronounced *ev-*), attached to *agkalos* (in case you've forgotten: "armful"), you've got a cheerful combination: "good (or pleasant) to embrace," and what could be nicer? *Cheerful little armful* is a phrase out of my all-too-distant past, evoking those nostalgic reminiscences of enthralling adolescent love. Ah, me! "Youth's the season made for joys, Love is then our duty ... "

évolué (ay vol yooh AY) *adj. n.* This word is the past participle of the French verb *évoluer* (to evolve) and is used as both an adjective and a noun. As an adjective modifying the word *nation*, it means "advanced" (as opposed to *backward*); modifying *person*, it means "enlightened" or "progressive." But it has come into use as a noun, rather chauvinistically, it would appear, to designate an African from a part of the continent that was formerly under French or Belgian control, who has been educated along European lines and has thus become Europeanized in his or her thinking and reactions. In this context, it is used adjectivally to mean, in effect, "Europeanized." J. Parker, in *Apes and Ivory* (1953), gives a rather class-ridden definition: "Exactly what is an *évolué*? A Native of some education—a clerk or an office worker." In 1956 K. Hulme, in *A Nun's Story*, writes: "A first generation to work with whites ... that queer lonely society of the *évolués* which was neither black nor white." In 1961 P. Mason wrote, in *Common Sense about Race*: "The man who had become entirely '*évolué*' or assimilated to Western ways," and nine years later, in *Fanon*, D. Caute wrote of "the Black French *évolué* (the relatively educated, Europeanized and privileged native)." As time goes on, the term will, it is to be hoped, be deemed racist and pejorative and be considered of historical interest only.

exclaustration (eks klos TRAY shuhn) *n*. *Claudere* in Latin means "to shut." The neuter of its past participle, *clausum*, is used as a noun meaning "enclosed place." The related noun *claustrum* means, inter alia, "enclosure" and is the source of our *cloister*. When monastic vows are taken, one retires from the outside world and enters a monastery or a convent, but those vows are sometimes renounced and the individual re-enters the world outside the walls. Latin *ex-* (from) and *claustrum* (enclosure; in this case, cloister) plus the noun ending combine to give us *exclaustration*, the "resumption of secular life by one who has been released from his or her vows." This doesn't happen very often, and that may explain why *CH* appears to be the only dictionary that deals with the word.

exequies (EKS ih kweez) *n. pl*. There is a singular, *exequy*, but *CH* comments "usually in plural," while the *O.E.D.* states "now always in plural," and that's the way I've always seen it, except in the fine poem by Bishop Henry King (1592–1665), "*Exequy* upon His Wife." *Exequies* are "funeral rites." The word comes from the Latin *exsequiae*, taken from the verb *exsequi*, meaning literally "to follow (a corpse) to the grave" and formed of the prefix *ex-* (from) and *sequi* (to follow), the principal component in the derivation of *consequent, subsequent,* etc. Note the dropping of the *s* in *exequies*, which sometimes happened in the Latin as well (*exequiae*). We are more familiar with *obsequies*, a word whose meaning "came about by accident," to quote from the comment in my *1000 Most Important Words*. The "accident" was the confusion of *exsequiae* with *obsequium*, the Latin word for "compliance, submission," which had nothing to do with funerals and resulted in the Late Latin error *obsequiae*. Strange, that we went along with the error and the "accident" and hardly ever use the "right" word, *exequies*. Our word *obsequiousness*, in the sense of "servile deference," the kind shown at funerals we never wanted to attend but felt we had to, probably had something to do with our attraction to *obsequies*.

exogamy   See **endogamy.**

expiscate (eks PIH skate, EKS-) *vb*. If you knew that *piscis* meant "fish" in Latin, you might jump to the conclusion that to *expiscate* was to "rid (e.g., a body of water) of fish," but you would have jumped in the wrong direction. *Expiscate* comes from the Latin *expiscatus*, the past participle of *expiscari* (to fish out), based on *ex-* (out) plus *piscari* (to fish), from the *piscis* mentioned at the outset of this etymological exercise. It sounds slangy, but to *expiscate* is exactly that, to "fish out" in the sense in which *fish* is used in the colloquialism *fishing expedition*, a phrase cried out by politicians who are quite properly being investigated. In this context, then, our verb means to "find out by skillful examination and close scrutiny." The activity is called *expiscation* (eks pih SKAY shuhn), and the adjective describing it is *expiscatory* (eks pih SKAT uh ree, eks PIH skuh toh ree). An 1829 issue of *Blackwell's Magazine* used the expression *"expiscatory curiosity,"* and Thomas Carlyle wrote of *"expiscatory questions."* As a nonce-word, *expiscate* has been used in the "wrong" sense warned of above: to "rid" or "exhaust of fish": An 1858 issue of the *Saturday Review* stated that *"Norway is nearly expiscated."* With the reckless methods of contemporary fishing, the nonce use might well be revived and put into circulation by conservationists.

extrapunitive   See **intropunitive**.

famulus (FAM ooh luhs) *n*. In the first stages of the study of Latin, we learn about the declension of nouns. *Puella* is the model of the "first declension," nouns ending in *-a*. *Servus* is the usual model of the "second declension," masculine nouns ending in *-us*. *Puella* means "girl" and *servus* "slave." *Servus* is related to the verb *servire* (to be a slave), and we learn that our words *serve, servile*, etc., stem from the Latin root *serv-*. What has this to do with *famulus*? Well, a *famulus* in old Roman times was a special kind of slave, a "household servant, an attendant, especially one attached to a scholar or a magician"— very special indeed. In some dictionaries, *famulus* is defined as a "private secretary or factotum." In others, he is simply an "attendant." They all stress the relationship to magicians and scholars, a rather restricted function. Domestic slaves were a feature of Roman society. Some were well educated and became instructors. Except for their status as owned chattels, the *famulus* class had little in common with the ordinary *servus*. Incidental intelligence: Did you know that our word *slave* comes from the *Slavs*, who lived on the banks of the river Dnieper, and in Eastern Europe called *Slavi* and, who, as captives, spread through many parts of early medieval Europe as *slaves*?

farthingale (FAR *thing* gale) *n*. Except in films about the Old South, *farthingales* aren't much in evidence these days. They were frameworks made of hoops, generally constructed of whalebone worked into textile of some sort, or otherwise padded rolls, used to bell out women's dresses to form a hoop skirt or crinoline. The word could also mean "hooped petticoat." In Old French it was called a *verdugale* or *vertugalle*, a corruption of the Spanish word *verdugado*, based on *verdugo*, a word with a great many meanings, including "hoop" or "ring." John Ray, in *Observations Made in a Journey through Part of the Low Countries, Germany, Italy and France, with a Catalogue of Plants Not Native of England* (1673) wrote: "The Women wear great *Vardingales*, standing ... far out on each side." In Charles Reade's *The Cloister and the Hearth* (1860), we read:

"Whatever he [Gerard, the hero of the novel, the father of Erasmus] was saying or doing, he stopped short at the sight of a *farthingale*," and well he might have, for that attire is very fetching, don't you think? And come to think of it, isn't *fetching*, the present participle of *fetch*, a strange extension of the usual meaning of that verb?

fartlek (FART lek) *n.* I assure you that this word has nothing to do with gastric disturbances, the kind that embarrass one at dinner parties, even though *The Oxford Pocket Book of Athletic Training* (Duncan and Bone, 1957) defines it as " ... a pleasant ... form of *wind* sprints across country" (emphasis mine). The truth is that *fartlek* is the Swedish training technique for middle- and long-distance running, in which the athlete runs cross-country in a mixture of fast and slow pace. The August 18, 1958, issue of *The Times* (London) refers to it as " ... the *Fartlek* or run-as-you-please training which originated from Sweden in the 1940s." The word is made up of Swedish *fart* (speed) and *lek* (play), and the running manual *Tulloh on Running* defines it in these terms: "*Fartlek*, meaning 'speed play' ... is a continuous run in which patches of fast striding are interspersed with jogging." It does sound like fun and is said to be an effective form of training. The common meaning of the German noun *Fahrt* is "journey," but in nautical parlance, it is the equivalent of "speed," as in *halbe Fahrt* (half speed), *kleine Fahrt* (slow speed), etc., so we see that Swedish *fart* has impeccable connections. As to the American variety, most authorities trace it to Middle English, and some to Greek *porde*. Its German equivalent is *Furz*, which, like the American term is marked "vulgar" in the respective dictionaries. (And I hope I have offended nobody's sensibilities in this learned discussion.)

fauve See **favism.**

fauvism See **favism.**

fauvist See **favism.**

favism (FAH viz'm) *n. Favism* is an "acute, extremely severe allergic reaction caused by eating broad beans or inhaling broad-bean pollen." The reaction takes the form of acute hepatitis, hemolytic (i.e., causing the breaking down of red blood cells and the releasing of hemoglobin) anemia, jaundice, diarrhea, fever, etc., and is said to be suffered particularly in southern Italy. The word was taken from the Italian *favismo*, from *fava* (bean, especially broad bean); *fava* figures in the Italian expression *prendere* (or *pigliare*) *due colombi a una fava*, meaning "to kill two birds (literally "doves") with one stone"; *fava* is from Latin *faba*, "broad bean," a word used by the Roman writer of comedies Terence in the sentence *Istaec in me cudetur faba*, meaning literally, "That broad bean of yours will be threshed in me," and idiomatically, "I shall have to suffer for this." The broad bean, according to my *British English, A to Zed*, is the approximate equivalent of our *lima bean*, and its identity is clarified (?) by the following comment: "Similar, but larger, darker and with a coarser skin. The British variety is the seed of a vetch known as *Vicia faba*; the American, that of the plant known as *Phaseolus limensis*." When I said "The British variety ... ," as I later discovered, I should have said, "The British and European (and for all I know, the South American and other) varieties." "A dictionary-maker," in the immortal language of Fowler, " ... must deal with a great many matters of which he has no first-hand knowledge." Be all that as it may, the *Vicia* in *Vicia faba* is Latin for "vetch," a word dear to the hearts of those who concoct (I might have avoided the **circumbendibus** "those who concoct" by using the word *concocters*, but that sounds like the plural of the word for a highly specialized component of a complex piece of automatic industrial machinery and in any case has a nasty sound) American (as opposed to British) crossword puzzles. I say " ... as opposed to ... " because there is a vast difference, and Americans who tangle with the British variety run the risk of premature death from frustration *cum* exasperation. If you care to know what a *vetch* is, you can look it up in any standard dictionary and become entangled in enough Linnean terminology to take a day's untangling. Caution: Never confuse *fava* or *favism* with *favus* or *favose*, *favus* being a fungal scalp disease resulting in a honeycombed appearance; and *favose* means "honeycombed." These come from Latin *favus* (honeycomb). Second caution: Never, never confuse any of the foregoing terms with *fauve, fauvist* or *fauvism*. A *fauve* is member of a group of early-20th-century painters (Matisse was the most prominent) who conceived a painting primarily as a two-dimensional colored decoration, rather than as an imitation of nature. *Fauvist* is a synonym of *fauve*, and *Fauvism* is the label applied to that school of painting. All of those words come from French *fauve* (wild beast). We've come a long way from broad beans, but that's how things go at times.

favose   See **favism.**

favus   See **favism.**

feck (FEK) *n.* We often use negative words, quite common ones, without stopping to think that they are based on positive words that are uncommon and unfamiliar. Everyday examples are words like *impeccable, untoward, ruthless, uncouth* and *disgruntled*. We almost never give a thought to the positive terms in the senses that form the basis of the familiar negatives: *peccable* (liable to error), *toward* (propitious), *ruthful* (compassionate). So it is with *feckless*, meaning "ineffective, incompetent, feeble, helpless." It must be obvious that there would be no such word unless there were also the word *feck*, and there is such a word, as unfamiliar or obscure as it may be. *Feck*, a mainly Scottish term that is also heard in the north of England, has a number of meanings, including "efficacy, efficiency," and by extension, "energy, vigor." It is deemed to be an aphetic form of *effect* (*aphetic* being the adjective from *aphesis*, the linguistic phenomenon of the loss of an unstressed initial vowel or syllable). *Feck* gives rise to the adjective *feckful*, meaning "vigorous, efficient, powerful." In Robert Willan's *List of Ancient Words at Present Used in the Mountainous District of the West Riding of Yorkshire* (1811), *feckful* is defined as "strong and brawny." Hence our word *feckless*; and it all goes back to *feck*. This is a different term from the slang *feck* (origin unknown) used by James Joyce in the sense of "swipe" or "pinch." In *Portrait of the Artist as a Young Man* (1916) he describes persons who " ... *fecked* cash out of the rector's room," and in *Ulysses* (1922) he writes of "fecking matches from counters." Nothing to do with the *feck* we've been discussing. A word about *aphesis* (AF uh sis) and *aphetic* (uh FET ik): *Aphesis* comes from the Greek, meaning "letting go," based on the verb *aphienai* (to set free), built of the preposition *ap-*, a variant of *apo-* (away) plus *hienai* (to send); cf. *aph(a)eresis* in my *1000 Most Challenging Words*.

feckful   See **feck.**

fetial, also **fecial** (FEE shul) *n., adj.* In ancient Rome, there was a college of priests known as *fetiales* who were charged with conducting the rites involved in the declaration of war and the conclusion of peace. A member of that group was known in Latin as a *fetialis*, from which we got the noun *fetial*. As a Latin adjective, *fetialis* means "pertaining to the *fetiales*," and by extension, "ambassadorial." The *fetial law* is the Roman law pertaining to the declaration of war and to peace treaties. The *O.E.D.* tells us that the form *fecial* came from an erroneous spelling of the Latin word and that the latter is of unknown origin. *W III* suggests that *fetial* comes from an "assumed" Old Latin noun, *fetis*, meaning "statute" or "treaty." Its definition of *fetial* as a noun is somewhat wider than the above, ascribing to that college of priests the responsibility for overseeing diplomatic relations in general and giving *diplomatic* as a synonym for the adjective. Sir William Segar, in *Honor, Military and Civil* (1602), tells us that "It was not lawful for ... any Souldier to take Armes, until the *Faecials* had so commanded or allowed." One wonders, did the *Consules* of the *Respublica* (the two annually elected chief executives of the republic of Rome) ever bypass the *fetiales* the way President Truman initiated the "police action" in Korea or President Johnson used the Tonkin Gulf Resolution to justify the bombing of North Vietnam, in each case bypassing Section 8 of the Constitution, which gives "The Congress ... [the] power ... To declare war ... "? There is no record of a "War Powers Act" in the annals of Rome. Suggested reading: *Original Intent and the Framers' Constitution*, by Leonard W. Levy (New York: Macmillan Publishing Company, 1988).

fidimplicitary   See **quisquilious.**

flabellate   See **flabellum.**

flabellation   See **flabellum.**

flabelliform   See **flabellum.**

flabellum (fluh BEL uhm) *n. Flare* is Latin for "to blow" and can be used transitively, as in "blow a horn," or intransitively, as in "the wind blows." The related noun *flabrum* means "breeze," and its diminutive is *flabellum*, "small fan," which we took intact into English to denote a ceremonial fan of the sort used in religious rites or formerly displayed on state occasions as an appurtenance of the pope, a bishop or a royal personage. *CH* says that it was "anciently used to drive away flies from the chalice during the celebration of the eucharist." *Flabellum* has certain uses in biology far too technical to go into here. Related adjectives are *flabelliform* and *flabellate*, meaning "fan-shaped," and *flabellation* is "the act of fanning."

fletcherism (FLEH chuh riz'm) *n.* There is also the word *fletchery*, and though the two are often confused, they have nothing whatever to do with each other. An American author named Horace Fletcher (1849–1919) preached the virtues of small bites and thorough mastication, 32 to the mouthful, if I correctly remember my mother's urgent pleas. Followers were known as *fletcherites* (FLEH chuh rites). Whether or not *fletcherization* (fleh chuh reye ZAY shun) contributed to health, it certainly prolonged mealtimes. In *Strictly Business,* O. Henry used the verb metaphorically, writing of a certain Annette who " ... *Fletcherized* large numbers of romantic novels." *Fletchery* (FLEH chuh ree), on the other hand, is the name given to the wares made or sold by a *fletcher,* a maker or vendor of arrows or bows and arrows. It is derived from *flèche,* French for "arrow." It is never safe to guess; such are the snares and pitfalls of amateur etymology.

fletcherite   See **fletcherism.**

flincher   See **vellinch.**

flitch (FLICH) *n.* Like so many words of Teutonic, rather than Greek or Latin ancestry, *flitch* has been found in a number of different spellings. The word goes back to Old English *flicca* and Old Norse *flikki* and designates a side of hog that is salted and cured, i.e., a side of bacon. One must be careful, in discussing *bacon,* to differentiate between British and American usage. To a Briton, *bacon* is what an American would call "Canadian bacon," and what we in America call "bacon" is generally referred to as "streaky" (a right descriptive name!) in Britain. We read, in Jephson and Reeve's *Narrative of a Walking Tour in Brittany* (1859): "From ... the ceiling hung a ... row of ... flitches of bacon," and Robert Herrick, in his poem *Hesperides,* applied the word jocularly to the human frame when he wrote (1648): "He ... walks with dangling breeches ... / And shewes his naked *flitches.*" In days of yore, a *flitch* could be claimed once a year at Dunmow, Essex, by a man and wife who could present proof that they had lived in married peace for a year and a day. A 1615 record indicates that a certain Richard Wright claimed the "Bacon of Dunmow," and "there was delivered unto [him] one *fleech* of Bacon"; and in 1820 William Combe, in *The Tour of Doctor Syntax in Search of Consolation*, wrote: "They might have claim'd or I'm mistaken/ With conscience clear one *Flitch* of Bacon." We are mostly concerned here with bacon and conjugal harmony and need not dwell on other uses of *flitch* as applied to the cutting of whale blubber or halibut, the sawing of timber and carpentry. Sufficient unto the *flitch* is the reward of marital peace!

florilegium (flohr ih LEE juhm), also **florilegy** (floh RIL uh jee) *n*. A *florilegium* is an "anthology, a collection of choice pieces of literature." Literally, it is a "collection of flowers," formed of Latin *flor-*, the stem of *flos* (flower) and *legere* (to collect, gather, cull). *Florilegium* is a literal translation of Greek *anthologia*, built of *anthos* (flower) plus *logia* (collection), akin to *legein* (to gather), cognate with Latin *legere*. Originally, *anthology* was applied to a collection of the "flowers of verse," i.e., small select poems, especially epigrams, but the term was extended to cover any collection of literary pieces. James Russell Lowell, in *My Study Windows* (1871), wrote: "We have made but a small *florilegium* from Mr. Hazlitt's remarkable volumes," referring to the writings of the English critic and essayist William Hazlitt (1778–1830). The *O.E.D.* tells us that *florilegium* was formed "after the analogy of *spicilegium*." When we get to that word, we find that it is formed of Latin *spica* (ear of corn; but caution: *corn*, in British English, is a generic term analagous to American *grain*, and definitions in the *O.E.D.* are set forth in British English) plus *legium* (see above) and means "gleaning," literally, but "collection" or "anthology" figuratively. It also turns out that *spicilegium* has not been "naturalized" (i.e., taken into English), that its equivalent *spicilegy* is obsolete and that the proper form now is *spicilege* (SPIH suh lej). Somewhat complicated; better stick with *anthology*.

foehn   See **moazagotl.**

forisfamiliation (for is fah mil ee AY shuhn) *n*. This term denotes the procedure under Scottish law by which it is recognized that a child has flown the family nest and is prepared to set up on his or her own account. The verb is *forisfamiliate* (for is fa MIL ee ate), and it can be used both transitively and intransitively. When a parent *forisfamiliates* a child, the parent emancipates the heir from parental authority and in effect portions the heir off so as to exclude him or her from any claim to future inheritance; when the heir *forisfamiliates*, it amounts to the acceptance of a present gift and renunciation of any share of future parental inheritance. In short, *forisfamiliation* amounts to "exclusion from inheritance," whether by act of heir or parent. Both noun and verb stem from the Late Latin verb *forisfamiliare*, constructed of the adverb *foris* (outside) plus *familia* (family). This is all to warn you that if the subject arises, play it safe and consult your Scottish lawyer, especially since there are not only lots of subsidiary wrinkles, but, as I have recently (June 15, 1988) been informed by the Deputy Secretary of the Law Society of Scotland, many of the wrinkles are " ... in the melting pot at the moment [how's that for mixing metaphors—wrinkles in the melting pot?] as the Scottish Law Commission has the question under review."

fricatrice (FRIK uh truhs) *n*. *Fricare* means "to rub" in Latin, and the noun *fricatrix*, which the *O.E.D.* describes as "a word or form not actually found, but of which the existence is inferred," means, literally, "female rubber," i.e., "a female who rubs"; hence, the *O.E.D.* defines *fricatrice* as "a lewd woman." It is defined the same way in *W III*, which goes on to include "harlot" and "female homosexual," calling attention to the Latin and Greek noun *tribas*. Under *tribadism*, in my *1000 Most Challenging Words*, I dealt with the words *tribadism* (lesbianism), *tribade* (a lesbian, "usually in the sense of a homosexual female who assumes the male role, the 'active partner'"), *tribadic*, the adjective for the person and the practice, the Greek noun *tribas* (rubbing) and the Greek verb *tribein* (to rub). If all this brings to mind the implications of the modern institution known as the "massage parlor," so be it. In *Volpone* (1605), Ben Johnson puts these words into the mouth of "A patron": "To a lewd harlot, a base *fricatrice*." Robinson Ellis's translation of *The Poems and Fragments of Catullus* (1871) contains the line "Like slaver [saliva] abhorr'd breath'd from a foul *fricatrice*." Some dictionaries state that the word is archaic; others do not. The practice certainly isn't.

frippery   See **frippet**.

frippet (FRIH puht) *n*. This is a slang term for a "flashy or frivolous young woman." W. Chetham Strode's novel *Sometimes Even Now* (1933) gives us this sentence: "I'll invite him—and he can bring all his 'lovelys' and *'frippets'* with him." Apparently, the term, though pejorative, did not connote too harsh a judgment upon the young person in question. In *Sick to Death* (1971), David Clark writes: "Quite a nice bit of *frippet*. But too young for me. I like a mature woman." The phrase "rather enticing bit of *frippet*" appears in Sheed's *Middle Class Education* (1960). Both the *C.O.D.* and *O.E.D. Supplement* say "origin unknown" about this word. It would seem to me, however, to have something to do with the noun *frippery* (FRIH puh ree), the immediately preceding entry in the *C.O.D.*, defined there as "finery, needless or tawdry adornment esp[ecially] in dress ... "; in the *O.E.D.* as (inter alia) "finery in dress, *esp*[ecially] tawdry finery ... tawdry ornamentation in general ... tawdry style; frivolity" and as an adjective "trifling; frivolous ... "; and in *CH* as (inter alia) "tawdry finery; foppish triviality," all of which have some connection (even if remote) with "flashy and frivolous" young women. But who am I to argue with the beloved *W III* and *O.E.D.*?

frondeur (fron DUR) *n*. *Fronde* is French for (inter alia) "sling," and *frondeur* is French for "slinger, fault finder, rioter, dissident, member of the *Fronde*." *Fronde* was the name given to as series of civil wars in France (urban riots, peasant revolts, battles, etc.) during the minority of Louis XIV, and by extension, it was applied to any malcontent party or to any violent political opposition. The name *frondeur*, in the sense of "slinger," was given to the "parliamentarians" (really lawyers) who participated in the revolt, because they were compared to schoolboys who used their slings only when the teacher wasn't looking. In other words, they were sneaky. An article in the *Daily Telegraph* (London) of September 22, 1880, inquired: "Are the French, then, incurable *frondeurs*? incorrigible revolutionists, who must attack a Minister simply because he is 'in'?" *Fronde* and *frondeur* have nothing to do with the botanical term *frond*, denoting the leaf of a palm or fern.

fustigate (FUS tuh gate) *vb*. You think you've never *fustigated* anybody? Well, probably not, in the literal sense. In Latin, a *fustis* is a stick, especially a knobbed stick, a cudgel or a club, and the unpleasant word *fustuarium* meant "clubbing to death," a common punishment for desertion. *Fustigare* meant "to cudgel to death" (this is a very disagreeable subject), and its past participle *fustigatus* gave us *fustigate*, but our verb by no means implies capital punishment: just a "beating, or another sort of severe punishment." So far, so literal. The figurative meaning is much attenuated: "to criticize harshly, to castigate," with no hint of corporal, let alone capital, consequences. Somehow, the clubbing aspect got lost in the Romance descendants of the Latin ancestor. In French *fustiger* means "to whip"; the Italian *fustigare* and the Spanish *fustigar* have the same effect: no sticks, clubs or cudgels, just whips, though I wouldn't want to be forced to choose; and the figurative sense seems not to have caught on in those tongues. The *O.E.D.* takes the "sting" out of *fustigate* by characterizing it as "now humorously pedantic."

fusuma (FOOH suh mah) *n*. A house in the Occident, whatever its size, has a finite number of rooms, anywhere from 1, in a shanty, to the 375 or so in Knole, the Sackville-West castle in Sevenoaks, Kent, England—and there are palaces with even more. Not so in Japan, where the houses are equipped with *fusamas*, sliding screens of opaque paper that run along grooves in the floor and ceiling and divide a single space into a number of rooms. E. S. Morse, in *Japanese Homes* (1886), defined *fusamas* as "movable partitions between the rooms." Very useful, one would think, in case of the arrival of unexpected guests, provided they didn't make too much noise.

futhork, also **futhorc** or **futhark** (FOOH thork) *n*. I suppose most people realize that the word *alphabet* got its name from *alpha* and *beta*, which are the first and second letters of the Greek alphabet and the basis of the Greek word *alphabetos*. We generally think of the alphabet in terms of *a, b, c*, etc., but there are many different alphabets, such as the Hebrew, Arabic, Russian, German (before the adoption of Western-type characters), Sanskrit (Devanagari) and others. *Futhork* is the name given to the Runic alphabet, fashioned from its first six letters: *f*, *u*, *th*, *o*, *r* and *k*. In the variant name *futhark*, *a* takes the place of *o*. What is the Runic alphabet? *Runic* describes anything written in *runes*, i.e., letters of the ancient Germanic alphabet, which was used by Scandinavians and Anglo-Saxons from the third to the twelfth centuries. *Runes* were formed by modifying Roman or Greek characters to facilitate carving them in inscriptions on wood or stone. *Rune* has other meanings as well: a secret, a mystic symbol, spell or song, any song or canto. There aren't many about who can write or read *futhork*, but *rune* and *runic* were no strangers to the poets of the last century. Wrote Dante Gabriel Rosetti (*The Sybyl*):

> 'I saw the Sibyl at Cumae'
> (One said) 'with mine own eye.
> She hung in a cage, and read her *rune*
> To all the passers-by ...'

and Matthew Arnold (*The Grande Chartreuse*):

> ... Thinking of his own Gods, a Greek
> In pity and mournful awe might stand
> Before some fallen *Runic* stone ...

while Poe (*The Bells*) gave us the chilling lines:

> Keeping time, time, time
> In a sort of *Runic* rhyme ...

and Emerson (*Woodnotes II*) told us that

> ... nature beats in perfect time
> And rounds with rhyme her every *rune* ...

fylfot, also **filfot** (FIL fot) *n.* A *fylfot* is a type of swastika, also known as a *gammadion* and a *cross cramponée*. First, some derivations: *Swastika* comes from the Sanskrit *svastika*, which is in turn based on *svasti* (well-being), from *su* (good) plus *asti* (he is). *Gammadion* (guh MADE ee uhn) gets its name from its resemblance to four Greek uppercase *gammas* set at right angles. *Cross cramponée* (kross kram pah NAY) is a term in heraldry, based on the French noun *crampon*, a metal bar bent in the form of a hook and used as a grappling iron; thus, *cramponée* describes a cross with a square hooklike bend at the end of each of its four limbs. So much for *fylfot*'s other names, but how about *fylfot* itself? This word appears to have occurred only once, in a 15th-century manuscript known as the *Lansdowne*, but, judging from its context in the manuscript it is believed to be a nonce spelling of *fill-foot*, a pattern or device for "filling the foot" of a painted window. The *fylfot* or swastika is a mystical symbol that is found worldwide and goes back to prehistoric times. It has been discovered on Etruscan tombs, Celtic monuments, Buddhist inscriptions, Greek coins, Byzantine architecture and American Indian artifacts and was the hateful badge of Nazism.

galdragon (GAL druh guhn) *n*. If you saw this word and didn't know where the accent was, you might think it was a slang term for a female dragon, but you'd be wide of the mark, unless you want to stretch a point. To end the suspense, *galdragon* is what the people of the Shetland Islands used to call a sorceress or witch. The word has nothing to do with dragons in the sense of the legendary fire-breathing variety. The Shetlanders took the word from Old Norse *galdra-kona*, a combination of *galdra* (incantation, crowing, or witchcraft generally) and *kuna* (woman). A crowing woman may resemble a "dragon" in the slang sense of an intimidating beady-eyed old female, but the etymology is as stated.

galligaskins (gal ih GAS kinz) *n. pl.* This was the name given to a kind of wide hose or breeches worn by men in the 16th and 17th centuries. It degenerated into a humorous name for any type of loose breeches. The word was a corruption of the 16th-century French adjective *garguesque*, a variation of *greguesque* resulting from metathesis (transposition of letters), which itself was taken from the Italian noun *grechesca*, based on the feminine form of the adjective *grechesco* (Greek), this fashion having been described in the 16th century as *alla gregescha* (in the Greek manner). *Grègues* is still French for "breeches" of any variety; in Spanish it is *griega*. The English poet John Philips (1676–1709), a pioneer in blank verse at a time when the standard form was the heroic couplet, wrote these lines in "The Splendid Shilling," a parody of Milton:

> My *galligaskins*, that have long withstood
> The winter's fury and encroaching frosts …

Philips also wrote the poem "Cyder" about apple growing and cider pressing, in imitation of Virgil's *Georgics*. Laurence Sterne 1713–68) in *Tristram Shandy* wrote naughtily: "His whole thoughts … were taken up with a transaction which was going forwards … within the precincts of his own *Galligaskins*." The article of attire is mentioned as well in Trollope and Browning. If you come across a pair in the attic, hold on to them: Old styles keep coming back. You never know.

gammadion   See **fylfot**.

gavage (gah VAHZH) *n*. This word, which in French means "cramming (of poultry)" or "gorging," has been taken into English to mean "forcible feeding (generally)" by means of a force pump through a tube leading into the stomach. *Gaver* is the French verb for "to cram with food," and *gave* is the French word for a "bird's crop." The French origin of the word has obviously to do with the production of *pâté de foie gras*, which is produced by a rather brutal process of stuffing food into geese so as to enlarge their livers unnaturally. It is a treat for gourmets but doesn't do the geese much good. Lawrence Durrell, in *Holiday* (1963), wrote: "In goose country, where the practice of force-feeding geese (*gavage*) is in operation, there are always a goodly number of casualties." A Doctor Turnier of Paris, according to *Buck's Handbook of Medical Science* (1889), "advocated the method of *gavage* in infants prematurely born." Sir William Osler, the Canadian physician and professor of medicine, in the 1905 edition of his *Principles and Practice of Medicine*, recommended *gavage* in cases of persistent anorexia. History records some ghastly cases of the *gavage* of hunger-striking British women in their struggle for women's voting rights. Ugh! And today they have not only suffrage, but *Mrs.* Thatcher!

gavelkind   See **Borough-English.**

gematria (guh MAY tree uh, gee muh TREE uh) *n.* From Rabbinical Hebrew *gee mah TREE yah*, taken from Greek *geometria* (geometry), came the term *gematria*, denoting a cabalistic system of interpretation of the Hebrew Scriptures. The *cabala* (spelled in a variety of ways) was a mystical system of scriptural interpretation developed by Hebrew religious scholars of the Babylonian academies from the sixth to the eleventh centuries. In both the Greek and Hebrew alphabets, the letters had numerical equivalents (Greek alpha=1, beta=2, etc.; Hebrew aleph=1, beth-2, etc.) By adding the numerical equivalents of the letters of a word in the Hebrew scriptures, the scholars arrived at a total and found another word the numerical equivalents of whose letters added up to the same total. Then, by interchanging the words, they arrived at a mystical interpretation of the original word and thus found its "hidden meaning." In his *Astro-meteorologica, or Aphorisms and Discourses of the Bodies Celestial, their Natures and Influences* (1686), John Goad wrote: "I am persuaded ... that there may be something in Cabala, *Gematry*, something in the mysterious Force of Numbers, in Critical Days, Climacteric Years & c." I have a sneaking suspicion that those early scholars were much akin to today's numerologists and readers of tea leaves.

gemel   See **gemellion.**

gemellion (juh MEL ee uhn) *n.* This word, taken from medieval Latin *gemellio*, based on the Latin adjective *gemellus* (twin), is one of a number of words that go back to that Latin source. It is the name of either of a pair of usually identical basins used for washing the hands before a meal. The water is poured over the hands from one *gemellion* into the other. It was applied especially to one of a pair of basins so used for the ritual washing of hands at the Mass. The word is sometimes spelled *gemellione*, giving it an Italian twist. *Gemellus* gave the French *jumeau* (male twin) and *jumelle* (female twin) and shows up closer to the Latin in such terms as *grossesse gémellaire* (twin pregnancy) and *école géminée* (coeducational school); in such Italian words as *gemello* and *gemella* (male twin, female twin); and similarly in Spanish *gemelo* and *gemela*. Getting back to English, a *gemel* is a pair of bottles blown individually and then fused together with the necks pointing in different directions, so that the halves can contain different liquids, such as oil and vinegar. As an adjective, *gemel* means "paired" or "twin." A *gemel window*, for example, is one that fills two openings. How that Latin keeps rearing its lovely head!

Geneva bands (juh NEE vuh bands) *n. pl.* You doubtless know that *Geneva* is a city in Switzerland, but you may not know that its name is often used attributively with reference to matters connected with Calvinistic doctrine, because it was to Geneva that Calvin (a Frenchman) went, in 1536, to devote his life to the work of the Reformation. *Geneva bands*, to those unfamiliar with the customs of the Swiss Calvinist clergy, might at first blush be taken for those Swiss musical groups that play rather noisy brass instruments, featuring selections of the oompah variety. In fact, *Geneva bands* are part of the ecclesiastical dress of some Protestant clergymen, consisting of a pair of narrow white cloth strips that hang down from the front collar of the robe. English barristers also wear bands. These *bands* or strips are modeled after those worn by the Swiss Calvinist clergy. The *Geneva gown* is a flowing large-sleeved black gown of the academic model worn as a vestment for preaching by the Calvinistic clergy of Geneva and widely adopted by Protestant ministers. What, then, does *Geneva movement* mean? A religious crusade? Wrong again: It is a device for producing intermittent motion, whereby a cam on a driving wheel engages slots on a driven wheel; also known as *Geneva motion* or *bar movement*, an old type of watch movement too complex to go into here. And speaking of *movement*, we certainly have moved far from *bands* on ecclesiastical dress, though we've managed to stay in Geneva.

Geneva motion   See **Geneva bands.**

Geneva movement   See **Geneva bands.**

geotaxis (jee oh TAX is) *n. Geotaxis* applies to *motile* cells, spores, etc.—i.e., organisms capable of spontaneous movement—and denotes their response to the stimulus of gravity, whether toward or away. *Geotaxis* is formed of the Greek nouns *ge* (earth, as in *geology, geography*, etc.) and *taxis* (arrangement). It is synonymous with the biological term *geotropism*, "movement or growth with respect to the force of gravity," based on *ge* plus *tropos* (turning). Getting back to *motile*, that word is used as a noun in psychology for a person whose mind creates distinct motor images, as opposed to auditory or visual images, motor images being those involving muscular movement. (I'm not sure what this is all about, either. "A dictionary-maker," said H. W. Fowler in his preface to the *C.O.D.*, "unless he is a monster of omniscience, must deal with a great many matters of which he has no first-hand knowledge." I am not a monster of omniscience.)

geotropism   See **geotaxis.**

gephyrophobia (GUH fye ruh FOH bee uh) *n.* We are acquainted with *phobia* as both a noun and a ubiquitous (these days, anyway) suffix indicating fear or dread or terror of something or other, as in *acrophobia* (dread of heights), *agoraphobia* (fear of open areas), *claustrophobia* (dread of confined places) and *xenophobia* (fear—or hatred—of foreigners or strangers or of anything foreign or strange, a morbid condition that accounts for lots of the troubles in our world). *Gephyrophobia* is formed of the Greek noun *gephyra* (bridge—the kind that crosses rivers and valleys, not the card game that makes evenings at cousin Harriet's bearable, or the contraptions installed by dentists or the raised structure on ships) and our old friend *phobia*. An example of this rare condition is set forth in the following news item in *The Times* (London) of October 3, 1987, which is my authority for the spelling of this headword.

'BRIDGE TOO FAR' STOPS DRIVER
By Thomson Prentice, Science Correspondent
Gephyrophobia—a terror of crossing bridges—brought traffic to a halt for 45 minutes on the A45 yesterday.

The prospect of crossing the three-quarters of a mile long Orwell Bridge, near Ipswich, Suffolk, was too much for a middle-aged woman driver. She came to a halt in the middle of the A45 approach road and refused to budge.

The woman told police that she was terrified of crossing bridges and had planned her route to avoid them, but had taken a wrong turning on her 100 mile journey from Felixstowe to London.

Rush-hour traffic built up into a long tailback while police tried to find a solution.

Eventually PC Ian Lankester took over at the wheel and the woman, whose identity has not been disclosed, crouched in the back seat with her hands over her eyes during the fearful crossing.

The bridge is Britain's longest single-span concrete bridge and has a drop of 150 feet. However, the woman's problem was not caused by a fear of heights, but by gephyrophobia, one expert said.

Mr Norman Lee, president of the National Council of Psychotherapists, said: "The sufferer cannot bear the responsibility of crossing from one side to another, and opts out of the decision."

Ghibelline   See **Guelph.**

glebe (GLEEB) *n.* This is a term having to do with British ecclesiatical life, denoting a portion of land that is part of a clergyman's benefice and furnishes him a revenue. In Britain, *benefice* (BEN eh fis) is used to designate a "church living," i.e., a position granted to a clergyman, especially a rector or vicar, that guarantees a fixed amount of property or income, or the revenue itself. *Glebe* is also used poetically to mean "earth," "land" or "field" in Britain, but in that sense, it is archaic in American English. The term comes from Latin *gl(a)eba* (clod, land) and is sometimes expanded to *glebe land*. *Glebe* can also denote a parsonage without the real property appurtenant. Thackeray tells us in *The*

Virginians (1859): "Virginia was a Church of England colony; the clergymen were paid by the State and *glebes* allotted to them." Using the word poetically in the sense of "cultivated land" or "field," Tennyson, in an 1833 poem, wrote of "Many an … upland *glebe* wealthy in oil and wine." In that use, the term had no ecclesiastical connotation whatever. If you run across the word, before deciding how it is being used, better look over the territory and see if there are any clergymen lurking about.

glossolalia (glos oh LAY lee uh), also **glossolaly** (glos oh LAY lee) *n*. From Greek *glosso-*, the combining form of *glossa* (tongue), plus *-lalia* (-speaking), from *laleein* (to speak), we get *glossolalia*, also known as the "gift of tongues." In Frederic W. Farrar's *Life and Work of St. Paul* (1879), we read of " … those soliloquies of ecstatic spiritual emotion which were known as *Glossolalia*, or, 'the Gift of Tongues.'" In *Early Days of Christianity* (1882), Farrar wrote: "In Corinth the terrible abuses of *glossolaly* had led to outbreaks which entirely ruined the order of worship." William S. Lilly, in an 1898 issue of the monthly review *The Nineteenth Century*, discussed " … those of the disciples who possessed that singular gift of *glossolaly*, or speaking with tongues." Practitioners of *glossolalia* were known as *glossolalists* (glos oh LAY lists), who are referred to in Farrar's *St. Paul* in these words: " … the rivalry of unmeaning sounds among the *glossolalists*." The *gift of tongues* is more explicitly defined as "unintelligble ecstatic 'speech'" uttered in religious services of various denominations that assign more importance to emotional fervor than to intelligibility, although the worshipers may have some notion of what they are "talking" about. I would imagine that their thoughts flow heavenward together with their sounds, thus improving on the prayers of King Claudius at the end of Act III, Scene 3 of *Hamlet*, who rises and says: "My words fly up, my thoughts remain below: /Words without thoughts never to heaven go."

glossolaly   See **glossolalia**.

gongorism (GONG gor iz'm) *n*. This word comes from the name of the Spanish poet Luis de Góngora y Argote (1561–1627) and denotes a florid, pedantic, affected style of writing introduced into Spanish literature in the 16th century. Góngora was roughly contemporary with the English writer John Lyly (1554–1606), the father of *euphuism* (YOO fyuh iz'm), a "flowery, affected, precious, high-flown style of language," written or spoken. Lyly was much imitated at the end of the 16th century. He was best known for his two-part didactic romance *Euphues, or the Anatomy of Wit*, and *Euphues and his England*, a work advocating a reform of education and manners. *Euphuism* utilized preciosity, alliteration, antithesis and other similar devices. A literary review in 1886 noted that "Euphuistic language corresponded in date and character with *Gongorism* in Spain." The name of Lyly's protagonist was fashioned after the Greek adjective *euphues* (well-bred), formed of the Greek prefix *eu-* (well) and *phue* (growth). I have not succeeded in learning whether these two writers knew each other. Probably not, in view of the difficulty of traveling in those days. Strange, the way these innovations seem to pop up simultaneously in distant places.

gradatio   See **anaphora.**

grager (GRAH guhr—rough *r* as in French) *n.* We know from the Book of Esther that the villainous Haman, a prince in the court of King Ahasuerus (better known as Xerxes I), plotted to kill all the Jews in the kingdom. Seems he was particularly eager to get rid of Mordecai, the cousin and guardian of Ahasuerus's beautiful Jewish Queen Esther, and built a gallows 50 cubits (about 85 feet) high for the purpose. But Mordecai, who had become popular with Ahasuerus by foiling a plot to assassinate the king, found out, and told Esther, and she told the king. He not only overruled Haman but ordered him hanged on those very gallows. (See my discussion of *petard* in *1000 Most Challenging Words* for an explanation of Shakespeare's *hoist with his own petard*, where I mention Haman's fate as an illustration.) The deliverance of the Jews is celebrated in the annual Hebrew festival of Purim. During the religious service, children use a rattle or other noisemaking contrivance to drown out the hated name of Haman whenever it is mentioned. That apparatus is known as a *grager*, a Yiddish word derived from the Polish noun *grzegarz*, meaning "rattle." *Gragers* come in various models, the usual form having a handle around which some form of noisemaking contraption is swung with great gusto. For once, the kids have a lot of fun during the service instead of the usual wiggling around and the struggle to stay awake.

graveolent (gruhv EE oh luhnt) *adj.* You would want to stand as far away as possible from anything (or for that matter, anybody) that could be so described, for *graveolent* means "rank-smelling, fetid" and applies to whatever or whoever emits a strong offensive odor. This wonderfully dignified substitute for *stinky* is composed of Latin *grave*, the adverb formed from the neuter of *gravis* (heavy) plus -*olent*, the stem of *olens*, the present participle of the verb *olere* (to smell). Rotten eggs are as good an example as any of a *graveolent* substance, and the next time you are tempted to say, "Something smells fishy around here!" you might with more dignity exclaim, "I detect something *graveolent* hereabout!"

griffin (GRIH fin) *n.* A good many Anglo-Indian words have found their way into the vocabulary of people, especially Englishmen, who have never been within a thousand miles of India. A few examples: *bungalow, dhobi* (washerman/woman), *dhoti* (loincloth), *guru, pukka(h)* (genuine), *punkah* (ceiling fan), *sahib* (gentleman; term of respect); *swami, walla(h)* (-man, person employed in something, as in *typewriter-wallah*, a person who repairs typewriters). *Griffin* is such an Anglo-Indian word, of uncertain origin, meaning "greenhorn" as applied to a European newly arrived in India (in the old days, when India was the Jewel in the Crown), a "novice, newcomer" who had to get used to Indian ways. "Quiz" (a pseudonym), in *The Grand Master; or Adventures of Qui Hi? in Hindustan* (1816), wrote: "Young men, immediately on their arrival in India, are termed *griffins*, and retain this honour until they are twelve months in the country." In a letter (1834) he included a note reading: "N. B. *Griffin* means a freshman or freshwoman in India." *Griffinage* is the term for the condition of being a *griffin*, or a person's first year in India. Edward H. D. E. Napier (not the famous general), in *Scenes and Sports in Foreign Lands* (1840), wrote: "A large detachment who, like myself, all in their *griffinage*, had but lately landed in Madras." *Griffin*, in this sense, is usually explained as a figurative use of the same word as the name of a mythical beast with the head and wings of an eagle and the body and hindquarters of a lion, but the *O.E.D.* says that " ... there is no evidence for this." Yet the hybrid nature of an Anglo-Indian is a tempting basis for this bit of popular etymology, no?

griffinage   See **griffin.**

grimthorpe (GRIM thorp) *vb.* To *grimthorpe* an ancient building is "to remodel or restore it without proper grounding or knowledge of its authentic character or without exercising care to remain faithful to its original quality and uniqueness." *Grimthorping* implies lavish expenditure without appropriate skill or decent taste. The eponym of this peculiar word is Sir Edmund Beckett, first Baron *Grimthorpe* (1816–1905), an English lawyer and architect whose restoration of St. Albans Cathedral generated severe censure and a storm of controversy. The July 23, 1892, issue of *The Athenaeum* (the literary review founded by James Silk Buckingham in 1828 that was incorporated with *The Nation* in 1921, which merged with *The New Statesman* in 1931, which merged with *New Society* in 1988), spoke of " ... St. Albans and other great national fabrics that have been '*Grimthorped*,'" and the July 28, 1900, issue used the expression " ... *grimthorping* with a vengeance." Prince Charles is a champion of ancient monuments and would be the first to be concerned about the dreadful practice of *grimthorping*. Poor Baron Grimthorpe: What a way to be remembered!

Guelph (GWELF) *n.* If anyone at all familiar with the political scene during the late Middle Ages hears the word *Guelph*, the word *Ghibelline* (GIB uh leen, -lin) springs to mind, because the *Guelphs* and the *Ghibellines* were major opposing political factions during that period. The Guelphs got their name from the German dukes, named *Welf* or *Guelph*, who ruled in Saxony and Bavaria. They were rivals of the Hohenstaufens, whose center was a castle named *Waiblingen*, which was garbled into *Ghibelline* when both factions showed up in Italy, where they kept fighting, with the *Guelphs* on the side of the Pope and the *Ghibellines* favoring the great noble families, each party seeking political dominance. After a while, these party names lost their original connotations. In Florence, the Guelphs expelled the Ghibellines and themselves split like an amoeba into Black and White Guelphs. The curious and sad fact is that they kept feuding more or less for the hell of it, because neither faction represented any special ideology or social stratum. The magnificent Dante Alighieri (1265–1321), author of *The Divine Comedy* and other prose and poetic gems, whose writing fixed the character of modern Italian, joined the White Guelphs, and when the Black Guelphs rose to power, he was banished, at the age of 37, and spent the rest of his life, 19 years, wandering throughout Italy. His unhappiness gave rise to these immortal lines from the *Inferno*: "There is no greater sorrow than to recall a time of happiness in misery," echoing the doleful lines of the Roman philosopher and statesman Boethius (?475–525) from his *Consolation of Philosophy*: "For truly in adverse fortune the worst sting of misery is to *have been* happy." Gone and mostly forgotten are the *Guelphs* and the *Ghibellines* and the Whites and the Blacks and their senseless warring and feuding and banishments, while Dante's moving words remain immortal.

gynogenesis   See **androgenous.**

Habdalah, also **Habdala, Havdala, Havdallah** (hav DAY luh) *n.* Orthodox Jews take the Commandment regarding the Sabbath very seriously: " ... the seventh day is the Sabbath of the Lord thy God ... the Lord blessed the Sabbath day, and hallowed it ... " In the household of my childhood, the Sabbath, from nightfall Friday to nightfall Saturday, was truly a time of rest. The house was thoroughly scrubbed, no work was done (and *work* was a most inclusive term) and special prayers were said. The Sabbath so differed from the other days that it was truly "separated" from them; hence the Hebrew word *habdalah* (separation, division) was the source of the *Habdalah*, the Jewish religious rite that celebrates the conclusion of the Sabbath, and the name of the prayer recited at that ceremony. Michael Friedländer's *The Jewish Religion* (1891) tells us: "On Sabbath evening, after the close of the Sabbath, we recite the *Habdalah*, in which God is praised for the distinction made between Sabbath and the six week-days." In Israel Zangwill's *Children of the Ghetto* (1893), we find the words: "*Havdalah*, ceremony separating conclusion of Sabbath ... from the subsequent days of toil." Beth-Zion Abrahams, in her translation of her own *Life of Glückel of Hameln 1646–1724* (1962), writes of an incident that occurred " ... at the close of Sabbath, while my husband was reciting the *Habdalah* ... " Yes indeed, the Sabbath was quite distinct from the subsequent days of toil in my youth, and I still miss the distinction.

haboob (hah BOOHB) *n.* Like so many words transliterated from the Arabic, this word is found in a variety of spellings: *habbub, haboub, hubbob, hubbub,* etc.

I ran into it, or it ran into me, when a fellow passenger on a tour told me about an awful *hubbub* that he experienced in northern Africa. I wondered why he put the stress on the second syllable of this familiar word for "tumult" or "uproar" and asked what the trouble had been about. After a bit of confusion, he explained that this *hubbub* was a sandstorm that had blinded him and his fellow travelers. Eventual reference to the dictionaries revealed that a *haboob*, in whatever spelling, is a "violent windstorm that occurs principally in the Sudan," bringing with it desert sands. *Haboobs* also occur in Arabia, on the plains of India and in the United States as well. The word is from the Arabic *habu*, meaning "blowing furiously" or "violent wind." The *Daily News* (London) in 1897 described a *haboob* as "a tornado of sand and small stones," and Ralph E. Huschke's *Journal of Meteorology* (1959) defines *haboob* as "a strong wind and sandstorm or duststorm in the northern Sudan, especially around Khartum, where the average number is about 24 a year." As to those nearer home, a 1973 issue of *Scientific American* tells us: "The American *haboobs* are not so frequent as the Sudanese (two or three a year at Phoenix as compared with perhaps 24 a year at Khartoum)." I experienced one in 1953 on the way from Santa Fe to the oil fields of southeastern New Mexico. It brought our car to an instantaneous halt, pitted the windshield, got into our hair, eyes, ears and mouths and scared the daylights out of us. Incidentally, the Arabic word *habu* has nothing to do with its Japanese twin, which is the name of a poisonous pit viper *Trimeresurus flavoviridis* native to certain Pacific islands. However, it has one thing in common with the *haboob* described above. According to an 1895 issue of the *Geographical Journal*, "The poisonous Trimeresurus ... , called *habu* by the natives ... is an object of universal fear."

haecceity   See **proprium.**

haiku   See **cinquain.**

hamesucken (HAME suk'n) *n.* In Old English this was spelled *hamsocn*, from *ham* (rhymes with *game*), meaning "home" plus *socn*, meaning "seeking" or "attack." *Hamesucken* is the crime of "assaulting a person in his or her own house or wherever he or she resides." This is a specific offense only under Scottish law (which is quite distinct from English law). Laws of other countries lump it with assault generally. The word has been spelled in various ways through the years. Thus, we read in John Erskine's *Institute of the Law of Scotland* (1773): "*Haimesucken* ... is the crime of beating or assaulting a person within his own house." There is a German word, *heimsuchung*, which is variously defined as "visitation" or "affliction," but a German friend tells me that this seldom-heard word means something much closer to "retribution" or "punishment" for past offenses." One is "sought out" by one's nemesis and "gets what he deserves." The German word appears not to involve anything in the nature of beating or assault per se, though retribution might on occasion happen to take that form.

hammada, also **hamada(h)** (huh MAH duh) *n.* Most people think of the desert as a sea of sand, undulating and marked by dunes. It is so pictured in painting, song and story. But many parts of it are flat rocky areas from which the sand has been stripped by the winds. This is typical of the Sahara. Such an area is known as a *hammada*, an Arab word taken intact into English. The *McGraw-Hill Encyclopedia of Science and Technology* (1966) describes it in these terms: "Ordinarily, a *hammada* is a bare rock surface composed of relatively flat-lying consolidated sedimentary rocks from which overlying softer sediments have been stripped, principally by wind erosion." The 1886 edition of the *Encyclopedia Brittanica* speaks of " ... undulating surfaces of rock (distinguished as *hammada*)." Some travel writers have described the *hammadas* as "plateaus," but from other authorities one gets the impression that this is true of only some of the rocky areas. In my travels in Egypt I noticed, to my surprise, that my romantic notion of the desert as an unbroken sea of spotless sand was anything but justified: In many areas, the desert was strewn with pebbles and larger bits of blackish stone that belied what I remembered from my youth as background of *The Sheik of Araby* ("Into your tent I'll creep,/At night when you're asleep ... " etc.). Nor was the sand spotless, alas.

hanap (HAN ap) *n.* From Old French *hanap*, Old English took *hnap*, related also to Old High German *(k)napf* and Dutch *nap*, and in all those languages the meaning was "wine cup, goblet." In antiquarian circles, a *hanap* is a "richly carved medieval goblet, often with a cover or lid." From Robert Fabyan's *Newe Cronycles of England and of Fraunce* (1494), we learn that "Kyng Rycharde gaue vnto the Frenshe Kyng a *hanap* or basyn of golde ... ," and Alexis Soyer tells us, in his *Pantropheon: or History of Food and its Preparation* (1853), that "Charles the Bald gave to the Abbey of St. Denis a *hanap*, said to have belonged to Solomon." (After looking in vain for *Pantropheon* in all my dictionaries, the best I could come up with was the Greek noun *trophe* (nourishment) and a number of *tropho-* words having to do with aspects of nutrition, all very technical and specialized.) One Charles Dickens, Jr., wrote a *Dictionary of London* (1884) in which he spoke of "a ... collection of mazers and *hanaps* and cups." A *mazer* (MAY zer) was a bowl or goblet without a foot, originally made of "mazer" wood [maple or other hard wood], often richly carved and mounted with silver or gold or other metal, but the term was also applied more generally to a bowl made entirely of metal or anything else. The related word *hanaper* (HAN uh per) was the name of a case for one or more *hanaps*, or a baize-lined plate basket in which silver flatware was kept, or a container for valuables or money. The name was also applied to a round wicker case or small basket for keeping documents. Up until 1832, *hanaper* was the name of a department of the Chancery in London to which fees were paid for the sealing and filing of charters and other documents. *Hanaper* gave rise to the modern word *hamper*, the familiar wickerwork container, usually equipped with a cover, for laundry or picnic fare.

hanaper   See **hanap.**

hapax   See **hapax legomenon.**

hapax legomenon (HAH pahks leg GO muh non) *n*. This phrase, taken from the Greek and literally meaning "(something) said once," is used to denote a word, or form of a word, of which only one instance has been recorded in the entire work of an author or a whole literature. *Hapax* means "once" and *legomenon* "said." In *Poetic, Scientific & Other Forms of Discourse* (1956), Joshua Whatmough points out: "The *hapax legomenon*, although statistically it hardly differs from a word of very low occurrence ... is nevertheless anomalous just like the *scazon* (SKAY zon) in Greek comedy." To understand what he is driving at, I must tell you that a *scazon* (from Greek *skazon*, a nominative use of the present participle of *skazein*, to limp), is an alteration of the commonest Greek iambic meter (a line of six iambs—an *iamb* being a foot consisting of an unstressed followed by a stressed syllable) in which a *spondee* (i.e., two stressed syllables) or a *trochee* (i.e., a stressed followed by an unstressed syllable) replaces the final *iamb*. There were those who disapproved of *scazons*, like Obadiah Walker, who said, in *Of Education, Especially of Young Gentlemen* (1673), "Archilochus and Hipponax two very bad Poets ... invented those doggerel sorts of Verses, Iambics and *Scazons*." Well, you can't please everybody. To go back to our headword for a moment, *hapax legomenon* is sometimes shortened to just *hapax*.

haplography (hap LOG ruh fee) *n*. I discuss *haplology* in my *1000 Most Challenging Words*, as denoting the loss of a syllable from the middle of a word (*conservatism* for *conservativism, syllabication* for *syllabification*, etc.) I should have added that *haplology* relates to the spoken word: It is an "omission in utterance." A related phenomenon is *haplography*, the "inadvertent omission in writing of one of two or more adjacent similar letters, syllables, words or passages." *CH* defines it tersely: "the inadvertent writing once of what should have been written twice." But that definition doesn't cover the case of the stenographer or copyist whose eye wanders in the following circumstance (an experience I have encountered more than once in my legal career): A paragraph of a contract begins, "If the parties agree on the price and the date of delivery ... " The next paragraph begins, "If the parties agree on the price but leave the date of delivery open ... " The stenographer types those initial words of the first of the paragraphs and is then interrupted by, for example, a telephone call. The call ended, she goes back to the draft and her eye catches the first few opening words of the second paragraph; she continues with that one and omits the first one in its entirety. Alas! (But the boss is a kindly soul and all is forgiven; happy ending.) The *haplo-* element is the combining form of *haplous* (single), and the familiar *-graphy* is from *-graphia*, the combining form of *graphe* (writing). *Caveant scriptores*!

Hasid   See **Mitnagged.**

hebenon   See **posset.**

heeltap   See **supernaculum.**

hegemon   See **hegumen.**

hegumen (hih GYOOH muhn) *n*. This is a general term in the Greek Orthodox (or Eastern) Church for a leader of a religious community. More specifically, a *hegumen* is the "head of a minor or second-class monastery." *Hegumen* can also denote the second in authority in a major monastery in the Greek Orthodox Church, corresponding to a prior in the Western Church. The word comes from the Greek *hegoumenos*, the present participle of *hegeisthai* (to lead, command) used as a noun, and is sometimes used as a title of honor for certain monks who are also priests, known as *hieromonks* (HEYE roh muhnks). Further up in the hierarchy of the Greek Orthodox Church is the *archimandrite* (ark uh MAN drite), a word composed of the prefix *archi-*, from the Greek verb *archein*, related to the nouns *arche* (beginning) and *archos* (ruler), plus *mandra* (monastery) (literally, "fold"). *Archimandrite* is the title of the superintendent or abbot of a major monastery. It may also be bestowed by a *patriarch, catholicos* (kuh THA luh kos) or bishop upon monks who are heads of a group of monasteries (corresponding to *superior abbots* or *provincial fathers* in the Western Church), and upon prominent *hieromonks*. Some definitions: In the Eastern Church, a *patriarch* is the spiritual head of certain independent churches, such as the Russian, Syrian and Coptic churches. A *catholicos* has the same position in certain other independent churches, like the Armenian Church. Neither of those titles is used in the Greek Orthodox Church. It's as clear as mud to me but was clear as a bell to a priest of an Eastern Church who explained it all to me over a plate of hot borscht in the basement of his church. In any case, do not confuse *hegumen* with *hegemon* (HEE juh mon, HEH-), meaning "paramount power" in international politics, from the familiar word *hegemony* (he JEH muhn nee), and taken intact from the Greek, where it means "leader" and is thus related to *hegumen*, though only in derivation.

helminth (HEL minth) *n*. A *helminth* is a "worm," especially a parasitic worm, like a tapeworm. The word comes from the Greek noun *helmins*, with *helminth-* as its stem. The adjective is *helminthic* (hel MIN thik), and the science of worms, especially of the parasitic type, is *helminthology* (hel min THAH lo gee). The pathological condition caused by the presence of worms in the body is *helminthiasis* (hel min THEYE uh sis), a word taken, via New Latin, from the Greek verb *helminthian* (hel MIN thee in), "to suffer from worms." Medicine administered to rid the body of parasitic, especially intestinal, worms, is described as *anthelmint(h)ic* (an thel MIN t(h)ik), composed of the prefix *anti-*

(*ant-* before a vowel or *h*, against) plus *helminth*, followed by the usual *-ic*. *Worm* is a peculiar word, in that as a noun, a *worm* is, zoologically speaking, a "long, slender, soft-bodied, legless bilateral invertebrate," but as a verb, *to worm*, apart from *worming* one's way out of a situation or into someone's favor, or *worming* a secret out of a weak-willed soul, is really "to free from worms," i.e., to *deworm*. If you have pimples, you don't *pimple* them, and if you have a rash, you don't *rash* it. With *worm*, the same little word covers both the problem and the remedy. Think about this linguistic aberration next time you take Fido to the vet.

helminthiasis   See **helminth.**

helminthic   See **helminth.**

helminthology   See **helminth.**

hemeralopia   See **nyctalopia.**

hemiepes   See **prosodion.**

hemiola (heh mee OH luh) *n.* This was the term in medieval music (sometimes spelled *hemiolia*) for a perfect fifth, based on the fact that it was produced by shortening a string to two-thirds of its length. It also denoted a triplet, i.e., a rhythmic alteration of three notes in place of two, or vice versa. The word was taken intact via Late Latin from the Greek, being the feminine of *hemiolos* (in the ratio of 1 ⅓ to 1), based on the prefix *hemi-*, "half," plus *-olios*, from *holos*, "whole." The adjective *hemiolic* (heh mee OL ik) in classical prosody described an accent characterized by the proportion of 3 to 2, a *hemiolic* foot being one distinguished by that ratio between *thesis* and *arsis*, which mean, respectively, (1) "downbeat," the accented part of a musical measure, taken intact via Latin from the Greek, where it meant, inter alia, "downbeat of the foot in keeping time," from the verb *tithenai* (to place or lay down); and (2) "upbeat," the unaccented part of a musical measure, taken via Late Latin from the Greek, where it meant "lifting of the foot in keeping time," from the verb *aeirein* (to lift). A foot where three notes take the place of two is called a *paeon* (PEE uhn) in prosody, consisting of one long or stressed syllable and three short or unstressed ones that take the place of two, and this is known as a *paeonic* foot. Via Latin *paeon*, the word comes from Greek *paion*. There is some question about the derivation of *paeon*. It is generally thought to be an Attic variation of *paean*, a hymn of thanksgiving to Apollo after a victory or a war song addressed to Ares (the Roman Mars), but the first-century Roman rhetorician Quintilian derived it from the alleged inventor of the form, a physician named Paeon. Hard to settle the argument at this late date. I hope this little discussion has not diminished your interest in classical prosody. If so, I apologize and hope to be forgiven.

hemiolia   See **hemiola.**

hemiolic   See **hemiola.**

hemistich (HEM ih stik) *n. Stich*, from the Greek *stichos*, means "verse" or "line" of poetry," and a *hemistich*, as you might suspect, is half (or approximately half) of such a line, as divided by a *caesura* (a break or pause between words within a metrical foot—discussed briefly under **dolichurus**). *Hemistich* can also be applied to any line of verse of lesser length than that of the poem generally. Abraham Cowley, in *Davideis* (1638), included a note to the effect that he disagreed with those "who think that Virgil himself intended to have filled up these broken *Hemestiques.*" In *The Spectator* (issue 39, 1711), Joseph Addison wrote: "I do not dislike the Speeches in our English Tragedy that close with an *Hemistick* or Half Verse." Henry Hallam, the literary and constitutional historian, expressed the opinion (1847) that "the occasional *hemistich* ... [broke] the monotony of [measures]." It would appear, then, that *hemistichs* had the approval of English literati, and why not, pray?

heresiarch (huh REE zee ark, he-, -see-, HER uh see-) *n.* We get this word via Late Latin *haeresiarcha* from Greek *hairesiarches* (leader of a sect or school), based on *hairesis* (heresy) plus the suffix *-arches* (-arch, ruler). It means "originator or chief advocate of a heresy" or "leader of a group of heretics." In Horace Walpole's *Anecdotes of Painting in England, with Some Accounts of the Principal Artists; Collected by G. Vertue* (1786), we read: "Jargon and austerities are the weapons that serve the purposes of *heresiarcs* (sic) ... " A related word is *heresimach* (huh REE zee mak, he-, -see-, HER uh see-), an "antiheretic," using the Greek suffix *-machos*, from the verb *machesthai* (to fight). *Heresiography* (huh ree zee AH gruh fee) is "a treatise on heresies or a description of them," and a *heresiologist* is "one who writes about heresies or against them." The word *heresy* itself has an interesting etymology. It is based, via Late Latin *haeresis*, on Greek *hairesis*, which has a number of meanings, among them "taking, choice, school of thought, philosophic principle or sect, religious sect," all going back to *haireisthai* (to take for oneself, choose), that being the "middle voice," a verbal "voice" not found in Latin or English, of the verb *hairein* (to take). *Heresy* is used in the realm of science as well as religion. Many "scientific *heresies*" are now accepted as scientific truths.

heresimach   See **heresiarch.**

heresiologist   See **heresiarch.**

heresiology   See **heresiarch.**

heriot (HEH ree uht) *n.* This is an English legal term that dates back to feudal times, when it denoted a death duty payable to the lord of the manor upon the death of a tenant. Originally, the duty or tribute so payable consisted of the horses and arms that had been lent by the lord to his tenant, but later the duty consisted of the best beast or chattel owned by the tenant. Later, in the case of *copyhold tenures* (of which more later), the death duty consisted of whatever chattel the custom of the particular manor provided or of a payment of money. *Heriot* comes from Old English *heregeatwe* (military equipment, from *here*, army, plus *geatwe*, equipment), which was shortened in Middle English to *heriet* or *heriot*. In exceptional cases, the duty might be payable on a change of tenant or even a change of lord. The word was used figuratively (and imaginatively) by Bishop John Hacket in *Scrinia Reserata, a Memorial Offer'd to the Great Deservings of John Williams, Archbishop of York* (1692) in these words: "His body was interred ... in Langeday, the *heriot* which every son of Adam must pay to the Lord of the Mannor of the whole Earth." (*Scrinia reserata* means literally, in Latin, "cases of papers opened," freely, "files examined.") In relatively recent times, an 1896 issue of the *Daily News* reported this item: "In the Court of Appeal yesterday ... Sir Thomas claimed that either by *heriot* custom or *heriot* service he was entitled to a *heriot* of the best beast of the deceased tenant." As to *copyhold*, that was a type of tenure or holding of land constituting a parcel of the manor at the will of the lord in accordance with the customs of the particular manor as inscribed in the *copy*, i.e., the transcript of the manorial court roll, which contained the names of the tenants and the customs of the manor affecting such tenure. *Heriot* was clearly distinguished from *relief*, a system whereunder a sum of money was paid by the heir of a deceased tenant to the lord for the right to assume the estate, which otherwise would have reverted to the lord. A special form of *heriot* was *thirdings*, which consisted of one-third of the corn or grain growing on the tenant's parcel at the time of his death. Historical novels are replete with terms like these.

hermitage   See **supernaculum**.

hesychasm   See **hesychast**.

hesychast (HEH zuh kast) *n*. *Hesychast* was the name given to a member of an Eastern Orthodox sect of ascetic mystics that arose in the 14th century among the monks of Mount Athos, the easternmost prong of the peninsula of Chalcidice, in northeastern Greece. They formed a school of *quietists* practicing a method of contemplation for the purpose of attaining a beatific vision or a like mystical experience. Their practice was known as *hesychasm* (HES uh kaz'm); the adjective describing their method of solitary meditative mysticism is *hesychastic* (heh see KAS tik). *Hesychast* is derived via medieval Latin *hesychasta*, from ecclesiastical Greek *hesychastes* (quietist, hermit), related to the verb *hesychazein* (to keep quiet, be still) and the adjective *hesychos* (quiet, still). As early as the sixth century, the term *hesychastic*, in addition to describing their practices, took on the meaning "soothing, calming," without reference to any order of monks; it was also an ancient Greek musical term descriptive of a melodic system that tended to calm and appease the mind. Getting back for a moment to *quietism* (KWEYE eh tiz'm), that is the general term for a type of religious mysticism founded on the doctrine that the essence of religion is the withdrawal of the soul from all external objects and the fixing of the mind solely on the contemplation of God. Followers, known as *quietists* (KWEY eh tists), subscribed to the tenet that when one has attained the mystic state by inner, mental prayer, his transgressions will not be considered sins, since his will has been extinguished in the course of the contemplation of God to the exclusion of all externals. This would appear to be a comfortable way of avoiding retribution for all one's transgressions. The monk Gregorius Palamas, later canonized as St. Gregory Palamas, an intellectual leader of the *hesychasts*, pled the cause of his party at the councils of Constantinople in 1341 and 1351 with such fervency that his fellow sectarians acquired the name of *Palamites* (PAL uh mites), now considered synonymous with *hesychasts*. According to the *Oxford Dictionary of the Christian Church* (1959, 2d ed. 1974), in the second half of the 14th century, *hesychasm* was accepted by the entire Greek Church, and its adherents were also known as *Palamites*.

hesychastic   See **hesychast.**

hetaera (heh TEER uh), also **hetaira** (heh TIRE uh) *n.* This word, from the Greek *hetaira*, the feminine form of *hetairos* (companion), has several shades of meaning. It is generally understood to have meant "courtesan" or "mistress" in ancient Greece. *RH* defines the term as a "female paramour" or "concubine" but goes on to widen the definition to include "any woman who uses her charm to gain wealth or social position." *CH* starts off with a different slant: "in Greece, a woman employed in public or private entertainment" (a female somewhat like a geisha in Japan, especially the "private entertainment" aspect, the audience consisting, in both cases, of men); but *CH* goes on to include "paramour, concubine, courtesan (especially of a superior class)" as well. *W III* equates the term with "demimondaine" and then defines that term as "a woman of the demimonde; a kept woman." The *O.E.D.* definition includes "a female companion or paramour, a mistress, a concubine; a courtesan, harlot." That definition covers a lot of distance, all the way from "female companion" (seems innocent enough) to "harlot" (not so innocent). The *O.E.D.* quotes *LS*: "In Attic [Greek] mostly opposed to a *lawful wife*, and so with various shades of meaning, from a *concubine* (who might be a wife in all but the legal qualification of citizenship) down to a *courtesan*." It is evident that the word must be understood in context and used carefully, in view of the variety of its meanings. There were *hetaerai* who acquired great renown. Phryne, an Athenian *hetaera* of the fourth century B.C. famous for her beauty (she was the model for Praxiteles's Cnidian Venus), became so rich that she offered to rebuild the walls of Thebes if the authorities agreed to put on them the inscription: "Alexander destroyed them, but Phryne the *hetaera* rebuilt them." The offer was not taken up. The story goes that when the defense was doing badly during her trial on a capital charge, she was acquitted on the spot when she bared her uniquely beautiful bosom to the judges. One offshoot of the word comes as a surprise: Going back to the original Greek root, *hetairos* (companion), the term *hetairia* means a "club" or "society"; but another related word *hetearocracy* (heh teer AH cruh see), also *hetairocracy* (heh tire AH krah see), which can mean the "rule of courtesans" (cf. **pornocracy**), has another meaning as well: the "rule of fellows (of a college)"! James Bowling Mozley, in *Essays, Theological and Historical* (1878), wrote of "the '*hetairocracy* ' of Oriel Common Room." (Oriel is an Oxford College, and a *common room* is a room in a college available to members for business or social purposes.) Based on its Greek origin, one might be forgiven for guessing that still another related word, *hetaery* (heh TEE reye), denoted a sort of Playboy Club, teeming with Bunnies, but no: It comes from *hetaireia* (companionship) and means an "oligarchical club" formed in ancient Athens principally for political and judicial purposes—nothing the least bit naughty.

hetaerocracy   See **hetaera.**

hetaery   See **hetaera.**

hetairia   See **hetaera.**

heteronomous   See **heteronym.**

heteronomy   See **heteronym.**

heteronym (HET ur oh nim) *n.* Most of us are familiar with *synonym, homonym* and *antonym*, but how about *heteronym*, built of the Greek prefix *heter-* (other, different) plus *-onym*, the combining form of *onoma* (name)? A *heteronym* is a "word of the same spelling as another but with a different pronunciation and meaning." Examples: *lead* (to conduct) and *lead* (a metal); *sow* (to scatter seed, to plant) and *sow* (an adult female swine); *desert* (arid region) and *desert* (to abandon); *refuse* (to decline to accept) and *refuse* (rubbish, trash). Be careful not to confuse *heteronym* with *heteronomy* (het uhr OH noh mee), the state of being under the rule or control of another, as opposed to the more familiar term *autonomy*. The adjectival form of *heteronym* is *heteronymous* (het uh RON uh muhs), to be carefully distinguished from *heteronomous*, the adjectival form of *heteronomy*, meaning "subject to different laws." Note that *heteronymous* and *heteronomous* do not qualify as a pair of *heteronyms*, because they are *not* pronounced differently, unlike the *heteronymous* examples shown above.

heteronymous   See **heteronym.**

heteroscian   See **amphiscian.**

heterozetesis (hed uh roh zuh TEE sis) *n*. This word was found only in *W III*, which gave as its derivation the Greek prefix *hetero-*, the combining form of *heteros* (other, different) plus *zetesis* (search, inquiry), related to the verb *zetein* (to seek, inquire), and gave as its definition simply "*ignoratio elenchi*," letting it go at that. If we look up that phrase, we find: "L[atin], lit[erally], ignorance of proof; trans[lation] of G[reek] *elenchou agnoia*." Under the headword *elenchus* in my *1000 Most Challenging Words*, after explaining that an *elenchus* is a "logical refutation, an argument that refutes another argument," I say that *ignoratio elenchi* means "ignoring the argument ... the fallacy of ignoring the point in question and arguing to the wrong point," which is pretty close to the *W III* definition: "a fallacy in logic of supposing that the point at issue is proved or disproved by an argument based on such a fallacy." There is a passage in Vita Sackville-West's *Pepita* about a will contest in which her mother testified against the charge of undue influence. The judge was Sir Samuel Evans, and counsel for the contestants was the able F. E. Smith. Here is a bit from the transcript:

> The Judge: You are fencing with each other prettily, but these are all speeches to the jury.
> Mr F. E. Smith: My Lord, the lady puts it on me.
> The Judge: Your experience ought to enable you to cast it off.
> Mr F. E. Smith: If I do, my Lord, I shall get no answer, because the lady answers another question every time, which I have not asked.

I cannot remember coming across a prettier example of *ignoratio elenchi*, i.e., *heterozetesis*.

hierodule (heye AIR uh dyoohl) *n*. From the combining form of the Greek adjective *hieros* (holy, sacred) came the prefix *hiero-*, which (dropping the *o* before a vowel) is found in words like *hierarchy* and *hierocracy* (the latter denoting government or rule by ecclesiastics, like what is going on in Iran these days). *Doulos* is Greek for "slave," so that a *hierodoulos* was a "slave (of either sex) who dwelled in a temple and was dedicated to the service of a god." According to *LS* the term *hierodoulos* "was especially applied to the public courtesans or votaries of Aphrodite at Corinth." The Greek geographer and historian Strabo (63 B.C.–A.D. 21, but the dates are uncertain) was the authority for that special application. The April 27, 1893, issue of *The Nation* would appear to have been somewhat off base in its use of *hierodule*, when it spoke of "The Amazons ... the warrior priestesses, or *hierodules*, of the Cappadocian Hittites." Warriors? Courtesans? What's going on here? Anyway, I'd love to know just what went on when a devotee of Aphrodite paid a visit to that temple at Corinth.

hieromonk   See **hegumen.**

hip(s)   See **hypo.**

hippiatric (hip ee AY trik) *n., adj. Hipp-* is a combining form of Greek *hippos* (horse), and *-iatric* comes from *iatros* (physician); together they formed *hippiatrikos*, the adjective from *hippiatros*, meaning "horse doctor," although the *O.E.D.* definition, "veterinary surgeon," would appear to indicate that the practice of a *hippiatros* was not necessarily limited to the treatment of equine ailments. The plural form, *hippiatrics*, means "treatment of diseases of horses," or, in context, "farriery," which denotes anything from the mere shoeing of horses to the treatment of horse diseases to veterinary surgery in general; but *hippiatrics* can cover, as well, a study or treatise on the diseases of horses. *Hippiatry* is a synonym of *hippiatrics* (hip ee AY trix) and *hippiatrist* (hip pee AY trist) is another word for *hippiatric* used as a substantive to mean "horse doctor." None of the above has anything to do with hippies.

hippocamp   See **hippodame.**

hippocampus   See **hippodame.**

hippocrene (HIP uh kreen) *n.* Usually capitalized, *Hippocrene* was the name of a fountain in ancient Greece that burst forth, according to legend, at the spot on Mount Helicon (the abode of the Muses) struck by a hoof of Pegasus, the winged horse ridden by Bellerophon when he rode against the Chimera, a monster, according to Homer, with a lion's head, a goat's body and a dragon's tail. (*Chimaira* is Greek for "female goat.") *Hippocrene* was known as the Fountain of the Muses and was believed to be a source of poetic inspiration, whence it acquired the meaning "poetic or literary inspiration." George Daniel, in *Polylogia; in Severall Eclogs* (1638–48), wrote: "And *Hippocrene* it selfe is but a Tale/To countenance dull Soules who drinke not Ale." Keats, in *Ode to a Nightingale* (1820), cried, "O for a beaker ... Full of the true, the blushful *Hippocrene.*" In *The Goblet of Life* (1841), Longfellow wrote of "maddening draughts of *Hippocrene.*" In 1880 James Russell Lowell complained, "We shrink from a cup of the purest *Hippocrene* after the critics' solar microscope," and Oliver Wendell Holmes (the elder), in 1891, wrote of "a loiterer by the waves of *Hippocrene,*" so we see that the fabulous spring was on the minds of poets over the centuries. It got its name from Greek *hippokrene*, composed of *hippos* (horse) and *krene* (fountain). Fortunate are those who have found it and drunk of its waters.

hippodame (HIP uh dame) *n.* This is a word erroneously used by Spenser in *The Faerie Queene* for *hippocamp*, a shortened version of *hippocampus*, when he wrote of "Infernell Hags, Centaurs, feendes, *Hippodames*," and later of "His [Neptune's] swift charet ... Which foure great *Hippodames* did draw." *Hippocampus* is also the term in ichthyology for the sea horse, and in anatomy for a certain part of the brain that supposedly resembles the sea horse. I have gone into all this lest, in reading *The Faerie Queene*, you ran into *hippodame* and thought it denoted a female horse, or mare, and got confused. In fact, *hip-*

podame is an obsolete form of *hippodamist* (hih POD uh mist), which means "horse tamer," i.e., one who breaks in horses, taken from the Greek word based on *hippos* (horse) plus the stem of *damazein* (to break in). Samuel Warren, in *Ten Thousand a Year* (1841), wrote: "The present famous *hippodamist* at Windsor, by touching a nerve in the mouth of a horse, reduces him to helpless docility." That's not the way I've seen it done out West!

hippodamist   See **hippodame.**

hipps   See **hypo.**

hircine (HUR sine, -sin) *adj. Hircus* is Latin for "billy goat"; the adjective *hircinus* means "goatlike," and more specifically, "smelling like a goat," which isn't a very good way to smell. From *hircinus* we get *hircine*, with both those meanings, as well as a meaning of its own: "lustful," in view of that legendary aspect of a goat's character. Cf. "old goat," a slang pejorative for an aged lecher. *Cervus* is Latin for "stag" (cf. French *cerf*, Italian *cervo*, Spanish *ciervo* and our adjective *cervine*), and the combination of *hircus* and *cervus* gave us *hircocervus* (hur coh SUR vuhs), the name of a fabulous beast, half goat, half stag. This was a translation from the Greek *tragelaphos*, built of *tragos* (billy goat) and *elaphos* (stag), from which the Romans got *tragelaphus*, a kind of antelope, and we got *tragelaph* (TRA juh laf), the name of a large African antelope, also called *strepsiceros* (strep SIS uh ruhs), from the Greek *strephein* (to turn) plus *keras* (horn), indicating that this particular type of antelope has twisted horns. Apparently the ancients thought that an antelope was part goat, part deer. It's a long way from smelly goats to antelopes with twisted horns, but this is the sort of thing that happens once you begin delving into dictionaries, especially in the field of biological classification.

hircocervus   See **hircine.**

hirple (HUR p'l, HIR-) *n. To hirple* is "to walk or run lamely, to drag a leg, to hobble." As a noun, a *hirple* is a "limping or crawling sort of gait." It is a chiefly Scottish word but is heard as well in the north of England, or, as the British put it, south of the border. (That phrase, *south of the border*, to American ears, means "south of the border with Mexico," i.e., south of the Rio Grande. *The border*, in Britain, refers to the one with Scotland, and the British generally use *frontier* for an international border.) The dictionaries present those doleful words "origin unknown" for this word. This may be a wild guess, but the Greek verb *herpein* (to move slowly, to creep) which is cognate with Latin *serpere* (to creep, crawl), whose present participle *serpens* gave us *serpent*, may somehow have crept into *hirple*. (The cognate relationship may become clearer if we compare the first-person singular present indicative forms of the verbs: *herpo/serpo.*) The *O.E.D.* gives a rather feeble assent in saying of *hirple*: "Its coincidence in sound and sense with Gr[eek] *herpein* is noticeable." In Sir

Walter Scott's *The Pirate* (1821), we find the sentence: "They will be waiting for him, *hirpling*, useless body." Lord Cockburn's *Memorials of his Time* (1821–30) speaks of " ... a slow stealthy step—something between a walk and a *hirple*." *Shamble* may be as good a synonym as any.

hokku   See **cinquain**.

hominist   See **hominization**.

hominization (hom uh nih ZAY shuhn) *n*. This word was taken from the French *hominisation*, as used by P. Teilhard de Chardin in his *Le Phénomène Humaine* (1948). Latin *homin-*, the stem of *homo* (man), is the basis of the word, which denotes the development, through evolution, of traits, particularly those mental and spiritual characteristics that distinguish man from the rest of the animal world. In Julian Huxley's *Evolution in Action*, we are told: "The original stock of pre-human apes differentiated into many species, all showing a trend toward what has been called *hominization*—the acquisition of more human characters." In Bernard Wall's translation of de Chardin's work, entitled *The Phemenon of Man* (1959), we find these words: "*Hominisation* (note British alternative spelling with *s*) can be accepted in the first place as the individual and instantaneous leap from instinct to thought, but it is also ... the progressive phyletic spiritualisation in human civilisation of all the forces contained in the animal world." [*Phyletic* means "relating to a line of descent."] In the same translation, Wall uses the participial adjective *hominized*: "Are not the artificial, the moral and the juridical simply the *hominised* (note *s* again) versions of the natural, the physical and the organic?" A 1973 issue of the *Times Literary Supplement* spoke of the " ... *hominized*, secularized world." *Hominization* has nothing to do with *hominist* (HOM uh nist), as used by Bernard Shaw (1903) in the preface to his *Man and Superman* (1903): "The wildest *hominist* or feminist farce is insipid after the most commonplace 'slice of life.'" *Hominist* is the word for one advocating equal rights for men, the way their opposite numbers, the feminists, seek them for women. The poet Rupert Brooke (1887–1915) wrote, in a letter published in 1968: "If feminists are 'women' trying to be men, I suppose 'men' trying to be women are *hominists*."

homolog(o)umena   See **antilegomena**.

horn-mad (horn MAD) *adj*. The *O.E.D.* tells us that this word applied originally to beasts equipped with horns and in that context meant "enraged so as to be ready to horn anyone," i.e., to gore the offender. But it was extended to describe persons "enraged, furious, boiling over with anger." An earlier form was *horn-wood*, now obsolete. Examples are given in which the *horn-* element was spelled *horne-*, and the *Shorter Oxford English Dictionary* explains the *-wood* by listing *wood* as an obsolete adjective meaning, inter alia, "violently angry," or "irritated"; "enraged, furious," giving as an example an excerpt from the speech of Demetrius in *A Midsummer Night's Dream* (Act IV, Scene 1): " … and here am I, and wood [*wode*, in my edition] within this wood, because I cannot meet my Hermia." Thomas Nashe, the English dramatist, novelist and satirical pamphleteer, in *Have with you to Saffron-Walden* (1596), wrote of "a bull … bellowing and running *horne mad* at every one in his way," and Robert Louis Stevenson, in *Catriona: a Sequel to Kidnapped* (1893), tells of a lady who "would be driven *horn-mad* if she could hear of [something or other]." But this adjective also has an altogether different meaning, involving *horn* as a symbol of cuckoldry. This goes all the way back to Latin *cornu* (horn), which is reflected in Italian *cornuto*, Spanish *cornudo* and French *cocu*, all names bestowed upon the poor deceived husband. In this context, *horn-mad* means "enraged at being cuckolded," a sense that the *O.E.D.* attributes to "word-play." Both senses show up in *The Comedy of Errors* (Act II, Scene 1), when Dromio of Ephesus says to Adriana, "Why, mistress, sure my master is *horn mad* … I mean not cuckold-mad; but sure, he's stark-mad." And in *The Ring and the Book* (1868), Browning uses the *cuckold* sense: "Somebody courts your wife, Count? Where and when? How and why? Mere *horn-madness*: have a care!" In his delightful little book *The Whole Ball of Wax and Other Colloquial Phrases* (1988), the American lexicographer Laurence Urdang (William Safire calls him "America's Samuel Johnson") deals with *horn-mad* and has (as is his usual practice) interesting things to say. I urge the reading of his book for supplementary information about this curious term, as well as all sorts of fascinating data about our wonderful language.

humuhumunukunukuapuaa (HOOH mooh HOOH mooh NOOH kooh NOOH kooh AH pooh AH uh) *n.* Yes, this *is* a word, the name of either of two triggerfishes that swim among the coral reefs of the tropical Indian and Pacific oceans. The lovely name is generally applied to one of the two species known to ichthyologists as *Rhinecantus aculeatus*. Beyond that, it is the name of the state fish of Hawaii. Each of our 50 states has a state flower, a state tree and a state bird. Some have a state insect, dog, grass or even fossil, and a fair number have a state fish. If you say *humu* … etc. fast, you can almost hear the steel guitars twanging and see the wahines swaying. A few examples of other state fishes: Alaska, the king salmon; California, the golden trout; Pennsylvania, the brook trout—but they all sound rather prosaic alongside Hawaii's *humu* … If your state lacks a state fish and that bothers you, select one and send a specimen of your nominee to your congressperson, senator or governor along with your complaint.

hydria   See **krater.**

hyle (HEYE lee) *n. Hyle* is Greek for "wood" and "matter" in the sense of physical substance in general as opposed to incorporeal things such as mind, spirit, qualities and actions. *Hyle* figures in numerous compounds: *hylic* (HEYE lik), "material, corporeal"; *hylicism* (HEYE luh siz'm) and *hylism* (HEYE liz'm), "materialism"; *hylicist* (HEYE luh sist) and *hylist* (HEYE list), "materialist"; *hylogenesis* (heye loh JEN uh sis), "the origin of matter"; *hylopathism* (heye LOP uh thiz'm), built of *hyle* and Greek *pathos* (sensation), the doctrine that matter is sentient (a case of *pathetic fallacy*, as discussed in my *1000 Most Challenging Words?*); *hylopathist* (heye LOP uh thist), denoting a follower of that doctrine; *hylophagous* (heye LO fuh guhs), built of *hyle* and *phagein* (to eat), "wood-eating," as applied, e.g., to termites; *hylotheism* (heye LOH thee iz'm), built of *hyle* and *theos* (god), "the doctrine that God and matter are identical"; *hylotheist* (heye LOH thee ist), denoting one who follows that doctrine; *hylotomous* (heye LOT uh muhs), built of *hyle* and *temnein* (to cut), "wood-cutting," as applied to insects; *hylozoism* (heye loh ZOH iz'm) built of *hyle* and *zoe* (life), "the doctrine that all matter is endowed with life" (more pathetic fallacy? Incidentally, there is a technical term used in psychology for the pathetic fallacy: *psychomorphism* (seye koh MORF iz'm), from Greek *psyche*, soul, plus *morphe*, form, meaning the "attribution of mental and spiritual processes, such as feeling, knowledge and purpose, to animals or inanimate objects); *hylozoist* (heye loh ZOH ist), denoting a follower of that doctrine; and *hylozoical* (heye loh ZO uh kuhl) and *hylozoistic* (heye loh zoh IST ik), adjectives descriptive of that doctrine. There are more *hylo-* compounds, but they would get us into philosophical concepts and doctrines too abstruse for even this book.

hyleg (HEYE leg) *n.* This is a term in astrology, the "science" that claims to interpret the influence of the heavenly bodies on human affairs. The astrology and horoscope business beguiles millions of people and relieves them of millions of dollars (pounds, francs, lire, etc., but not rubles, as far as I know). *Hyleg* is variously defined (a multiplicity of dictionaries can cause a combination of enlightenment and confusion). It is said to be the "ruling planet at the moment of birth," the "astrological position of the planets at the hour of birth," etc. *Hyleg* appears to be a modification of Persian *hailaj* (which means "material body," according to *W III*, but "calculation of astrologers by which they obtain evidence of the length of an infant's life" according to the *O.E.D.* Persian lexicographers, according to the *O.E.D.*, say the word is originally Greek and means "fountain of life.") Some dictionaries give *apheta* (AH fuh duh) as a synonym of *hyleg*. When we investigate that word, we find it to be a New Latin word taken from Greek *aphetes*, literally "one who lets go"; figuratively, "heavenly body determining the vital quadrant," from the Greek verb *aphienai* (to send forth), meaning in English "the ruler of life in a nativity." Phew! This has nothing to do with *aphetic*, the adjective from *aphesis*, also derived from *aphienai*, denoting the loss of a short unaccented vowel (i.e., "one let go") at the beginning of a word, as in *lone* from *alone*, *special* from *especial*, *squire* from *esquire*, etc. *Aphesis* is synonymous with *aph(a)eresis*, discussed at length in my *1000 Most Challenging Words*. (My astrologer assured me that this was an ideal day to write up this entry.)

hylic   See **hyle.**

hylicism   See **hyle.**

hylicist   See **hyle.**

hylism   See **hyle.**

hylist   See **hyle.**

hylogenesis   See **hyle.**

hylopathism   See **hyle.**

hylopathist   See **hyle.**

hylophagous   See **hyle.**

hylotheism   See **hyle.**

hylotheist   See **hyle.**

hylotomous   See **hyle.**

hylozoical   See **hyle.**

hylozoism   See **hyle.**

hylozoist   See **hyle.**

hylozoistic   See **hyle.**

hyp(s)   See **hypo.**

hypaethral (hi PEE thrul, heye-), also **upaithric** (ooh PYE thrik) *adj.* Any structure without a roof is *hypaethral*, i.e., "roofless, open to the elements." The Harvard Stadium, the Yale Bowl, the countless meeting places of those stalwart college and professional football teams, are *hypaethral*, with the exception of those few covered arenas like the Astrodome. How we have shivered and suffered in those *hypaethral*, or if you prefer, *upaithric* structures in the late autumnal and early winter contests! The noun for one of those open stadia is *hypaethron* (hi PEE thron, hye-) but I can't think of any one of them that calls itself that. The adjective comes from two Greek words: *hypo* (beneath) and *aether* (sky), which gives us *ether, etherial*, etc. The other form in the headword is simply a matter of spelling, having the same root and the identical meaning.

hyperbaton   See **metaplasm.**

hyperborean (heye pur BOH ree uhn, -buh REE uhn) *n., adj.* In both Latin and Greek, *boreas* means "north"; in classical mythology, *Boreas* was the god of the north wind. By combining *hyper-*, from Greek *hyper* (over, beyond) with *borean*, formed from *boreas* by adding the English *-an* ending, we get *hyperborean*, meaning "pertaining to, or inhabiting an extreme northern region"; also used as a noun denoting, literally, an inhabitant of the extreme north, and, informally and figuratively, one who lives in any northern climate. According to Greek legend, the *Hyperboreans* were a happy race who enjoyed perpetual sunshine and plenty in the realms beyond the north wind. In Maurice Keating's *Travels through France and Spain to Morocco* (1816), we read: "At six in the morning the yokes of oxen were going to their work a field; and nearly three hours advantage ... of active life is possessed [in France] over us *Hyperboreans.*" As an ethnological term, a *hyperborean* (sometimes capitalized) is a "member of an Arctic people," like the Eskimos, or the Koryak and Chukchi of northeastern Asia. The 17th-century Puritan clergyman John Davenport used the adjective figuratively to mean "frigid" when he wrote of being "dragged ... out of our *hyperborean* gloom into the South." Davenport was one of the founders of New Haven, Connecticut, and those of us who suffer through winters in that part of the world know what he was talking about.

hyperdulia   See **dulia.**

hypnagogic   See **hypnopedia.**

hypnobate   See **hypnopedia.**

hypnogogic   See **hypnopedia.**

hypnology   See **hypnopedia.**

hypnopedia (hip nuh PEE dee uh) *n. Hypnos* is mentioned in **thanatism,** but only briefly. He was the Greek god of sleep, the twin brother of Thanatos, the god of death. *Hypno-* is the combining form and has served as a prefix in a number of words in our language. *Hypnosis* is the most familiar of them. *Hypnopedia*, combining *hypno-* with the *paid-* of Greek *paideuein* (to teach, instruct), is "learning or conditioning by repetitive recorded sound during sleep" (sometimes semiwakefulness). A *hypnobate* (HIP nuh bate) is a "sleepwalker." Here, the prefix is combined with *-bates* (walker). *Hypnology* (hip NOL uh jee) is the "scientific study of the phenomena of sleep and hypnosis." *Hypnopompic* (hip nuh POMP ik), using *pompe* (sending away), means "dispelling or disturbing sleep" or "having to do with the condition of semiconsciousness preceding sleep." *Hypnophobia* obviously means "dread of sleep."

Hypnogogic (sometimes *hypnagogic*, built of *hypn-*, omitting the *o* before a vowel plus *-agogos*, from *agein*, to lead), the opposite of *hypnopompic*, means "relating to the drowsiness preceding sleep." A *hypnagogic* or *hypnogogic* image is a hallucination occurring when one is falling asleep or extremely fatigued. A *hypnoscope* (HIP nuh skope), using the suffix -scope, from *skopos* (watcher), is an "instrument used by hypnotists to ascertain whether the subject is capable of being hypnotized." It is to be hoped that this discussion has been more *hypnopompic* than *hypnogogic*.

hypnophobia   See **hypnopedia.**

hypnopompic   See **hypnopedia.**

hypnoscope   See **hypnopedia.**

hypo (HEYE poh) *n.* This word takes a number of forms: *hypo, hyp* (usually, *the hyp* or *the hyps*), *hip* and *hipps*. They all go back to *hypochondria*, a familiar word, but perhaps you don't know its origin; via Late Latin, from the Greek neuter plural of *hypochondrios* (pertaining to the upper abdomen, once believed to be the seat of melancholy). I dealt with the archaic word *hip* in *British English, A to Zed*, giving as its American equivalent "the blues," and said: "As a noun, it is sometimes spelled *hyp*, revealing its derivation (hypochondria)." *Hypo* and its variants mean "pathological depression," and it is found in the plural as well. Herman Melville, in *Moby Dick, or the Whale* (1851), used it in the expression "when my *hypos* get the upper hand of me," and in *Oldtown Folks* (1869), Harriet Beecher Stowe used it the same way: " ... alleging as a reason that' 'twould bring on her *hypos*.'" In the introduction to *Polite Conversation* (1738), Jonathan Swift writes sarcastically: "Some Abbreviations exquisitely refined; as ... *Hypps*, or *Hippo*, for Hypochondriacks." Robert P. Ward, in *Tremaine; or the Man of Refinement* (1825), has this to say: "Belmont was a melancholy place, and I was dying there of *hyp*!" A 1710 issue of *The Tatler* contains this bit of tattling: "Will Hazzard has got the *Hipps*, having lost to the Tune of Five Hundr'd Pound." In *John de Lancaster* (1800), Richard Cumberland has a character say: "You have caught *the hip* of [i.e., from] your hypochondriac wife," thus clearly revealing the derivation of *hip*. Whether *hypo, hypos, hyp, hyps, hip* or *hips*, it is (or they are) a condition much to be deplored. So, cheer up!

hypocaust (HEYE poh kawst) *n.* The Greek verb *hypokaiein* means "to light (a fire) under (something)"; it is built of the prefix *hypo-* (under) plus *kaiein* (to burn). *Hypokaustos* (heated by a *hypocaust*) has the neuter form *hypokauston*; used as a noun, it led to Latin *hypocaustum* or *hypocauston*, which is the name given to the central heating system of an ancient Roman building, usually a villa or public bath, consisting of a space below the floor containing a furnace and a series of flues for the distribution of the heat. Every ancient Roman villa excavated thus far in Britain contains the remains of a *hypocaust* that follows the pattern described by the first-century Roman architect and engineer Vitruvius. The sense of the word was extended, by transference, to include the meaning "stove," as indicated by a passage in Scott's *Anne of Geierstein* (1829): "The *stube* [room, chamber, apartment] of a German inn derived its name from the great *hypocaust*, or *stove*, which is always strongly heated, to secure the warmth of the apartment in which it is placed." But the original meaning of *hypocaust*, and Vitruvius's description, just go to show that there is nothing new under the floor.

hypocorism (hip OK ur iz'm, hipe-), also **hipocorisma** (hip ok uhr IZ muh, hipe-) *n*. From Greek *hupokorisma, -mos* (pet name), built of *hypo* (in the sense of "somewhat" or "slightly") plus *koros* (boy), *kore* (girl), and related to the verb *hypokorizesthai* (to act like a child, to use child talk), we get *hypocorism*, meaning "pet name"; and from *hypokoristikos*, as used in the phrase *onoma hypokoristikon* (pet name, diminutive), we get *hypocoristic* (hip ok uhr IS tik), meaning "like a pet name," and by extension, "pertaining to the inclination to use endearing terms and euphemisms." Thus, Samuel Pegge (the elder) in *Anonymiana; or Ten Centuries of Observations on Various Authors and Subjects* (1809) wrote: "Harry ... is the free or *hypocoristic* name for Henry." (Strangely enough, the *Oxford Dictionary of English Christian Names* says that *Harry* is the original English form of the name.) That seems obvious but is a clear example of the use of *hypocoristic* and its noun. *Abe, Ben, Chet, Don*—one could run through the alphabet and come up with *hypocorisms* all the way to *Zeke*.

hypocorisma   See **hypocorism**.

hyponoia (heye puh NOY uh) *n*. Occasionally one runs into a word on whose definition dictionaries differ—usually narrowly, on a matter of nuance, once in a while widely, because of divergent etymologies. *Hyponoia* is a case of the latter. *RH* defines it as "dulled mental activity; diminished function of thought" and is satisfied with "HYPO- + -NOIA" as its etymological background. In that dictionary, *hypo-* is traced to Greek *hypo* (under, below), and *-noia* to *no-*, the stem of *noos* or *nous* (mind) + *-ia*; and *-ia* is described as a noun suffix applying in various fields, including diseases. I set great store by *RH*, but I always turn to the *O.E.D.* for support and additional etymological material. Lo and behold: *Hyponoia* is tucked away in a very long list of *hypo-* words and is defined as "underlying meaning." The derivation given is Greek *hyponoia*, from the verb *hyponoein* (to suspect). *CH* tells us that *hypo-*, in composition, means "under; defective; inadequate," and if you connect "defective" with Greek *noos* (mind) you get "defective mind," in harmony with the *RH* definition. But if you then go to *LS*, you find *hyponoia* defined as "a hidden meaning or sense: a suspicion, conjecture, guess, supposition, fancy: the true meaning which lies at the bottom of (a thing)," and see that it comes from the verb *hyponoeein*, meaning, inter alia, "to think covertly, suspect." If you look up *suspicion* in the Woodhouse *English-Greek Dictionary*, you find its Greek equivalent to be our old friend *hyponoia*, supporting the *O.E.D.* and differing from *RH* and *CH*. There used to be a department in *The New Yorker* magazine entitled "What Paper D'ya Read?," in which wildly differing versions of the same news event were quoted from various newspapers. I propose (timidly) to our leading American lexicographer, Laurence Urdang, editor of the language quarterly *Verbatim*, a column entitled "Which Dictionary D'ya Read?," but I suspect (*hyponoeo*) that my proposal will be politely (Laurence is always polite) rejected because of the dearth of material.

hyponymy (heye PON uh mee) *n.* This is a term for a relationship between a pair of words or concepts, one of which is included in the other but the other of which is not included in the first. Example: *horse/quadruped; horse* is included in *quadruped*, in that the term *quadruped* includes *horse*, but it doesn't work the other way around. *Hyponym* (HEYE puh nim) will be discussed later. In *Structural Semantics: An Analysis of Part of the Vocabulary of Plato* (1963) by John Lyons, who has written a number of instructive works in the fields of linguistics in general and semantics in particular, we find a definition of *hyponymy* and some examples: "*Hyponymy* is the relation that holds, for instance, between *scarlet* and *red*, or between *tulip* and *flower* ... It may be defined in terms of unilateral implication [a very helpful phrase: *tulip* implies *flower*, but *flower* does not imply *tulip*; the key word is *imply*]. Thus *X is scarlet* will be understood (generally) to imply *X is red*; but not conversely." To put it another way, *hyponymy* is not a vice-versa relationship. *Hyponym* and *hyponymy* are formed from the Greek prefix *hypo-* (under, shortened to *hyp-* before a vowel) plus *onoma* (name), which figures in *antonym* and *synonym* and other *-nym* words. In another part of his book, Lyons says: "I say that *scarlet* is a *hyponym* of, or is included in, *red*." Note that here, Lyons uses the word *include*, rather than *imply*. In view of the meaning of *hyp(o)-* given above, I would tend to modify the *O.E.D.* definition of *hyponym*: "One of two or more words related by *hyponymy*" so as to make it clear that *hyponym* applies to the word that is *included* (i.e., by *implication*), not the *including* (i.e., general or generic) word. Thus, *scarlet* and *tulip* are *hyponyms*, being *included* in *red* and *flower* respectively, while *red* and *flower* are not *hyponyms*. And note the *two or more* in that definition, which is very helpful, because one might infer, from the examples and quotations under *hyponymy*, that only two words are involved. Obviously, that is not the case: The examples might just as well have been *red, scarlet* and *vermilion*, or *flower, tulip* and *rose*, with the latter two words in each case serving as *hyponyms*.

hypos   See **hypo**.

hypotaxis (heye poh TAX is) *n.* In my *1000 Most Challenging Words*, I discussed *parataxis* (par uh TAX is), the "omission of a connective between clauses or sentences," and gave examples like "Don't worry, I'll see to everything." Here is a famous one: "I came, I saw, I conquered." In *parataxis* (taken intact from the Greek noun meaning "placing side by side"), there are no connectives indicating the relation between the clauses, i.e., whether they are coordinate or subordinate. *Hypotaxis* is the opposite construction, in which a connective is used to indicate the relationship between clauses, which is one of subordination, a dependent arrangement. Example: *I went to Venice because I love the place.* In *parataxis*, it would have been put this way: I went to Venice, I love the place. *Taxis* is "arrangement" in Greek; *para-* is "beyond," *hypo-* is "under," whence we get *subordination.* Don't confuse *hypo-* and *hyper-*, meaning "excessive." Thus, *hypertension* is high blood pressure; *hypotension* is low blood pressure.

hypozeuxis   See **anaphora.**

hypselotimophobia   See **xenodochiophobia.**

ichabod (IK uh bod) *interj.* The first thing that comes to mind on meeting this word (usually capitalized), unless one is unusually familiar with I Sam. 4:21, is Ichabod Crane, the headless horseman of Washington Irving's *Legend of Sleepy Hollow.* But there was a much earlier *Ichabod.* When the pregnant daughter-in-law of the priest Eli heard of the Philistines' defeat of Israel, the deaths of Eli and her husband Phineas and the taking of the ark together with the Torah, her labor pains began, and on giving birth, she named the infant *Ichabod,* from the Hebrew word *i-khabhodh,* meaning "The glory is departed." That word has ever since been used as an exclamation of regret for the good old days. The adjective *Ichabodian* was later coined to mean "regretful" or "lamentable."

ichnite (IHK nite) *n. Ichnos,* in Greek, means "track, footprint"; its combining form is *ichno-, ichn-* before a vowel. *Ichnite* means "fossil footprint," especially that of an animal preserved in a rock. The synonym *ichnolite* (IK noh lite) comes from a combination of *ichno-* with *lithos* (stone). *Ichnology* (ik NOL uh jee) and *ichnolithology* (ik noh lith OL uh jee) both mean the "study of fossil footprints," a subsection of paleontology, but they can also denote the *ichnological* features of a given area, i.e., the fossil footprints characteristic of a district, in the same way *flora* and *fauna* are used. *Ichnomancy* (IK noh man see), according to Edward Smedley in *The Occult Sciences* (1855), "is the art of finding out the figure, peculiarities, occupations, &c. of men or beasts by the traces of their posture, position and footsteps." That word combined *ichno-* with a suffix derived from Greek *manteia* (divination). One might think that *ichnography* (ik NAW gruh fee) was the written lore pertaining to fossil footprints, but that is not so: It means "groundplan" or "plan or map of a place." Charles Merivalle, in *A History of the Romans under the Empire* (1865) wrote about "the *ichnography* of the wall of Antoninus," and the word was used in a figurative sense in an 1830 issue of *Fraser's Magazine*: "The theatre is, as it were, the *ichnography* (ground-plan) of a people."

ichnography   See **ichnite.**

ichnolite   See **ichnite.**

ichnolithology   See **ichnite.**

ichnology   See **ichnite.**

ichnomancy   See **ichnite.**

ignoratio elenchi   See **heterozetesis.**

impolder   See **empolder.**

impunitive   See **intropunitive.**

inchoative   See **adscititious.**

inclusio   See **anaphora.**

infangthief (IN fang theef) *n.* In Old English, this was spelled *infangentheof*, and the word was built of the adverb *in-* (in), plus *fangen*, the past particple of the verb *fon* (to seize) plus *theof* (thief). Its literal meaning was thus "thief seized within." *Infangthief* denoted the jurisdiction over a thief caught within the territorial limits of the lord of the manor and the lord's right to try and punish him. This was distinguished from *outfangthief*, the lord's right to pursue a thief, if the miscreant were attached to the manor, bring him back to the lord's own court for trial and keep his forfeited chattels on conviction. This latter right was defined in various ways and circumscribed in the 13th century, by which time its meaning became arguable. Of course, all this is old stuff, and these practices are obsolete. This leads me to make a point: A practice or an artifact may be obsolete, but the word denoting it may not necessarily be so. Thus, a chariot is an obsolete vehicle, but the word *chariot* isn't. The same applies to a penny farthing (the old bicycle with an outsize front wheel), or a biplane or a battle-axe. I make this point to demonstrate that there is a difference between *obscure* and *obsolete* and that a word like *infangthief* may be obscure but isn't obsolete. Otherwise, writers would be unable to produce those interminable historical novels in which people exclaim "Egad!" and "Gadzooks!" and "Tush! Tush!," which are obsolete but not obscure.

inlaut   See **anlaut.**

intimism (IN tuh miz-m) *n.* According to Peter and Linda Murray, in their *Dictionary of Art and Artists* (1959), *intimism* is "a form of Impressionist technique applied to the depiction of everyday life in domestic interiors rather than to landscape. The work of Bonnard and Vuillard is usually meant." This form of painting is based on the selection of intimate and familiar scenes and occasions from the daily routine of the painters themselves, and the term was obviously based on the adjective *intimate.* Another word for the same type of painting is *genre,* which I define in my *1000 Most Important Words* as "an artistic style," which, as applied to painting, "has the special meaning of 'scenes of everyday life,' that tell a story in realistic terms." An *intimist* (sometimes *intimiste*) is a "painter who practices *intimism.*" One meets the term in newspaper art criticism and reviews of painting exhibitions, and it is occasionally used attributively or adjectivally as well.

intimist   See **intimism.**

intinction (in TINK shuhn) *n.* This is the term for a manner (especially in the Eastern Church) of administering Holy Communion by means of dipping the bread into the wine and giving it, thus moistened, to the communicant. This custom was followed in the Western Church from the seventh to the twelfth centuries. Gasquet & Bishop, in their *Edward VI and the Book of Common Prayer* (1890), called *intinction* a "purely oriental rite" but in 1965, it was once more authorized by the Roman Catholic Church as a permissible method. Meaning no disrespect, this practice would appear to be a timesaving but soggy method of delivering the ingredients. The word comes from Late Latin *intinctio* (immersion), based on Latin *intinctus,* the past participle of *intingere* (to dip in), based on the prefix *in-* (in) plus *tingere* (to dip, wet, moisten).

intropunitive (in troh PYOOH nuh tiv) *adj.* Three relatively modern terms in psychology end in *-punitive* and deal with blame, in the sense of censure, reproach: *intropunitive* (sometimes *intrapunitive*), *extrapunitive* and *impunitive.* The *-punitive* ending comes from the Latin *punitus* (the source of our *punitive*), the past participle of *punire* (to punish, chastise); the prefixes are self-explanatory. *To be intropunitive* is "to blame oneself rather than others or external events; to give way to an excessive feeling of responsibility for frustrations or other misfortunes." *Extrapunitive* (ek strah PYOOH nuh tive) applies to persons who blame other people or events unreasonably and react aggressively to frustration. *Impunitive* describes those who are resigned to frustration and blame neither themselves nor others unreasonably. Henry Alexander Murray discussed these psychological problems in *Explorations in Personality* (1938):

> ... He [the patient] may react with emotions of guilt and remorse and tend to condemn himself as the blameworthy object. This type of reaction

may be termed *"intropunitive ."* ... He may manifest the emotion of anger and condemn the outer world ... for his frustration, adopting an attitude of hostility toward his environment. This type of reaction may be termed *"extrapunitive."* ... He may experience emotions of embarrassment and shame, making little of blame and emphasizing instead the conciliation of others and himself to the disagreeble situation. In this case he will be more interested in condoning than condemning and will pass off the frustration as lightly as possible by making references, even at the price of self- deception, to unavoidable circumstances. This type of reaction may be termed *"impunitive."*

John Michael Argyle, in *Religious Behavior* (1958), sums it up this way: "A ... personality variable is that of *punitiveness*: people are said to be *extrapunitive* if they react to frustration by aggression directed outwards, *intropunitive* if the aggression is directed inwards, and *impunitive* if they do not react aggressively at all." That's putting it in a nutshell.

iotacism   See **mytacism.**

ipseity   See **proprium.**

isagogic (eye suh GOJ ik, -GOG-) *adj.* This adjective means "introductory." Add an *s* and you have *isagogics*, a plural noun treated as a singular (like *economics, physics,* etc.), which is a division of theological study *introductory* to exegesis, which is defined in my *1000 Most Important Words* as "interpretation, especially of Scripture, but applicable generally." In the context of *isagogics,* we are of course speaking of Biblical interpretation. *Isagogic* is derived from the Greek noun *eisagoge* (introduction), based on the prefix *eis-* (into) plus the verb *agein* (to lead); while *exegesis* (ek suh GEE sis) was taken over intact from the Greek, which was based on the verb *exegeisthai* (to explain), formed of the prefix *ex-* (out) plus *hegeisthai* (to guide). There is no point to studying *isagogics* unless you are going into Biblical *exegesis.*

isodomon (eye SOD uh mon), also **isodomum** (eye SOD uh mum) *n.* This is a form of classical Greek masonry in which uniform blocks are laid in courses of equal height in such a way that the vertical joint between two blocks is placed exactly over the middle of the block below. I remember a film of Churchill in his garden building a brick wall in just that way, and my question to a contemporary bricklayer about this method evoked the reply, "Natch." It does seem logical. The adjective is *isodomous* (eye SOD o muhs) or *isodomic* (eye so DOM ik). *Isodomos* is Greek for "equal-coursed." *Isodomon* is its neuter form, and the word is built on the prefix *iso-,* the combining form of Greek *isos* (equal) plus *domos* (course), related to the verb *demein* (to build).

itacism   See **mytacism.**

ithyphallic (ih thee FAL ik) *adj.* An *ithyphallus* is an "erect penis," from the Greek *ithys* (straight) and *phallos* (penis). As an adjective, *ithyphallic* has a number of meanings. Most commonly, it applies to statues and graphic representations displaying that part of the anatomy in that state or to meter employed in hymns sung at ancient festivals honoring Bacchus, the Greek and Roman god of revelry. The technical description of that meter is *trochaic dimeter brachycatalectic*, as to which we shall attempt to enlighten you without introducing too many new terms: *Trochaic* (troh KAY ik; discussed under **dolichurus**) applies to a foot of two syllables, one stressed followed by one unstressed, as in *spinach*; a *dimeter* (DEYE mee tur) is a verse containing two measures; *brachycatalectic* (brak ee kat uh LEK tik) designates the omission of two syllables at the end of a verse composed of larger metrical units like *dipodies* (DIP uh deez), measures of two feet in which the stress of one is stronger than that of the other—but, unless you're about to write poetry in the classical manner, enough already! Getting back to *ithyphallic* for a moment: It can also apply to the Bacchic festivals of yore or the gigantic phallus carried in those processions. However, getting away from festivals and Bacchus, the adjective, used in a more general or literal way, can apply to the erect phallus itself, and from there it was extended (the meaning, not the phallus) to mean "lustful" and "obscene," which hardly seems fair, for where would the animal world be (nowhere!) without the *ithyphallus*? Incidentally, *ithyphallic* can be used as a noun denoting a poem in *ithyphallic* meter, or more widely, any licentious poem, like (if they can be called poetry) so many of our best limericks.

jabble (JAB'l) *n., vb.* This is British English for "turbulance on the surface of water, choppiness, rippling, splashing" and figuratively, "emotional turmoil, agitation of the mind." As a verb, *to jabble* is "to splash or splatter liquid," whether water in a usually placid pool or tea in a saucer, where, of course, it shouldn't be if you're careful and well mannered. The figurative use to denote emotional disturbance or mental agitation brings to mind the colloquial expression "Don't make waves," meaning "Don't start trouble," often given as advice to someone to avoid bringing up a certain subject that will cause "troubled waters." That, in turn, is an image that brings to mind the hideous old joke about a group of sinners in hell, punished (in the manner of the ingenious tortures fashioned by Dante in *The Divine Comedy*) by having to stand eternally in a brimming cesspool, the surface of which reaches just below their lower lips. A visitor (it might be Dante, led by Virgil) approaches and hears a constant murmuring, almost inaudible, issuing from the cesspool. As the visitors near, the murmur becomes louder and louder, and finally becomes intelligible. They are murmuring to one another: "Don't make waves! Don't make waves!" People in that position, then, shouldn't *jabble*.

jack-leg, jackleg (JA kleg)*n., adj.* A *jack-leg* is an "incompetent person," lacking not only ability and skill but scruples as well. As an adjective, *jackleg* describes such a person, and both noun and adjective express contempt. The British use the term *cowboy* in much the same vein. I define that term in my *British English, A to Zed*, as a "self-employed workman ... who undercuts a skilled man and does a job of awe-inspiring incompetence," a quite different application from the American usage: a "reckless driver." The *O.E.D. Supplement* tells us that it is "freq[uently] used [in American] of lawyers and preachers," and this is borne out in a number of examples supplied, relating to those professions and to carpenters and army officers as well. (The term seems to have originated in Texas.) In a 1974 issue of *American Speech*, we read: "One innovation possibly attributable to population shift is *jackleg preacher* ... " In R. Ottley's *New World A-Coming* (1943), the author tells us about a cult that was " ... augmented by a number of herb doctors, clairvoyants and '*jackleg*' preachers." The *jack-* part of the word seems to come from the name *Jack*, the common nickname for the ubiquitous *John*, hence a generic term for the "common man," while the *-leg* appears to be an echo of that in the pejorative term *blackleg* for "scab." The *Decca Book of Jazz* (1958) speaks of "wandering evangelists and '*Jack-leg*' preachers," and from what we have discovered in recent days about evangelists—those who wander not on foot but by television——*jackleg* seems much too mild a pejorative.

jampan (JAM pan) *n.* In the hill country of India, a vehicle of transportation for ladies is the *jampan*, a type of sedan chair carried by four men. The chair is large and clumsy; it has poles attached to the sides and sometimes a top from which curtains are hung. This contrivance is not nearly as elegant as the sedan chair once used by the French aristocracy before the revolution, with richly attired carriers on either side. The Indian carrier is known as a *jampani* or *jampanee*. *Jampan* and its several variants (*jampaun, jompon*, etc.) come from Bengali *jhampan* and Hindi *jhappan*. John Lang, in *Wanderings in India* (1859), describes "ladies and gentlemen on horseback, and ladies in *janpans* [sic]—the *janpanees* dressed in every variety of livery," and *The Times* (London) of August 17, 1879 tells us: "Every lady on the hills keeps her *jampan* and *jampanees*, just as in the plains she keeps her carriage and footmen." India fanciers, including my wife, tell me that transportation by *jampan* is a very comfortable way of mounting staircases.

jampani   See **jampan**.

jerque (JURK) *vb.* This term may be related to the Italian verb *cercare*, meaning "to search." In view of its form and sense, it seems like a pretty good guess. The *O.E.D.* says that "historical evidence is wanting," but it's the best we can do. *To jerque* is "to search a vessel for smuggled goods" or "to examine its papers in order to ascertain whether its manifest and the custom office's cargo lists are in agreement, and to make sure that all the cargo has been properly entered and accurately described." A *jerquer* is a "custom-house officer charged with the duty of examining a ship's papers to verify that all is in order with respect to the manifest." An 1867 *Sailor's Word-book* defines *jerquing a vessel* as "a search performed by the *jerquer* of the customs, after a vessel is unloaded, to see that no unentered goods have been concealed." Nowadays a lot more *jerquing* might well be in order, with respect to aircraft as well as vessels, to root out the importation of narcotics.

jumart (JOOH mart) *n.* Fabled monsters of many descriptions have long existed in legend, mythology and the imagination of people throughout the world. They "exist" in many ancient religions, especially Egyptian and Greek. The sphinx is probably the best known in the world; the griffin, with the head and wings of an eagle and the body of a lion, and the unicorn are familiar legendary monsters. The *jumart* was at first taken quite seriously: a hybrid, the offspring of a bull and a mare or a female ass, or that of a horse or ass and a cow. No less a person than the philosopher John Locke (*An Essay Concerning Human Understanding*, 1690) considered such a union possible: "We have Reason to think this not impossible, since Mules, and *Gimars* [Locke's spelling], the one from the mixture of an Horse, and an Ass, the other from the mixture of a Bull, and a Mare, are so frequent in the World." Locke erred, of course, and by 1809 an article in *The Philosophical Transactions of the Royal Society* mentioned "a *jumart* [JOOH mart; taken from the French; formerly *jumare*, an adaptation of modern Provençal *gemerre, gemarre*, origin unknown] ... the *pretended* offspring of the mare and the bull." Except for rare aberrations by man, animals are pretty fussy in their choice of mates.

kalyptra   See **zucchetto.**

karakia (ka ra KEE uh) *n., vb. Karakia* is a Maori incantation. The word comes up in a number of books about Maori customs and culture. The clearest definition appears in Peter Henry Buck's *The Coming of the Maori* (1949):

> The priests established oral communication with their gods by means of *Karakia*. A *Karakia* may be defined as a formula of words which was chanted to obtain benefit or avert trouble ... They cover a range which exceeds the bounds of religion. It is therefore impossible for one English word to cover adequately all the meanings of *Karakia*. All *Karakia* are chants but there are a number of chants ... which are not *Karakia* ... Probably incantation is the nearest in general meaning.

It might be well to define *incantation*: "magical formula, spell, charm; the chanting of words purporting to have magical power." This word comes to us via Late Latin *incantatio*, from Latin *incantare* (to chant, enchant, bewitch). Such incantations are of course not peculiar to Maoris; they are used and heard in many, if not most, primitive cultures. Stage "magicians" (to go from the sublime to the phony) use them all the time: *hocus-pocus* is a pretended incantation used in magic and juggling shows; *toutous talontus* and *vade celerita jubes* were additional ridiculous mock Latin incantations reeled off by conjurors in the old vaudeville days, and though I can't find it in the dictionaries, *abracadabra* was favored as well. These silly "incantations" are not intended to denigrate the serious *Karakia* or the incantations of any culture. *Karakia* is used as a verb as well: intransitively, "to chant *karakia*"; transitively, "to put a spell on (someone) by so doing."

kelebe   See **krater.**

klismos (KLIZ mos, -muhs) *n.* In ancient Greece, this was the name of a chair designed with a concavely carved back rail that curved forward from the back and with legs that curved upward and inward from the floor, in the form of a shallow letter *c.* The name was taken intact from Greek *klismos* (chair, couch), akin to the verb *klinein* (to lean, recline). The style of the *klismos* was often imitated during periods of classical Greek revival and was popular in the early 19th century. Specimens of the revival imitations can still be found in antique shops and at auctions. I have sat in one and found it rather uncomfortable, but then, though I don't like the way they look, I like to snuggle into the overstuffed variety.

kobold (KOH bold) *n.* We have taken this word intact from the German, where a *Kobold* is a "hobgoblin, elf or sprite." The etymology is uncertain, but some relate the word to Dutch *kabouter* and Middle Dutch *cobout.* A *kobold*, a character in German folklore, is a household sprite, sometimes rather tricky and slippery, and not always to be trusted. He is akin to a brownie, who can be very helpful when nobody's looking and assist a great deal with the household chores, scoring "brownie points" in recognition of services rendered, like a good husband who does the dishes or bathes the kids even after a hard day at the office. Another version of the *kobold* in folklore is that of the gnome that dwells undergound, haunting caves and mines. James Russell Lowell, in *Among My Books* (1870), used the term in a quite dramatic figurative sense; "There in the corner is the little black *kobold* of a doubt making mouths at him." Doubts *can* be as disturbing as little black imps making mouths at one.

krater, also **crater** (KRADE ur, KRAH tur) *n.* The Greek word *krater* means "mixing bowl" for mixing wine and water, i.e., diluting the wine. The bowl was used in ancient days by Greeks and Romans. Unlike the more or less familiar amphora, the *krater* had lower handles, a much wider mouth, a much more capacious body and a flat round base. It came in various sizes. One variety of *krater*, known as a *kelebe* (KEL uh bee), was ovoid in shape, with handles that dropped straight down to the shoulder of the jar from horizontal extensions of the rim. That word came from the Greek *kelebe*, which R. M. Cook, in *Greek Painted Pottery* (1960), called "a conventional name for a *column crater.*" Our word *crater*, in the sense of "volcano opening," came from the Latin *crater* or *cratera* (mixing vessel, wine or punch bowl), which in turn came from the Greek *krater*. Other types of Greek jars were the *hydria* (HEYE dree uh), based on *hydros* (water), a large jar in which water was carried, having two, sometimes three handles; and the *stamnos* (STA mnos), based on *sta-*, the combining form of *istanai* (to cause to stand), a two-handled jar with a neck shorter than that of the *hydria*. One finds examples of some of these jars not only in the museums but while wandering in Greek villages, a highly recommended form of exercise.

kwashiorkor (kwah shee OR kur) *n*. This is a term native to Ghana denoting those terrible cases of malnutrition in infants and children, causing stunting, skin and hair color changes, edema (abnormal puffy swelling), liver degeneration, anemia and the type of apathy one sees in those horrifying television films of starvation in African countries. The underlying cause is a diet lacking in protein and excessively high in carbohydrate. No doubt there are as many obscure words to designate this condition as there are regions where it exists (there's not much point in going into Ethiopian and Sudanese dialects), but the very fact that there is even a word for it is horrifying in itself. Let's hope that this word (and its equivalents in other regions) will one day be not only obscure but obsolete, or at least of only historical interest. An article in *The Times* (London) as far back as December 2, 1959, wrote of a " ... hospital doctor [who] described the incidence of *kwashiorkor* as 'needless slaughter' which could easily be prevented by funds for milk and other proper nourishment." In 1971 a Cape Town journal called *Progress*, writing of a medical research organization, wrote: "One of the unit's major achievements was to prove that the cure of *kwashiorkor* ... could be initiated by the administering of a synthetic skimmed milk." Need more be said?

labarum   See **chi-rho.**

lallation   See **psellism.**

latria   See **dulia.**

lazaret   See **clapperdudgeon.**

lazaretto   See **clapperdudgeon.**

lazar-house   See **clapperdudgeon.**

levirate (LEV uh ruht, LEEV-, -rate) *n. Levir* is Latin for "brother-in law" but only in the restricted sense of "husband's brother," as opposed to "sister's husband." It was compulsory among the ancient Hebrews for a brother, or if none existed, the next of kin of a deceased husband, to marry a childless widow. This curious custom, known as the *levirate*, prevailed in certain other nations as well. The word can be used attributively, as in *levirate marriage*, but the adjective *leviratic* (lev uh RAT ik) or *leviratical* (lev uh RAT uh kuhl) is used as well; and the term *leviration* (lev uh RAY shuhn) denotes such a marriage. We find these words in Renan's *Life of Jesus* (1863) which reads in translation: "The Mosaic code had consecrated this patriarchal theory by a strange institution, the *levirate* law." Matt: 22:24 is cited as the authority for the ancient rule that the firstborn son of such a marriage is deemed the son of the deceased brother: " ... Moses said, If a man die, having no children, his brother shall marry his wife, and raise up seed unto his brother." When a younger brother of the deceased marries the widow, the marriage is known as a "junior *levirate*." *Polygyny* (the custom of having multiple wives) was common in ancient societies, including the Hebrew. *Sororal polygyny* from Latin *soror* (sister) is one in which the wives are sisters. Another custom quite apart from *levirate* is *sororate* (suh ROH ruht) denoting marriage with two or more sisters, usually successively, after a first wife has been found to be barren, or after her death. These ancient marriage arrangements so alien to modern societies were considered quite normal in ancient times.

leviratic(al)   See **levirate.**

leviration   See **levirate.**

lickerish (LIK ur ish) *adj.* It sounds like that chewy black stuff that comes in long strips and blackens your tongue, but it isn't. That's *licorice* or *liquorice*. *Lickerish* describes one fond of good food, not necessarily a gourmet or an epicurean: just somebody who likes good eating and is rather eager to savor the experience. Its meaning has been expanded to reflect the desire for other things, such as wine, women and song—i.e., "desirous" generally—and in context, subject to lustful cravings, even to the point of serving as a synonym for *lecherous*, with which it appears to have an etymological connection. There was a time when *lickerish* meant "tempting" (to the appetite) and "dainty," but those uses are now obsolete. The word appears to have come from the obsolete adjective *lickerous*, from Old North French, as a variant of Old French *lechereus*. There are a number of variant spellings, the most frequent of which is *liquorish*. In connection with the enjoyment of fare, we find in W. E. Heitland's *Quintius Curtius* (1879) the description of one who drank "rather by good fellow-ship than from a *liquorish* appetite." In the sense of "desirous" or "greedy" generally, Jonathan Swift, in *A Tale of a Tub* (1704), wrote of "a *liquorish* affection to gold." In *The First Part of King Edward the Fourth* (1600), Thomas Heywood wrote: "Go to Hell … ye may be caught, I tell ye: these by *liquorish* lads," using this versatile word in the sense of "lecherous, lustful." A useful and dramatic word; too bad it has gone out of style.

liquorish   See **lickerish.**

literal (LIT uh ruhl) *n*. In its common function as an adjective, *literal* is hardly an obscure word. A *literal translation* is a "word-for-word translation." The *literal meaning* of a word is its "primary or strict meaning," as opposed to its figurative or metaphorical sense. Thus, *thunder* is the loud, explosive noise resulting from the expansion of air heated by lightning; that is its *literal* meaning. But the *thunder* of hoofs or of applause has nothing to do with this meteorological phenomenon; there, *thunder* is used in its figurative sense of a resounding noise like the one associated with lightning. But *literal* has another, entirely distinct use as a noun. A *literal* is a "misprint of a letter in type or writing," the kind proofreaders are supposed to ferret out when they *reed* a *manuescript*. This is a usage that appears more often in British than American English. In either sense, *literal* comes, via Late Latin *litteralis*, from Latin *littera* (letter of the alphabet; in the plural, *litterae*, an epistle, or "letters" in the sense of "literature").

lithodipyra (lith oh duh PEYE ruh) *n*. In 1769 the Coade family took over a factory in Lambeth, a borough of South London, where a type of artificial stone had been made and continued to be made until about 1837. They gave it the name *lithodipyra*, forming the word from *litho-*, the combining form of Greek *lithos* (stone), plus *di-*, the combining form of *dis* (twice), plus *pyr* (fire): stone twice fired. This was the process of manufacture of the artificial stone made in that factory, which was also called *Coade Stone*. The manufacturer claimed that the artificial stone was more resistant to both heat and frost than natural stone. The product was used quite extensively for monuments, statues and fancy stone work in general. The firm advertised in 1778: "Coade's *lithodipyra* or artificial stone manufactory. For all kinds of statues, capitals, vases, tombs, coats of arms, & architectural ornaments &c. &c." A monument to Edward Wortley Montagu (d. 1761), the ambassador to Turkey and husband of the English writer Lady Mary Wortley, is in the cloisters of Westminster Abbey. Friends who have have seen the statue say that it is in excellent condition and looks like natural stone. The name *lithodipyra* attests to some knowledge of classical Greek on the part of the Coade family, an attribute far more common in those days than would be the case today.

lithonthryptic   See **lithotrity.**

lithontripist   See **lithotrity.**

lithontriptic   See **lithotrity.**

lithontriptor   See **lithotrity.**

lithotripist   See **lithotrity.**

lithotripsy   See **lithotrity.**

lithotripter   See **lithotrity.**

lithotriptic   See **lithotrity.**

lithotriptor   See **lithotrity.**

lithotrite   See **lithotrity.**

lithotritic   See **lithotrity.**

lithotritist   See **lithotrity.**

lithotritize   See **lithotrity.**

lithotritor   See **lithotrity.**

lithotrity (lith OT rih tee), also **lithotripsy** (LITH oh trip see) *n*. These nouns are alternative terms for the surgical operation of crushing stones in the bladder into particles small enough to be passed through the urethra. *Lithotrity* is formed of the Greek noun *lithos* (stone) plus *tritus*, the past participle of the Latin verb *terere* (to rub, wear away), thus forming a hybrid word, one formed from elements taken from different languages. *Lithotripsy* comes from the same *lithos* plus Greek *tripsis* (rubbing). The surgical instrument used in this operation has a variety of names, formed from the above sources: *lithotrite* (LITH oh trite), *lithotritor* (lith oh TREYE tuhr), *lithotriptor* (lith oh TRIP tuhr) and *lithontriptor* (lith on TRIP tuhr; *lithon* is the genitive plural of *lithos*). The adjectives are *lithotritic* (lith oh TRIT ik), *lithotriptic* (lith oh TRIP tik), *lithontriptic* (lith on TRIP tik) and *lithonthryptic* (lith on THRIP tik; *thryptika* means "breakers," related to *thryptein*, to shatter). All four adjectives are also used as substantives denoting medicines that produce the same result. To *lithotritize* (lith OT ruh tize) a patient is to perform the operation on him or her. *Lithotritist* (lith OT rih tist), *lithotripist* (lith oh TRIP ist) and *lithontripist* (lith on TRIP ist), as you might predict, are all terms for the surgeon performing the operation. Now that we have gone into all those variations relating to a surgical procedure practiced since the 19th century, we must introduce the term *lithotripter* (note the *e*), an instrument currently in use for reducing kidney stones to tiny particles, using shock waves instead of resorting to surgery to produce the same result. The derivation is the same as that of *lithotriptor* (note the final *o*), the vowel being changed merely to distinguish between the old surgical device and the new technique.

litotes (LEYED uh teez, LID-, leye TOHD eez, and some authorites prefer *t* to *d* in all cases) *n. Litotes*, however you choose to pronounce it, is one of the many kinds of figures of speech, i.e., expressive or fanciful forms of language using words in other than their literal sense, as in "apple of his eye," "a horse of a different color," "a different kettle of fish," and "forever chasing rainbows." There are many different kinds of *tropes* as such figures are called. In previous books I have dealt with some of them: In *1000 Most Important Words* I discussed *euphemism, hyperbole, metaphor* and *simile*; in *1000 Most Challenging Words*, *hyperbaton, metonymy* and *synecdoche*. Now comes *litotes*, meaning an "understatement, especially one in which an affirmative is expressed by the negative of its contrary" (the opposite of *hyperbole* or exaggeration). Examples: *Not bad*, meaning "very good"; *not easy*, for "very difficult." The British use their own brand of *litotes*: *not half*, which is discussed in my *British English A to Zed*, from which I quote: " … In describing the boss's reaction when he came in and found everybody out to lunch, a porter might say, 'He *didn't half* blow up,' meaning that he did blow up about as completely as possible. In other words, *not half* is used ironically, meaning 'not half—but totally.'" *Litotes* was taken, via New Latin, from the Greek, where it was a diminutive of *litos* (simple, plain, meager). It might be said that some of the discussion in this book is *not at all brief*.

locofoco (loh koh FOH koh) *n.* This peculiar concoction appears to have been fashioned from the *loco-* of *locomotive* (under the mistaken notion that *locomotive* meant "self-propelled") plus a rhyming corruption of the Italian word *fuoco* (fire). Says the *O.E.D.*: " … the inventor would hardly think of Latin *focus* (hearth), which is the source of the modern Roman word for 'fire.'" Whatever the source, the word is the name of a match or cigar invented in the 19th century which could be ignited by being rubbed against any rough surface. It was described in the Springfield, Massachusets, *Union* as "a decided improvement over the lucifers," matches tipped with antimony sulfide and potassium chloride, which could be ignited by friction against a hard surface. But now comes the amusing part: *Locofoco*, usually capitalized, became the name of the "Equal Rights" or radical section of the American Democratic Party as a result of an event at a meeting on October 22, 1835, of New York City Democrats.

The radical members were forewarned of a plot by the opposition to break up the meeting by putting out the lights; they came armed with *locofoco* matches and candles and thus foiled the plot. This happened at Tammany Hall, and immediately after the event the *Courier and Examiner*, a Whig newspaper, and the *Times*, a Democratic journal, gave the name *"Locofoco Party"* to the radicals, and the label soon thereafter was applied to the whole Democratic party. This is, of course, fairly ancient American political history, but one must be fond of words that come to designate things as disparate as self-igniting matches (or cigars) and political parties.

longanimity (long uh NIM uh tee) *n.* This word denotes patience, fortitude, forbearance and especially the long-suffering endurance of hardship. The adjective that describes one exhibiting such qualities is *longanimous* (long AN uh muhs), and that is surely an apt description of Job in his hardship and patience. The derivation is from Late Latin *longanimitas*, built on Latin *longus* (long) and *animus* (mind, spirit, soul). Another word involving *animus* is *parvanimity* (pahr van IM it ee), meaning "meanness," the quality of having a little or ignoble mind or spirit, and this word involves Latin *parvus* (little). *Parvanimity* is obviously the antithesis of the more familiar quality of mind known as *magnanimity*, but nowhere do I find a listing of *"parvanimous"* as the antithesis of *magnanimous*. Nonetheless, I hereby coin the adjective *parvanimous* and without publishing their names, hereby confer it upon several people I know.

longanimous   See **longanimity.**

lorimer (LAWR ih mur) also **loriner** (LAWR ih nur) *n.* We start with Latin *lorum* (thong, strap), then via Late Latin *loramentum* (harness) proceed to Old French *loremier*, French *lormier* (from obsolete French *lorain*, the straps, often studded with metal or gems, that were used in the harness and trappings of a horse), and arrive, finally, at *lorimer*, "one who makes metal parts of horse harnesses," like bits, metal mountings for bridles, spurs and, more generally, small ironware and works of wrought iron. (Those who specialize in the making of spurs are known as *spurriers*.) People don't commonly speak of *lorimers* by that name today, and it persists only in the title of one of the livery companies. And what are livery companies? They are the descendants of the old city of London craft guilds. (The City of London, presided over by the Lord Mayor, and sometimes known as the "square mile," is the financial district of London.) The name *livery company* derives from the fact that their members used to wear distinctive livery, i.e. uniforms, on special occasions. These companies date back to the early 14th century. I have attended a number of annual livery company dinners, very formal affairs involving evening dress, huge dinners, speeches and loving cups—large drinking vessels with two or more handles, unhygienically passed around at banquets. There are 12 "great companies" and more than 70 "lesser companies." Many of them still maintain halls in the City and contribute to charities, almshouses and schools. The *Lorimers'* Company is one of the lesser category. John Holland wrote a book entitled *A Treatise on the Progressive Improvement and Present State of the Manufacture in Metal* (1833) in which he informs us that "The manufacture of all the metallic parts of horse furniture was carried on ... by artisans, incorporated under the denomination of *loriners* and *spurriers*." (Note the alternative spelling *loriners*.) This was the *Company of Lorimers*.

lulab   See **ethrog.**

lulal   See **ethrog.**

lulov   See **ethrog.**

lumpectomy (lump EK tuh mee) *n*. This quite unpleasant-sounding medical term for the excision of a lump from the body, usually involving the female breast, is a horrible example of a hybrid word, i.e., one built of components taken from different languages. (*Hybrid* itself comes from the Latin *hybrida*, a variant of *hibrida*, and applies to anything composed of elements from heterogeneous sources, like the offspring of animals or plants of different species, or persons whose parents come from different ethnic groups, or words like *lumpectomy*.) Hybrid words are unpopular among linguistic purists, who commonly offer *television* as an example, *tele-* being of Greek origin (*tele*, far) and *vision* of Latin origin (*visio*, view). In the case of *lumpectomy*, we have *lump-*, from Middle English *lumpe*, and believed to be cognate with Early Dutch *lompe* (piece) and certain Scandinavian words, while *-ectomy* is a combining form meaning "excision," taken from New Latin *-ectomia*, based on Greek *ek* (out of) plus *-tomos* (cutting). I have no objection to hybrids, whether in the animal world (I love mules), the plant world (I am a hybrid rose fancier) or the world of language, provided that the result has a pleasant sound. Would all-Latin *proculvision* or all-Greek *teleopsis* roll off the tongue more smoothly than good old *television*? But *lumpectomy*? No, especially when *tylectomy* (*tulos*, Greek for "lump") might fill the bill. Let's excise the *lump-* from *lumpectomy* and fill the space with *tyl-*.

lungi, also **lungyi, longye** (LOON gee, -jee) *n*. From the Hindu word, which in turn came from Persian, a *lungi* is a type of cloth, usually cotton, used for such articles of attire as sarongs, skirts and turbans, as seen especially in India, Pakistan and Burma. In India it also has the special meaning of a piece of cotton cloth between two and three yards long, wrapped around the waist several times and worn as a loincloth. It lends a particular grace to the body that somehow cannot be imitated by Western people. Strangely, on a Western man or woman, no matter how young, slim and graceful, it just doesn't look right; in fact, it looks conspicuously wrong. *Lungis* have changed over the years. In 1634 Sir Thomas Herbert (*A Relation of Some Yeares Travaile Begunne Anno 1626,* *into Afrique and the Greater Asia*) described it in these terms: "A *lung* to conceale their privy members." Not long thereafter, in a 1662 travel book that included a translation of "*the travels of J.A. de Mandelslo from Persia into the East-Indies,*" John Davies of Kidwelly wrote of "Some Common-cloaths ... of those kinds which are commonly called ... *Longis* ... &c." In 1698 John Fryer (*A New Account of East India and Persia*) wrote: "The Peer as well as Peasant, wrapping only a *Lunga* about his middle ... " and (not quite consistent about his spelling—or was it the printer?) a little later in the same book wrote: "The Men and Women came down together to wash, having *Lungies* about their wastes only." Things got somewhat more elaborate by 1727 when, in *New Account of the East Indies*, Alexander Hamilton wrote: "His Dress was only a Silk *Lungie* or Scarf made fast by a Girdle of Gold Plate, about his Middle." Silk, mind you! And by 1901 an item in the *Daily News* (London) told of "Indian soldiers ... wearing *lungis* of beautifully woven silk." The *lungi* hangs down only to the knee, leaving the legs exposed, and presents a much neater appearance than the *dhoti*, the long loincloth worn by Hindu men. As for Hindu ladies, I'll take the sari any day.

lycanthropy   See **zoanthropy.**

macaronic   See **swasivious.**

macroscian (ma KROH shee uhn) *adj., n.* As an adjective, this word describes anyone or anything casting a long shadow. It comes from the Greek *makroskios*, built of *makro-*, the combining form of *makros* (long) and *skia* (shadow). As a noun, it means (according to the *O.E.D.*) "one having a long shadow, an inhabitant of the polar regions." See **amphiscian**, where I discuss *periscian* and define it as "one who resides in a polar circle, whose shadow moves around him in a complete circle on those days on which the sun does not set." Here we have a bit of a conflict, i.e., between *macroscian* and *periscian*, unless it be the case that the *periscian*'s shadow not only moves around him but is also a long one. Osbert Sitwell used *macroscian* metaphorically in the expression "that *macroscian* day which I had dreaded for so long," apparently a day far ahead on which something dire was bound to happen. *W III* tells us that *macroscian* has to do with long shadows but is silent on the matter of polar regions. Under *macroscian*, the kindly *O.E.D.* refers us to the entry *antiscian*, an adjective pertaining to the *antiscii*, who are those who dwell on the same meridian but on opposite sides of the equator, with the result that their shadows at noon fall in opposite directions. (The derivation of *antiscian* is surely obvious.) Better study this discussion together with that covering **amphiscian** to get the whole thrilling story.

macroscopic (mak ruh SKOP ik) *adj.* You ought to be able to figure this one out, but you never can tell. It's really quite simple: Since *microscopic* is an everyday word whose everyday meaning is "tiny," literally, "so tiny that you can't see it without the use of a microscope," but loosely just "very small," *macroscopic* is an antonym whose meaning is what you might expect: "large enough to be visible to the naked eye." It has a synonym, *megascopic*, which happens to be used especially in the study of rocks, and denotes those whose physical features are visible to the unaided eye. Why so? Nobody knows, as far as my pumping of geologists could determine. Anyway, it should be predictable that the *micro-* in *microscopic* is the combining form of Greek *mikros* (small) and that the *macro-* in *macroscopic* bears the same relationship to Greek *makros* (long). As for *megascopic*, we are all too dismally familiar with the prefix *mega-*, the combining form of Greek *megas* (large, great), from the terrifying word *megaton*, which has to do with the destructive force of the H-bomb. (A megaton—pay attention, class—is an "explosive force equivalent to that of a million tons of TNT.") All of these *-scopic* words make use of the combining form of the Greek verb *skopein* (to look at). The *-ton* in *megaton* is just plain old *ton*, from Middle English *tonne*, so that *megaton* is one of those hybrid words (words composed of elements drawn from different languages, like *television*) that outrage linguistic purists. (Television outrages me for other reasons as well.)

malapert (MAL uh purt) *adj.* A *malapert* person is "impudent, bold, saucy, forward, presumptuous"—quite a collection of unpleasant traits. In Old French, it meant "unskillful," based on *mal*, from Latin *malus* (bad) plus *appert* (a modification of *espert*, from Latin *expertus*, "tested, approved, experienced," but understood in English as if *apert*, old French for "open, outspoken," from Latin *apertus*, frank, straightforward). Shakespeare liked the word. In *Twelfth Night*, Act IV, Scene 1, Sir Toby Belch and Sebastian are having it out. Says Sebastian: "If thou dar'st me further, draw thy sword." Sir Toby answers: "What, what! Nay then, I must have an ounce or two of this *malapert* blood from you." (*Draws.*) In Act V, Scene 5 of *Henry VI, Part 3*, George, Duke of Clarence, chides Prince Edward: "Untutor'd lad, thou are too *malapert*." Queen Margaret, in Act I, Scene 3 of *Richard III*, tells Dorset: "Peace! Master marquess, you are *malapert* ... " In each case, it was impudence that was being checked. In Scott's *The Bethrothed* (1825), a lass is told: "You are too *malapert* for a young maiden." Ben Jonson used the word as an adverb in *Epicaene: or the Silent Woman* (1609): "It angred me to the soule, to heare hem beginne to talk so *malapert*." Steele, in *The Tattler* (1709), used it as a noun: "The *Malapert* knew well enough I laughed at her." In his *Comedies of Terence Translated into Blank Verse* (1765), George Colman (the elder) made the same use of the word: "Away, you *malapert*! Your forwardness/Had well nigh ruined me." However the word is used, the person in question obviously deserves to be taken down a peg or two.

malison   See **catmalison.**

malversation (mal vur SAY shuhn) *n.* The general meaning of this word is "breach of trust in public office, or in any position of trust; corrupt administration," details of which have been filling many a news column these troubled days (but wasn't it always thus?). According to all the dictionaries I have consulted, the term covers just about every aspect of misbehavior (extortion, bribery, embezzlement, misappropriation, disloyalty) in positions of public or private trust. The word was taken over intact from the French, where it appears to mean "peculation" or "embezzlement" generally, with no particular reference to public office or trust. The French took it from two Latin words: *male* (badly) and *versatus*, the past participle of *versare* (to keep turning about, twist around), whose passive form, *versari*, means "to behave, keep busy, occupy oneself." *Versare* is itself an interesting word, in that it is the frequentative of *vertere* (to turn). And what, pray, is a frequentative? As explained in my *1000 Most Challenging Words*, a *frequentative* is a verb that "serves to express the frequent repetition" of an action covered by another verb. In other words, to *versare* (as it were) is to *vertere* (as it were) repetitiously, i.e., to keep on *vertere*-ing. Even the innocent-sounding verb *vertere* itself had a sinister extended meaning as used by Cicero, in the expression *vertere ad se* (to turn [something] to oneself; in other, more direct, words, to appropriate, or in less delicate terms, to steal, swipe, snitch or pinch [somebody else's property]). If you keep doing that you qualify for the frequentative, and jail.

Manichaean (man ih KEE uhn) *adj., n.* This is a somewhat overworked, voguish, little understood and both loosely and improperly applied adjective and noun that stem from the Persian religious teacher Manichaios, also known as Mani and Manes (c. 215–275), who began his teaching c. 240. Properly, this word applies to his doctrine holding that the world was controlled by two antagonistic powers, Good (light, God and the spirit) and Evil (darkness, Satan or chaos and the body.) Only through total asceticism could the pure spirit be freed from physical sensuality. He claimed that Jesus Christ had been sent into the world to banish darkness and restore light (i.e., to do away with evil and make goodness triumphant), but that his apostles had perverted that doctrine and he, Manicaios, had been sent to Earth as the Paraclete (the intercessor—a term applied to the Holy Ghost) to set matters right. Manichaeism influenced many Christian sects (St. Augustine was a Manichaean for nine years) and was denounced as a heresy, though it survived into the 13th century in Asia and elsewhere. In his "On Language" column in the *New York Times* of June 12, 1988, William Safire had much to say about the unrestrained and oversimplified use of *Manichaean* by American political pundits in phrases like "an unending *Manichaean* East-West death struggle," "a *Manichaean* view of the world that he [Nixon] sees as divided between the bad Soviet Union and the good United States" and "Reagan's *Manichaean* division of the world into the Good and Evil Empires." "Whence," asks Safire, "this voguish evocation of an obscure figure fogbound in the mists of history?" (Admirable Safirian evocative eloquence, if I may say so!) He quotes William F. Gavin as follows: "We all know that politicians don't have a clue about the esoteric complexities of *Manichaean* theology ... Accusing a politician of harboring a *Manichaean* view of the world is a shorthand way of saying this poor chucklehead lacks sophistication, is ignorant of nuances, and doesn't know—yokel that he is—that there is no black or white, but only shades of gray." Gavin suggests " ... a moratorium on applying theological labels to political figures who, poor souls (so to speak), have enough trouble with ordinary language ... " Amen.

maniple   See **phelonion.**

manticore (MAN tih kor) *n.* This is the name of a mythical beast, part lion, part scorpion, with the head of a man. Also in the form *manticora*, the word comes, via Latin *manticora*, from Greek *mantichoras*, apparently an erroneous reading of *marti(o)choras*, an old Persian word for "man eater." In some versions, the beast is equipped as well with porcupine's quills, and in heraldry, with dragon's feet and spiral horns: however you look at it, a complex and terrifying beast. In *The Water Babies*, the English novelist and clergyman Charles Kingsley writes of "unicorns, firedrakes, *manticoras*." A *firedrake*, in Germanic mythology, was a fiery dragon; in *Beowulf*, we read of "fyr-draca," and in *Hereward the Wake* the same Kingsley wrote: "He expected the enchanter to enter upon a *fire drake*." Obviously, Kingsley liked mythical beasts, especially *firedrakes*, and why not?

manualiter   See **pedaliter.**

mast   See **pannage.**

matrass (MA truhs) *n.* This word, pronounced, as you can see, just like the *mattress* of a bed, has two distinct meanings. The principal one is a "glass flask with a round or oval body and a long neck, once used to dissolve substances by heating the bottle, or for distilling." The other meaning is "bolt" or "bolt head," also called "quarrel," a short, thick, square- or blunt-headed arrow to be shot from a crossbow. (The strange use of *quarrel* in this connection derives from Old French *quar(r)el*, which the *C.O.D.* relates to a conjectural Romanic noun *quadrellus*, diminutive of Late Latin *quadrus*, square.) *W III* gives only the first definition but adds "—also called *bolt head*." The *O.E.D.* gives both definitions, "quarrel or bolt for the cross-bow" and one similar to the first one given above (the glass vessel with a long neck ...) and adds the note: "By some considered to be a transferred use of *matrass* [in its meaning of 'bolt' or 'quarrel' to be shot from a crossbow] with reference to the shape of the vessel." Other possible derivations are suggested, but I like the "transferred use" bit, which goes a long way to explain how one word, which sounds like a bed mattress but isn't one, can have two such wildly disparate meanings. The byways and back alleys of etymology never cease to amuse and bemuse. By the way, a special type of crossbow is the *arbalest* (AR buh luhst), which had a steel bow instead of a string. It was used in medieval times as a weapon and was capable of shooting balls and stones as well as quarrels. This word was derived from the *ar-* of Latin *arcus* (bow) plus Latin *ballista*, a Roman military device for projecting large stones and the source of our term *ballistics*.

matroclinous (mat roh KLEYE nuhs), also **matroclinal** (mat roh KLEYE nuhl), **matroclinic** (mat roh KLIN ik) *adj.* All of these forms mean the same thing (in the field of genetics, not the inheritance of worldly goods): "inherited from the mother or the maternal line." The derivation is from either Latin or Doric Greek *mater* plus Greek suffix *-klines* (leaning), from the verb *klinein* (to lean) or Latin *clinare* (to lean). In any event, put the Latin and Greek elements together; don't mix them and get a hybrid word like *television*, in which the prefix *tele-* is from the Greek and the rest is from the Latin. As you might expect, dad is not neglected, for we have as well *patro-* words matching those *matro-* forms listed above, with the derivation based on Latin or Greek *pater* and the same suffixes. In the case of both *matro-* and *patro-* types, we also have the words *matrocliny* and *patrocliny*, each accented on the third syllable, *-KLEYE-*, and denoting, respectively, resemblance to mother or dear old dad.

matrocliny   See **matroclinous**.

mazer   See **hanap**.

megascopic   See **macroscopic**.

melisma (muh LIZ muh) *n.* The original meaning of *melisma* was "song, melody, air." Grove's *Dictionary of Music* excludes from its definition "recitative or any passage of purely declamatory nature," and says that it is not entirely correct to use *melisma* in the sense of "fioritura" (florid musical embellishment) or "cadenza" (a parenthetic flourish that interrupts an aria or other solo, usually performed by the soloist toward the end of a concerto, sometimes improvised and always technically brilliant regardless of authorship). *Melisma* was taken intact from the Greek meaning "song" or "melody," and is based on the verb *melodein* (to sing), from *melos* (song), which plays a part in the etymology of *melody*: *melos*, plus *-oidia*, from *adein* (to sing; the Greeks had more than *a* word for it). But usage changes: *W II* included in its definition "a grace or melodic embellishment ... less correctly, a cadenza," and *W III* extended its definition to include "melodic embellishment or ornamentation" and "cadenza," as well as a "group of notes or tones sung to one syllable in plainsong," defining *plainsong* in various ways, including "nonmetrical monophonic chant ... used today in some liturgical churches," viz., *Glo-o-o-ria in Excelsis Deo*, the Christmas hymn. Grove based its definition on the Greek, but, based on further investigation and discussions with a number of musician acquaintances, it is safe to say that *melisma* now has as its principal meaning "musical ornament," or "ornamental melody," an affectation particularly common in the Renaissance/Baroque transition, as heard often in the music of Monteverdi (1567–1643) and his contemporaries. The *C.O.D.* cautiously steers a middle course, content with "melodic music or tune." The Grove definition is understandable in view of the etymological background of the word, but is now too limited in view of the extensions that have crept in over the years.

mendacious   See **mendicity.**

mendacity   See **mendicity.**

mendicancy   See **mendicity.**

mendicity (men DIS ih tee), also **mendicancy** (MEN dih kan see) *n*. Both terms mean "beggary," i.e., the state of being a begger or *mendicant* (MEN dih kuhnt), or the practice of begging. *Mendicity* is from Latin *mendicitas* (beggary), *mendicancy* from Latin *mendicans*, the present participle of *mendicare* (to beg), which is also the basis of *mendicity*. One must avoid confusing these words with *mendacity* (men DAS ih tee), which is "untruthfulness," from Late Latin *mendacitas* (falsehood), a synonym of *mendacium*. The sweet little Latin noun *mendaciunculum* (a little lie) is the sort we might call a "fib" or in certain cases a "white lie," as when you tell Aunt Elizabeth that her horrible new hat suits her beautifully. These *mendac-* words go back to Latin *mendac-*, the stem of *mendax* (lying, untruthful), which gave us *mendacious*, a rather high-class way of saying "lying, false" when you want to seem less blunt, though it all amounts to the same thing. What you say is either true or false; a little bit false is like a little bit pregnant: you is or you ain't. These words should not be all that obscure, but I thought it well to include them to make sure you never confuse them. Archbishop Frederick Temple (1821–1902) certainly knew the difference when he observed, at a meeting of the Ecclesiastical Commissioners (as quoted in *Years of Endeavor* by Sir George Leveson Gower, 1902): "There is a certain class of clergyman whose *mendicity* is only equalled by their *mendacity*."

menhir (MEN heer) *n*. A *menhir* is an "ancient (usually prehistoric) single standing stone or monolith." The word comes from two Breton words: *men* (stone) and *hir* (long). *Men* has kindred words in Welsh (*maen*) and Cornish (*men* with a long *e* or *medn*), and *hir* has one in Old Irish (*sir* with a long *i*). *Menhirs*, the *O.E.D.* tells us, have been discovered in "various parts of Europe, and also in Africa and Asia." In my *1000 Most Challenging Words*, I deal with *dolmens*, which are Celtic prehistoric structures generally considered to be tombs, constructed of a capstone laid on top of two or more large vertical stones, and *cromlechs*, their Welsh counterparts (though that term applies equally to any circular group of large upright stones lacking a capstone). There are many *dolmens* and *cromlechs* in Britain. Although the *C.O.D.* omits "Britain" specifically as one of the locations where *menhirs* are found, a 1904 book by Sir Bertram C.A. Windle, *Remains of the Prehistoric Age in England*, tells us that "The Dartmoor row begins with a circle and ends with a *menhir*." Apparently the *O.E.D.* must have meant to include *England* in the term "Europe" in its list of *menhir* locations, thus anticipating England's actual participation in the E.C. by some years.

menology (min OH luh jee) *n.* This is the name given to a calendar of saints' days, especially of the Greek Church, giving biographies of the saints. The word comes via Late Latin *menologium* from Greek *menologion*, formed from *men* (month) plus *logos* (account). Philemon Holland, in his 1610 translation of William Camden's 1586 *Britannia siue Florentissimorum Regnorum, Angliae, Scotiae, Hiberniae, Chorographia Descriptio*, entitled in English *Britain, or a Chorographicall Description of England, Scotland, and Ireland*, wrote: "They report … upon the authority … of the Greeks *Menology*, that St. Peter came hither." The term has been applied to an Anglo-Saxon metrical church calendar that was first printed in 1705. The word *menologium* (min uh LOH juhm) is often substituted for *menology*. A *menologist* (muh NOL uh jist) is a compiler of a *menology*.

merchet, also **marchet** (MAHR chuht), **marcheta** (mahr KAY duh) *n.* In feudal times, all sorts of restrictions were placed by the overlord upon the vassal's freedom to act. One of these was the limitation of the vassal's right to marry off a son or daughter, especially when the marriage was to one outside the overlord's jurisdiction. In addition, the vassal had to contend with the lord's *droit du seigneur* (right of the lord), also known as the *jus primae noctis* (right of the first night), a handy little arrangement that gave the lord the right to deflower the bride of a vassal or the vassal's daughter in prospect of her wedding. The *merchet* was a "fine imposed upon the vassal for marrying off his child or for waiving the *droit du seigneur*." One wonders what the lord's wife thought about that *droit* or *jus*, but that's just a passing thought. What the vassal thought about it didn't matter, and customs being customs, especially in those days, he probably took it in his stride, as did his womenfolk—and in any case nobody could do anything about it. The derivation is, via Middle English and Anglo-French, from Latin *mercatus* (trade). Some trade!

merdivorous (mur DIV uh ruhs) *adj.* When I looked into *RH* to make sure of the meaning of this word, I found the definition "coprophagous," and the same thing happened when I peeked into *W III*. Why such delicacy, since when one gets to *coprophagous* (koh PROF uh guhs), one's educated guess is confirmed: Both mean "dung-eating," *merdivorous* from Latin *merda* (dung, excrement) plus *vorare* (to eat, devour, swallow greedily), and *coprophagous* from Greek *kopros* (dung) plus *phagein* (to eat, devour). In *RH*, the definition is qualified by the phrase "as certain beetles," and the *O.E.D.* skips the Greek equivalent and is content with "(said of insects)," but *WIII* tells the awful truth under the related entry *coprophagy*: "the ... eating of dung ... that is normal behavior among many insects, birds and other animals but in man [aha!] is a symptom of some forms of insanity." Why didn't these fine lexicons come out with an English definition in the first place, instead of giving us the term derived from Greek, and why didn't *RH* go on to inform us of the human aberration? Let's not dwell on this esoteric subject; nothing about the human race surprises me; *de gustibus* etc. But this little exercise in etymology shows us that if you knew your Latin stems you needn't have wandered into Greek territory—and vice versa, or as the old Greeks said it, *enantios, empalin, toumpalin* or *anapalin*. Did I hear anyone say, "The Greeks had *four* words for it?"

merry-andrewize   See **pantropragmatic.**

metacism   See **mytacism.**

metaplasm (MET uh plaz'm) *n*. Apart from a special use in biology not relevant here, this word has a number of applications in rhetoric and grammar. It comes from Greek *metaplasmos*, defined by *LS* as "the formation of noun cases or verb tenses from stems that vary from those of the nominative or present," as the case may be. An example is found in the Latin verb *fero*: infinitive *ferre*, perfect tense *tuli*, supine *latum*. (Don't worry about irregular Latin verbs: This example is given simply to support dear friends *LS*.) *Metaplasmos* was built from the prefix *meta-*, which has lots of meanings and most often denotes change, and *plasma* (something molded), akin to the verb *plassein* (to form, mold). In rhetoric, *metaplasm* is the "shifting of the position of words from their normal order," also known as *hyperbaton* (heye PUR buh ton), fully discussed in my *1000 Most Challenging Words*, where I give examples, to which I now add *By Love Possessed* and *God Almighty*. In grammar, *metaplasm* is the "changing of a word by adding, extracting or transposing letters or syllables." The erroneous insertion of a sound is also known as *anaptyxis* (an ap TIK sis), applying only to vowels—both terms relating to insertions within the mutilated word—and *paragoge* (PARE uh goj') covering additions of sounds at the end of mangled words. In the case of the transposition of sounds in words, we find the synonym *metathesis* (me TA thuh sis). I shouldn't belabor the point, but *epenthesis, anaptyxis, paragoge* and *metathesis* are all dealt with in that same previous work of mine, complete with examples. If you've exhausted your funds by buying this book, you can get the other one out of the library. (Is that okay with you, Dear Publisher?) (Ed. note: Certainly.)

metathesis   See **metaplasm.**

metaxy (meh TAK see) *n. Metaxu* is Greek for "between." The Greek upsilon can be either *u* or *y* in transliteration, so when I found the word in Professor Elizabeth Dipple's profound work on the novels of Iris Murdoch (*Iris Murdoch, Work for the Spirit*, the University of Chicago Press, Chicago, and Methuen & Co. Ltd., London, 1982; see also a reference to that book in **alieniloquy**) and came to the conclusion that *metaxy* meant "betweenness," or "indecision" or "confusion," I thought that Dipple had coined the word and wrote her to that effect. But she hadn't, she told me. I quote from her letter: "*Metaxy* is a word used by the political philosopher Eric Voegelin in his *Anamnesis* and elsewhere. Obviously a Platonic realist, Voegelin sees humankind existing in an inescapable middle place between materiality and spirituality, and he names this condition *metaxy*." As to Voegelin's title *Anamnesis*, that word is dealt with in my *1000 Most Challenging Words*, where I say, inter alia: "In Platonic terms, it is the recollection of a previous existence. *Anamnesis* comes intact from the Greek, where it means 'remembrance' generally ... Anything that recalls to mind earlier experiences may be described as *anamnestic*." *CH* includes in its definition "the recollection of the Platonic pre-existence." Please don't jump to the conclusion that I believe in transmigration or previous existences; once is enough!

misapodysis   See **tyrosemiophile**.

Misnagid   See **Mitnagged**.

Mitnagged (mit nah GED), also **Misnagid** (mis NAH guhd) *n.* These terms are taken from Hebrew *mithnagged* and Yiddish *misnaged*, meaning "opposing, opponent," and denote an Orthodox Jew opposed to the creed of the Chasidim or Hasidim. The latter is a Jewish sect founded in Poland about 1750 by Rabbi Israel ben Eliezer to revive the practices of the earlier Chasid sect, itself founded about the third century B.C. to counter Hellenistic influences. They were then known as the *Assideans* or *Hasideans* and were devoted to strict observance of purification and adherence to Hebrew law. (*Chasid* is pronouced CHA sid, the plural cha SEED im; the *ch* being pronounced as in German. *Hasid* is a common alternate spelling.) They are found in many countries and are conspicuous for their costumes and hair styles. The usual attire is a broad-brimmed black hat and a long black cloak; the hair style is characterized by long, curled sideburns known in Yiddish as *peyes* (PAY uhs, from Polish *pejsy*). Today's Chasidim, on the theory that if you're not with us you're against us, apply the term *mitnagged* or *misnagid* to any Jew who is not a Chasid, which is true of the vast majority of Jews.

mixobiosis   See **phylacobiosis**.

mizmaze (MIZ maze) *n. Mizmaze*, a reduplication of *maze* (for a full explanation of *reduplication* see **nid-nod**), means "labyrinth or maze." In John

Harman's translation of Master Beza's *Sermons upon the Three First Chapters of the Canticle of Canticles* (1587) we read: "Solomon ... hath walked us through the whole labyrinth and *mizmaze* of this life." The poet John Davies of Hereford wrote in *The Muses Sacrifice* (1612): "Errors *misse-maze*, where lost is Veritie, / Or blinded so, that still wrong course it takes." Thus far, the examples indicate that the word was used in an abstract sense, rather than to denote a physical maze of the sort one gets lost in at Hampton Court. Again, in the 1624 collection of the *Sermons* of Bishop Miles Smith, the word is found in its figurative sense: "In this distraction, and *miz-maze*, I think the middle-way to be the best way." Bishop Thomas Percy, in his *Reliques of Ancient English Poetry* (1794), uses the word in its literal sense: "On the top of Catharine-hill, Winchester (the usual play-place of the school), was a very perplexed and winding path, running in a very small space over a great deal of ground, called a *Miz-maze*"; but *mizmaze* is usually found in the figurative sense of "confusion, perplexity, bewilderment." An 1875 issue of the *Quarterly Review* speaks of " ... the physico-theological *mizmaze* which ... clouded the perception of those who were following immediately in the wake of Newton." Louisa Parr, in *Adam and Eve* (1880), treats us to this sentence: "I want to be a bit quiet—my head seems all of a *mizmaze* like." In Margaret A. Courtney's *Glossary of Words in Use in Cornwall* (West Cornwall by Miss Courtney; East Cornwall by Thomas Q. Couch), Couch defines *mizmaze* as "bewilderment." It's an unintentionally almost onomatopoeic word for the buzzing that goes on in one's head when in a state of confusion, with a distant accidental cousin in *mishmash* (another reduplicative, this time of *mash*, one of whose meanings is "muddle"). These etymological treasure hunts can leave one in a thorough (the British would say "proper") *mizmaze*.

mizpah (MIZ pah) *n. Mizpah* is the name of the place in ancient Palestine where, according to Gen. 31, 41–49, Jacob and Laban built a cairn, a heap of stones to memorialize their covenant, after they had settled the quarrel between them. Laban said, "This cairn is witness today between you and me." *Mizpah* is Hebrew for "watchtower"; that is why the cairn was named *Mizpah*, "for Laban said, 'The Lord watch between me and thee.'" That word is now used as a term or token of agreement and remembrance, either as an adjective or attributively as a noun, to identify an ornament with the inscription *Mizpah*, given, for example, by a lover to signify remembrance. Hence the term "*Mizpah* ring, bracelet, brooch, etc." H. G. Wells, in *Babes in the Darkling Wood* (1940), uses the expression "*Mizpah*, as they say inside the engagement rings ... Like most English people they thought that was a pledge between two young lovers." An 1898 catalogue of T. Eaton & Co., a jewelry firm, listed the item "*Mizpah* ring." In *Images and Shadows: Part of a Life* (1970) Iris Origo writes: "He gave me the gold Victorian locket—engraved with the word *Mizpah*, 'God watch between us two'—which he had given to his fiancée." I remember a silver brooch worn by my mother bearing the inscription *Mizpah* engraved in Hebrew letters. When I asked her what it meant (this was long after my father's death), she answered something like "I'll never forget (or forsake) you" and said he wore a ring with the same inscription, though I don't remember ever seeing it.

Mizrachi (miz RACH ee—*ch* as in German, e.g., *machen, lachen*, or Scottish, e.g. *loch*) *n*. This is the name of an Israeli religious and political group created in 1902 as the Orthodox wing of the Zionist movement. The group strives to promote traditional Judaism within the Zionist movement and to protect Hebrew fundamentalism against secularization. Many followers of events in Israel are familiar with the *Mizrachi* movement but ignorant of the derivation of the name. *Mizrach*, sometimes spelled *mizrah*, is from Hebrew *mizrah*, meaning "east, the place of sunrise," based on *zarah* (to rise, come forth), and has a number of meanings: "the east," "the direction of Jerusalem," "facing toward Jerusalem in prayer," and more tangibly, a "sacred picture" hung on the eastern wall of a house, i.e., toward Jerusalem; also, the "eastern wall of a synagogue." Israel Zangwill, in *Children of the Ghetto* (1892), writes of " … a crudely-coloured *Mizrach* on the east wall, to indicate the direction towards which the Jew should pray." A 1911 issue of *The Zionist* states: "The *Mizrachi* profess to see in such work [ardent secular Zionism] a danger to orthodox Judaism of which they claim to be the bulwark in Zionism." James Joyce was familiar with *Mizrach* (and just about everything else!); in *Ulysses* we read: "His gaze turned in the direction of *Mizrach*, the east." Though relatively small in numbers, the *Mizrachi* members of the Knesset, under the proportional representation system in Israeli elections, wield disproportionate influence. In the Antwerp home of an ardent *Mizrachi* aunt of mine, I was found reading the *Divine Commedia* in bed one night. (I had majored in Italian literature at Harvard.) "Why," she asked, "do you read a Catholic work when there is so much to find in our Talmud?"

moazogotl (moh aw tsuh GAW duhl) *adj*. This mouthful of an adjective can claim two distinctions: It serves exclusively as a modifier of the noun *cloud*, and it is not to be found in any dictionary that I have come across except *W III* and that includes the *O.E.D.* Well, what is a *moazogotl* cloud, and whence comes this lovely word? A *moazogotl* cloud is a "cloud bank that is created under foehn conditions on the lee side of a mountain." And what, pray, are foehn conditions? *Foehn* shares with *moazagotl* the distinction of appearing in no other dictionary than the same old *W III*, which informs us that it comes to us from Latin *favonius* (warm west wind—related to *fovere*, to warm), via the tortuous route of Vulgar Latin *faonius*, Old High German *phonno* and German *föhn*, in which form it does appear in the *O.E.D.* and its supplement. Fair enough, but what is *foehn*? It is a "warm, dry wind that blows down the side of a mountain" and is like a *chinook*, which is a "warm, dry *foehnlike* wind that blows down the eastern slopes of the Rockies." So back we go from *chinook* to old friend *foehn*, also known as square one. *Moazagotl* and *Chinook* are usually capitalized.

motile   See **geotaxis.**

mousmee, mousmé (MOOHS may) *n.* This comes from the Japanese word *musume* and means "unmarried girl." It is applied especially to a waitress or tea girl and is by no means a disrespectful term of address. Quite the contrary: Henry C. St. John, in *Notes and Sketches from the Wild Coasts of Nipon* (1880), writes of "the gentle kindness and pretty ways of the *mousmees.*" In Pierre Loti's *Madame Chrysanthème*, it means what you would expect: a girl hired as a temporary wife à la *Butterfly*. From what I have been told by those who have traveled in Japan, and from my recollection of the old days in Britain, *mousmee* is close to the obsolescent British slang term *nippy*, a word originally confined to the nimble waitresses at Lyons Corner Houses, a restaurant chain that (alas!) has gone the way of so many cozy institutions, but then became generic for *waitress*. In my *British English, A to Zed* (1987), I observe that "*Nippy* is just about on its way out." One summons a waitress in Germany as *Fräulein*, in France as *mademoiselle*, in Italy as *signorina* and in Spain as *señorita*, but all we can muster is the rather pale *miss*, and that's about all that's left in Britain. I like *mousmee*; it sounds affectionate.

moxa   See **moxibustion.**

moxibustion (moks uh BUS chuhn) *n.* A *moxa* (MOK suh) is a "cone- or cylinder-shaped mass composed of the downy surface of the dried leaves of wormwood, sunflower pith (similar to the white inner skin of an orange) or a similar substance such as absorbent cotton or spider's web," burned on a patient's skin as a counterirritant in the treatment of gout and other ailments. Modeled after *combustion* because of the burning process, *moxibustion* is "cauterization by the application of a burning *moxa.*" *Moxa* is from the Japanese *mokusa*, which is pronounced MOK sah. There is also the synonym *moxocausis* (moks uh KOW suhs), formed by combining *moxa* and the Greek noun *kausis* (burning), akin to *kaein* (to burn). Could there be a better example of a hybrid word than this—the union of a Japanese noun with a Greek one? A July 1965 issue of the *New Scientist* refers to *moxibustion* as "the burning of a herbal [the *h* is sounded in Britain] mixture on part of the body to transfer the site of irritation from one place to another." In an April 1974 issue of *Scientific American*, mention is made of the adoption by the West of "certain traditional [Chinese] techniques: the use of herbal preparations ... and of two related treatments, *moxibustion* and acupuncture." I shuddered at the thought, but my doctor says they both work.

moxocausis   See **moxibustion.**

multipara   See **primipara.**

multiparity   See **primipara.**

multiparous   See **primipara.**

mumpsimus (MUMP sih muhs) *n.* No, this has nothing to do with the infectious disease whose main symptom is the swelling of the parotid and other glands. It is a word taken from an old story about a priest who, in conducting the Mass, always read "quod ore *mumpsimus*" instead of "sumpsimus." The correct Latin expression means "which we have taken into the mouth," *sumpsimus* being the first-person plural perfect of the verb *sumere* (to take, receive). When the old illiterate priest's error was pointed out, he is alleged to have replied, "I will not change my old *mumpsimus* for your new *sumpsimus*." In one version, the old priest referred to his missal, which was incorrectly printed. In another, a fly speck in the missal made the first *s* in *sumpsimus* look like an *m*. In any event, the old man had read it that way for 40 years or more and just wasn't going to go in for any newfangled alterations. In *Impenetrability*, Robert Graves gives *mumpsimus* as an illustration of the coining of new words by simple declaration. In a speech from the throne in 1545, Henry VIII gave *mumpsimus* his blessing as signifying "an erroneous doctrinal view obstinately adhered to," stating: "Some be too stiff in their old *mumpsimus*, others be too busy and curious in their *sumpsimus*." Although *Brewer's Dictionary of Phrase and Fable* gives *mumpsimus* the narrow definition "an established manuscript-reading that, though obviously incorrect, is retained blindly by old-fashioned scholars," modern dictionaries define it variously and much more generally as "an error cherished after exposure; stubborn conservatism; an antiquated person" (*CH*); "one who obstinately adheres to old ways, in spite of the clearest evidence that they are wrong; an ignorant and bigoted opponent of reform; ... an old fogey; ... a traditional custom or notion obstinately adhered to however unreasonable it is shown to be; ... (as a quasi-adjective) stupidly conservative" (*O.E.D.*); "a bigoted adherent to exposed but customary error; a custom or tenet adhered to by a *mumpsimus*" (*W III*). Would anybody agree to coining a Latin verb *mumere* by back formation: *mumo, mumere, mumpsi, mumptum*, from which we derive *mummify* (to preserve)?

mutualism   See **phylacobiosis.**

myrmecoxene   See **symphile.**

mytacism (MITE uh siz'm) *n.* You mightn't think there would be a word denoting the erroneous or excessive use of the letter *m* in writing or of the *m* sound in defective speech, but there it is, in all its glory and obscurity: *mytacism*. *W II* is content to give as its derivation the Greek *mytakismos* but warns us to "cf. *metacism*," which we'll get to in a moment. *W III* omits reference to *metacism* but adds the information that *mytakismos* is "irregular from *my* [*mu*, the Greek letter] plus -*ismos* -ism" (this seems somewhat obscure); it doesn't offer *myism*, which isn't listed in that dictionary (or any other, so far as my explorations indicate), so apparently there ain't no such animal. Let's first get rid of *metacism*, which cannot be found in *W III* but shows up in *W II*, with the pronunciation MET a siz'm and the derivation "Late Latin *metacismus*, from Greek *mytakismos* [same as for *mytacism* in both *W's*]: fondness for the letter *m*," and the alternative meanings "putting a word ending in *m* before one beginning with a vowel—considered an error in Latin prose"; and "pronunciation [in Latin] of a final *m* that precedes a word beginning with a vowel, in which case the *m* should be elided [i.e., not pronounced]." *W II* has the decency to warn us to take a look at *mytacism*. Enough, now (if not too much) of *metacism*. *Mytacism* is one of several cases of **psellism**, but in my comment on that word, defined as "any defect in pronunciation," I include several examples of types of *psellism* but omitted both *mytacism* and *metacism*. I find *mytacism* particularly obscure, expecially because my efforts to find an example of it have thus far met with no success. Any exemplification will be most welcome.

I feel it is time to point out that in transliteration from Greek into English via Latin, the letter *upsilon* (20th in the Greek alphabet) becomes *y*. (Thus, for example, Greek *muthos* is English *myth*; Greek *lura*, English lyre.) As to its form, the *upsilon* in uppercase resembles *Y*, in lowercase *u*.

LS defines *mutakismos* as "fondness for the letter *mu*," and the verb for this mysterious abuse is *mutakizein*, defined as "to be fond of the letter *mu*," with the explanation "formed like *iotakizein*." Going to that verb, one finds it defined (predictably) as "to lay too much stress upon the *iota*," and the next entry is *iotakismos*, "the above fault in pronunciation." In the definition of the verb, examples are given: *Troiia* for *Troia*, *Maiia* for *Maia*. *Iota* is the ninth letter of the Greek alphabet, and the smallest; for this reason it is used in Greek, as well as English, French, Italian and German—possibly also in other languages unfamiliar to me—to mean a "very small bit (of something)." It corresponds to Hebrew *yodh* and is the origin of English *jot* (cf. "jot or tittle" in Matt.5:18). As long as we are discussing *iota*, we might as well (irrelevant though it may be) mention the fourth-century ecclesiastic Arius (d. 336), the founder of Arianism. This doctrine states that God is alone and separate from every created being, while Christ is a created being and so not fully God, though as maker of all other creatures he might be worshiped as a secondary divinity, who assumed a body but not a human soul and thus was neither truly God nor truly man. Arius was excommunicated for his pains. He and his followers (who for a time included a large part of the Church and several Germanic rulers) held that Christ was not of the same nature or essence (*homoousios*, rendered in Latin as *consubstantialis*) as God the Father but only of similar nature (*homoiousios*). The dispute may be compared to that between Trinitarians and Unitarians. It aroused much violence, and some mockery in subsequent ages, at the shedding of blood "for the sake of an *iota*." Arius's doctrine was condemned at the Council of Nicaea in 325, presided over by the Emperor Constantine, who was not yet a Christian. According to William J. Turner, in the winter 1988/89 edition of the magazine *Free Inquiry*, the slight spelling variation between the two Greek words gave rise to the saying "I don't care an *iota*." Maybe, but to me it sounds apocryphal. The use of *iota* in the sense of "jot" is good enough for me. Getting back to more mundane matters, for abuses of the sounds of certain other letters of the alphabet, see **psellism** and **lallation** in this book and *rhotacism* and *pararhotacism* in my *1000 Most Challenging Words*. (I still find myself wondering why some ancient Greeks "were fond of" or "laid too much stress on" *mu*s and *iota*s.) From *iotakismos* we get *iotacism* (excessive use of *i*) and the variant *itacism* used especially for the tendency, which has prevailed in modern Greek, to pronounce several vowels like *i* (English *ee*] instead of with their original value. Come to think of it, a fair number of not-so-good-English-speaking people tend to make excessive use of poor little *i*: cf. mischievious, ancilliary, heinious, municipial.

nasute   See **phylacobiosis.**

niddle-noddle   See **nid-nod.**

nidicolous (nih DIK uh luhs) *adj.* From Latin *nidus* (nest) and *colere* (to inhabit, dwell) we get *nidicolous*, which denotes young birds that linger for some time in the nest. This condition is common to birds whose young are hatched in a state so immature and helpless as to need tender loving care for quite a time. Birds with that habit are known as *altricial* (al TRISH uhl), an adjective derived from Latin *altrix* (female nourisher) and *altor* (male nourisher), both from *altus*, the past participle of *alere* (to nourish). The opposite of *nidicolous* is *nidifugous* (nid DIF yuh guhs), from *nidus* and *fugere* (to flee), an adjective that describes birds that abandon the nest soon after hatching—such as the chicks of chickens and other gallinaceous birds—because they can do without parental care at a very early stage. Such birds are also known as *precocial* (pree KOH shuhl), formed, via Latin *praecox* (early ripening, precocious), from New Latin *precoces*. So, in the avian department, *nidicolous* youngsters are *altricial* and *nidifugous* kiddies are *precocial*, and if you can't resist concocting a limerick whose first line ends with *nidicolous* and whose second or final line terminates in a misspelling of *ridiculous*, go ahead; and remember, there's always *pediculous* (puh DIK yuh luhs), meaning "infested with lice," from Latin *pediculus*, diminutive of *pedis* (louse), a happy coincidence because it can apply to fledglings.

nidifugous   See **nidicolous.**

nid-nod (NID nod) *vb.* To *nid-nod* is "to keep nodding, from drowsiness, boredom or sheer fatigue." This is a reduplicative form, based on *nod*. In *reduplication*, a word formation that occurs quite frequently, the initial element is joined to a rhyming element (as in *helter-skelter, hocus-pocus, hurly-burly* and *mumbo-jumbo*) or a second element in which the vowel changes (as in *fiddle-faddle, flimflam, seesaw, skimble-skamble* and *zigzag*). This occurs in other languages as well: cf. French *zigzag*, German *zickzack*. Robert Burns used *nid-nod* effectively: "We're a' noddin, We're a' noddin, *nid nid noddin* ... at our house at hame." Like *nod*, *nid-nod* may be used transitively, with *head* as the object. Susan Ferrier used *nid-nodding* as a participial adjective in *The Inheritance* (1824), writing of " ... that odd little *nid-nodding* face." The word was used figuratively as a gerund in an 1896 issue of *Blackwell's Magazine*: "The *nid-nodding* of the red rose ... " A related word is *niddle-noddle*, meaning "to nod rapidly or unsteadily back and forth." It, too, may be used transitively, with *head* as the object. This sentence appears in an 1845 issue of *Punch*: "He continually *niddle-noddles* his head like a toy mandarin." Writing about obscure words and reduplicatives in my quiet country study may at times be drudgery, but I much prefer it to the *hustle-bustle* of the big city.

noctivagant (nok TIV uh guhnt) *n., adj.* A *noctivagant* is "one who wanders in the night"; as an adjective, the word applies to any such person—a "night wanderer." It is formed of Latin *noct-*, the stem of *nox* (night) plus *vagant-*, the stem of *vagans*, the present participle of *vagari* (to wander), which gave us *vagabond* and *vagary*. There is a synonym, *noctivagous* (nok TIV uh guhs), formed of *nocti-* plus *vagus* (wandering), which gave us *vague*, but it is used only as an adjective, never as a noun. *The Pageant* (1843) by Francis E. Paget contains this amusing sentence: "Beasts of prey, burglars, and ladies of fashion are the only three kinds of *noctivagous* mammalia." Thomas Adams, in *The Sinner's Passing-Bell; or a Complaint from Heaven of Man's Sins* (1614, reprinted in his *Works*, 1861), wrote: "The lustful sparrows, *noctivagant* adulterers, sit chirping about our houses."

noctivagous   See **noctivagant.**

nolt-tath   See **tath.**

nosocomial (nos oh KOH mee uhl) *adj.* Anything pertaining to a hospital may be described by this adjective, from the Greek *nosokomeion* (hospital), built on *nosos* (disease) plus *komein* (to tend). A *nosocomial* sickness is one originating in a hospital, like the frightening Legionnaires' disease contracted by a number of hospital patients, which has resulted in numerous fatalities. This type of phenomenon brings to mind the adjective *iatrogenic*, with which I deal in my *1000 Most Challenging Words*, in connection with the headword *iatric*. *Iatros* means "physician" in Greek, and the suffix *-genic* means "producing," so that *iatrogenic* describes any illness "produced" by a doctor (wrong treatment, mistaken diagnosis, etc.). This discussion is not intended as a charge leveled against the medical profession or hospitals, but accidents do happen, and they have to have a name.

noyade (nwah YAHD) *n.* Jean Baptiste Carrier was a French revolutionist, a member of the National Convention that proclaimed the Republic on September 22, 1792 and was the governing body of France until October 1795. He was notorious for the brutality with which he carried out the sentences of the revolutionary tribunal in Nantes and was himself guillotined in 1794. His method was *noyade,* wholesale drowning, and the ferocity of the measure was referred to in an 1822 issue of *Blackwell's Magazine:* "They choked their rivers with their *noyades.*" John Adams, in one of his *Familiar Letters,* made a peculiar use of the word in commenting on " ... The *noyade* of the tea in Boston harbor." Thomas Carlyle, in *The French Revolution,* used the word correctly in writing (1837) of "sounds of fusillading and *noyading.*" *Noyade* means "drowning" in French and is based on the verb *noyer* (to drown), which came from the Latin verb *necare* (to kill, put to death), which acquired the sense of "drown" in Late Latin. Carrier's practice on the Loire was to cram boats full of the condemned and then have the plugs pulled. There is no record of anybody's escape by swimming. (The victims were bound together.)

nunatak (NUN uh tak) *n.* This is an Eskimo word for a "rock peak that protrudes above the inland ice of a region." It was first mentioned by the Swedish arctic explorer and geologist Baron Nils Adolf Erik Nordenskjöld (1832–1901), whose work was carried on by his nephew Nils Otto Gustav (1869–1928) and extended to the antarctic regions. An 1877 issue of the *Quarterly Journal of the Geological Society* speaks of *nunataks* in various parts of Greenland. J. D. Whitney, in *Climatic Changes* (1882), describes a *nunatak* rising almost a mile above sea level. Six years later, an article in the *Times* (London) contained this bit of poetic prose: "The '*nunataks*' which rise like skeletons above the frozen waste." A 1900 issue of *Time* spoke of " ... *nunataks*, or ... sea-cliffs, with *talus* beaches here and there." *Talus* (TAY luhs), from Late Latin *talutum,* from Latin *talus* (ankle), is a geological term for a sloping mass of fragments of rock at the foot of a cliff. In *South with Scott* (1921), E. R. G. R. Evans wrote about a *nunatak* 2,800 feet high. The word appears in a number of works of exploration and geology in various regions, including Norway. This Eskimo word is now a respected geological term in our language.

nuppence (NUH pens) *n.* This is British slang for "no money" or "nothing," as in *It's worth nuppence,* or *He's living on nuppence.* The word is fashioned after *tuppence,* on which I comment as follows in my *British English, A to Zed*: "*Twopence* and *twopenny* are pronounced TUPPENCE and TUPPENNY, and are sometimes slangily spelled that way." There have been a number of changes in British coinage in the last 20 years, most notably the decimalization of the currency on February 15, 1971, when shillings were abolished and the pound thenceforth consisted of 100 "new pence." The pound formerly consisted of 240 pence; hence, the new penny was worth 2.4 times as much as the old penny. Nowadays *two pence* is written, "two pence" or "two pee" but the term *tuppence* stays on, without reference to its actual cash value, in the figurative sense of a "trifle." An 1886 issue of *Longman's Magazine* complained: "The Americans can get our books, and do get them, and republish them and give us nothing—that awful minus quantity, *nuppence!*" In 1964 *The Observer* used the expression "Living on *nuppence.*" But even after the old penny became the new penny, or *p.*, the *Times Literary Supplement*, in 1973, contained the sentence: "For the appreciation of the novel, this information matters little more than *nuppence.*" Partridge, in his *Dictionary of Slang and Unconventional English* (7th edition—1970) has the entry: "**nuppence.** No money: from ca. 1885; ob[solete]. Ex *no pence* after *tuppence.*" *Nuppence* was still alive in 1973, but it may well be obsolete now: I had to explain it to an English friend in 1988.

nyctalopia (nik tuh LOH pee uh) *n.* One shouldn't encumber a book of this sort with those weird medical terms for all sorts of rare diseases, but this one hits home, because I suffer from it, and so do many of my coevals. *Nyctalopia* is what is vulgarly known as "night blindness," but the term covers any degree of reduced vision in low light indoors or out. There was a time when … were sadder words e'er spoken? But things could be worse, thanks to Mr. Edison. The term comes intact from New Latin, from Middle Latin, from Latin *nyctalops* (incapable of seeing at twilight), in turn taken intact from Greek, based on the Greek prefix *nyct-*, the combining form of *nyx* (night), plus *alaos* (blind) plus *ops* (eye). *Hemeralopia* (hem uh uh LOH pee uh) is related but quite different: a visual defect causing reduced vision in bright light, a condition vulgarly known as "day blindness." This term was taken intact from New Latin, from Greek *hemeralops*, based on *hemera* (day) and the same *alaos* and *ops*. Predictably, the adjectives are respectively *nyctalopic* (nik tuh LOP ik) and *hemeralopic* (hem uhr uh LOP ik). Here, too, things could be worse: One can always wear dark sunglasses or stay indoors. If these remedies prescribed by Dr. Schur don't help, see your eye doctor.

nystagmic   See **nystagmus.**

nystagmiform   See **nystagmus.**

nystagmoid   See **nystagmus.**

nystagmus (nuh STAG muhs) *n.* Via New Latin, from Greek *nystagmos* (drowsiness), related to *nystazein* (to sleep, doze), we get this term in pathology denoting involuntary rapid oscillation of the eyeballs, usually accompanied by dizziness, occurring during and after bodily rotation or after being struck on the back of the brain or the central cavity of the labyrinth of the ear. The oscillation is usually lateral but can be vertical or rotatory. This condition is most frequently found among miners. The movements of the eyeballs are ceaseless and give the impression that the eyes are vainly attempting to glimpse the light. The adjective is *nystagmic* (nuh STAG mik), *nystagmoid* (nuh STAG moyd) or *nystagmiform* (nuh STAG muh form). In view of the condition's frequent occurrence among miners, the Greek *nyx* (night) may enter into the derivation. Wherever it's found, and whatever the cause, it's a good thing not to have.

obmutescence (ob myooh TEH sens) *n.* The *-mute-* in this word might give you a hint of its meaning: "the act of becoming mute or speechless," with the implication that it is a stubborn, willful act, or "remaining silent, unreasonably and obstinately." The Latin preposition *-ob* can either mean "toward" or "to" or simply act as an intensive; *mutescere* is Latin for "to become silent," from *mutus* (silent), and *mutescens* is its present participle; hence, *obmutescence*. The adjective is *obmutescent*, and it describes perfectly the willful, obstinate witness who keeps his or her mouth firmly shut, or the stubborn child who won't 'fess up. William Paley, in *A View of the Evidence of Christianity* (1794), wrote of "the *obmutescence*, the gloom and mortification of religious orders," and an 1827 issue of *Blackwell's Magazine* described someone as "subject to habitual and invincible *obmutescence*." I like that "invincible"; it puts one in mind of the Mafia code of *omertà* (literally, a legal term in Italian, meaning "connivance," but applied by the Mafia to the "pledge of silence" when a member is questioned by the authorities about the activities of any other member).

obnounce (ob NOUNS) *vb.* The Latin prefix *ob-* is the combining form of the preposition *ob* and has many uses in combination with Latin verbs. One of these is to indicate that the action is "against" something or "objectionable" or "unfavorable." *Nuntiare* is Latin for "to announce"; *obnuntiare* is an intransitive verb meaning, in the idiom of *augurs* (soothsayers), "to report an unfavorable omen" for the purpose of avoiding or stopping some action of the state. That, in turn, gave us *obnounce*, with the same meaning. *Obnunciate* (ob NUN see ate) is a synonym of *obnounce*, and *obnunciation* (ob nun see AY shuhn) is the noun. Henry Cockeram's *The English Dictionarie, or an Interpreter of Hard Words* (1623) contains the item: "To Tell ill newes, *Obnunciate*; a Telling thereof, *Obnunciation*." ("Interpreter of Hard Words" sort of rings a bell, in this here book!) A listing in Thomas Blount's *Glossographia, or a Dictionary Interpreting Such Hard Words ... As Are Now Used* (1656—there goes that bell again, folks) reads: "*Obnunciation* ... as the ancient Romans were wont to dissolve their Assemblies (which dissolution they called *obnunciation*) when soever any evil token was seen or heard, either by the Magistrate or Augur." Did Blount have that right—that the Romans called the *dissolution* an *obnunciation*? According to Cockeram, the *telling* of bad news was the *obnunciation*, not the *dissolution*; and that makes more sense, if you go back to *obnuntiatio*, which my Latin dictionary defines as "in the language of augurs, the *announcement* of an unfavorable omen." Blount either disagreed with Cockeram or failed to read him; in either case, his Latin must have been somewhat shaky.

obnunciate   See **obnounce.**

obnunciation   See **obnounce.**

obreption (ob REP shuhn) *n.* Somehow, this word looks like a misprint, but it isn't. It denotes the attempt to obtain or the actual obtaining of something by making a false statement or expression of deceit. It is derived from Latin *obreptio* (stealing or creeping upon), related to the verb *obrepere* (to creep or crawl up to, steal up on). The word has a special meaning in ecclesiastical and Scottish law, where the object sought to be obtained in this way is a dispensation or gift, as the case may be. Randle Cotgrave's *Dictionarie of the French and English Tongues* (1611) defined it as "the creeping, or stealing to a thing by craftie meanes." McDouall's *Institute of the Laws of Scotland in Civil Rights* (1752) speaks of " … checks against subreption or *obreption, i.e.* their [speaking of dispensations] being obtained by concealing a truth, or expressing a falsehood." This introduces the somewhat related word *subreption*, which differs from *obreption* in that the former involves concealment, the latter outright falsehood. I dealt with *subreption* in my *1000 Most Challenging Words*, under (of all things) the headword *sarcophagus*. There, I explained the use of *subreption* in the sense of the semantic change or shift that occurs when a word continues in use, though what it signifies undergoes change; the example given in that book was: " … *pen* is derived from *penna* (feather) and was used originally when pens were made of quills. The name stuck even after the object underwent change." That, however, is a special use of *subreption*. Its general meaning is the gaining of a gift or an advantage by concealing the truth. Both these "craftie meanes" are equally reprehensible; there's little to choose between them. *Subreption* is from Latin *subreptio*, related to the verb *subrepere* (to creep under, steal into). But note: Whereas *obreption* comes from the combination of the preposition *ob-* (toward, to, against) and *reptus*, the past participle of *repere* (to creep), *subreption* is obtained by yoking the preposition *sub-* (under) and *raptus*, the past participle of *rapere* (to snatch). Talk of minding your *p*s and *q*s? How about *a*s and *e*s?

occamy (OK uh mee) *n.* This appears to be a corruption of *alchemy*, which meant, inter alia, an "alloy imitating gold," known as "alchemy gold." *Occamy* was an "alloy imitating silver." Thomas Nashe, in *Have with you to Saffron-walden* (1596), writes of " … a tongue of copper or *ochamie* (meerly counterfetting silver) such as organe pipes and serjeants maces are made of." Sir Richard Steele (of Addison and Steele) in *The Guardian* (1713) described a " … thimble and an *occamy* spoon." In Sir Francis Palgrave's *History of Normandy and of England* (1857) the word is used figuratively in the sense of "sham" or "counterfeit": "the dawning spirit of conventional honour gilding the *ockamy* shield of Chivalry." This *occamy* is in no way related to *Occamism*, the doctrine of the English philosopher William of Occam (d. 1349), the *Doctor Singularis et Invincibilis* known popularly as the "Invincible Doctor," who is fully discussed in my *1000 Most Challenging Words* under the headword *Occam's razor*. (He "dissected" all questions as with a razor, hence the term *Occam's razor*.) Thus, an *Occamist* was a disciple of Occam, not a counterfeiter of silver.

ochlocracy (ok LOK ruh see) *n*. There are a fair number of words ending in -*cracy* that are quite common and familiar—*aristocracy, autocracy, democracy, plutocracy*, etc.—each with its concomitant ending in -*crat* and each built of a word derived from the Greek (*aristos*, best; *autos*, self; *demos*, people; *ploutos*, wealth) plus the suffix -*kratia*, from *kratos* (power). There are less familiar words such as **pornocracy**, *ochlocracy* and *stratocracy*, each with its related terms utilizing suffixes from the Greek. *Ochlocracy* is "mob rule," from *ochlokratia*, built of *ochlos* (crowd) and *kratos*. Related words are *ochlocrat* (one who advocates mob rule); *ochlocratic* (describing that attitude) and *ochlophobia* (dread of crowds). *Stratocracy* from *stratos* (army) and *kratos*, is "rule by army, military despotism." A *stratocrat*, predictably, is an adherent of that type of government, and *stratocratic* is the adjective. These words are included because they *are* obscure. Should they be? No: The problem is the elimination of the classics from our curricula, a condition much to be deplored.

ochlocrat   See **ochlocracy.**

ochlophobia   See **ochlocracy.**

omadhaun (OM uh don, -thon) *n*. This is (or was) an Irish term of abuse: To call a person an *omadhaun* is to label him a fool. In Irish, the spelling is simpler: *amadán*, cognate with Latin *amens*, i.e., "mindless." Hall Caine spelled it differently in *The Manxman* (1894) when a character accused another in these terms: "You dobmouthed *omathaun*" (perhaps it is a Manx form), and Jane Barlow used still a different spelling in *Strangers at Lisconnel* (1895), writing of "Hugh McInerney, whom people were apt to call an *omadhawn*." An Irish friend of advanced years tells me that the term is rarely heard, and in his experience, the final syllable is always pronounced -*thon* (soft *th*). It is a very abusive term, he says, and is equivalent to "blithering idiot" or even "madman."

onychocryptosis (on nee koh krip TOH sis) *n*. *Onyx* is the Greek for "nail"—as in fingernail, toenail—or "claw," as well as the veined gem used in semiprecious jewelry. *Kryptos* is the Greek for "hidden." *Onycho-* is the combining form of *onyx*; thus, *onychocryptosis* is the logical form for "ingrown toenail," since the ingrown sides, the parts that cause the pain and sometimes the infection, are "hidden." There is a shorter word—*onyxis*—denoting the actual ingrowing of the nail. We also find other *onycho-* combinations: *onychomancy*, "divination by observation of the nails," the *-mancy* coming from *manteia* (divination); *onychophagy*, "nail biting," *-phagy* being the combining form from *phagein* (to eat); and *onychophagist*, a "nail biter." It seems the Greeks suffered from the kind of nervous attack that prompted Noël Coward to deduce the armlessness of the famous statue of Venus de Milo as the terrible effect of long-term nail biting.

onychomancy   See **onychocryptosis.**

onychophagy   See **onychocryptosis.**

onyxis   See **onychocryptosis.**

opisthograph (uh PIS thuh graf) *n.* This is a "manuscript written on both sides of the paper, parchment or papyrus." The term includes as well a tablet inscribed on both sides. Via Latin *opisthographus*, from Greek *opisthographos* (written on the back), built of the prefix *opistho-*, the combining form of *opisthen* (behind) plus *graphos* (written), related to the verb *graphein* (to write), we got the noun *opisthograph* and the adjective *opisthographic*. The *Encyclopedia Britannica* in 1876 commented, with respect to slabs with a pagan inscription on one side and a Christian one on the reverse, "These are known as *opisthographs*." In his 1816 *Researches into the History of Playing Cards*, Samuel W. Singer used the phrase " ... *opisthographic*, or printed on both sides of the vellum." The adjective *anopisthograph* (an uh pis thuh GRAF), formed of the Latin and Greek prefix *an-* (not, without, lacking) plus *opisthograph*, means "without writing or printing on the back; inscribed on one side only." There is also the form *anopisthographic* (an uh pis thuh GRAF ik), which would seem the more usual form for an adjective. E. G. Duff, in *Early Printed Books* (1893), discussed certain books printed "on one side only ... or, as it is called, *anopisthographically*.

opsigamy (op SIG uh mee) *n.* You've heard of *bigamy*, an illegal second marriage, and there is **digamy**, a legal second marriage, and even **trigamy**, the meaning of which you can guess. Then what is **opsigamy**? *Opse* means "late" in Greek, and *gamos* means "marriage." From these the Greeks concocted *opsigamia*, "marriage late in life," from which we got *opsigamy*. In his 1824 book *The Highlands and Western Isles of Scotland*, John Macculloch wrote: "Nor is there any danger of Donald's being flogged for *opsigamy* by the Highland nymphs as the Spartans were of old." Flogged for *opsigamy* in Sparta of old? You learn something every day!

opsimath (OP sih math) *n.* From Greek *opsimathes* (late in learning) we get this lovely word for "one who acquires knowledge late in life." It is based on Greek *opse* (late) and *mathe* (learning). *Opsimathy* (op SIM uh thee) is the learning thus acquired. An 1883 issue of the *Church Times* contains these words: "Those who gave the name were not simple enough to think that even an *opsimath* was not something better than a contented dunce." An issue of the *Saturday Review* of the same year had this to say: "[He] is what the Greeks called an *opsimath*: not ignorant, but a laggard in learning." Back in 1656, one John Hales, in *Golden Remains*, wrote: "Therefore *Opsimathie*, which is too late beginning to learn, was counted a great vice, and very unseemly." In 1889 *Harper's Weekly* proclaimed: "The figures alone betray the inevitable weakness of *opsimathy*." Why all this denigration? How about "better late than never?" And "adult education?" And Cato the Elder, the great Roman statesman, soldier and writer, who in very advanced age took up the study of Greek and two years later was proficient in it? I'm all for *opsimathy* and am still adding to my store of lore, such as it is, at an age when wheelchair catalogues are many persons' most important reading.

opsimathy   See **opsimath**.

opsomania   See **opsophagy**.

opsony   See **opsophagy**.

opsophagy (op SAW fuh jee) *n*. *Opson* is Greek for "cooked meat, relish, rich food generally, delicacies of all sorts," and *phagein* means "to eat," from which came the suffix -*phagos* (eating, eater). Thus, *opsophagy* is the "eating of delicacies" and in most cases, especially fish. There are related words: *opsony* (OP suh nee), denoting anything eaten with bread to give it flavor, in Greece and Rome of old chiefly fish, from Greek *opsonion* and Latin *opsonium*; and *opsomania* (op suh MAYE nee uh), taken as is from the Greek, a "pathological or morbid yearning for delicacies or for some specific food." Pregnant women are said to acquire acute longings for delicacies like grapefruit or pickles or almost any arbitrary selection. In Robley Dunglison's *Medical Lexicon* (1842, 1858, 1867, 1874, 1893), *opsomaniac* was defined as "One who loves some particular aliment to madness." Well, we do say things like "I'm simply *crazy* about olives" (or caviar or oysters or whatever). Thus, there's nothing new about *opsomania*.

oreo (OH ree oh) *n*. This is U.S. slang for a "black person with a 'white' mentality," who thinks like a white or tries to join white society. It is, of course, a derogatory term, especially as used by other blacks who spurn such pretensions. *Oreo* is the name of a popular commercially prepared cookie consisting of two round chocolate wafers enclosing a white sugar-cream filling—"black" on the outside, "white" on the inside. The application of the name of that cookie to a black person with a "white mentality" is apt but cruel. Thoughtful blacks heartily dislike and reject the term. An article in the magazine *Black*

World, June 1971, stated: "Every Black man or woman who refers to his Black brother or sister by a derogatory label such as *Tom, nigger* or *oreo* is deliberately walking into the enemy's trap." It's a sad world that has to invent such derisive labels. This one is reminiscent of the days when a secretly dissident Nazi was called "rare roast beef"—brown on the outside, red on the inside—and they were "rare" indeed, in more senses than one.

orihon (OH ree hon, AW-) *n.* This is the name of a Japanese form of book produced by the accordion-folding of strips of paper, vellum or other material in such a way as to divide the written or printed text on one side into columns or pages. It is usually provided with covers and laced down one side with some type of cord. The entire text appears on one side of the paper or other material, leaving the reverse side blank. The etymology is uncertain, but most dictionaries agree that it is "probably" from Japanese *ori* (fold) plus *hon* (book), and a "fold book" it surely is. The Chinese follow a similar procedure in the production of *orihons*. The *O.E.D.* calls it "the link between the roll and the book." In a book entitled *Greek Papyri* (1968) E. G. Turner tells us that "books of this kind (termed *orihon*) are still in everyday use in China and Japan." The Japanese are adept at the art of folding paper into intricate shapes. This craft is known there as *origami* (awr ih GAH mee) and has been handed down from generation to generation for ages. In the *Manchurian Candidate* (1960), Richard Condon writes of one expert who "amused them [his audience] or startled them or flabbergasted them with the extent of his skill at *origami*." I have watched one of my sons engage in this art, producing all kinds of things, from houses, bridges, chairs, animals of various species, boats and flowers to birds that could be made to flap their wings by pulling their beaks. Many books have been published on the art of *origami*, a word of Japanese origin formed of *ori* plus *kami* (paper).

orogeny   See **diastrophism.**

outfangthief   See **infangthief.**

Paduanism   See **Patavinity.**

paenula   See **phelonion.**

paeon   See **hemiola.**

paeonic   See **hemiola.**

Palamite   See **hesychast.**

pancratian   See **pancratium.**

pancratiast   See **pancratium.**

pancratic   See **pancratium.**

pancratium (pan KRAY shuhm), also **pancration** (pan KRAY tee uhn) *n.* This is the name of a sport combining boxing and wrestling from the Greek *pankration,* combining the prefix *pan-* (all) and *kratos* (strength). The adjective is *pancratian,* and the noun *pancratiast* denotes a competitor or victor in the sport. The related adjective *pancratic,* literally "pertaining to the *pancratium,*" means, by extension, "excelling in all types of athletics," and by further extension, "excelling in all types of accomplishment," a pretty broad territory indeed. Nathan Bailey's *Universal Etymological English Dictionary* (1731) defines *pancratick* (sic) as "all-powerful, almighty." James Russell Lowell's *Bigelow Papers* (1848) spoke of " ... the advantages of a *pancratic* ... education." A special use of *pancratic* is found in the field of optics: A *pancratic* eyepiece is one capable of various degrees of power. It was invented in the early 19th century and was brought out under the name of *Pancratic Eye Tube.* Edward H. Knight's *Practical Dictionary of Mechanics* (1884) described the *Pankratic* microscope as having " ... a sliding tube containing the eye-piece, by which its distance from the object glass may be changed, and various degrees of enlargement ... obtained without change of glasses." It is interesting to see how *power,* which goes all the way back to Latin *posse* (to be able), has a special use in optics, in the way Greek *kratos* developed a special use in the same field. Janet Van Duyn, in her excellent book *The Greeks, Their Legacy,* in the McGraw-Hill *Early Cultures Series* (1972), gives us a vivid description of the *pankration* as it was fought in the Olympic Games in ancient Greece:

> The *pankration,* a blend of wrestling and boxing, was probably one of the most brutal legally sanctioned sports on record. In this contest the two opponents punched, kicked, and strangled each other until one of them raised a finger to acknowledge defeat. Nearly every kind of maiming blow man could deliver was allowed, with the exception of gouging and biting. Breaking an opponent's fingers, easy enough under the circumstances, was also frowned upon. If further rules existed, they have not come down to us.

(Don't you like that "frowned upon?") Today's "professional" wrestling seems to have taken *pankratium* a step or two further. A bit later in her book, Ms. Van Duyn tells us: "Wrestling the *Pancratium* was a feature of the Olympic Games. A rough and brutal form of athletic contest in which almost no holds were barred, it was a favorite with Greek audiences." There is a marvelous bas relief of two contestants in this "sport" exhibited in the National Archaeological Museum in Athens.

pannage (PAN uhj) *n.* This word has a number of meanings, all associated with the pasturing of swine (sometimes other animals as well). *Pannage* is the "pasturing of swine (or other animals) in a forest" or the right or privilege to do so. It can also denote the payment made to the owner of the forest for that privilege, or the profit made by the owner of the woodland. It is a term that relates to the customs of medieval England and covers as well the material on which the swine fed: mainly acorns and beechnuts, known collectively as *mast*. An 1882 issue of *The Athenaeum: Journal of Literature, Science, and the Fine Arts* speaks of " ... herds of wild ponies and droves of wilder pigs thriving on the *pannage*." A little-used meaning of *mast* is "nuts, especially beechnuts and acorns, amassed as detritus on the forest floor; the accumulation of such matter used as feed for hogs and other animals." In this usage, *mast* is derived from Middle Dutch and Old high German *mast*, meaning "food," and Old English *mete* with the same meaning. One of Charles Lamb's essays that appeared under the signature *Elia* in an 1822 issue of *The London Magazine*, entitled "In Praise of Roast Pig," speaks of " ... the swineherd, Ho-ti, having gone out into the woods ... to collect *mast* for his hogs." As for *pannage*, the derivation is from Latin *pascio* (pasturing), related to the verb *pascere* (to feed, lead to pasture) and its past participle *pastus*, which led to medieval Latin *pas(ti)naticum*.

panpharmacon (pan FAR muh kon) *n.* This is a synonym of *panacea*, a "universal remedy, a medicine for all poisons and diseases." It was taken intact from the Greek, built of the prefix *pan-* (all) plus *pharmakon* (drug), and related to the adjective *panpharmakos* (skilled in all drugs). It was defined in Thomas Blount's *Glossographia, or a Dictionary Interpreting Such Hard Words ... as are Now Used* (1661) as "a medicine for all diseases," and William Salmon, in *Pharmacopoeia Bateana, or Bate's Dispensatory* (1694), in describing a certain remedy, was careful to say: "It is used by some as *Panpharmacon*, but what Diseases it will absolutely cure I think is scarcely determin'd." *Panacea* is a familiar word, but a little discussion may be of use. It was taken, via Latin, from Greek *panakeia*, based on the adjective *panakes* (all-healing), built of *pan-* plus *akos* (cure), akin to the verb *akeisthai* (to heal). In Greek mythology, Panacea was the daughter of Aesculapius, the Latin form of Greek Asklepios, the god of healing and medicine. His symbol is a snake entwined around a staff, based on his legendary introduction to Rome, during a 293 B.C. plague, in the form of a serpent. Alchemists in the Middle Ages searched for panaceas, and legend has given us a variety: Achilles's spear, which could heal wounds; Promethean unguent, which made the body invulnerable to fire and military arms; Prince Ahmed's apple, a remedy against all ills (superior to those others, which were effectively only against certain ailments—but you can't win 'em all), to name a few. A *panpharmacon* that could handle AIDS would be welcome.

panspermatism (pan SPUR muh tiz'm), also **panspermism** (pan SPUR miz'm), **panspermy** (pan SPUR mee), **panspermia** (pan SPUR mee uh) *n.*

Panspermatism is derived from the Greek prefix *pan-* (all), plus *spermat-* (root of *sperma*, seed) plus *isma* (state, condition). In opposition to the theory of spontaneous generation, a biogenetic theory was propounded in the 19th century holding that the atmosphere teems with germs that develop whenever and wherever they meet a favorable environment. Believers were known as *panspermists*. In the words of the *Sydenham Society Lexicon of Medicine and Allied Sciences* (1893), *panspermia* is "the physiological system according to which there are germs disseminated through all space which develop when they encounter a suitable soil." In ancient times, the Roman poet and philosopher Lucretius (99–55 B.C.), in *De Rerum Natura* (On the Nature of Things), wrote: "Nil posse creari de nilo" (Nothing can be created from nothing), and the Roman satirist Persius (A.D. 34–62) agreed: "De nihilo nihilum, in nihilum nil posse reverti" (Nothing can come out of nothing, nothing can go back to nothing)—beating the *panspermists*, in their opposition to spontaneous generation, by a good many centuries. It's difficult to say what those old boys might have thought of the "germs everywhere" doctrine, but they certainly would have agreed in disbelieving in spontaneous generation. The *panspermists* theorized that life could be diffused throughout the universe through germs carried by meteorites. We haven't discovered life on any other planet yet, but who knows?

panspermia   See **panspermatism.**

panspermism   See **panspermatism.**

panspermy   See **panspermatism.**

pantagamy (pan TAG uh mee) *n.* This is the term for a marriage practice in certain communities, a "free-for-all," in which every man is considered the husband of every woman and vice versa. Sounds pretty messy, but it has a history. One of the more amusing aspects of the word is the disagreement among dictionaries as to its derivation from Greek components. *W III* gives it as *pant-* plus *-gamy*, short and sweet. *Pant-* is a combining form of *pas* (all, every), and *-gamy* is from *-gamia*, based on *gamos* (marriage). *RH* omits the entry (out of delicacy?). When we get to the *O.E.D.*, we find something quite elaborate: "An illiterate formation for *pantogamy*, from Greek *PANTO-* all plus *-gamia*, from *gamos*, marriage. (*Pantagamy* is etymologically, from Greek *agamia* celibacy, 'universal or total celibacy.')" (Note: The *a* of *agamia* means, literally, "no marriage," i.e., "celibacy.") In its definition, the *O.E.D.* refers to the practice of "the Perfectionists at Oneida Creek in U.S." More about them later. *CH* gets the prize for its pawky Scottish humor. (*Pawky* gets the following treatment in my *British English, A to Zed*: " ... Its usual application is to Scottish humor. The Scots have spread two legends about themselves which are not borne out by the facts: 1. that they are stingy; 2. that they are humorless. Simple jokes are sometimes referred to by the English as 'easy jokes for Scotsmen.' *Pawky humor* is Scottish humor according to their own *pawky* legend, the kind that encourages the victim to make a fool of himself." Note the address of the *CH* publisher: "No. 11 Thistle Street, Edinburgh. The thistle is the national emblem of Scotland.) All that *CH* has to say about the derivation of *pantagamy* is: "Greek *gamos*, marriage, *agamia*, bachelorhood." Its definition: "A word that ought to mean universal bachelorhood applied with unconscious irony to the universal marriage of the Perfectionists, in which every man is the husband of every woman." It is now time to get to the *Perfectionists*. They were a sect founded in 1839 by John Humphrey Noyes, who lost his license to preach because of his "perfectionist" doctrine, a name taken from Matt.5:48: "Be ye therefore perfect, even as your Father which is in heaven is perfect." Beginning in 1846, his sect began the practice of "complex marriage," so arousing the neighborhood (Putney, Vermont) that in 1846 they fled to Oneida, New York. By 1879, internal problems and outside hostility forced Noyes to emigrate to Canada, where he spent the rest of his life. Noyes's basic premise was that man's innate sinlessness could be regained through communion with Christ, and such communion made communal marriage sinless. The sect was dissolved in 1881. The Mormons were established in 1831. It was only 15 years later that Noyes out-Mormonized them, combining polyandry and polygamy. Must have been confusing.

pantaleon (pan TAL ee on), also **pantalon** (PAN tuh lon), **pantalone** (PAN tuh lun), **pantaloon** (pan tuh LOOHN) *n.* Despite the ultimate variant, this word has nothing to do with lean old dotards wearing spectacles low on the nose, slippers or pantofles and tight trousers—i.e., the character that originated in the *commedia del' arte* of Venice. The word, which denotes a type of stringed instrument, comes from the unusual first name of *Pantaleon* Hebenstreit. And who was he? A German musician who, in 1705, invented a musical instrument, a large dulcimer with from 100 to 250 strings of gut and metal wire, struck by wooden mallets held by the player. Hebenstreit died in 1750. The instrument that bears his name is described in the venerable *Grove's Dictionary of Music* (1880 edition) under the heading *Pantaleon* or *Pantalon* as follows: "A very large Dulcimer invented and played upon in the early part of the last century by *Pantaleon* Hebenstreit, whose name was transferred to the instrument by Louis XIV. The name was also given in Germany to horizontal pianofortes with the hammers striking downwards." So far, so good; but why would anyone name a son *Pantaleon*? (All I have been able to dig up is that *Pantaleon* figures in the Roman Missal at July 27, and *Pantileimon* in the Byzantine one at the same date.)

pantopragmatic (pan toh prag MAT ik) *n., adj.* Thomas Love Peacock, the English novelist and poet who was one of Shelley's closest friends and eventually his executor, wrote satirical novels full of wit and eccentricity. One of them, *Gryll Grange* (1860), concerned an imaginary society devoted to *pantopragmatics*, the "'science' of universal benevolent interference." As an adjective, *pantopragmatic* describes one who meddles in everybody's business; as a noun, it denotes a universal busybody. The word is derived from Greek *panto-*, the combining form of *pas* (all), plus *pragmatikos* (active and skilled in business, businesslike). From Peacock's book: "Two or three ... arch-quacks have taken to merry-andrewizing in a new arena, which they call the Science of *Pantopragmatics.*" (*Merry-andrewize* is a nonce verb made from *merry andrew*, a buffoon, a clown; originally a quack or charlatan's assistant.) Peacock gave the president of his society the name "Lord Facing-both-ways." I'm sure you've run into a *pantopragmatic* or two; I have, and they are to be avoided like the plague, though they mean well. They have nothing else to do; their "advice" is spontaneous, thoughtless, generally irritating. It's lovely to have a word for their kind.

pantoum (pan TOOHM) *n. Pantoum* is an erroneous French spelling of the Malay word *pantun*, which is the name of a complicated verse form consisting of a series of quatrains built as follows: in the first, let's say the rhyme is *abab*; in the next, the second rhyme (*b*) recurs as the first, so that the rhyme is, say, *bcbc*; and in the next, the same system is followed, giving *cdcd*, and so on and so on, until we get to the final quatrain, where the initial rhyme of the series (*a*) recurs as the second rhyme, thus: *xaxa*. Complicated, isn't it? The August 2, 1897, issue of the *Daily News* contains a reference to this verse form: "Very few people know what a *Pantoum* is; it ... is a Malay form of verse patented by Mr. Austin Dobson [English poet, biographer and essayist, 1840–1921]." The *Encyclopedia Britannica* of 1883 defines this verse form, under the heading *pantun*, thus: "improvised poems, generally of four lines, in which the first and third and the second and fourth rhyme. The meaning intended to be conveyed is expressed in the second couplet, whereas the first contains a simile or distant allusion to the second, or often has, beyond the rhyme, no connexion with the second at all." This "explanation" seems even more complicated than the rhyme scheme set forth above, based on the definition given in *W III*, which is an expanded version of the one in *W II*. To muddle the situation, *RH* says that the second and fourth *lines* (not *rhymes*) of each quatrain are repeated as the first and third *lines* of the following one. Anyone desiring to improvise a *pantoum* please raise his hand.

pantun   See **pantoum.**

paphian (PAY fee uhn) *n., adj.* Paphos is the name of an ancient city in Cyprus that was the center of worship of the Greek goddess of love Aphrodite (Venus in the Roman hierarchy of gods) and the site of a great temple to that deity. *Paphos* gave rise to the Greek adjective *paphios*, which became Latin *paphius* andour *paphian*, usually capitalized. The adjective describes anything or anyone relating to *Paphos* or characteristic of the place or its people. In view of this city's devotion to the cult of Aphrodite, the adjective came to be used of anything relating to love, especially illicit love, so that it eventually took on the meaning of "wanton." As a noun, it meant, at first, "a native of Paphos," later "a worshiper of Aphrodite" and eventually, "prostitute," hardly a way to show one's repect to the lovely goddess.

parabasis See **epirrhema.**

paragoge See **metaplasm.**

paragraphia (par uh GRAF ee uh) *n.* This word, which might be mistaken for an exotic plural form of the common word *paragraph*, has nothing to do with paragraphs except for its derivation. It is, to make matters a bit more confusing, variously defined as a "condition of mental disorder or brain injury in which the sufferer writes words or letters other than those intended" or (in British) the "actual writing of wrong words or letters resulting from disease or brain injury." Either way, it's a sad state of affairs. The adjective is *paragraphic*, but that is also the adjective from *paragraph*. Both *paragraphia* and *paragraph* are derived from the Greek prefix *para-* (beside or beyond) and the verb *graphein* (to write). An example of *paragraphia*: When a friend of mine staying with me arrived at the breakfast table having had (as proved to be the case) a slight stroke in the night, he found himself unable to articulate. On being offered pencil and paper, he wrote, "Is there anything *right* with me?" We departed quickly to the nearest hospital. (This sturdy fellow was fine the next day.)

parallelepiped (par uh lel uh PEYE puhd, -PIH-, -le LEH puh ped, -luh LEH puh ped), also **parallelepipedon** (par uh leh luh PIH puh dawn, -duhn), **parallelopipedon** (par uh leh luh PIP uh dawn, -duhn) *n.* I didn't think enough people used the word to involve that many pronunciations or spellings! Anyway: This word, in the first spelling given above, was taken intact from the Greek, based on *parallelos* (parallel) plus *epipedon* (plane surface), the neuter of *epipedos* (level), from prefix *epi-* (upon) plus *pedon* (ground). May I say "Whew!?" So what is it? It is nothing more or less than a "six-faced polyhedron (a multfaced solid figure), all faces of which are parallelograms (quadrilaterals, i.e., four-sided figures with four sides and four angles) placed in pairs of parallel planes." So—why all the geometry all of a sudden? Two reasons: It's a wildly obscure word that you will never meet, let alone use, in all likelihood (that alone qualifies it for inclusion); and it was a term of abuse, meaning "blockhead," arbitrarily hurled at his students by a high school mathematics teacher, according to a telephone call that came in while I was broadcasting about obscure words on a talk show. Happy now? In his *History of Ancient Pottery and Porcelain* (1858), Samuel Birch wrote of bricks that were " ... *parallelopipeda*, of Nile-mud or clay of a dark loamy colour, held together by chopped straw." Note the plural in *-a* and the spelling with *o* after the third *l*, said by the *O.E.D.*, like one with *i* in that position, to be incorrect. I wonder how many readers caught this egregious error.

pararhotacism   See **psellism.**

paroemia (puh REE mee uh) *n.* A *paroemia* is a "proverb, adage, old saw"—though *old* would appear to be equally applicable to *proverb* and *adage,* or superfluous in all cases, because you don't run into new *paroemiae.* They're all old, except some that Ambrose Bierce invented and listed under the heading *Saw* in his *Devil's Dictionary,* some examples of which follow:

> A penny saved is a penny to squander.

> A bird in the hand is worth what it will bring.

> Think twice before you speak to a friend in need.

> Strike while your employer has a big contract.

> Where there's a will there's a won't.

Bierce also invented some beautiful examples under his rubric *Epigram.* *Paroemia* is derived, via Latin, from Greek *paroimia,* based on the prefix *par-* (near, beside) plus *oimos* (road), i.e., "heard commonly, in small talk by the road." Incidentally, I have something in common with Ambrose Bierce, who commented on his "famous obscurity," a lovely oxymoron, when he wrote: "My, how my fame rings out in every zone—/ A thousand critics shouting: 'He's unknown!'"

parvanimity   See **longanimity.**

pataphysics (PAT uh fiz iks) *n.* This is the name of the "science of imaginary solutions," an invention of the French dramatist Alfred Jarry (1873–1907). Jarry wrote symbolic farce, which led to the theater of the absurd, which I dub "murder mysteries," because it is a mystery to me how the authors of that type of theater get away with that kind of murder. Jarry was a familiar Paris figure, famous for his eccentric and dissolute behavior. He preached the superiority of hallucinations over rational thought. The hero of his satirical farce *Ubu Roi* (Ubu the King) is cowardly and repulsive, an authentic antihero. His surrealistic verse narratives are witty, blasphemous and scatological. The system of *pataphysics* is ludicrous but amusing, if your tastes run in that direction.

Patavinity (pat uh VIN uh tee) *n.* This word comes from Latin *Patavinitas,* from *Patavinus,* the adjective relating to *Patavium,* the Latin name for what is now Padua. That was the birthplace of the Roman historian Livy (Titus Livius, 59 B.C.–A.D. 12). His writings revealed dialectal characteristics peculiar to Patavium, and *Patavinity* came to mean "provincialism" in writing generally. Hence arose the noun *Paduanism* (PAD yooh un iz'm) as well, denoting the dialectal peculiarities of that part of the country, and a term that became a synonym for "patois." Certain Roman critics censured Livy for *Patavinity* in his historical writings. They considered it a stylistic weakness, especially compared with the elegance of the work of the more sophisticated city fellers of Rome.

patriarch   See **hegumen.**

patroclinous   See **matroclinous.**

patrocliny   See **matroclinous.**

pawky   See **pantagamy.**

pedaliter (peh DAL uh tuh, -tur) *adv.* This is a direction in organ music meaning "to be played on the pedal keyboard"; *manualiter* (man yuh WAL uh tuh, -tuhr) is in the same category, meaning "to be played on the manual keyboard." If you have watched an organist perform on a large organ fitted with a pedal keyboard, you will have noticed that while most notes are played on the manual keyboard, operated by the musician's fingers, some very low notes issue from the pedal keyboard, operated by the player's feet. *Pedalis* in Latin, means, literally, "a foot long (or wide)," based on *ped-*, the stem of *pes* (foot), but it was used in the more general sense of "relating to the foot." In New (i.e., postmedieval), Latin the adverbial suffix *-ter* was added to form the organ direction first mentioned. Latin *manualis*, based on *manus* (hand), meaning literally "fitted to the hand," used as well in the general sense of "manual," got the same treatment, resulting in *manualiter*, the other organ direction described above. The playing of an organ fitted with pedals requires an extraordinary degree of bodily coordination, and the sight of a gifted organist playing one of Bach's great preludes and fugues always fills me with wonder at not only the musicianship but also the sheer physical dexterity of the performer, using all four appendages in wondrous coordination.

perdurable   See **perdure.**

perdurance   See **perdure.**

perdurant   See **perdure.**

perdure (pur DYOOR) *vb.* The *O.E.D.* originally marked this verb as "now *rare,*" but the *Supplement* says, "Delete now *rare* and add later examples," which it does. *To perdure* is "to continue, last, keep going, endure," but, unlike its close relative *endure*, *perdure* can be used only intransitively. The *per-* element is here used as an intensive; the *-dure* is from Latin *durare* (to harden, endure), based on the adjective *durus* (hard). *Perdure* is somehow more forceful than *endure*. The same goes for the participial adjective *perduring*. In *A Dissertation on Metaphysics* (1890), John Skinner writes, "The Soul is revealed intuitively as a *perduring* living agent or entity." In M. León-Portilla's *Time and*

Reality in the Thought of Maya, translated by Boilès and Horcasitas (1973), it is stated that "For longer than a millennium and a half, not a little of Maya symbolism has *perdured.*" The Summer 1977 issue of the magazine *Daedalus* contains these words: "The assignment and reassignment of meaning must be investigated as processes in the domain of resilience possessed by each population recognizing itself to be culturally *perduring.*" Predictably, we have the adjective *perdurable* (pur DYOOR uh bl, PUR dyoor-), "lasting a long, long time or indefinitely." The English novelist and critic Sir Arthur Quiller-Couch declared that "our literature is going to be our most *perdurable* claim on man's remembrance." *Perdurance* is "persistence, permanence," and *perdurant* is a synonym of *perdurable.* Shakespeare used *perdurable* twice. In *Henry V* (Act IV, Scene 5), the Dauphin, on learning of his defeat, cries, "O *perdurable* shame!— let's stab ourselves!" Incidental note: This comes only a few lines after Orleans shouts, "*O seigneur! le jour est perdu, tout est perdu.*" ("O Lord! the day is lost, all is lost.") In the innocence of youth I somehow connected *perdurable* with *perdu* and for years thought of *perdure* as a French word meaning "loss." Now I—and you—know better. Iago says to Roderigo in *Othello* (Act I, Scene 3): "I have professed me thy friend, and I confess me knit to thy deserving with cables of *perdurable* toughness." *Perdurably* shows up as well. In *Measure for Measure* (Act III, Scene 1), after Isabella refuses to yield her body to Angelo to save her brother Claudio from the death sentence imposed upon him for getting the fair Juliet with child, he exclaims: "Why would he for the momentary trick [trifle]/Be *perdurably* fin'd?" (Death is certainly *perdurable*, if anything is!)

Perfectionist   See **pantagamy.**

periscian   See **amphiscian.**

perispomenon   See **properispomenon.**

perissology (pehr uh SOL uh jee) *n. Perissology* is "redundancy, superfluity of words, pleonasm." I discuss *pleonasm* in my *1000 Most Challenging Words*, with many examples (*free gift* and *obviate the necessity of* are two of my pet hates), but I must now add *the hoi polloi*, an all-too-frequently heard bit of *perissological* illiteracy. If you're going to go in for a little fancy Greek, please remember that the *hoi* in *hoi polloi* is the definite article, making the *the* a *perissology. Fowler's Modern English Usage* has something to say about this: "These Greek words for the majority, ordinary people, the man in the street, the common herd, etc., meaning literally 'the many,' are equally uncomfortable in English, whether *the* (= *hoi*) is prefixed to them or not. The best solution is to eschew the phrase altogether, but it is unlikely to be forgotten as long as *Iolanthe* is played. "Twill fill with joy and madness stark the *Hoi Polloi* (a Greek remark.)'" *Perissology* is formed via Late Latin *perissologia*, taken intact from the Greek, based on the adjective *perissologos* (speaking too much), built on *perissos* (redundant) plus *logos* (word). George Campbell, in *The Philosophy of Rhetoric* (1776), says: "If we should say *the alcoran* we should fall into a gross *perissology*." Campbell is right, of course, *al* being *the* in Arabic, but just as *Fowler* regrets that *the hoi polloi* is here to stay, *the Alcoran* shows up in high literary places. In *The Hind and the Panther*, Dryden writes: "The jolly Luther, reading him, began/T'interpret Scriptures by *his* Alcoran" (the *his* constituting as much a *perissology* as a *the* would be). And before that, Francis Bacon, in his *Essay on Atheism*, said: "I had rather believe all the fables in the legend, and the Talmud, and *the* Alcoran, than that the universal frame is without a mind." And how about these words, all of which contain the Arabic definite article: *alchemy, alcohol, alcove, alembic, algebra, alkali, arsenal, artichoke, azimuth* and even *lute*, which goes back, via Middle English, Middle French, Old English and Old Provençal *laut* to Arabic *al ud* (the wood); and as an effect of the Muslim conquest, the Spanish words *alcalde* (mayor), *alcázar* (castle, fortress), *Alhambra, almacén* (shop, warehouse) and many more? Despite Dryden, Bacon and all the users of *the hoi polloi*, never use a redundant, pleonastic, tautological, *perissological* word if you can help it, because it is needless, unnecessary, plethoric, superfluous, entirely *de trop* and in bad taste.

perjink (puhr JINGK), also **perjinkety** (puhr JINGK uh tee), a Scottish word, *adj.* To call a person *perjink* or *perjinkety* is to praise him or her for being precise or minutely accurate, or to complain that he or she is prim or finical. The context must decide whether praise or criticism is intended. The word is sometimes spelled *prejink*, and its origin is unknown. John Jamieson's 1808 *Etymological Dictionary of the Scottish Language* has this entry: "*Perjink*, 1. Exact, precise, minutely accurate ... 2. Trim, so as to appear finical." In *The Life of Mansie Wauch, Taylor in Dalheith* (1839), David M. Moir described a character as looking " ... as *prejinct* as a pikestaff [a walking-stick with a spike at the bottom to prevent slipping]." That would seem to indicate primness to the point of finicalness. To be *on one's perjinks* is to be "on one's best behavior," "meticulous about details." *Perjinkities* or *prejinkities* means "niceties, proprieties," or "exact details," depending again on the context. John Ruskin, in *Praeterita: Outlines of Scenes and Thoughts ... in my Past Life* (1887) wrote: "[She] had always what my mother called '*perjinketty*' ways, which made her typically an old maid in later years." That may give the exact flavor: fussy, prim, insistent on precise details and niceties; spinsterish. The *Praeterita* in Ruskin's title means "things past"; it is the neuter plural of the past participle *praeteritus* of the Latin verb *praeterire* (to pass by). Ah, those Latin elegancies!

perjinkety   See **perjink.**

perjinkities   See **perjink.**

per stirpes   See **stirp.**

petasus (PET uh suhs) *n*. Hermes, whose Roman counterpart was Mercury, was a most versatile god: god of science, commerce, eloquence, games and feats of skill; patron of thieves, rogues, travelers and vagabonds. He is represented as wearing a low, broad hat, sometimes winged, known in Latin as a *petasus* and in Greek as a *petasos*; also *talaria* (tuh LA ree uh), winged sandals or wings attached to the ankles, from the neuter plural of the Latin adjective *talaris* (pertaining to ankles), based on *talus* (ankle); and carrying a *caduceus* (kuh DYOOH see uhs, -shee uhs), a wand or staff of the sort borne by heralds (often pictured with two serpents twined around it and two wings at the top—in addition to his many other attributes, he was the messenger of the gods). So if you happen to run into a good-looking chap wearing a *petasus* and *talaria* and sporting a *caduceus*, and if you are a thief, rogue or vagabond or happen to be traveling, you couldn't be in better company.

petrology   See **Zingg.**

pharmakos   See **polypharmacy.**

phelonion (fuh LOH nee uhn) *n*. This is a vestment worn by priests of the Eastern Orthodox Church, similar to a *chasuble* (CHAZ yuh buhl) worn by the celebrant at Mass in the Western Church. *Phelonion* was taken intact from Late Greek, where it had a variant *phailonion*, an alteration of *phainolion* resulting from an erroneous transposition of consonants. The term *phainolion* came from Latin *paenula* (cloak), a sleeveless garment with an opening for the head alone, covering the entire body. The 1753 Supplement to Ephraim Chambers's *Cyclopedia; or, an Universal Dictionary of Arts and Sciences* describes the *paenula* as " ... among the Romans, a thick garment fit for a defence against cold and rain," but by 1868, it was more fully described in Wharton B. Marriott's *Vestarium Christianum: the Origin and Gradual Development of the Dress of Holy Ministry in the Church*, particularly as to " ... its gradual exaltation from the garb of slaves or of peasants to one which even emperors might wear in travelling, and which was expressly prescribed in the fifth century of our era as the dress of senators." Thus, the *paenula* eventually rose from its humble origin to an ecclesiastical vestment, and was taken into English.

phenakistoscope (fen uh KIST uh skope) *n*. This is the name of a scientific toy that produces the illusion of moving pictures. It consists of a disk with figures representing a moving person or object arranged about the center in successive positions. When the disk is turned around rapidly and the figures are viewed through a fixed slit, or their reflections are seen in a mirror through a series of slits cut into the rim of the disk itself, the continuity of the successive images produces the illusion of actual motion. The name of the gadget is derived from Greek *phenakistes* (deceiver), based on the verb *phenakizein* (to deceive) and the noun *phenax* (deceiver). According to the 1838 edition of the *Encyclopedia Britannica*, the device was invented by a Dr. Roget and then improved by a succession of people. It has been called by various other names, including *stroboscope* (STROH buh skohp) and *magic disk*. Another optical toy based on the same principle is the *zoetrope* (ZOH uh trope), from Greek *zoe* (life) plus the suffix *-tropos* (turning), based on the verb *trepein* (to turn); also called *zootrope* (ZOH oh trope), *zoo-* (ZOH oh) being the more normal combining form of *zoe*. With this optical toy, successive figures on the inside of a rapidly revolving cylinder are viewed through slits in its circumference and give the appearance of a single animated object or person. This toy was also known as the "wheel of life." In the *"Bab" Ballads* (1869), W. S. Gilbert wrote these lines: "And also, with amusement rife/ A 'Zoetrope, or Wheel of Life ...'" An 1881 edition of *The Athenaeum* explained: "By a *zoetrope* ... figures are projected on a screen ... exhibited as in motion ... with all ... changes of position." Ah, the simple pleasures that preceded the movies and television!

philologaster (fil OL uh gas tur) *n.* In my *1000 Most Challenging Words*, I explain that the suffix *-aster* forms nouns denoting "inferior versions of the real thing." Thus, a *poetaster* (POE uh tas tuhr) is a "second-rate poet; a rhymester, a versifier"; and I give other examples of *-aster* nouns. One I omitted is *philologaster*, a lovely mouthful, and as you have already guessed, it means an "incompetent philologist," a mere "dabbler in philology," a "petty philologist" or a "would-be philologist." While the Latin *philologus*, taken from the Greek *philologos* means "student of literature" or "scholar," *philologist* has a narrower meaning: "one versed in *linguistics*, the science of language." *Linguist* used to mean (and still can, in context) "one skilled in a number of languages, a polyglot," but with the development of *linguistics*, it has taken on the meaning of "specialist in linguistics," or "linguistician," and the result can be somewhat confusing, expecially to older people who grew up before *linguistics* developed. I prefer *linguistician*. I pray that *-aster* will never be attached to any noun denoting an activity of mine. *Philologaster* and *etymologaster* (I just made that one up) is fightin' words.

phit   See **phut.**

phlogiston (flo JIST on, -GIST-, -uhn) *n.* Until the 1770s and the development of the theory of oxygenation, *phlogiston* was believed to be an element, a material substance, that separated from any combustible body in the course of burning. Metals were supposed to be created from the union of their *calces*, the *friable*, i.e., ashy, residue left after *calcination* (i.e., heating to a high temperature), with *phlogiston*. In short, *phlogiston* was a nonexistent chemical thought to be released during combustion. The chemist James B. Conant (he was my organic chemistry professor at Harvard in 1924–25, and president of Harvard from 1933 to 1953) asked, logically enough, "What manner of substance or principle could *phlogiston* be that when it was added to another material the total mass or weight diminished?" The French scientist and pioneer in chemistry Lavoisier (1743–94) disproved the *phlogiston theory*, which had held that every combustible substance was a compund of *phlogiston*, liberated through combustion, leaving the other constituent as a residue. The word was taken via New Latin from the neuter of Greek *phlogistos* (burnt, inflammable), a verbal adjective from *phlogizein* (to set afire), based on *phlog-*, the stem of *phlox* (flame), related to *phlegein* (to burn). It was from *phlegein* that *Phlegethon*, the river of liquid fire in Hades that flowed into the river Acheron, took its name. In *Paradise Lost*, Milton writes of "Fierce *Phlegethon*/Whose waves of torrent fire inflame with rage." My memory may be faulty, but I remember wearing a little sack, hanging by a loose cord around my neck and containing a bit of substance smelling of camphor, as a preventive during the influenza epidemic of 1918. The substance was called, unless I am much mistaken, "antiphlogiston," though I can't see any earthly connection with the long-discarded *phlogiston theory*; but mother insisted, and I didn't get influenza. As to *friable*, mentioned above. I quote from my *1000 Most Challenging Words*: " ... like *ply* and *pliable*, *fry* and *friable* are unrelated. *Friable* describes anything easily crumbled or broken ... from ... Latin *friabilis*, based on *friare* (to crumble) ... Col. Sanders should not come to mind when you see ... *friable*."

phrontist   See **phrontistery**.

phrontistery (FRON tis tur ee) *n*. The Greeks gave the name *phrontisterion* to a "place for thought and study," a "thinking-shop," according to one of the O.E.D. definitions; would the modern "think tank" be such a place? Aristophanes applied it in ridicule to the school of Socrates. It may now be used to denote any institution of learning, though it is rarely in evidence. The Greek noun was derived from *phrontistes* (philosopher, profound thinker, one with intellectual pretensions) from the verb *phrontizein* (to reflect), based on *phrontis* (thought, reflection). The word *phrontist* applies to a "deep thinker," a "person involved in study, reflection, meditation," and it, too, in its Greek form, was applied ironically by Aristophanes to Socrates. In the early days of its history, Oriel, the Oxford college founded in 1326, was called "the *phrontisterion*," half in earnest, half in ridicule. The ridicule part shows that anti-eggheadism is nothing new.

phut (FUT) *adv., n., interj*. This is the way it is pronounced in the expression *to go phut* (more later, in the discussion of other uses). *To go phut* is "to break, become useless, unserviceable, to come to nothing. According to the O.E.D., *phut*, in this use, comes from Hindustani *phatna* (to split). There is yet another *phut*, pronounced differently (F'T): an imitative or onomatopoeic word indicating a thud, a dull sound, as of the impact of a bullet or the explosion of a distant shell. It has been used, for example, to indicate the thud of a tennis ball against the racket. As an interjection, it indicates a feeling of hopelessness: "We'll do all we can to help, but if it doesn't work, *phut!*" The O.E.D. calls it "echoic; an imitation of a sound" and gives an example from Steevens's *With Kitchener to Khartoum* (1898): "Thud! went the first gun, and *phutt!* came faintly back, as its shell burst on the zariba." But the *O.E.D. Supplement* corrects the *O.E.D.*'s etymology, stating that the two *phuts* are one and the same. So much for *phut*; as for **zariba**, see that entry. A related word is *phit* (FIT), which is an imitation of various sounds. An 1894 issue of the American magazine *Outing* describes a bear that " ... gave a soft *'phit!'* of startled recognition, pricked up his ears and turned his head askew." An 1896 issue of the *Daily Chronicle* wrote of "the pert crack of the Lee-Metford, the *'phit'* of whose bullet is lost in the whirr of a lead-coated stone from the Matabele arsenal." If you hear *f't!* or *fit!* from fairly close by, duck!

phylacobiosis (FIL uh koh beye OH sis) *n.* This is a term in entomology for the arrangement whereby a particular species of ant dwells in a termite nest and apparently performs the service of the soldier class of termite known as the *nasute* (NAY sooht) caste, whose function is to guard the nest against predator insects. *Phylacobiosis* comes from *phylak-*, the stem of Greek *phylax* (guard), plus *-biosis*, a suffix denoting "way of life," from *bios* (life), related to *bioun* (to live). We are more familiar with the prefix *bi-* or *bio-*, from the same Greek source, as in *biology, biopsy*, etc. *Phylacobiosis* is one type of *mixobiosis*, a general term (you guessed it) that denotes a form of relationship known as *mutualism*, in which organisms (such as ants) of different species live together in common or composite colonies, in an arrangement benefiting both. *Mixobiosis* is built of *mixo-*, the combining form of *mixis* (mixing), from the verb *mignunai* (to mix), plus *-biosis*. *Nasute*, from Latin *nasus* (nose), describes any organism with a well-developed proboscis and applies specifically to the class of modified soldier termites mentioned above, so called because their jaws have receded, and the tops of their heads form a type of snout which ejects a sticky fluid that entraps attacking insects. Now that the linguistic exegesis has somehow developed into a short entomological sermon, you can stop worrying about those vulnerable termites and begin worrying about your vulnerable wooden house.

phyle   See **taxiarch.**

piacular (peye AK yooh lur) *adj.* This adjective would appear to have two antithetical meanings: "expiatory," i.e., atoning for; and "requiring expiation," i.e., extremely bad, atrocious, sinful, wicked. In other words, a *piacular* act is either one that is good, in the sense that it atones for a bad act, or one that is bad, in that it requires an act of atonement. The word comes from Latin *piacularis* (atoning, expiating), based on *piaculum* (a means of atoning for sin, for appeasing a deity—but Horace and Livy both used it in the opposite sense: an act requiring expiation, i.e., a sin or crime). It all goes back to the verb *piare* (to propitiate, to seek to appease by an offering) and the adjective *pius* (dutiful; more generally, honest, upright). It is obvious that care must be taken to make clear the sense in which *piacular* is being used (if you care to use it!). John R. Macduff, in *Memories of Patmos* (1871), wrote of " ... the great brazen altar of burnt offering, where *piacular* or bloody offerings were alone presented," using the adjective in the sense of "expiatory," while De Quincy, writing on *Whiggism* (1857), used the word in the opposite sense, describing a politician in terms of "[leaving] no stone unturned to cleanse his little ... fold from its *piacular* pollution." Strange (and dangerous!) for a word to signify two opposite things.

Pierian (peye EER ee uhn) *adj.* Literally, this adjective applies to *Pieria*, a district in northern Thessaly in Greece, the reputed home of the Muses and by extension, to the arts, expecially poetry and learning. To refresh your recollection, there were nine muses in Greek mythology, patron goddesses of the arts, daughters of Zeus and Mnemosyne (memory): Calliope (epic poetry and eloquence), Euterpe (music and lyric poetry), Erato (love poetry), Polyhymnia (oratory and sacred poetry), Clio (history), Melpomene (tragedy), Thalia (comedy), Terpsichore (dance and choral song) and Urania (astronomy). Paintings at Herculaneum show them in their special attributes. Early in Greek history the Muses were worshiped in *Pieria*, for which reason they were also known as the *Pierides*, and there were springs in various districts considered sacred to them. Pope's famous line "A little learning is a dang'rous thing" is followed by "Drink deep, or taste not the *Pierian* spring"; and John Addington Symonds wrote: "*Pierian* Muses! hear my prayer." A *pierid* (PEYE uh rid) is any butterfly of the family *Pieridae*, typical of which is the *Pieris* (PEYE uh ris), the cabbage butterfly.

pilliwinks (PIL ee winks) *n.* This word, which sounds carefree and charming, like a children's game or a mischievous prank, is actually the name of a hideous instrument of torture designed to crush fingers—ugh! The *O.E.D.* lists a fantastic variety of spellings of this delightful gadget, 16 of them, in fact, all the way from *pyrwykes* to *pinniwinkis* to *pirliewinkles*, and notes that one of the variant forms, *pyrewinkes*, "coincides with the contemporary spelling of *periwinkle* (the flower)" but hastens to assure us that "there is no obvious connexion [note spelling] of sense." "Origin unknown" is the final verdict—an observation maddening but not unfamiliar to etymologists. Specialists in this category of artifact state that the *pilliwinks* were supposed to resemble thumbscrews, also known in the good old days as "thumbikins" or "thumbkins," another name that sounds like delightful woodland sprites beloved of little children.

pilpul (PIL poohl) *n.* This is an Aramaic word for "vigorous, keen argumentation and debate among rabbinical scholars" on the subject of proper interpretation of Talmudic principles and rules, particularly with respect to moral and religious matters. The word is related to the verb *pilpel* (to search, debate). *Aramaic* is a Semitic tongue that goes back to at least the ninth century B.C. It spread all over southwest Asia as a commercial lingua franca. After the Babylonian Captivity, it was adopted by the Jews and replaced Hebrew. The

Talmud, the focal point and the most important influence in Jewish life over its long history, is a collection of civil and religious laws, moral doctrine and ritual. There were two editorial revisions, the Palestinian, produced in the mid-fourth century A.D., and the Babylonian, completed at the end of the following century. The later revision was three times as large as the earlier one and is considered the more important version. The study of the Talmud and Talmudic disputation were for centuries the focal point of Jewish education and life.

pimp (pimp) *n.* Well you may wonder at the inclusion, in a dictionary of obscure words, of such a simple and familiar term, until you learn that there are two vastly dissimilar types of *pimp* in this world, or at least in that part known as the southern counties of England—or some of them. The familiar *pimp* is the pander or procurer, who lives off the earnings of prostitutes. The other type is—well, let me explain. Some years ago, as I entered the ironmonger's [British English for *hardware store*] in the village in the County of Kent, England, where I live about half of the time, I noticed a sign in the window: Pimps—2 for 5 d. (that was before the radical change, on February 15, 1971, in the British currency system, when *d*, the symbol of "pence," was changed to *p*). Naturally, that stirred not only my curiosity, but also my amazement. The shop was run, in the occasional absence of the young manager, by a somewhat slow-witted elderly couple, and this was one of those days. Setting aside, for the moment, the original object of my visit, I innocently asked for two *pimps*. After a certain amount of chin scratching, the old woman announced that they were out of them. That put me in a difficult position, but I forged ahead and asked, "What *are pimps*? The not-so-slow-witted woman stared at me for a moment or two and asked, intelligently enough, "Begging your pardon, sir, but if you didn't know what they were, how did you know you wanted them?" Trapped, I confessed, "I didn't really want any *pimps* and was only trying to find out what they were." At this juncture, the old man emerged through a little door saying, "I found one; here it is," and displayed a little bundle of kindling in cylindrical form, about ten inches long and eight inches in diameter, tied with wire. "A *pimp*, sir, is a bung o' firewood, and you can have this one for nothing if you want it." *Bung*, in this context, was a new one on me as well, and I hadn't heard *firewood* used to mean "kindling" before, but I let that pass and asked the old gentleman whether *pimp* was heard all over England or only locally. (I was sure the innocent twain hadn't run into the other kind of *pimp*.) "Oh, no, sir, not everywhere, only here in Kent, and maybe in Sussex, but only just across the border." The border between those two counties has always seemed rather vague in that part of the country. So I accepted the gift, and since I was writing an Anglo-American dictionary at that period of my life, hastened home to make some notes. Later on, reading Vita Sackville-West's *The Edwardians*, I found a passage in which the young nobleman, Lord of the manor, " … looked into the *pimping-shed*, where old Turnour [one of the domestic staff] was chopping faggots." I rejoiced in this confirmation of the philological advice supplied by the sweet old couple at the ironmonger's.

pisé   See **tapia.**

plagiary   See **plagium.**

plagium (PLAY jee uhm) *n. Plagium* is Latin for "kidnapping," and it was taken intact into the English language to denote that felony. It was based on the Latin *plaga* (net for hunting). The Romans coined the word *plagiarius* for "kidnapper," and the Roman poet Martial used it in jest for "literary thief," i.e., "plagiarist." Another English word for "kidnapper" is *plagiary*, taken directly from *plagiarius*. What has come down from all this in modern usage are the words *plagiarism* and *plagiarist*, based squarely on Martial's jocular metaphorical extension. Samuel Johnson, in a 1758 issue of *The Idler*, wrote of "compilers and *plagiaries* ... who give us again what we had before," a wonderfully succinct gibe at "literary thieves."

pledget   See **dossil.**

pollicitation (puh lis ih TAY shuhn) *n.* The Latin noun *pollicitatio* means "offer" or "promise"; the verb *polliceri* means "to make an offer"; *pollicitari* means "to keep promising" and is the frequentative of *polliceri*. (A *frequentative* of a verb, as explained under that heading in my *1000 Most Challenging Words*, is a related verb that "expresses the continual repetition of the action of the original verb.") *Pollicitatus* is the past participle of *pollicitari* and is the origin of *pollicitatio*, the Latin ancestor of our headword. Why *pollicitatus* was preferred to *pollicitus*, the past participle of *polliceri* (which would have produced *pollicitio* in Latin and *pollicition* in English) is hard to explain, except for reasons of pronunciation. As to *polliceri*, that arose by combining *pro* (forth) with *liceri* (to bid). In Roman times, a *pollicitation* was "an informal offer, not yet accepted by the promissee and unenforceable, except in the case of a promise of *dos*," the property contributed to the husband by the wife or by a third party on her behalf. That contribution originally became the husband's absolutely but was later made legally returnable to the original donor on the termination of the marriage by death or divorce. In English law, *dos* (Latin for "dowry, marriage portion") denoted the property settled by or on behalf of a wife upon her husband at the time of the marriage; it is the origin of the term *dower*, which could mean either the "property settled by the wife upon the husband," or the converse, as the case might be. These practices are now obsolete. (The way things are going these days, the same is beginning to be true of marriage itself!)

polypharmacy (pah lee FAR muh see) *n. Poly-* is the combining form of Greek *polys* (many), and *pharmakon* is Greek for "drug, medicine," so that the combination *polypharmacon*, New Latin from Greek *polypharmakon*, designated a remedy consisting of many ingredients. *Polypharmacy* denotes the administering of numerous drugs concurrently, especially for the treatment of the same ailment. In current health officers' slang the word is used to indicate a situation whereby a patient has been administered such a multiplicity of drugs that it is impossible to ascertain which drug is causing what or the overall effect of the combination. This definition comes from Dr. Melvin Konner's *Becoming a Doctor* (1987). Allegedly overheard: "Well, Freddy's really ridin' the rollercoaster of *polypharmacy*, an' I don't know what's doin' what to what." This tendency of some doctors today is known as "pill-happiness" (meaning no offense—some of my best friends and saviors are doctors). And while we're at it, look out for *pharmakos* (FAR muh kos), somehow and probably irregularly derived from *pharmakon* but having nothing whatever to do with pharmacology. It is a word for a "scapegoat" of a rather specialized variety, in the form of a person, usually one already condemned to death for some crime or other, sacrificed according to ancient Greek custom as a means of purification or atonement for a community or city. Though *pharmakos* is technically unrelated to *pharmakon*, I suppose that the purification involved was somehow felt to be "remedial" in a way, since atonement and purging are at least metaphorically related.

Polypheme (POL ih feem) *n.* This is the anglicized form of *Polyphemus*, one of the Cyclopes (from the Greek *kyklops*, formed of *kyklos*, circle, plus *ops*, eye), a fabled race of giants who inhabited chiefly Sicily. They had one eye in the middle of the forehead and figured in *The Odyssey*. *Cyclops*, with a lowercase *c*, is used allusively to mean "giant" or "monster" generally. Their occupation was the forging of iron for the god Vulcan. According to Ovid's *Metamorphases*, Acis, beloved of Galatea, a sea nymph (not the Galatea beloved of Pygmalion), was the rival of *Polyphemus*, who in a jealous rage crushed him to death with a huge rock. Acis was then transformed into the river Acis. (*Metamorphoses*, as the name indicates, relates tale after tale about mythical transformations, which intrigued Ovid.) The bereaved Galatea threw herself into the sea, joining her sister nymphs. Handel composed an opera entitled *Acis and Galatea*, first performed in 1720 but rarely heard these days, like (sadly) so many of his operas. Homer tells us that when Odysseus landed in Sicily, *Polyphemus* captured him and twelve of the crew and ate six of them. Odysseus managed to blind him and get away with the survivors. *Polyphemus* has lent his name to the *Polyphemus moth*, a large yellowish-brown silkworm species (*Telea Polyphemus*) with a prominent eyelike spot on each of its hind wings, and to certain one-eyed animals. The name *Polyphemus* was taken from the Greek adjective *polyphemos*, meaning literally "figuring in many tales or legends, much spoken of," and, as we have seen, the adjective suited him.

polyphloisbic (pol ee FLOIS bik) *adj.* We all know that the prefix *poly-* indicates muchness, being the combining form of the Greek adjective *polys*, meaning "many," "much," "heavy," "great," "large," "wide" or "long" (I must stop somewhere), as the context requires. *Phloisbos* is Greek for "din," and the combination of the two plus the usual adjectival suffix *-ic* gives us the delightful adjective *polyphloisbic*, modifying anything that makes a hell of a noise. Homer used it to describe the sea (*thalassa*) as "loud-roaring" (*polyphloisboio thalasses* in the genitive case), and Thackeray concocted *poluphloisboiotatotic* as though from a Greek superlative form with the ending *-otatos*. But there is no reason why you shouldn't use it to describe the rush of a New York subway express train or the "music" of a frantic rock group who, in the deathless prose of Woody Allen (*Hannah and Her Sisters*) "looked as though they wanted to stab their mothers."

polyptych (POL uhp tik) *n.* A work of art, often an altarpiece, consisting of four or more panels that are hinged and fold together, is called a *polyptych*, from Greek *polyptychos* (having many folds, folded a number of times), built of *poly-* (many) plus *ptyche* (fold, layer). The reason this term applies only to a work of four or more panels is that there are specific terms for those consisting of a smaller number, viz., *diptych* and *triptych*. A *diptych*, as you might have guessed from the prefix *di-* (two, in both Latin and Greek), consists of two pictures, also usually forming an altarpiece, hinged and folding together. But *diptych* has several other meanings as well. The ancient Romans used waxed tablets on which they wrote with a pointed instrument called a *stylus*. They sometimes used a two-leaved hinged tablet that folded together to protect the writing on the easily damaged waxed surfaces. That double tablet was known in Late Latin as *diptycha*, a plural noun, from the neuter plural of Greek *diptychos*. *Dyptychs*, from the Latin plural *diptycha*, became the name of a two-leaved tablet with a list of the names of the living on one side, and on the other, the names of the dead commemorated in eucharistic services. *Dyptych* is applied also to a literary work with two contrasting parts (e.g., the same tale from two different points of view, as in the Japanese classic *Rashomon*, which, however, included the versions of more than two persons). Finally, the same word is used for any work consisting of two matching parts covering complementary or contrasting illustrations of two aspects of a single general topic—e.g., the flora and fauna of a particular region. Then we get to *triptych* (also *triptich*), the three-leaved waxed writing tablet used by the ancient Romans; or a picture (sometimes a carving) with three hinged and folding parts, usually an altarpiece, consisting of a central panel and two side panels each half its size that fold over it. The term can also apply to a literary or musical work with three matching or contrasting sections. Of the same origin is *triptyque* (also *triptique* or *tryptyque*), from the French *triptyque*, taken from Greek *triptychos*, denoting a customs pass for the temporary importation of a car into a particular country, or a general international pass for a car. What is the explanation of that use? Do those passes consist of three leaves, or is it a pun on "trip-ticket?"

polysemant (pol ee SEE muhnt) *n*. From Late Greek *polysemantos* (having many meanings), based on the prefix *poly-* (many) plus *semainein* (to mean), from *sema* (sign), we get *polysemant*, meaning a "word with more than one meaning." The adjective is *polysemantic* (pol ee suh MAN tik), and that puts us on somewhat more familiar ground, since *semantic* and *semantics* are met with quite frequently. A related adjective, *polysemous* (pol ee SEE muhs, puh LIS uh muhs), describing words having many meanings, comes from Late Latin *polysemus*, taken from Greek *polysemos*, built of *poly-* plus *sema*. *Polysemy* (pol ee SEE mee, puh LIS uh mee), from New Latin *polysemia*, means "multiplicity of meanings." You will find many words in this book that qualify as *polysemants*. It is my habit to describe them as *versatile*. One doesn't have to search for *polysemants* among obscure words: Just look up *cow* and *how* in any unabridged dictionary, and you'll be amazed at their *polysemia*!

polysemantic   See **polysemant**.

polysemous   See **polysemant**.

polysemy   See **polysemant**.

pornocracy (por NOK ruh see) *n*. We are all quite familiar with the noun *pornography*, but few of know how that word came about. Here's the story: *Porne* is Greek for "whore," and *graphein* is the Greek verb for "to write." That led to the noun *pornographos* (describing prostitutes and their profession), so that the original force of *pornography* was literature on that interesting subject. But the scope of the word grew to include obscene writing, art, photography, etc., especially that without artistic merit or "redeeming social value," as the courts put it. Then what about *pornocracy*? We know that the suffix *-cracy*, as in *democracy, autocracy, technocracy*, etc., indicates ruling force; it comes from Greek *kratos* (rule). And *porne* is our old friend "whore." The rule of whores? Actually, their influence, especially over (for shame!) the papal court in the early half of the tenth century. History says so, and who are we to deny it?

posset (POS uht) *n*. Once upon a time, a *posset* was served either as a delicacy or as a medicinal potion to people suffering from colds or other ailments. It was a warm drink of milk curdled with a liquor, usually ale or wine, sweetened with sugar and spices and sometimes thickened with bread or eggs. The poet Robert Herrick, in *Hesperides: or the Works both Humane and Divine of R.H.* (1648), says in a poem to Phillis: "Thou shalt have *possets*, wassails fine;/Not made of ale, but spiced wine!" In that case, Phillis wasn't ill; the *posset* was a delicacy, not a medicine. But Frances E. Trollope (sister-in-law of *the* Trollope), in *A Charming Fellow* (1876), expresses concern about an invalid: "I do wish he would try a hot *posset* of a night, just before going to bed." The word was used as a transitive verb meaning "to make curdle" or, as Oliver

Wendell Holmes used it, "to pamper, with delicacies," writing of one "cosseted and *posseted* and prayed over"; and intransitively meaning "to make a *posset*," as George Meredith used it in *The Ordeal of Richard Feverel* (1859): "She broke off to go *posseting* for her dear invalid." *Posset* pots are two-handled vessels used in making *possets*, and *posset* cups have two handles, usually a cover and a spout for feeding *possets* to invalids. They are rare now and are sought after by collectors of 17th- and 18th-century curios. In *Hamlet*, the ghost, in Act I, Scene 5, tells Hamlet how he was poisoned by Claudius:

> Upon my secure hour thy uncle stole,/With juice of cursed hebonon [a drink containing a poisonous juice, possibly henbane (*Hyoscyamus niger*), a poisonous plant of the deadly nightshade family or of the German *Eibenbaum*, yew-tree]/in a vial,/And in the porches of mine ear did pour/The leperous distilment; whose effect/Holds such an enmity with blood of man/That, swift as quicksilver, it courses through/The natural gates and alleys of the body;/And with a sudden vigour it doth *posset*/And curds ... /The thin and wholesome blood: so did it mine...

A happier kind of *posset* is mentioned in *Merry Wives of Windsor* (Act I, Scene 4), when Mistress Quickly says to Simple: "Go; and we'll have a *posset* for't soon at night, in faith, at the latter end of a sea-coal fire." And in the same play (Act V, Scene 5), Page says to Falstaff: "Yet be cheerful, knight: thou shalt eat a *posset* to-night at my house ..." Eat? That *posset* must indeed have been greatly thickened with bread! Delicacy or remedy, the *posset* sounds like a good drink. It came from Middle English *posschote, poshote, possot*; origin unknown, though there may be some connection with *posca*, a mixture of weak wine, water and vinegar once used as a remedy.

posslq (POS 'l kyooh) *n*. One evening, a dinner guest was telling us about his recent Christmas party. In listing the guests, he got to: "Then there was my son Bert and ... er ... the ... er ... woman he's living with and my daughter Anne and ... er ... the ... er ... man she's living with—but surely, there must be a better way of saying this!" That brought on a general discussion in which all the guests took a hand at trying to concoct a less awkward term for the person one's child is ... er ... living with. *Boyfriend* and *girlfriend* were dismissed without hesitation for inexactitude, as not necessarily implying cohabitation. His *woman*? Her *man*? Too crude; too suggestive of Tarzan and Jane. *Mistress, lover*? Too much like *Madame Bovary* or *La Bohème*. *Live-in companion, live-in friend, housemate, partner* and Lord knows what else were turned down as inexact or tasteless or stiff or loose or whatever. One of those present, well versed in Briticisms, including archaisms, came up with *tally-husband* and *tally-woman*, based on the obsolete slang or dialect expression *to live in tally*, and that caused general derision until this trustworthy fellow swore that the expression was defined by the *O.E.D.* as "to cohabit without marriage." That suggestion was, understandably, howled down. However, despair not. The California tax authorities have come to the rescue: *posslq*! This is an official term, an acronym considerably more difficult to pronounce than *Nato* or *Opec*, constructed as follows: *P*erson of the *O*pposite *S*ex *S*haring *L*iving *Q*uarters. It is officially defined as "either of two persons, one of each sex, who share living quarters but are not related by blood, marriage or adoption"; in other words, a man and a woman who have forgone "the benefit of clergy" (in popular but inexact meaning of that phrase). This rather quaint acronym, however, would seem not to cover the case of a homosexual ménage (note the "one of *each* sex" in the official definition). To remedy that situation, simply change the *O* (for *opposite*) to *S* (for *same*) in *posslq*, and you come up with *pssslq*) (PSS 'l kyooh), which is even harder to pronounce than *posslq*. If, to avoid the rather ominous hissing sound of *psssql*, you substitute *identical* for *same*, you wind up with *pisslq*, which is easier to pronounce but might prove embarrassing. To cover the case of a bisexual housemate, we would have to change *posslq* to *bpslq*—which has the advantage of being one letter shorter but the disadvantage of being unpronounceable—or to *possdcslq* (person of the opposite or same sex depending on circumstances sharing living quarters), which may be all-embracing (no pun intended) but is self-evidently unacceptable, leaving the alternative *peossslq* (person of *either* the opposite or same sex sharing living quarters), but that may be unclear and in any event involves excessive hissing. When it comes to a *ménage à trois*, we would get two *posslqs* in one package, if you follow me, which I'm having a hard time doing myself. In the rare case of the live-in buddy's being a hermaphrodite, whom the relevant authorities might designate a person of *indeterminate* sex, we would once more be stuck with the awkward *pisslq*, but surely there would be a creative linguist languishing somewhere in the labyrinthine quarters of the authority who would be quick to replace *identical* with *unclassified* or *unclassifiable* or something or other beginning with *u* and come up with *pusslq*. Not to worry, as the British say.

poteen   See **boreen.**

pradakshina (prah dah KSHEE nah), also **pradakshna** (prah DAH kshnah) *n.* This word is taken from Sanskrit, where it is built of *pra* (in front) plus *dakshina* (right, cf. Latin *dexter*, English *dexterous*, etc.) and is the name of the Hindu and Buddhist religious rite of walking around something in a clockwise direction. In *Sinhalese Social Organization: The Kandyan Period* (1956), Ralph Pieris writes of one who "reverentially performs *pradakshina* three times to the diagram." Monier Monier-Williams, in *Religious Thought and Life in India* (1833), narrates an elaborate instance of this form of worship: "A pilgrim … sets out from the source of the Ganges … and walks by the left bank of the river to its mouth … ; then, turning round, he proceeds by the right bank to [the point] … whence he departed. This is called *Pradakshina*." There is a moving scene in the film of M. M. Kaye's *The Far Pavilions* where the widow circumambulates her dead husband's funeral pyre clockwise, reciting the words "Ram Ram" over and over, preparing herself to join the corpse in the rite of suttee. In my *British*

English, A to Zed, I include the headword *withershins, widdershins,* meaning "counterclockwise," with the comment: "It is said to be bad luck to walk around a church *withershins,* a practice that sounds like one of those tiresome routines developed in black magic or withcraft." Somehow, the preference for the right over the left extends to favoring clockwise to its opposite. The Latin adjective *sinister* literally means "left, on the left," but figuratively "wrong, improper, unlucky, unfavorable." And there are more than 80 British dialectal terms, all of them more or less pejorative, for *left-handed,* including *bawky-handed, coochy-gammy, cow-pawed, scroochy* and *cuddy-wifted,* to name a few. No such prejudice prevails against *southpaws* in baseball.

praecipitatio   See **virga.**

precentor (pree SEN tur, prih-) *n.* This was the title of a person who led or directed the singing of a church choir or congregation. In some cathedrals, he was a member of the chapter (general assembly of canons, who attended to the business of the cathedral) ranking next to the dean (head of the chapter), and his duties were deputed to a *succentor* (suhk SEN tuhr), sometimes known as a *subchanter* (sub CHAN tuhr), who acted as the *precentor*'s deputy. We read in Walter A. Hook's *Church Dictionary* (1871): "Formerly the *precentor* in most of the Cathedrals ranked next to the Dean. Now he is usually a minor canon." Things do change, even in ecclesiastical hierarchies. All of these terms are based on the Latin verb *canere* (to sing), preceded by the appropriate prefix *prae-* (before, in front) or *sub-* or *suc-* (under), as the case may be. Now, if you find yourself in a cathedral and want to present yourself to the choir director, you'll know how to address him or her, and won't bungle.

precocial   See **nidicolous.**

prejink   See **perjink.**

presbycusis (prez buh KYOOH sis, pres-) *n.* This is the technical term for "loss of hearing in advancing age" and a good example of a word containing an element with which we are more familiar in other combinations: *presby-,* as in *Presbyterian. Presby-* is the combining form of Greek *presbys* (old). Thus, a *presbyter,* an "elder in the Presbyterian church," is based on Greek *presbyteros,* from *presbys* plus *-teros,* the comparative suffix. I have already dealt with *presbyopia* in my *1000 Most Challenging Words.* It means "farsightedness," another annoying ocular affliction of old age, and involves the suffix *-opia,* from Greek *ops* (eye). What about *-cusis,* then? Here we combine *presby-* with *(a)kousis,* Greek for "hearing," related to the verb *akouein* (to hear), the source of our *acoustic(s).* These things do come together if you look far enough. *Presbyopia, presbycusis,* ah me! "Last scene of all,/That ends this strange eventful history,/Is second childishness, and mere oblivion,/Sans teeth, *sans eyes,* sans taste, sans everything." Shakespeare (end of Jaques's speech in *As*

You Like It, Act II, Scene 7) left out the *ears* by name, but *everything* includes them, doesn't it?

primipara (preye MIP ur uh) *n*. From Latin *primus* (first) plus *parere* (to bring forth, bear) we get *primipara*, a "woman who has given birth to her first child or is about to do so." Some dictionaries define the word as applying to female animals as well. Others include the definition a "woman who has given birth to only one child," with the implication that there aren't going to be any more. This would describe the majority of women in China, which now favors the one-child family. The adjective is *primiparous* (preye MIP uhr uhs), the condition *primaparity* (preye mih PAR uh tee). As you might expect, a *multipara* (mul TIP uh ruh) is a "woman who has borne more than one child," and *multiparous* (mul TIP uh ruhs) and *multiparity* (mul tuh PAR uh tee) are the corresponding adjective and noun, except that they include as well the phenomenon of giving birth at any one time to multiple offspring and clearly apply to animals as well as women. *Multiparity* in women has become fairly frequent in recent days as the result of the administration of fertility drugs to women previously incapable of conception—variously described, in the joke about the group of recently arrived refugee German gynecologists, as "inconceivable," "unbearable," "impenetrable," "impregnable," and (climactically) "insurmountable." You have to supply the exaggerated phony accents.

primiparity   See **primipara**.

primiparous   See **primipara**.

proceleusmatic (proh suh loohz MAT ik) *n., adj.* This word has two distinct yet interestingly related meanings. As an adjective, it means "inciting, animating, rousing," and its Greek derivation explains this use. It comes, via Late Latin *proceleusmaticus*, from Greek *prokeleusmatikos*, based on *prokeleusmat-*, the stem of *prokeleusma* (incitement), from the verb *prokeleuein* (to urge on, give orders to), built of the prefix *pro-* (for—as opposed to against; cf. *pros* and *cons*) plus *keleuein* (to urge, command, drive on). As a noun, a *proceleusmatic* is a term denoting a metrical foot consisting of four short syllables, and it is used as an adjective as well, describing such a foot. The connection between the two meanings is found in the fact that in ancient times, such four-syllable or *proceleusmatic* feet were used in songs by which, according to Dr. Samuel Johnson in *A Journey to the Western Islands of Scotland* (1775), "the rowers of [ancient] galleys were animated." In *The History of the Crusades*, by Charles Mills (1818), we are told that "In an army ... there were as many *proceleusmatick* words as there were banners." Carl Engel, in *Introduction to the Study of National Music* (1866), confirming Johnson, writes of "the oar song of the Hebridians, which resembles the *proceleusmatic* verse by which the rowers of Grecian gelleys were animated." As to the two "distinct meanings" first mentioned, the "inciting" or "urging" came first, as specifically relating to the rhythmic beat inflicted, as it were, on those poor galley slaves, and the general prosodic application followed.

properispomenon (proh per ih SPOH muh non) *n., adj.* If you are not interested in classical Greek grammar, you might do well to sit this one out, because we're going to go on to discuss *perispomenon* (pa rih SPOH muh non) as well. But you never know: You might just bump into one or even both of them. A *properispomenon* is a term in Greek grammar for a "word having a circumflex on its penult," and the same term serves as an adjective describing such a word. It is the neuter of the passive participle of the verb *properispan* (to put a circumflex on the penult). You know, of course, that the penult is the next-to-the-last syllable of a word, like the -*tan*- in *titanic*. A *perispomenon*, on the other hand, is a "word with a circumflex on its *last* syllable." It is formed of the Greek prefix *peri*- (around) plus the verb *span* (to pull, stretch), which we have already met in the discussion of our old friend *properispomenon*, and like that word, it can function as an adjective as well. Since I'm sure you know what a circumflex is, we don't have to go into that. If you need any more information about *properispomena* or *perispomena* and want to find examples of them, please consult your *O.E.D.*.

proprium (PROH pree uhm) *n.* This word, the neuter of the Latin adjective *proprius* (literally, one's own special, particular, peculiar; by extension, peculiar to, characteristic of, a person or thing), means a "distinctive characteristic," an "attribute that is essential to someone or something." It is "selfhood," or "essential nature" or "individuation in personality." I went into the meaning of *quiddity* in my *1000 Most Challenging Words* and called it "the essence of a thing or person, the whatever-it-is that makes a thing or person what he, she, or it is." I spoke, too, of its synonym *haecceity*, "that which gives something its unique quality or characteristic," pointing out that *haecceity* was a "partial synonym," in that *quiddity* applied to both persons and things while *haecceity* was used only of things. I could have included a related word with which, at the time, I was unfamiliar: *ipseity* (ip SEE uh tee), from Latin *ipse* (self), meaning "individual identity." As many have pointed out, true synonyms do not exist, since although two or more words may mean just about the same thing, the connotations of a word may make any one of the "synonyms" inappropriate in a given situation. A search through the dictionaries and thesauri and books like the Rodale *Synonym Finder* (Laurence Urdang, editor in chief) will help to set you straight. *Proprium, quiddity, haecceity, selfhood, ipseity*—each has its place, but heed the warning.

proseuche (pro SOOH kee, pro SYOOH kee), also **proseucha** (pro SOOH kah, pro SYOOH kah) *n.* A *proseuche* or *proseucha* was an "oratory, a place of prayer"; a word taken from the Greek, based on the verb *proseuchesthai* (to offer prayers), constructed of the prefix *pros*- (toward) plus *euchesthai* (to pray), from the noun *euche* (prayer). Among the ancient Hebrews, the *proseuche* was usually a roofless structure, as distinct from a synagogue of orthodox construction. In the *Works* of Joseph Mead or Mede (1672) a *proseucha* was described as " ... a plot of ground encompassed with a wall or ... other ... inclosure, and open above ... A Synagogue was ... a covered edifice ... Synagogues were within the Cities, as *Proseucha's* were without." But a translation of *Father Didon's Jesus Christ* (1892) says that the Jews "built synagogues and *proseuchae* at the entrances of towns." Whether within cities or at the entrances to cities, the Jews could say their prayers in synagogues or *proseuches*. On visits to Israel, I saw many offering their prayers at the Wailing Wall, which had neither enclosure nor roof. I can't imagine it makes any difference to the Deity, as long as the words are accompanied by thoughts. See the king's concluding speech in *Hamlet*, Act III, Scene 3: "Words without thoughts never to heaven go."

prosodetic   See **prosodion.**

prosodiac   See **prosodion.**

prosodic   See **prosodion.**

prosodion (pruh SOH dee on) *n*. At first glance, this word appears to have something to do with *prosody* (the art or science of meter), but its proper meaning is "processional hymn," the kind sung by ancient Greeks as they approached a temple or the altar of one of their many gods. *Prosodios* is Greek for "processional," from *prosodos* (procession, formed of *pros*, "toward," and *hodos*, "way"). *Prosodion* is its neuter form, used as a noun. *Prosody* is another matter, formed of *pros* and *oide* (song). However, *prosodiac* (pruh SOH dee ak) is used as a synonym of *prosodic* (pruh SOD ik), meaning "relating to prosody," and also as a noun denoting the verse sung in a *prosodion*, this verse being an *enoplion* (eh NOP lee uhn) followed by a long or short syllable. An *enoplion* is an "*acatalectic hemiepes* preceded by one or two short syllables or one long one"; its name is formed from the neuter of *enoplios* (martial), based on *enoplos* (armed). As to *acatalectic* (a kad'l EK tik), that is a term in prosody meaning "a foot of verse complete in the number of its syllables," as opposed to *catalectic*, meaning "incomplete, lacking a syllable in the last foot." In this instance, I shall spare you the derivations but provide an illustration: "Tell me not in mournful numbers,/Life is but an empty dream!" This is a trochaic tetrameter, the first line *acatalectic*, the second *catalectic* (it drops a syllable). Warning: Never confuse *acatalectic* with *acataleptic* (ay kad'l EP tik), a term applied to one who refused to make a judgment, on the principle that certainty is impossible. Now we must deal with *hemiepes* (heh mee EP eez): a "dactylic tripody with a spondaic third foot or without the two short syllables of the third foot." (*Dactylic*, dak TIL ik: describing a metrical foot of three syllables, one stressed followed by two unstressed. *Tripody*, TRIP uh dee: in prosody, a group of three feet. *Spondaic*, spon DAY ik: describing a *spondee*,

SPON dee, a foot consisting of two stressed syllables.) Now that you have digested all the foregoing, caution: *Prosodetic* (pros uh DED ik) has nothing whatever to do with any of it. All it does is to describe the ligament of a bivalve mollusk. Forgive me: I got carried away. Dictionaries *are* distracting—and if you aren't bored, you haven't been listening.

prosopopoeia (pruh soh puh PEE uh) *n.* From Greek *prosopopoiia* (personification), built of *prosopon* (face, person), plus *poiein* (to make), we get this noun signifying two distinct rhetorical devices: (1) in which an absent or imaginary person is portrayed as speaking or acting—usually where a plausible but invented speech is put into the mouth of a real character; and (2) one in which an abstract quality is represented as a person or as having personal traits—a personification or embodiment of a quality or other abstraction. In category (1), characters who existed long before the age of video and tape recorders are quoted, particularly in historical novels, in words that seem to fit the occasion. "I am dying, Egypt," says Antony to Cleopatra in the play that bears their names, and he goes on to make quite a long speech before he dies. (Dying characters in drama and opera often take a long time dying and seem quite verbose on their deathbeds.) Antony's was a dramatically justified *prosopopoeia* if there ever was one. Here's another of my favorites: "One day, Abe, you'll grow up to be the finest president of these United States," said his stepmother Sarah Bush, "and it'll be you who'll keep them united!" That one is from a children's biography of the Great Emancipator, read many years ago and long since vanished from my bookshelves, but well remembered. And nobody will convince me that Napoleon ever said, "Not tonight, Josephine." In his novel *Ragtime*, E.L. Doctorow introduced a mixed bag of real people (long since dead) and fictional characters and put words into the mouths of both. But it remained for Iris Murdoch to present us with the most absorbing examples of *prosopopoeia* that I have ever come across introducing pretended speakers and putting words into the mouths of Socrates and Plato, in *Acastos, Two Platonic Dialogues*, "imagined dialogues between wise old Socrates and wild young Plato, with help from Acastos [Plato's fictional friend] and other friends," to quote from the dust jacket. *Art and Eros* is a dialogue about art; *Above the Gods* is a dialogue about religion. Dame Iris invented half a dozen participants who have much to "say" in these wonderful dialogues. *Prosopopoeia* has never been put to better use. Dr Robert Lowth, in *Lectures on the Sacred Poetry of the Hebrews* (G. Gregory's translation from the Latin, 1787), gave the following explanation of this type of *prosopopoeia*: "Of this figure there are two kinds: one, when action and character are attributed to fictitious, irrational, or even inanimate objects; the other, when a probable but fictitious speech is assigned to a real character." In category (2), a spotless character is represented as a knight in shining armor, or versatility as a Renaissance figure like da Vinci. In *Alciphron, or the Minute Philosopher* (1732), Bishop George Berkeley speaks of "Sentiments, and vices, which by marvellous *prosopopoeia* he converts into so many ladies." (It was not unusual for such figures to be ladies.) Sir George A Macfarren, in *Six Lectures* *on Harmony* (1876), describes a person who was "everywhere at once ... the *prosopopoeia* of ubiquity." Somewhat hard to pronounce, but a useful word nonetheless.

protreptic (proh TREP tik) *n., adj.* A *protreptic* is "an exhortation" or "pep talk" (which it rather sounds like), and the adjective means "hortatory, urging." The derivation, via Late Latin *protrepticus*, is from Greek *protreptikos*, related to the verb *protrepein* (to turn forward, urge on), based on the preposition *pro-* (forward) plus *trepein* (to turn). (The *-hort-* in *exhort* and *hortatory* is from the Latin verb *hortari* "to urge, encourage.") A stirring example of this form of address in literature is the opening speech of the king in *King Henry V*, Act III, Scene 1:

> Once more unto the breach, dear friends, once more ... imitate the action of the tiger; Stiffen the sinews, summon up the blood ... lend the eye a terrible aspect ... set the teeth, and stretch the nostril wide, Hold hard the breath ... On, on, you noblest English ... upon this charge/Cry "God for Harry, England and Saint George!"

That was some *protreptic*! And it worked!

proxemics (prok SEE miks) *n.* This is a new term in sociology coined by Dr. Edward T. Hall, concerning spatial relationships arranged by human beings. In *The American Anthropologist*, vol. 65 (1963), Dr. Hall defines it as follows: "The study of how man unconsciously structures microspace—the distance between men in the conduct of daily transactions, the organization of space in his houses and buildings, and ultimately the layout of his towns." The September 29, 1969, issue of *The Guardian* (London) had this to say: "Though territoriality and its effects has been studied for many years now in connection with animal life, Dr. Hall is ... the first person to link the concept direct with human beings and ... has coined a purely human word for it: *proxemics*." There is now also an adjective, *proxemic*, as in "*proxemic* behavior." The *Times Literary Supplement*, issue of June 4, 1971, states: "In man, '*proxemic*' behavior ranges from the distance two people maintain while engaged in conversation or the way a group of people arrange themselves, to architecture and city planning." Please bear all this in mind the next time you find yourself in a crowded elevator or in the subway during rush hour, and especially when planning a new condominium.

pschent, also *p-skhent* (PSKENT, SKENT, PSCHENT—*ch* as in German *ich*). *n.* This is an Egyptian word for the double crown worn by the pharaohs after Menes (fl. c. 3200 B.C.), the king of Upper Egypt, conquered Lower Egypt and unified the two countries. Despite the unification and centralization of Egypt that followed, the memory of the two former ancient kingdoms was preserved, especially in certain formalities of government and customs. Since the Nile flows from south to north, please remember that *Upper* Egypt is the name of the *southern* part of the country, and *Lower* Egypt the name of the *northern* part. This can be quite confusing but becomes clear when one remembers that *Upper* refers to the part near the source (or *lower* end) of the Egyptian part of the Nile (the Blue Nile) and *Lower* to the *upper* end, where the river flows into the Mediterranean. Before Menes's conquest and the unification, the pharaohs of Upper and Lower Egypt wore different types of crowns. After the unification, the pharaohs wore the double crown, or *pschent*. (If you want to see what the former separate crowns and the double crown looked like, there is an excellent diagram on page 1,829 of *W III*.) The word is formed of Egyptian *p* (the, the definite article) plus *skhent* (double crown, from the Greek transliteration of the demotic, i.e., the simplified form of ancient Egyptian hieratic writing, consisting of simplified hieroglyphics, used by the priests in record keeping; more about *demotic* and *hieratic* in my *1000 Most Challenging Words*). The word became known through the discovery of the Rosetta Stone in 1798. If you have ever been on a tour of Egypt and been blessed by a guide who told you all (or more than) you wanted to know about paintings on royal tomb walls, you undoubtedly often heard: " … and this is a representation of the pharaoh wearing the crowns of Upper Egypt and Lower Egypt, seen here smiting his enemies … " Those old pharaohs certainly did a lot of smiting, a polite Egyptian-guide-ism meaning "beating the hell out of."

psellism (SEL iz'm, PSEL-) *n*. From Greek *psellismos* (stammering—the verb is *psellizein*, the adjective *psellos*), the French got *psellisme*, though their common word is *bégayer*, and we got *psellism*, though our common word is *stammering*. *Psellism* covers any defect in enunciation, including lisping, **rhotacism** (substitution of the *r* sound for some other sound, the way the Japanese, for example, substitute *r* for *l*) and pararhotacism (the converse: substitution of some other sound for that of *r*, the way the Chinese pronounce *r* as *l*, for example). *Lallation* is another name for *pararhotacism*, but it denotes childish speech generally, as might be guessed from its source: Latin *lallare*, "to sing a lullaby." *Psellism* can result from malformation of the vocal organs or from nervous ailments (especially after attending Oxford?). I happen to find the "Oxford stammer" rather attractive, particularly in women, though it drives some people (probably Cantabrigians, i.e., students at Cambridge University) crazy.

psephism   See **psephology.**

psephology (see FOL uh jee, seh-) *n*. *Psephology* is the "statistical and sociological study of election results, isues and trends"; also known as *psephoanalysis* (see foh uhn AL uh sis). A related word, *psephism* (SEE fiz'm), denotes a decree of the Athenian assembly of classical times. Why *psephology* and *psephism*? Because the Greek noun *psephos* means "pebble," and the Athenian legislators voted with pebbles. The technical name for a pundit who specializes in the study of this aspect of the democratic process is *psephologist* (see FOL uh gist), as you might have suspected, but most of them would not be aware of that lofty label, I fear. We are all familiar with the ubiquitous suffix *-logy*, tacked on in this headword to our now, by this time, familiar *psephos*.

pseudepigraphy (syoohd uh PIG ruh fee) *n*. This is the word for the ascription of a written work, especially a book, to one other than the true author. Thus *The Pseudephigrapha* is the name of books ascribed to Old Testament characters but rejected as such by scholars versed in the subject. This headword is based on the Greek prefixes *pseud-* (or *pseudo-* before a consonant), from the adjective *pseudes* (false) and *epi-* (upon), plus *graphein* (to write). An *epigraphy* (eh PIG ruh fee) without the *pseud-*, or *epigraph* (EH pig graf), not to be confused with *epigram*, is "an inscription, especially on a building," or a "citation or motto at the beginning of a book or section of a book." Authors like to cite poetic or prose passages before the text proper as apposite introductions to what's ahead. Sometimes, alas, the *epigraph* is the best part of the book.

pseudocyesis (syooh doh sye EE sis) *n*. You doubtless know from familiarity with other *pseudo-* words, like *pseudonym* and *pseudointellectual*, that something phony or deceptive is afoot, but if you don't know that *-cyesis* comes from Greek *kyesis*, "pregnancy" (*kyein* means "to be pregnant"), you can't guess that *pseudocyesis* is "false or imaginary pregnancy in women," attributed by psychologists to an exceptionally strong desire or need for motherhood. In *pseudocyesis*, despite the lack of conception, many of the phenomena of actual pregnancy develop: Menstruation stops, the abdomen and breasts swell, lactation occurs and urine tests may even be falsely positive. Some women in this condition report the sensation of fetal movement. When finally the *commedia è finita*, the disappointment often causes severe depression. "Bloody Mary" (Mary Tudor, daughter of Henry VIII and queen of England, 1553–58) underwent this disastrous experience. Elizabeth I's accession would not have happened, and the history of England would have been quite a different story, but for the *pseudo-* in that *-cyesis*!

psilanthropism (psil AN throh piz'm) *n*. This word, taken from the ecclesiastical Greek adjective *psilanthropos* (merely human), based on the prefix *psilo-*, the combining form of *psilos* (bare, mere), plus the familiar *anthropos* (man), is the name given to the theological argument or doctrine that Christ was a mere man, and not divine. This book is not the vehicle for the discussion of that hotly contested dispute, which has plagued theologians for centuries. A *psilanthropist* (psil AN throh pist) is one who adopts this doctrine; the theological sense of *humanitarian* is synonymous with *psilanthropist*, and *anthropomorphite* is still another synonym for one who affirms the humanity but denies the divinity of Christ and claims that the Deity possesses a material body. *Psilanthropism* or *humanitarianism* (in this sense) has been a charge leveled at Unitarians for many years.

psychomorphism   See **hyle.**

psychopannychy (seye koh PAN uh kee) *n.* This is the "all-night sleep of the soul," the theological doctrine that the soul falls asleep at the time of death and does not wake until resurrection, the day of judgment. It comes from Greek *psych-*, the combining form of *psyche* (spirit, soul) plus *pannychios* (all night long), built of *pan-*, the combining form of *pan*, the neuter of *pas* (all), plus *nychios* (nightly, pertaining to night), from *nykt-*, the stem of *nyx* (night). This sleep of the soul is known as *psychopannychistic slumber* and the supporters of the doctrine as *psychopannychists*. The doctrine was much disputed. Calvin rejected it. Bishop John Gauden, in *Ecclesiae Anglicae Suspiria* [Sighs of the Anglican Church], *The Tears ... of the Church of England* (1659) wrote: "No more ... than the Saducees might deny and overthrow the resurrection against Christ; or the *Psychopannuchists*, the souls immortality." In Joseph Glanvill's *Lux Orientalis, or an Enquiry into the Opinion of the Eastern Sages Concerning the Prae-Existence of Souls* (1682), we find: "Unless we will be so dull as to fall into the drouzie dream of the *Psychopannychites*!" Carl W. Buch's (1847) translation of Hagenbach's *Compendium of the History of Doctrines* speaks of " ... a revival of the earlier notion of the death of the soul ... under the milder form of the sleep of the soul (*Psychopannychy*)." Death of the soul, sleep of the soul, existence of the soul, nature of the soul? Upon my soul, I don't know the first thing about it.

putto (POOH toh) *n.* There are several words in Italian for "boy" in the ordinary sense: *fanciullo, figlio, ragazzo*; but *putto*, from Latin *putus*, is the term for the representation of a child in Italian Renaissance painting and sculpture. The child is shown nude, sometimes in swaddling clothes, sometimes winged, often in the attitude of a cupid. The word is found more often in the plural, *putti*, than the singular, since it was customary for works of art to show them in groups. In an 1894 issue of *The Nation*, the art critic and collector Bernard Berenson wrote: "It was his passion ... for the expression of the joyful feeling that led Correggio to seize every chance to paint *putti*." A February 1973 issue of the *Daily Telegraph* (London) wrote of a painting "on one side [of which] are two coats of arms ... held together by ribbons in the hand of a flying *putto*." *Putti* are still a common sight on the walls and ceilings of great concert halls and other large rooms in public buildings.

pyrrhonism   See **zetetic.**

pyrrhonist   See **zetetic.**

pyrrhonize   See **zetetic.**

pyx (PIKS) *n., vb.* In Roman Catholic (and High Anglican) practice, the *pyx* is the "vessel or container in which the Host is contained after consecration, or in which it is carried to the sick." In the sixth century it took the form of a small round box with a conical lid and was usually suspended within the church. In about 1500 it took the shape of a standard box with a flat lid. In England it usually hung above the altar. The bishop determined its size, shape, color and material, whether lapis lazuli, iron, silver, brass or whatever else took his fancy, as well as its decoration, and that prevailed for the entire diocese. Antique church *pyxes* are hard to come by and are much sought by dealers and collectors. *Pyx* has another distinct meaning: the chest at the Royal Mint in London in which gold and silver coins are deposited for testing as to weight and purity at an annual ceremony known as the *trial of the pyx*, conducted by a jury of the Goldsmiths' Company. There is a similar chest in the United States Mint. *Pyx* also serves as a verb meaning "to put into a *pyx*" and more specifically, "to place the host into a *pyx*"; or "to place specimen coins into a *pyx*" and by extension, "to test coins as to weight and assay." Eventually, *pyx* came to mean "box" generally, but this is only a literary use. The container in the British Mint is usually known as the *pyx chest. Pyx* comes, via Latin, from Greek *pyxis* (box). Our word *box*, in the sense of "container" or "receptacle" comes, via Late Latin *buxis*, from Greek *pyxis*; and as the name of an evergreen shrub, it comes via Latin *buxus*, from Greek *pyxos*—lots of tricky little vowel changes to worry about. *Pixie* and *pixy* have nothing to do with *pyx* and are of "origin unknown," "origin obscure" or "[?]," depending on which dictionary you consult.

quean (KWEEN) *n.* At first sight, this word looks like a misprint, especially when you find out that it is a term for one or another type of female; but no, it is (or was) a perfectly good word, with a different ancestry from that of *queen*. The *C.O.D.* calles it an "impudent or ill-behaved woman" and labels it "archaic"—rightly so, as we shall see. Not so *CH*, which gives it a variety of meanings: "saucy girl"; "woman of worthless character"; and in Scots, just plain "girl." *W III* defines it as "disreputable woman" and in context, "prostitute." The *O.E.D.* lists a string of meanings: "female"; in early Middle English, "a term of disparagement or abuse"; "a bold, impudent, or ill-behaved woman"; "jade, hussy"; and specifically, "harlot, strumpet"; and in Scots, "a lass, usually denoting one of a robust and healthy appearance." *RH* gives "bold, impudent woman, shrew, hussy, prostitute," and in British dialect, "girl or young woman, especially a robust one." Not a hint of archaism in any of those save the good old *C.O.D.*, but wait: The *O.E.D. Supplement* says "Now archaic" and quotes Edith Sitwell in *Sleeping Beauty:* "My eyes are dim,—I yet can see You, lazy *quean!* Go work!" It also mentions Eric Partridge's definition: "a homosexual, especially one with girlish manners and carriage";

he calls it "low." I mentioned different derivations: *quean* is from Old English *cwene, queen* from old English *cwēn*—undoubtedly related, but not identical.

quiddity   See **proprium.**

quietism   See **hesychast.**

quietist   See **hesychast.**

quisquiliary   See **quisquilious.**

quisquilious (kwis KWIL ee uhs) *adj. Quisquiliae* is a Latin plural noun meaning "rubbish, refuse, sweepings," from which we get *quisquilious* and *quisquiliary* (kwis KWIL ee air ee), "of the nature of rubbish or refuse," i.e., "trashy, worthless." The Latin noun applies to people as well as things. An 1857 issue of *Fraser's Magazine* contained the sentence: "Besides garden fruit, insects and worms, the Jay's diet is sufficiently *quisquilious*." Jeremy Bentham's *Rationale of Judicial Evidence* (1827) declared: "The science is overloaded by the *quisquilious* matter they rake together." The author of an article in an 1817 issue of *Blackwell's Magazine* preferred the form *quisquiliary*. The piece, caricaturing the Scottish author and translator Sir Thomas Urquhart (1611–60), spun out this magnificent bit of prose, using two other words we shall have to deal with now: "Those shallow and *fidimplicitary* coxcombs, who fill our too credulous ears with their *quisquiliary deblaterations*." The O.E.D. characterizes *fidimplicitary* as a "nonce-word" (a word coined and used only for a particular occasion). It is based on the ecclesiastical Latin phrase *fides implicata* (implicit faith) and describes those who swallow whole whatever the other fellow says. (Urquhart had used the word in a work entitled *The Discovery of a Most Exquisite Jewel* (1652): "*Fidimplicitary* gown-men ... satisfied with their predecessors' contrivances ... ") For *deblaterations* we have to start with *deblaterate* (dih BLAT uh rate), meaning "to prate, blab," based on Latin *blaterare* (to babble, chatter), and go on to the noun. I trust that I will not be charged with *deblaterating* too much *quisquilious* matter in this brief treatise.

reckling (REK ling) *n.* A *reckling* is the "runt of a litter," or the "youngest or weakest child in a family." It has also been used as a synonym of "weakling" generally, without regard to litters or families, and as a synonym of "puny" in adjectival use. *Wreckling* is a variant spelling, but there would seem to be only the weakest connection with *wreck*, and no authority has attempted to explain its derivation. Tennyson used the word in *Vivien* (later renamed *Vivien and Merlin; Idylls of the King*, 1859): "On returning found/ Not two but three [babes]; there lay the *reckling one*/ But one hour old!" Sir Henry Taylor used the noun attributively in *Philip van Artevelde; a Dramatic Romance* (1834): "A mother dotes upon the *reckling* child/ More than the strong." I timidly suggest a connection between *wreckling* and a fusing of *wreck* and *weakling*, but you are entitled to your own flights of fancy.

relief   See **heriot.**

remugient (ruhm YOOH juhnt) *adj. Mugire* is Latin for "to roar, bellow" (cognate with Greek *mukasthai*), and *remugire* is "to bellow again, bellow back," with the Latin, like English, indicating repetition by the prefix *re-*. *Mugire*, by transference, took on the meanings "roar, rumble, groan." Its present participle is *mugiens*; the plural, *mugientes*, was used by Horace as a substantive meaning "oxen," literally "the bellowing ones." *Remugire*, by extension, took on the meaning "to resound." Its present participle *remugiens*, whose stem is *remugient-*, gave us *remugient*, meaning "resounding" (literally, "rebellowing"). Virgil used the verb in the sentence "Vox adsensu nemorum igeminata *remugit*" (The voice *resounds* magnified by the echo of the woods). Henry More, in *An Explanation of the Grand Mystery of Godliness* (1660), used the word in a dramatic passage when he wrote of "Trembling and tottering Earth-quakes accompanied with *remugient* Echoes and ghastly murmurs from below." Were *mugire* and *mukasthai* onomatopoeic in their first syllables?

retable   See **Churrigeresque.**

rhotacism   See **psellism.**

rhyparography (reye puh RAW gruh fee) *n.* From Greek *rhyparos* (filthy) plus *-graphos* (writing, painting; related to *graphein*, to write), we get *rhyparography*, meaning "painting, drawing, or writing about mean or sordid subjects." But the word has another meaning that has nothing to do with unworthy subject matter: "still-life or genre painting." It is hard to see the connection between the two meanings, since genre painting is simply a category that depicts scenes from everyday life, and still life includes anything from fruit or vegetables to guitars or tablecloths, and what's mean or sordid about them? So one must be careful to distinguish between the two meanings when meeting up with *rhyparography*. The faint connection might be that genre and still-life painting are removed from the romantic or elegant, but that hardly bespeaks filth or grossness. As has been noted before, strange are the ways of language and meanings; and as might be expected, there is an active noun, *rhyparographer* (reye puh RAW gruh fur), for a painter who practices *rhyparography* (again presumably in either sense of the word). The Greek ancestor *rhyparographos* means simply "painting sordid subjects"—nothing to do with genre or still life generally. In the early days, *rhyparography* was defined in the narrow sense. Sir William Smith's *Dictionary of Greek and Roman Antiquities* (1842) speaks of

"Rhyparography, pornography and all the lower classes of art," but a few years later John Leitch's translation of Mueller's *Ancient Art and its Remains* (1850) mentions " ... *rhyparography* (so-called still life ...)." Yet the taint of the seamy side of life remained, as seen in George Saintsbury's article in an 1886 issue of *The Academy*, where he criticizes a writer who " ... takes a sort of Naturalist delight in describing the most sordid ... features of the least attractive kind of English middle class life, and never misses a *rhyparographic* touch when she can introduce one"; and in 1885 J. E. Harrison, in *Studies in Greek Art*, wrote of the " ... mire of *rhypography*." Note the shorter form: *rhypography* (reye PAW gruh fee), from Greek *rhypos*, not to be confused with *rhypophagy* (reye PAW fuh jee), the "eating of filth," from *rhypos* plus -*phagia*, related to *phagein* (to eat).

rhypography   See **rhyparography.**

rhypophagy   See **rhyparography.**

rondel   See **sirvent(e).**

roquelaure (ROK uh lore) *n.* If you were in charge of the costuming of the male members of the cast in a play set in the 18th or early 19th century, you might dress one or more of them in a *roquelaure*, a "short cloak reaching to the knee," named for a fashion set by Antoine-Gaston, Duc de Roquelaure (1656–1738), a marshal of France. Laurence Sterne, in *Tristram Shandy*, referred to this garment in two passages: "I have a project ... of wrapping myself warm in my *roquelaure*, and paying a visit to this poor gentleman." Again: "Your honour's *roquelaure* ... has not once been had on since the night before your honour received your wound." Frederick Marryat, in *Japhet in Search of a Father* (1836), evidently conceived of the *roquelaure* as reaching some way below the knee, for he wrote, "I went out and purchased a *roquelaure*, which enveloped my whole person." In his *Biographical History of England; being a Continuation of J. Granger's Work* (1806: that work being James Granger's *Letters between G. and Many of the Most Eminent Literary Men of his Time*, 1805), Mark Noble noted: "The *roquelaure* cloak ... displaced the surtout." The *surtout* was a "man's overcoat," which, according to the *O.E.D.*, was a name taken from the French (*sur*, above, plus *tout*, everything) "applied c[irca] 1870 to a kind of single-breasted frock-coat with pockets cut diagonally in front." Getting back to this play and your job of dressing the male members of the cast, you might well be confused: If the *roquelaure* was worn only until the early part of the 19th century, how could it "displace" the *surtout*, which was not known as such until circa 1870? Wasn't it the other way around? And how about the diction-ary definitions that describe the *roquelaure* as reaching *to* the knee, and Marryat's telling us that it enveloped the "whole person?" It may be this sort of thing that results in the distasteful practice of doing period plays in modern dress, for fear of the carping of nitpicking critics.

roskopf (ROS kopf) *n*. This word denotes the type of watch described below. It is sometimes capitalized, as a sign of respect to G. S. Roskopf, a Swiss watchmaker (d. 1889) who designed it. It is a watch with a barrel (the flat cylindrical metal container that encloses the mainspring of a watch or clock) of greater diameter than the radius of the watch. This is a most unusual design, not especially attractive, but interesting. Horological friends have tried, without much success, to explain the advantages of Roskopf's innovation— something to do with greater accuracy, etc.—but the design itself hasn't much to recommend it.

rosmarine (ROZ muh rine) *n*. Three meanings are given for this word by the *O.E.D.*: "rosemary," "sea-dew" and "walrus." These three would appear to be pretty far apart: an herb, dew from the ocean and a marine animal. The walrus is a marine mammal of the genus *Odobenus rosmarus*, which does give us some connection with *rosmarine*. The word is used in the second sense mentioned above, "sea-dew," in Jonson's *Queenes Masque* (1616): "You shall ... steep Your bodies in that purer brine,/And wholesome dew call'd Ros-marine." It is used in the third sense in Spenser's *Faerie Queene* (1590): "The horrible Sea-satyre ... And greedy *Rosmarines* with visages deforme ... " Incidentally, *rosmaro* is Spanish for "manatee, sea-cow," and *rosmarino* in Spanish means "rosemary"; *ros* by itself is Latin for "dew," but *ros marinus* or *rosmarinus* in one word means "rosemary," and *ros maris* (dew of the sea) seems to be reserved for "sea-dew." Confusing. *CH* gives the definitions "rosemary," referring to Spenser; "sea-dew," referring to Jonson; and again referring to Spenser, "a walrus, or a sea-monster supposed to lick dew off the rocks." In "Word-Watching," the admirable definition-guessing game appearing daily in *The Times* (London), Philip Howard gives the definition "walrus." He goes on to explain: " ... once thought by old wives of both sexes to climb rocks by its teeth to feed on dew" and follows with the above chilling quote from Spenser. His "old wives of both sexes" echoes a quotation from *Tristram Shandy* that I used in my *1000 Most Challenging Words* under the headword *anile* when I ended the comment with: "Despite the remark in *Tristram Shandy* ... about 'the nonsense of the old women' (of both sexes), you can call an old woman *senile* but you can't call an old man *anile*." I don't know whether walruses like the taste of rosemary. If you run into *rosmarine*, I suggest you go along with Philip Howard and settle for "walrus."

rostrocarinate (ros troh KAR uh nate) *n*., *adj*. As an adjective, *rostrocarinate* is an archaeological term describing flint objects that resemble an eagle's beak, especially those found in East Anglia (i.e., the counties of Norfolk and Suffolk in southeast England, which were once an early English kingdom). They were at first believed to be artifacts of the late Pliocene era but are now recognized as natural, not man-made, formations. The term is derived from *rostro-*, the combining form of Latin *rostrum* (literally, that which gnaws; as an ornithological term, beak; as a nautical term, the curved end of a ship's prow, used for ramming) plus *carinatus*, from *carina* (keel); *carinatus* gave us *carinate*, meaning "keel-like" or "shaped like the keel or prow of a ship." As a noun, *rostrocarinate* means an object having the shape described above. *W III*, in an edition with a 1986 copyright, defines the word in terms of an artifact, whereas the *O.E.D. Supplement O to Scz*, copyright 1982, had already revealed that these flints, once believed to be hand tools, were now considered "natural forma-tions." As to the *W III* definition, one must remember the enduring statement of H. W. Fowler in his preface to the *C.O.D.*: "A dictionary-maker, unless he is a monster of omniscience, must deal with a great many matters of which he has no first-hand knowledge." Forgiveness is in order. Back in 1934 the *Journal of the Royal Anthropological Institute* contained these words: "Among these large *tools* ... a number of well-made *rostro-carinate* forms is to be distin-guished"; and J. K. Charlesworth's *Quaternary Era* (1957) states (referring to certain "Cromerian *implements*," i.e., artifacts of a period dating a million years back): "These *tools* ... include *rostrocarinates*." It was natural for the *W III* staff to rely on those authorities and very clever of the *Supplement* not to. Inciden-tally, in using the term "monster of omniscience," Fowler may well have had in mind the Latin noun *monstrum*, which means, inter alia, "wonder" or "miracle," not simply "monster."

rowen (ROU uhn) *n*. Also **rowan, rowing, rawing, rawn** and numerous other variants. Among other things, this word is interesting because of its synonyms, of which more later. Its general meaning is "second crop (e.g., of hay) in a season." It is Middle English, from Old French (and modern French as well) *regain*, meaning "second crop." In old French, *gain* meant, inter alia, "crop, harvest," and the prefix *re-* had the same force of "repetition" as in a number of modern languages (English and various Romance tongues). *W III* defines *rowen* as "a stubble field left unplowed till late in the autumn to be grazed by cattle" and gives "aftermath" as a second meaning, while *RH* tells us that a *rowen* is "the second growth of grass or hay in a season; and *CH* and the *C.O.D.* are content with merely "aftermath." The *O.E.D.* speaks of "second growth" and adds not only "aftermath" but also "eddish" and goes on to explain, in its usual helpful way, that "The precise application of the term (esp[ecially] with regard to the cutting of the aftergrowth or leaving it for pasture) varies to some extent in diferent localities." In a sense, "precise applications" of many terms "vary in different localities," do they not? As to *eddish*, the *O.E.D.* gives us "an aftergrowth of grass after mowing" and "stubble." I said above that *rowen* was interesting because of its synonyms. *Eddish* is a new one on me, but I found *aftermath* quite a surprise, because I had never run across that familiar word except in its generally understood meaning of "consequences," almost always with dire implications, as in "the aftermath of war," "the aftermath of widespread drought," epidemic, a stock market crash, etc. In their definitions of *aftermath*, most American dictionaries speak of "consequences" first and "second growth" second, while the British dictionaries do the reverse. In any event, I tried *aftermath* on a number of friends both British and American, and not one of them mentioned anything to do with second growths or crops. And only one American dictionary, *W III*, put the farming definition first and the "consequences" definition second. What's more, in its example of the second meaning, it mentioned "gratifying" effects rather than dire ones. Confusing, but interesting, I hope, to word buffs. As to the derivations of these synonyms, the *O.E.D.* tells us that *eddish* is "of obscure etymology," while in the case of *aftermath* in the agricultural sense, the *after-* is simple enough, but the *-math* is less obvious. *Math*, now dialectal British English meaning "mowing of a grass or hay crop" or the "gathered crop" itself, is an *assumed* Middle English term, from Old English *maeth* (crop of hay, grass mowing), derived from the root of the Old English verb *mawan* (to mow). The more familiar meaning "consequences" or "effects" is obviously a figurative extension, whether dire or gratifying.

rune   See **futhork.**

runic   See **futhork.**

scazon   See **hapax legomenon.**

scholiast   See **scholium.**

scholion   See **scholium.**

scholium (SKOH lee uhm), also **scholion** (SKOH lee uhn) *n.* A *scholium* or *scholion* is a "marginal notation in the nature of an explanatory note or comment," especially by an early grammarian on a Greek or Latin text. The word can also signify a note added by the author illustrating or developing a point discussed in the text and has been incorrectly used to mean a "trite saying" or "maxim," such as "familiarity breeds contempt," or, as a waggish friend of mine said about goings-on between male members of the staff and attractive females in a business office: "Familiarity breeds attempt." A *scholiast* (SKOL ee ast) is a "commentator" or "annotator." Another friend of mine collaborated on a *Key to Finnegans Wake*, with more text devoted to the *scholia* than Joyce allotted to the original. *Scholium* comes, via Modern Latin, from Greek *scholion*, a diminutive of *schole* (school).

scrag (SKRAG) *n., vb. Scrag* is a small word with an uncommonly large number of meanings. It is thought to be a modification of the obsolete *crag* in the senses of "neck, throat, neck of mutton or veal, a skinny person." The *O.E.D.* suggests that the initial *s* was added "due to some feeling of phonetic expressiveness" (to lend a touch of onomatopoeia?). In any event, *scrag* means "sheep's neck," "the lean, inferior part of a veal or mutton neck," "human neck" (slang) or "skinny person or animal" (pejorative); as a verb, it means, "to hang on the gallows" (slang), "to throttle," "to wring the neck of (a person or fowl)," "to tackle by the neck" (in soccer), "to kill, murder"; and to "bend" (a sheet of metal, for testing). A *scragger* or *scrag-boy* is a "hangman"; a *scragging-post* is "the gallows"; a *scrag-whale* or *scrag-tailed whale* is one with a knobbed back (i.e., any of a number of small whales without a dorsal fin but with protruberances on the dorsal ridge near the tail). A *scraggy* person, animal or limb is skinny and bony (pejorative); *scraggy* meat is lean meat; *scraggy* rocks are rugged rocks; a *scraggy* branch is knotted and full of projections; *scraggy* trees are stunted, ragged and of scanty growth. Getting back to this versatile noun, *scrag* can also mean "tree stump," a "rough projection on a tree trunk, a stump, a rock" or a "piece of rough, rocky, barren ground." Lots of work for a little word!

scrag-boy   See **scrag.**

scragger   See **scrag.**

scragging-post   See **scrag.**

scraggy   See **scrag.**

scrag-whale   See **scrag.**

scrutable   See **scrutate.**

scrutate (SKROOH tate) *vb.* *Scrutiny, scrutinize* and *inscrutable* are familiar words, owing their origin to Late Latin *scrutinium* (close examination) and Latin *scrutari* (to examine). Both these words are thought to come from *scruta* (broken bits, trash, rags), on the theory that *scrutari* implied a search so thorough that it even included an examination of rags and trash, reminiscent of the deseprate hunt for clues in modern detective stories. But *scrutate*, meaning "to search out, investigate," from *scrutatus*, the past participle of *scrutari*, is a quite unfamiliar form. So, too, is *scrutable* (SKROOH tuh b'l), meaning "decipherable, comprehensible, legible," while *inscrutable* is not quite its opposite, but means rather, "not quite comprehensible" and is generally understood as "mysterious," as in phrases like "the inscrutable East" and the popular character "the inscrutable Mr. Moto," of detective-story fame. I have in the past written about the peculiarity of usage in our language whereby the negative adjective is much more often used than the positive from which it is taken and is frequently not the exact opposite in meaning. Thus, for example, *impeccable* is used generally in the sense of "faultless, irreproach-able," as applied to dress, conduct and manners, while the rarely used *peccable* denotes liability to sin or gross error, though they both stem from Latin *peccare* (to go wrong, err, sin). The same goes for *steady* in its ordinary uses and *unsteady*, generally denoting shakiness of gait; and there are many more examples of this phenomenon. From Latin *scrutatio* we get *scrutation* (skrooh TAY shuhn), "minute search, examination, investigation," and we take Latin *scrutator* intact into English, meaning "investigator" generally, and more specifically "scrutineer," one who acts as inspector of votes at an election. *Scrutatory* comes into the picture as well, meaning "examining, searching, investigating." That about does it, except for the peculiar and apparently unrelated term *scruto*, a theatrical term of undetermined origin, meaning "trapdoor," flush with the stage, usually constructed of strips of wood or whalebone, and also known as *scruto-piece, sloat* or *slote*. A possible explanation of *scruto* or *scruto-piece* might have to do with "something one should have investigated," i.e., *scrutinized*, before falling into the trap; and *sloat* and *slote* may have had something to do with *slot*, the kind of opening things slip through—but, as I always say, beware of etymological guesswork.

scrutation   See **scrutate.**

scrutator   See **scrutate.**

scrutatory   See **scrutate.**

scruto   See **scrutate.**

scruto-piece   See **scrutate.**

securiform (sih KOOH rih form) *adj.* You might well be forgiven for thinking that this adjective has to do with *security*, but not after reading what follows. Our words *secure* and *security* are derived from Latin *securus* and *securitas*, which mean, respectively, "free from care, untroubled, secure" and "freedom from anxiety," "safety, security." Those Latin words are in turn based on the Latin prefix *se-* (without) and *cura* (care). Well and good; then how about *securiform*? Here we have a different story, for this word means "axe-shaped" (surprise!), because it is based on a different Latin word: *securis* (axe), based in turn on the verb *secare* (to cut) plus *forma* (form, shape). One may feel more secure carrying an axe than not, but that has nothing to do with the lack of etymological relationship between *securus* and *securis*. Mustn't let these little accidents fool you; appearances can be deceiving, particularly in etymology.

sermuncle (SUR munk'l) *n. Sermo* is Latin for "talk, discourse," and its diminutive *sermunculus* was formed in the usual way, by adding the diminutive suffix *-culus*, which incidentally caused the change of the *o* of the stem *sermon-* to *u*. (Cf. *carbuncle*, from Latin *carbunculus*, which originally meant "live coal," formed from *carbon-*, the stem of *carbo*, meaning "burned wood," plus the same diminutive suffix -*culus*, with the same change from *o* to *u*; *carbunculus* came to denote any red object and was applied to an inflamed tumor.) Latin *sermo* became *sermon* in English—a particular type of "discourse"—and, in more modern times, a short one became known as a *sermonette* (ocasionally *sermonet* or even *sermonettine*) with the addition of the familiar diminutive suffix -*ette*. It is a more readily recognizable synonym of *sermuncle*. By whatever name, these short sermons were devised to correspond to the shorter attention span of those members of the congregation endowed with much less patience than that of their forefathers.

sestet   See **sixain.**

sestina   See **sixain.**

sextain   See **sixain.**

sharia (shah REE uh) *n.* Taken from Arabic *shariah*, like most words of Arabic source this word has a number of variant spellings, always characteristic of transliterations from Eastern languages: *shariah, shariat, sheria, sheriah, sheriat*, etc. *Sharia* is the "Islamic religious law": the body of established law based primarily on the commandments of Allah as found in the Koran and revealed through the *sunna* (SOO nah)—the "words and deeds of Muhammad." Though this is the sacred law, it covers not only religious matters but also political, economic, civil and criminal areas and the general field of social and domestic affairs in Muslim countries. The *sharia* is usually supplemented by the traditional practices of a given region. A March 1979 issue of the *Guardian* (London) described the *shariah* as "a way of life remarkable for its homogeneity ... meaning simply the way or path," but doubtless the advent of the Ayatollah and the mullahs has brought about changes in the way of increasingly rigorous interpretation and enforcement. With every dispatch from some of the Islamic countries, we must evermore cherish our constitutions, whether written, as in America, or unwritten, as in Britain.

shebeen   See **boreen.**

Shekinah (shih KEE nuh), also **Schechinah** (shih CHEE nuh) *n.* This is a theological term, taken from Hebrew (*shuh CHEE nah—ch* as in *ach, loch*), signifying God's presence on earth or a manifestation thereof; also, a "refulgent light symbolizing the Divine Presence." *Shechinah* is used in the *Targums* in place of *God*; e.g., when He is said to dwell among the cherubim, in order to avoid any hint of anthropomorphism. *Targum* (TAR guhm) is Chaldean for "exegesis, interpretation," denoting an Aramaic translation or interpretation of a book of the Old Testament made after the Babylonian captivity (in the sixth century B.C.). That word gave rise to the verb *targum* (to interpret or paraphrase Scripture); the adjective *targumic* (tar GOOM ik), the noun *tar-*

gumist (TAR guhm ist, a translator and commentator who assisted in the compilation of, or one one versed in the literature of, the *Targums*), the adjective *targumistic* (tar guhm IS tik, pertaining to the *targumists*) and the verb *targumize* (TAR guhm ize, to make a *Targum* of a book of the Old Testament). George Eliot, in *Scenes of Clerical Life* (1858), wrote: "The golden sunlight beamed through the dripping boughs like a *Shechinah*, or visible divine presence." The term has also been applied to the presence of Jesus Christ on earth. It could be manifested by any natural or supernatural phenomenon, like the burning bush or the cloud on the summit of Mt. Sinai, by a mystical intervention in human affairs or through a sense of personal communion with God sensed by man.

shive   See **vellinch.**

sirvent(e) (seer VAWNT—the *A* pronounced nasally as in French) *n.* The ancestor of this word was Provençal *sirventes*, which was mistakenly taken to be a plural form, so that both the French and English form became the erroneous singular *sirvent(e)*. (I once heard someone say that so-and-so's accomplishments deserved a big *kudo*; same mistake!) Be that as it may, a *sirvent* is a "troubador's poem or lay, usually of a satirical nature." In *Ivanhoe* we read: "The knight ... asked his host whether he would choose a *sirvente* in the language of *oc*, or a *lai* in the language of *oui*." *Oc* was *yes* in the Romance dialects of southern France, and *Langue d'oc* was the name given to them. *Oil* or *oui* was *yes* in the Romance dialects of northern France, and *Langue d'oil* and *Langue d'oui* were names given to them. Bishop William Stubbs, in *Seventeen Lectures on the Study of Mediaeval and Modern History* (1886), writes of " ... some few *sirventes* or satiric lays that entitle Richard [I] to the name of a trouvère [a medieval narrative poet of northern France]." (Trouvère is the northern French form of the word, more familiar to us as *troubadour*.) In Browning's *Sordello* we find the couplet: "A notion of the Troubador's intent/In rondel, tenzon, virlai or *sirvent*." A *rondel* is a verse form of thirteen or fourteen lines on two rhymes, the seventh and thirteenth being identical with the first and the eighth, and the fourteenth (if present) with the second. A *tenzon* or *tenson* is a verse competition between two troubadors before a court of love (a judicial court to determine affairs of the heart in Provence in the days of the troubadors). A *virlai*, more commonly *virelay*, is a song or short lyric piece originating in 14th-century France, consisting of short lines in stanzas with two rhymes, the end rhyme of one stanza being the chief one of the next. Back to Browning for a moment: He had to pronounce *sirvent* in his own, arbitrary, way, to rhyme with *intent*. Things like that don't matter much to poets; they have enough troubles as it is.

sis(s)erary (sis ur AY ree), also **sassarara** (sas uhr AY ruh) *n.* Originally, this was a popular corruption of *certiorari*, the name of a writ issuing from a superior court calling for the record of a proceeding in an inferior court on an appeal. A petition for *certiorari* is the document filed with the Supreme Court of the United States on an appeal to that court. *Sis(s)erary, sassarara* and a large number of variant spellings are now all obsolete in this sense. *Certiorari,* incidentally, is the passive infinitive of the Latin verb *certiorare* (to inform), related to *certior* (surer), the comparative of *certus* (sure, certain). *Sis(s)erary* and its variants acquired the following meanings: "Severe rebuke," "scolding," "sharp blow," "torrent (of language)," "loud clang." The expression *with a siserary* (however spelled) means "with a vengeance," as used, for example, by Laurence Sterne in *Tristram Shandy*: "It was on a Sunday in the afternoon, when I fell in love all at once *with a sisserara.*" In *The Vicar of Wakefield*, Oliver Goldsmith used it this way: "'As for the matter of that,' returned the hostess, '... out she shall pack *with a sassarara.*'" Smollett used it in the sense of "rebuke," Scott in the sense of "torrent" (a *siserary of Latin*) and others with the meaning of "clang." In all its spellings, a versatile word!

sixain (suh ZANE, sik SANE) *n.* This is a term in poetry meaning a "stanza of six lines," taken over from French, where *sixain* is an alternative to the more frequently found *sizain*, which came from Old French *sisain*, based on *sis* (six). *Sextain* (SEK stane) is another word for a "six-line stanza." The related word *sestina* (seh STEEN uh) denotes a much more complicated form, a lyrical arrangement contrived by the troubadors of Provence in the 12th century consisting of six stanzas, each of six lines, originally unrhymed, with the six end words repeated in different order in each of the stanzas, and an envoy (sometimes spelled *envoi*; a short concluding stanza) of three lines, in which three of these end words occur in the middle of the line and the other three at the end of the line—a very elaborate scheme indeed! The *sestina* is not to be confused with the *sestet*, the last six lines of a sonnet in the Italian form, considered as a unit. This takes some explaining. A sonnet consists of fourteen lines, usually in iambic pentameter (each line containing five feet of two syllables, the first syllable unstressed, the second stressed). A sonnet in the Italian form, also known as the *strict form*, is divided into a group of eight lines considered as a unit and known as the major group or *octave*, followed by a group of six lines, the minor group, or *sestet*. The looser "Shakespearean" form of sonnet consists of three quatrains (groups of four lines) followed by a couplet (two lines), with a less exacting rhyme scheme. Look at the first quatrain of one of the most beautiful of Shakespeare's sonnets (number 18):

> Shall I compare thee to a summer's day?
> Thou art more lovely and more temperate:
> Rough winds do shake the darling buds of May,
> And summer's lease hath all too short a date ...

and read the rest.

sjambok (SHAM bok) *n.* Also found in the forms *sambock, shambok, jambok,* etc., this is the name of a heavy whip made of rhinoceros or hippopotamus hide, used in South Africa for driving cattle and whipping people—lovely thought! As a verb, *to sjambok* is "to flog with such a whip." This delightful instrument is described in a number of South African travel books (e.g., Thomas Pringle, *African Sketches*; Frederick Selous, *Travels and Adventures in South-east Africa*). The word originated in Cape Dutch, fashioned after Malay *samboq* and Persian and Urdu *chabouk* or *chabuk* (horsewhip). We have seen lots of pictures on television of South African police using heavy-looking whips on protesters. Do you suppose the whips were made of rhinoceros or hippopotamus hide? *Sjamboks?* Or is everything plastic these days?

skelder (SKEL dur) *vb*. *To skelder*, used intransitively, is "to beg, to live by begging, especially by passing oneself off as a wounded or discharged soldier." Shackerley Marmion (there's a name for you!), in his comedy *A Fine Companion* (1633), penned these words: " ... wandering abroad to *skelder* for a shilling." Transitively, *to skelder* is "to swindle, defraud, obtain (money) by cheating." Ben Jonson, in *Poetaster, or the Arraignmment* (1601), said: "A man may *skelder* yee, now and then, of halfe a dozen shillings, or so." Sir Walter Scott, in *Woodstock, or the Cavalier* (1826), wrote: "I have lived in a *skeldering* sort of way myself." The dictionaries agree that the origin of *skelder* is shrouded in mystery, differing only in whether to characterize it as "unknown," "obscure" or simply "cant." Perhaps *cant* needs an apostrophe and is simply short for "can't help you"?

skimmington (SKIM ing tuhn) *n*. *To skim* is "to clear a liquid" (of scum or any other unwanted floating substance). This is usually done with a skimming ladle, also known as a *skimmer*. A *skimmington* is a "boisterous, ludicrous procession, once common in the countryside, to ridicule or heap odium upon an unfaithful or abusive spouse," and the term was applied as well to the person in the procession who impersonated the cuckolded or abused spouse, whether the henpecked or cuckolded husband or his unfaithful or shrewish wife. To *ride (the) skimmington* was to hold such a procession. A *skimmity* (SKIM uh dee) or *skimmity ride* was another name for that kind of procession. Well may you wonder, what is the connection between *skimming* scum off the top of a liquid and boisterous processions shaming abusive spouses? Believe it or not, there is a simple explanation: The shrewish wife in the procession was usually represented as beating her unhappy spouse with a *skimming* ladle. Farfetched? Nothing in language is farfetched. Elementary, as Sherlock Holmes would have put it, on coming across the frontispiece of a 1696 publication entitled *Diveres Crabtree Lectures*, showing a woman beating her husband with a *skimming* ladle and bearing the caption *"Skimmington, and her Husband."* In *The Mayor of Casterbridge* (1886) Thomas Hardy wrote of "the rude music of the *skimmington* and the *skimmington ride*," and an 1865 issue of *St. James' Magazine* asserts: "The '*skymington*' (sic) is still in use for henpecked husbands and shrewish wives." Cf. *shivaree*, another type of noisy procession expressing disapproval, fully discussed in my *1000 Most Challenging Words*.

skimmity   See **skimmington.**

sloat   See **scrutate.**

slote   See **scrutate.**

smogger (SMOG ur) *n*. This is the tramps' cant word for their special road-sign code, said to have been initiated in England during the reign of Henry VIII (first half of the 16th century). Communication among vagabonds was achieved by chalk marks, which they called *"smogger"* (origin unknown), made on gateposts. For example: Two large overlapping or intersecting circles meant "tell a sob story, a sad tale of woe"; three circles in a row meant "soft touch for money here." Tramps read *smogger* as easily as Egyptologists read hieroglyphics. The symbols were usually taken by householders to be naive children's drawings. No one has demonstrated any connection between *smogger* and the much later *smog*, a portmanteau combination of *smoke* and *fog*.

smoot (SMOOHT) *n*. This is a unit of linear measurement equivalent to approximately 5 feet 7 inches. Its origin is one of the more esoteric bits of Harvard College history. Oliver R. Smoot was an M.I.T. (Massachusetts Institute of Technology) freshman in 1958. As a bit of fraternity hazing, he had to lie down 365 times as friends (?) painted *"smoot* marks" every tenth time to measure the length of the Harvard Bridge over the Charles River. It comes to about a half mile; i.e., 10 *smoots* = 1/2 mile. Not long ago (this is March 1989) *smoot* marks were threatened with obliteration. The bridge was to be renovated and the *smoots*, maintained and repainted over the years by freshmen, eradicated. However, bridge authorities ruled that the *smoots*, now a tradition, must stay. Indeed, a plaque honoring the *smoot* will be installed on the bridge this spring. Bravo! So far, the *smoot* has not been taken into everyday English, but in view of the multiplicity of Harvard men gaining high positions in our government, it may be adopted, and as a Harvard '27 man myself, two of whose older brothers were M.I.T. men, '16 and c. '19 respectively, I shall do my best to keep the *smoot* alive.

snuff (SNUFF) *n., vb*. In addition to denoting a preparation of powdered tobacco inhaled through the nostrils, *snuff* has a number of entirely distinct meanings: the "sooty, partly consumed, ill-smelling end of a lamp or candle wick that has to be trimmed:' a "candle end"; figuratively, "anything of no value"; a *"heeltap"* (see **supernaculum**); in Scotland, "umbrage, a huff or pet"; as a verb, "to sniff, to smell at something doubtfully, to remove the *snuff* from, to brighten"; *to snuff out* is "to put out (a lamp or candle) with *snuffers*." As slang, *to snuff it* or *snuff out* is "to die." The derivation is from German *Schnuppe* (snuff of a candle), and, in the sense of "something of no value," cf. German *Das ist mir ganz Schnuppe* (I don't care a rap). In Trollope's *He Knew he was Right* (1869) we read the words "going out like the *snuff of a candle*," i.e., on the way out, dying. Pepys used *snuff* in the sense of "umbrage" in his *Diary* (a 1662 entry): "Mr Mills ... I expect, will take it in *snuffe* that my wife did not come to his child's christening the other day." Stevenson used it in the sense of "huff" or "pet" in *Kidnapped*: "Dinnae flew up in the *snuff* at me." A very versatile word, *snuff*, quite apart from *snuff*-taking.

soc(c)age (SOK ij) *n.* This is one of those technical terms having to do with social and economic arrangements under the feudal English legal system. *Soc(c)age* was the "tenure of land for agricultural service fixed in amount and kind or by payment of rent in money," but in either case free of any obligation to render military service to the owner. *Soc* was a variant of *soke*, which denoted, among other things, jurisdiction over a defined territory or group of people; and a *sokeman* was a "tenant by *socage*," also known as a *socager*. The origin of these various terms was Old English *socn* (jurisdiction). Another form of tenure was *burgage*, in which royal land or that owned by the nobility in English *burghs* (boroughs) was held for an annual rent, and in Scottish boroughs for the service of "watching and warding," i.e., overseeing and guarding. The most distinctive feature of *socage* was freedom from "knight-service" (military service) in the lord's armed forces. Our conscientious objectors never suggested that type of proposition.

socager   See **soc(c)age.**

soke   See **soc(c)age.**

sororate   See **levirate.**

spicilege   See **florilegium.**

spiggoty, also **spiggity, spigotti**, etc. (SPIH guh tee) *n.* I disapprove of all ethnic pejoratives, but one does run into them, and I suppose they have to be explained. *Spiggoty*, then, is a derisive term for a Spanish-speaking native of Central or South America. The name seems to have originated during the digging of the Panama Canal, from the broken English "speekee (or spikka) de" in the expression "no speekee de Inglish," which was supposedly all the Panamanians could muster when addressed in English. Rex Stout, in *Fer-de-Lance* (1934), used the word in this passage: "'He's a dirty *spiggoty*.' 'No. Archie, Mr. Manuel Kimball is an Argentine.'" In *Harbor Nights* by H. Klemmer (1937) we see this unhappy sentence: "*Marijuana* is a popular *spiggoty* drug which has spread rapidly into the North during recent years." Harry La-Tourette Foster's *The Adventures of a Tropical Tramp* (1922) contains this bit of prose: "Just stood around the dock and jabbered a lot of *spiggoty* talk at me, like I could understand *spiggoty*. I don't know a word of this damned Spanish, and I'm glad of it!" We can see from these passages that *spiggoty* was a contemptuous term, and I'm happy to say that, so far as I can ascertain, it's extinct. But unhappily, *spic* or *spick*, also derived from *spiggoty*, still issues from the mouths of thoughtless people.

spondee   See **dolichurus.**

spurrier   See **lorimer.**

stamnos   See **krater.**

statocracy   See **ochlocracy.**

statocrat   See **ochlocracy.**

stenobathic (sten oh BATH ik) *adj.* From Greek *stenos* (narrow) we get the combining form *steno-*, which, combined with *bathos* (depth), gives us this term relating to aquatic life and describing those species capable of life within only a narrow range of depths. Combining the same *steno-* with *hals* (salt), we get the aquatic term *stenohaline*, designating a species capable of living only within a narrow range of salinity. *Steno-* plus *therme* (heat) produces *stenothermal*, describing animals capable of existing only within a narrow range of temperature. Greek *eurys* (wide) has the combining form *eury-*, which is combined with *bathos, hals* and *therme* to produce *eurybathic* and *euryhaline* to describe aquatic life capable of existence within wide rangers of depth and salinity, respectively, and *eurythermal* to designate animals that can survive within a wide range of temperature. One could, I suppose, combine additional Greek prefixes and environmental terms to increase the scope of biological terminology much more widely, but sufficient unto the day is the homework thereof.

stenohaline   See **stenobathic.**

stenothermal   See **stenobathic.**

stillicide (STIL ih side) *n.* This might well be taken for the name of one of those heinous crimes like *fratricide, matricide* or *regicide* whereby somebody gets killed, but people don't go around killing *stills*, except perhaps those mean "Feds" who destroyed the apparatus used in the moonshine industry romanticized in old movies. Actually, *stillicide* has nothing whatever to do with killing. The confusion arises because there are two distinct Latin verbs, *caedere* and *cadere*, from which we get the suffix *-cide. Caedere* means "to kill," *cadere* "to fall." The *-cide* of all those killing words comes from *caedere*; the *-cide* of *stillicide* comes from *cadere*. Now, *stilla* is Latin for "drop," as in *drop of water* (or any liquid), and *stillicidium* means "dripping moisture" generally, and in a special usage, "rain water dropping from eaves of houses." *Stillicide* developed as a legal term denoting the dropping of rain water from one's eaves upon the roof or land of a neighbor and was then applied to an easement (called a *servitude* in Scots law) permitting such dropping, which would otherwise be actionable. If your eaves protrude far enough to cause rain water dropping from them to moisten your neighbor's land, better talk it over with him and ask for an easement, but if he's stubborn, consult your lawyer, and if he can't work it out, get your carpenter to fit gutters and downspouts. Otherwise, the *stillicide* might result in a *vicinicide*, a word I just concocted to mean "killing of a neighbor," from *vicinus*, Latin for "neighbor," and the murderous type of *-cide*.

stirp (STURP) *n*. In Latin, *stirps* means literally the "stock or stem of a tree or plant," and by transference, figuratively, "stock, source, origin" relating to human beings; particularly, the "stock of a family, a line of descent." It is in the latter sense that the legal phrase *per stirpes* (pur STUR peez; *stirpes* is the plural of Latin *stirps*) is used in testamentary or trust documents. Distribution *per stirpes* is one that follows the lines of descent. For example, if a bequest is qualified as made *per stirpes* (as opposed to *per capita*) and the testator is survived by three children and the two children of a deceased child, the bequest would go initially four ways because there are four *stirpes*: one share to each surviving child and one share to the two grandchildren collectively, so that each of them would receive one-eighth of the bequest. In effect, the testator is saying: "I loved my four children with equal affection while they were all alive, and therefore allot that last fourth to the children of the one that died during my lifetime." As a practicing lawyer for more than half a century, I had to explain the shortcut technical term *per stirpes* a couple of thousand times or thereabouts. It was sometimes hard to keep the attention of the client, and I frequently had to resort to diagrams, but all in a good cause.

strangury (STRANG yur ee) *n*. This book contains few medical terms, which exist in the thousands and certainly are obscure to the layman, whom they generally terrify rather than inform, yet this word not only has an interesting derivation but also exemplifies one of those cases of dangerous etymological association. *Strangury* is the "painful retention of a difficulty of discharging urine." Via Latin *stranguria*, it comes from Greek *strangouria*, composed of *stranx* (drop, trickle) plus *ourein* (to urinate), from *ouron* (urine). It amounts to a slow, painful discharge, a drop at a time, caused by spasmodic contraction of the bladder and urethra. Our word *strain* is associated with *stranx* and the Greek adjective *strangos* (twisted, flowing drop by drop). This disorder goes back a long way, as indicated by the Greek and Latin nomenclature mentioned above, and as long ago as 1398 there appeared the following graphic description of the disease in John de Trevisa's translation of Bartholomeus de Glenville's *De Proprietatibus Rerum* (On the Properties [Peculiarities?] of Things): "He that hath that dysease ... that hyghte *Stranguria*, pysseth ofte ande lytyll." Laurence Sterne, in *The Life and Opinions of Tristram Shandy*, gives us this sentence: "I hope they have got better of their colds ... fevers, *stranguries*, [etc.]." Now comes the dangerous jump-to-conclusion exercise in association-type etymology: Some have believed that *strangury* is a disease caused by *strangling* (!) or choking, as a result of which it has been used figuratively (and erroneously) by no less great figures than George Farquhar in *Love and a Bottle*: "Is my countenance strain'd, as if my head were distorted by a *Stranguary* [sic] of thought?" and Thackeray in a contribution to *Punch*: "Everybody stopped. There was a perfect *strangury* in the street." The adjective is *strangurious* (strang YUR ee uhs), and damned be him who cries "I hold too much!"

strappado (struh PAH doh, -PAY-) *n*. This is the name of a terrible form of torture, in which the victim's wrists were tied behind his back and fastened to a pulley, by means of which he was hoisted and then let down partway with a jerk. The word served as well to denote the procedure and the instrument involved. In the bad old days, it was used to force confessions, evidencing, like the rack, catherine wheel, thumbscrew and a variety of other instruments of torture, the delightful combination of man's ingenuity and inhumanity to man. *Strappado* was a modification of Italian *strappata* (sharp tug), related to the verb *strappare* (to pull sharply), with the addition of the common quasi-Spanish suffix *-ado*. In H.C. Lea's *History of the Inquisition* (1888) we learn that "in some witch trials of 1474 in Piedmont the oath to tell the truth was enforced with excommunication and *'tratti di corde'* [literally, tugs of cords] or infliction of the torture known as the *strappado*." I have been unable to ascertain the number of wrists broken, or shoulders separated, in the course of this delectable exercise. The device was used in the Inquisition and for some time thereafter. It is mentioned as a contemporary form of torture in numerous works, some as late as 1688. Shakespeare was familiar with the term (what *wasn't* he familiar with?). In *Henry IV, Part I*, Act II, Scene 4, in the course of a hilarious and protracted argument at the Boar's Head Tavern involving Prince Hal, Coins, Francis, Bardolph, Peto, other rough characters and Falstaff, whose veracity in recounting a valorous deed is challenged by the Prince, Falstaff exclaims: "What, upon compulsion? 'Zounds! an I were at the *strappado*, or all the racks in the world, I would not tell you on compulsion."

strepsiceros   See **hircine**.

strigil (STRIJ uhl) *n*. The ancient Romans and Greeks used the *strigil*, a curved skin-scraper of metal or ivory, to scrape the sweat and dirt from the skin after exercise or a hot bath. The term was later applied to any type of flesh-scraping brush used for that purpose. *Strigil* was taken from Latin, based on the verb *stringere* (to touch lightly). A *strigil* was, so to speak, a "currycomb" used on human beings by themselves or others. The Italian noun *striglia*, the German *Striegel* and the French *étrille* all mean "currycomb" and attest to the persistent influence of the Latin term. John Evelyn's *Diary* has an entry for June 1645, telling of "being rubbed with a kind of *strigil* of seal's-skin, put on the operator's hand like a glove," and Richard Chandler, in *Travels in Asia Minor*

(1775), provides this information: "We were rubbed with a mohair-bag fitted to the hand, which, like an ancient *strigil*, brings away the gross matter perspired." *The Civil Engineer and Architect's Journal*, in an 1843 issue, tells this sad story: "One day Hadrian recognized an old companion in arms in poverty, scraping himself with a tile instead of the *strigil*." D. Maguire's *Art of Massage* (1887) shows that this scraping technique persisted well into the 19th century: "Our masseurs of to-day use an instrument similar to the *strigil* made of box or any other hard wood, and call it sometimes *strigil* or *raclette*." (*Raclette* is French for "scraper," synonymous with *racle*; *raclage* is "scraping," *racler* means "to scrape" and a *racleur* is a "scraper," and colloquially a "poor violinist," i.e., a bad "scraper of catgut.")

subchanter   See **precentor.**

subreption   See **obreption.**

succentor   See **precentor.**

sunna   See **sharia.**

supernacular   See **supernaculum.**

supernaculum (sooh pur NAK yuh luhm, syooh-) *n., adv., adj.* Before analyzing this word, you should know that it's a term of praise, something wonderful, a treat, and then you'll be on the right track (but perhaps for the wrong reason). As an adverb, *supernaculum* means "to the last drop" (which happens to be a phrase familiar from the extensive national advertising of an American brand of coffee). It is used chiefly in the expression "drink to the last drop," and this is why: The word is constructed of Latin *super* (over, above, upon) plus New Latin [*CH* says "sham Latin"; the *O.E.D.* "Modern Latin"; *W III* "New Latin"] *nagulum* or *naculum* (nail), meaning, literally, "on the nail." This curious expression arises from the German idiom *auf den Nagel trinken*, literally, "to drink upon the nail," figuratively, "to drink [liquor] to the last drop." The reference here is to the practice of turning the emptied glass upside down onto the left thumbnail, to demonstrate that all the liquor has been drunk, i.e., drunk to the last drop. In Disraeli's *Vivian Grey* (1827) we find the sentence: "As he withdrew the horn from his mouth, all present ... gave a loud cry of '*Supernaculum!*'" In Thomas Nash's *Pierce Pennilesse his Supplication to the Diuell* [Devil] (1592) there is a passage that makes the procedure absolutely clear: "Drinking *super nagulum*, a deuise of drinking new [newly] come out of Fraunce [wasn't it in fact Germany?]; which is, after a man has turned up the bottom of the cup, to drop it on his naile, & make a pearle with that is left; which, if it shed, and he cannot make stand on, by reason ther's too much, he must drinke againe for his pennance." (Not a harsh penance, by any means!) *Supernaculum*, as a noun, means an "alcoholic drink of the finest quality," or as *CH* puts it, "a liquor of the best kind, too good to leave heeltaps." *Heeltap* is a fine word itself, meaning a "bit of liquor left in the glass after drinking." We have to get back to *supernaculum* for a moment: There would seem to be a bit of uncertainty as to whether there should be nothing at all on the thumbnail or one drop that must "stand on" without "shedding," according to Thomas Nash. The only way to resolve this seeming inconsistency is to remember that *to* in the expression *to the last drop* might mean "up to" or "to and including," a dilemma that has worried legal draftsmen for centuries. In America, lawyers avoid the ambiguity by using *through* when the sense is "to and including" and the circumlocution seems cumbersome. There is an adjective from our fine headword: *supernacular*, said of excellent drink. Thackeray, in *The Book of Snobs* (1848) writes: "Some white Hermitage at the Haws (by the way, the butler only gave me half a glass each time) was *supernacular*." And what is *hermitage*? Apart from a "hermit cell" or any "retired abode," it is the name of a white wine made near Valence (Drôme) in France, the locality of a supposed hermit's cell. By the way, I wish that Thackeray had placed the "only" immediately before the "half" in his sentence. The position of *only* in our sentences is a matter of great distress to some. There is a popular song entitled "I only have eyes for you." It doesn't mean "I alone of all the people in the world," or "only eyes," as opposed to ears or other parts of the anatomy, which wouldn't have been true by any means, but "only you of all the inhabitants of this planet." The poor lyricist had to fit the words to the melody, with that unpardonable result.

surtout   See **roquelaure.**

swasivious (swa SIV ee uhs) *adj.* To my regret, this delightful word is marked "obs[olete], rare" in the *O.E.D.*, and the only etymological note is "f[rom] It[alian] SUASIVO plus -IOUS." The meaning is "agreeably persuasive," and *swasivious* deserves to be resurrected to take the place of that circumlocution. In any event, it rhymes with *lascivious*, and that would be of great convenience to limerick makers, especially in view of its meaning. The only reference to literature offered by the *O.E.D.* is "1592. R.D. *Hypnerotomachia* ... With pleasurable actions, maydenly iestures, suasiuious behauiours." The initials *R. D.* turn out, after some confusion, to be those of Sir Robert Dallington, of whom we shall have more to say later. It develops that *Hypnerotomachia* is an Italian work in macaronic Latin (more about *macaronic* below) written by a Dominican friar, Francesco Colonna, under the pseudonym Poliphilus some time before 1479 and published in Venice in 1499. The work is a mysterious allegorical romance with the full title *Hypnerotomachia Poliphili.* In 1592 the aforesaid Dallington published an English translation of part of it entitled *The Strife of Love in a Dream*, edited by Andrew Lang in 1890. The explanation of *Hypnerotomachia* is in the definition of three Greek elements: *hypn-* (the combining form of *hypnos*, sleep), *eroto-* (the combining form of *eros* (erotic love), and *mach* (conflict, battle). The more literal meaning of *hypnerotomachia* would be the "struggle between sleep and sexual desire," a problem most healthy males will quickly recognize. I promised to come back to *macaronic*. It is fully discussed in my *1000 Most Challenging Words*, where I explain it as "applied, in a narrow sense, to language characterized by a mixture of Latin and non-Latin words ... " The word has broader applications not relevant here. An up-to-date work about the good friar's book is a German tome by Linda Fierz-David published in Zurich in 1948 under the title *Der Liebestraum des Polifilo*. *Liebestraum* means "love-dream," and *Polifilo* is the Italian spelling of *Poliphilus*. Come back, *swasivious*. As to the *w*, Shakespeare used it in *King John*, Act V, Scene 5, when the Messenger says: "The count Melun is slain; the English Lords,/By his pers*w*asion, are againe falne off," and in *Twelfth Night*, Act III, Scene 4, where Antonio says to Viola: "Isn't possible that my deserts to you/Can lacke pers*w*asion?" Of course, it depends on which folio you read. *Perswaisive(ly)* appears often in 17th-century literature, including Milton. The Italian *suasivo* mentioned in the etymology is one of a group of three adjectives (*suadente, suasivo, suasorio*) meaning "persuasive," all going back to Latin *suadere* (to present in a pleasing manner), and the "pleasing" element clearly justifies the *O.E.D.* definition. There are a great many *sua-* words in Latin having to do with persuasion, recommending, advising, etc., and the *per-* of Latin *persuadere* is the intensive prefix, giving the effect of "thoroughly, utterly," suggesting that the *persuasive* effort has been so strong as to result in *convincing*.

symphile (SIM file) *n*. You wouldn't think that ants or termites kept guests in their nests, would you? Well, they do. A *symphile* is an "insect of another species, such as any of various beetles, living in the nests of social insects like ants or termites who feed and guard them for the value of their secretions, which are consumed as food by the hosts." This is an example of *commensalism*. (*Commensal* is discussed at length in my *1000 Most Challenging Words*, from which I quote: "When it is used of animals or plants, *commensal* describes types living together, or a type living on or in another, without harm to either.") *Symphile* is from Greek *symphilia*, formed of the prefix *syn-* (together) plus *philos* (friend), and has a synonym, *myrmecoxene* (mur muh KOK seen), from *myrmec(o)-*, the combining form of Greek *myrmex* (ant) plus *-xene*, the combining form of *xenos* (stranger, alien—from which we get our unhappy word *xenophobia*). In view of that bit of etymology, I am puzzled to find *myrmecoxene* defined, in the discussion under *symphile* in *W III*, as "true guest." I suppose every accommodating beetle in an ant's nest is a "true guest," but not every "true guest" is an ant's beetle.

symploce   See **anaphora**.

tabby   See **tapia.**

tabia   See **tapia.**

talaria   See **petasus.**

talion (TAL ee uhn) *n. Talion* means "like for like, retaliation" from Latin *talio* (like punishment, retaliation), based on the adjective *talis* (such, of such a kind), and it figures in the derivation of our word *retaliation*. In Exodus: 21:23–25, we read " ... life for life/Eye for eye, tooth for tooth, hand for hand, foot for foot/Burning for burning, wound for wound, stripe for stripe ... " This system of condign punishment is discussed under the headword *condign* in my *1000 Most Challenging Words*, where I also mention Gilbert's " ... punishment fit the crime ... " in *The Mikado*. In Roman times, this primitive penal code was known as the *Lex Talionis* (Law of Retaliation), freely (very freely, and quite crudely) translated "tit for tat," and that childish-sounding phrase has been variously traced to Dutch *dit voor dat* (this for that) and French *tant pour tant*. An extension of the *Lex Talionis* was the infliction on an unsuccessful plaintiff of the very punishment that the accused would have suffered if found guilty. In the Rollin-Tilton translation of Edmundo De Amicis's *Morocco* (1879) there is a tantalizing account (because the *O.E.D.* quotation doesn't tell us what went before) of a vindictive lady who " ... demanded that in virtue of the law of *talion* he [presumably the judge] should order the English merchant's two front teeth to be broken." A teeth for a teeth?

tallis   See **daven.**

talus   See **nunatak.**

tanka   See **cinquain.**

tantara   See **taratantara.**

tapette (ta PET) *n., adj.* In French, *tapette*, aside from its literal meanings "tap, type of hammer to push corks in, engraver's pad, marble game," is slang for "homosexual." The word has been taken into English by a number of writers. In Evelyn Waugh's *Vile Bodies* (1930) we find "My dear, he looks terribly *tapette*." Rebecca West, in *The Thinking Reed* (1936), has a character declare: "It will make my room look as if I were a *tapette*!" In *Another Country* (1963), James Baldwin describes a character who " ... had lived by his wits in the streets of Paris, as a semi-*tapette* and as a *rat d'hôtel* [hotel thief]." *Tapette* means "passive male homosexual," or in (objectionable) slang pejorative usage, "pansy." Its use has been widened to denote any effeminate man whose sexual tastes may be totally heterosexual, or "straight." I detest all derogatory labels in this area; some of my best friends ... etc.

taphephobia (ta fee FOH bee uh) *n*. In view of all the frightening news about earthquakes in the last few years, I'm sure *taphephobia* is on the increase. It means "morbid fear of being buried alive" and is based on Greek *taphe* (burial, grave), akin to *thaptein* (to bury, inter), plus Late Latin *-phobia*, indicating fear of something, from Greek *phobos* (fear, terror). (Does the derivation of Late Latin *-phobia* from Greek *phobos* save *taphephobia* from the somewhat pejorative designation *hybrid word*? I discuss that subject in my *Practical English: 1000 Most Effective Words*: "Figuratively, *hybrid* is applied to anything made from different elements. There are *hybrid* words, like *television*: *tele-* is derived from Greek, *-vision* from Latin.") *Taphephobia* brings to mind the superstitious expression *knock on wood* (*touch wood*, in Britain), said after an expression of satisfaction with the way things are going at the moment ("I haven't had a cold for years!"), in order not to tempt fate into reversing the course. It is said that *knock (on) wood* comes from the rather grim picture of a person accidentally interred alive knocking on the inside of the lid of his wooden coffin. After that kind of experience, the disinterred one would certainly be entitled to a lifelong case of *taphephobia*.

taphonomic(al)   See **taphonomy.**

taphonomist   See **taphonomy.**

taphonomy (taf ON uh mee) *n*. We are familiar with fossils and the phenomenon of fossilization, whereby organic material is replaced with mineral substances in the remains of an organism, affording clues of great importance in paleontology and paleobiology. The study of the processes involved in the fossilization of animal and plant remains is known as *taphonomy*, from Greek *taphos* (grave) plus the suffix *-nomia*, from *nomos* (law, custom). It was J. A. Efremov, in *Pan-American Geology* (1940), who coined this word: "I propose for this part of paleontology the name of '*Taphonomy* ', the science of the laws of embedding ... *Taphonomical* research allows us to glance into the depth of ages from another point of view." The March 2, 1974 issue of *The Times* (London) contained the following: "Russian scientists have brought together a team of geologists ... and a group of *taphonomists*: the last belong to a specialty created in Russia for studying the way animals and plants are preserved in their burial sites." A 1981 issue of *Nature* states: "Paleontologists ... are bringing their subject out of the museum through studies of the processes by which the fossil record forms (*taphonomy*)."

tapia (TA pyuh) *n*. In Spanish, *tapia* means "mud or adobe wall, wall fence" as well as a "wall measure of 50 square feet." Taken into English, it denotes a material used for walls, consisting of clay or mud, puddled (i.e., mixed with water to form an impervious mixture), beaten into solidity and dried. Hooker & Ball's *Journal of a Tour in Morocco and the Great Atlas* (1878) speaks of "the remains of massive walls of *tapia*." *Tabia* (TA byuh), probably a modification of *tapia*, is a somewhat different building material consisting of earth, lime and pebbles rammed between forms. It is an extremely durable material, especially in arid regions. Many of the castles in the northern Sahara are built of it and have proved to be long-lasting. Still another building material, known as *tabby* (derived from a number of words of African origin—'*tabi, tabax, ta'bo* and *ntaba*, all having to do with mud in one way or another) and made of lime, sand or gravel and oyster shells, was once used on the coasts of Georgia and South Carolina. This *tabby* hasn't a thing in the world to do with the noble creatures known as *tabby cats*. Finally, in this category, we have the word *pisé*, the past participle of the French verb *piser* (to beat, pound, stamp) used as a substantive in French meaning "masonry" (*pisé de terre* means "blocks of clay"; *mur en pisé* means "cob-wall," a wall built of cob, a composition of clay and straw); *piser* is from Latin *pinsere* (to beat, pound, stamp); alternative forms are *pisare* and *pinsare*. We use *pisé* to mean "stiff clay or earth kneaded or mixed with gravel" for use in the building of walls or cottages. The mixture is rammed between boards that are removed when it solidifies, a process used in France and in parts of England. *Pisé* can also be used to denote this mode of construction. Edward H. Knight's *Practical Dictionary of Mechanics* (1875) states that "The best material for *pisé* work is clay with small gravel-stones interposed through it." But Lord protect us from *pebbledash*, British for "pebble-coated stucco," which I describe in my *British English, A to Zed* as "a not very good- looking and all too frequent building surfacing in Britain … and one wonders how in the world this miserable invention ever came about."

tapis (TA pis) *n*. Late Latin took the noun *tapetium* and its variant *tapecium* from Greek *tapetion*, the diminutive of *tapes*, meaning "cloth woven with varicolored figures and designs." *Tapis* is a generic term for any cloth wrought with colored designs, such as tablecloths, curtains, rugs and carpets; it is French for "rug, carpet, tablecloth." The phrase *on the tapis* (from the French *sur le tapis*) means, literally, "on the tablecloth," which we shorten to "on the table," meaning "under discussion" or "being considered." Incidentally, where we use the verb *to table* meaning "to postpone consideration of at the moment," presumably for later action, the British use it meaning "to present for discussion." In my *British English, A to Zed*, I give the meaning of *table* (the verb) as "submit for discussion," with the comment: "This term means exactly the opposite of what it means in America, where to *table* an item is to *shelve* it or postpone discussion of it, perhaps hoping it will never come up again." Another use of *tapis* is in the phrase *tapis vert*, taken from the French, meaning literally "green carpet" but used to denote a grass walk, a long strip of lawn, as used by Mrs. Lyndon B. Johnson ("Ladybird") in her book *White House Diary* (1965) in the sentence "He wants to … preserve the *tapis vert*, the long green ribbon that stretches from the Capitol to the Lincoln memorial." In Wood's *Practical Garden Design* (1976) we find the phrase " … on either side of the *tapis vert*— 'green carpet,'" referring to a grass strip. *Tapis* once meant "to adorn with tapestry" or "to embellish (tapestry, etc.) with figures." It came to mean to "lie low so as to be hidden, to lurk or skulk," or, transitively, "to hide," and in a wholly different sense, "to adorn with tapestry," but those uses are obsolete. However, in the form *tapish*, now dialectal, especially in Sheffield, a city in the English county of Yorkshire, it is used to mean "to languish" or "to be mortally ill." In the 1891 supplement to Sidney Addy's *Glossary of Words Used in the Neighborhood of Sheffield* (1888), *tapish* is defined as "to waste or pine away" and an example is furnished: "He *tapished* and died." It's a long way from rugs and carpets to pining away and dying. Don't get the idea that the words have a common derivation, which they quite obviously haven't.

tapsell (TAP s'l) *adj*. When you think of a gate, you visualize a swinging barrier that closes an opening in a fence, hinged on one side or the other, moving inward or outward as best suits the particular need. Not so with a *tapsell* gate, which turns about a central post and thus admits entrance. It is a type of churchyard gate peculiar to the English county of Sussex, one of the Home Counties, those nearest London. The origin of the word is unknown, and though I have characterized it as an adjective, it might well be a noun, or, for all I know, the name of the inventor used attributively. H. Hall, the author of *Some Sussex Sayings & Crafts* (1957), says: "*Tapsell gate*, this ingenious gate is peculiar to Sussex, but nothing is known of its origin or its designer. Its special use is to prevent cattle entering churchyards, and to make room for coffin bearers to pass through easily ... Today there are only six in the county." However, the March 15, 1979 issue of the magazine *Country Life* tells us: "*Tapsell gates*, which turn on a central pivot, are peculiar to Sussex. It has been suggested that they are so-called after one Tapsell, a Sussex iron-master." In any event, Hall's mention of cattle brings to mind another type of gate that prevents cattle from trespassing, the *kissing-gate*, which I discuss in my *British English, A to Zed*:

> Kissing gates found in rural Britain are gates hung with the side away from the hinge swinging within a V- ... or U-shaped enclosure in such a way that people can get in but cattle can't. You push the gate away from the near side of the V or U, step into the latter, slide over to the other side, and push the gate back. This quaint device acquired its romantic name (or so one is told) because it was often the place where a swain said goodnight to his lady love, and a certain amount of lingering and incidental activity were in order.

Sounds like much more fun than *tapsell gates* and coffin bearing.

tar(r)adiddle (tar uh DID'l) *n., vb*. This rather happy-sounding flippant-seeming word means "fib," or "white lie" and can also, in context, mean "pretentious nonsense." The *-diddle* element apparently comes from the slang verb *diddle* (to swindle, cheat, cajole), of unknown origin, and the whole word is credited with no etymology except that reference to "diddle." In Mrs. Elizabeth Gaskell's novel *Wives and Daughters, an Every-day Story* (1865), we read the amusing passage: "Oh, don't call them lies, sister; it's such a strong, ugly word. Please call them *tallydiddles*, for I don't believe she meant any harm." Mrs. Gaskell came close. *Tar(r)adiddle*, as an intransitive verb, means "to fib," and transitively, "to impose upon by telling fibs." In that sense, it is quite close to the verb *diddle* without the *tar(r)a-*, but that element seems to give it a happy-go-lucky air, rather than a dark, deep, scheming atmosphere. Yet *tar(r)adiddling* may have serious consequences. An 1828 issue of *The Examiner, a Sunday Paper on Politics, Domestic Economy, and Theatricals*, of which Leigh Hunt was the original editor, wrote of a public figure whose enemies " ... squibbed, and paragraphed, and *taradiddled* him to death." So go easy on *taradiddling* your adversaries.

tarantism (TAR uhn tiz'm) *n.* This was the name of a hysterical disease that took the form of an irresistible need to go into maniacal dancing; it became epidemic in Apulia and neighboring parts of southern Italy from the 15th to the 17th centuries. The malady took its name from the *tarantula*, to whose sting or bite it was popularly attributed. The tarantula in question was a large, hairy poisonous spider, named from the town of Taranto, the Roman Tarentum, a seaport town in Apulia where it proliferated. Opinions differed as to whether the maniacal dancing was caused by the bite of the tarantula or was a cure for the disease. A popular form of the dancing was the *tarantella*, a lively, whirling dance native to southern Italy, done in triplets by one couple, and formerly believed to be a cure for *tarantism*. Getting back to the tarantula for a moment, there are several spiders that bear this name. The one discussed above is the wolf spider found in many parts of southern Europe, *Lycosa tarantula*; there are American tarantulas as well, sluggish types, whose bite is painful but usually not venomous. (They are ugly and scary, nevertheless.) An item in *Chambers's Encyclopedia* (1883) reads: "*Tarantism* may be defined as leaping or dancing mania, originating in, or supposed to originate in, an animal poison ... The gesticulations, contortions, and cries somewhat resembled those in St. Vitus's dance, and other epidemic nervous diseases of the middle ages." Apparently, the writer of that article didn't take the connection between *tarantism* and the tarantula very seriously.

taratantara (tah rah TAN tuh ruh) *n.* A lovely bit of onomatopoeia is *taratantara*, imitating and denoting the sound of a trumpet (though one has to indulge in a bit of imagination) and referring figuratively to "pretentious talk, grandiloquent language, flamboyant oratory." A similar word, *tantara* (TAN tuh ruh), sometimes extended to *tantarara, tantararara* and *tantaratara*, means a "flourish" on a trumpet, occasionally a drum roll or a like sound. We didn't invent *taratantara*: It appears in the writing of the Roman poet Ennius (239–169 B.C.) and was taken into Italian as well. Ouida (Mlle. de la Ramée), in *Pascarèl; Only a Story* (1873), wrote this romantic sentence: "Their Tirolean postilions roused the echoes ... with a *tarantarratara* upon their tassellated bugles." A nice elaboration of our word and an evocative bit of *taratantara* in itself, no?

Targum   See **Shekinah.**

targumic   See **Shekinah.**

targumist   See **Shekinah.**

targumize   See **Shekinah.**

tath (TATH) *n., vb.* This is the term for the "dung of cattle and sheep allowed to remain on the field on which they have been pastured, so as to improve the fertility of the land." John Cowell's *The Interpreter: or Booke Containing the Signification of Words*, as augmented by W. Kennett (1701), tells us that in Norfolk and Suffolk (counties of England) " ... the Lord of each Manor had the Privilege of having their Tenants (sic) Flocks of Sheep brought at Night upon their own Demesne Ground [i.e., estate], there to be fouled [i.e., confined?] for the benefit of their Dung, which liberty of so improving their Land is called *Tath*." The term applies as well to coarse tufted grass that grows on land manured in this manner. *Water-tath* has been applied by stock farmers to all grasses that are especially rank and luxuriant. They differentiate between *water-tath*, produced by excess moisture, and *nolt-tath*, produced by dung. (*Nolt* is a Scottish word for "cattle.") A *tath-field* or *tath-fold* is one in which cattle or sheep are confined for purposes of manuring the land. *Tath* is used as a transitive verb in Scottish or other dialects to denote the process of manuring land by confining cattle on it, and *water-tathing* is the flooding of land to improve its productivity. As an intransitive verb, *to tath* is a term applied to cattle meaning "to drop dung upon land and thus to manure it."

tath-field   See **tath.**

tath-fold   See **tath.**

tatpurusha (tat POOHR uh shuh) *n.* This Sanskrit word means, literally, "this servant," from *tad-* or *tat-* (that one) plus *perusha* (servant), and denotes a class of compound words in which the first component is a noun or noun stem that modifies the second component by relating to it as possessor (*horsehide*), thing possessed (*sailboat*), object of action (*lawnmower*), location (*heartworm*) or agent (*manmade*). A related but different kind of compound is the *dvandva* (DVAHN dvah), also a Sanskrit word, consisting of two components related as though joined by the conjunction *and*. The full grammatical name is *dvandva compound*, and here are some examples: *prince-consort, secretary-treasurer, bittersweet*. *Dvandva* means "pair" in Sanskrit, formed by the reduplication of the numeral *dva*, meaning "two," and etymologically related to the English word *two*. *Tatpurusha* (also called *determinative compound* in Sanskrit grammar) and *dvandva* bring to mind another type of compound word, also from the Sanskrit, with the pleasant name of *bahuvrihi*, which swam into my ken in the dark days before the other two did. It has the alternative name of *possessive compound* and is fully discussed in my *1000 Most Challenging Words*. *Bahu* and *vrihi* mean "much" and "rice" respectively; if the words are combined, the compound thus formed becomes an adjective or noun signifying "(one) possessing much rice." Compare, in English, *redcoat* (British soldier in colonial times), *graybeard* or *tightwad*, or in German, *Dummkopf*. Mahatma Ghandi's title meant literally "great soul," from *maha* (great) (cf. Greek *megas* and *maharajah*) and *atman* (soul). (And Rudyard Kipling bestowed the title *Greatheart* on Teddy Roosevelt, in a poem written after his death.) Philologists have gone to Sanskrit for terms like *tatpurusha* and *bahuvrihi*, perhaps because compounds of German-type length and complexity are common in that language, and Indian grammarians are assiduous in classifying them. Perhaps, too, our scholars, like the author (and, I hope the readers) of this book are susceptible to the glamor of exotic words.

tautonym (TOT uh nim) *n.* This would be an easy one to guess if you had a bit of Greek at your command. The prefix *taut-* or *tauto-* comes from the adjective *tautos* (same, identical), which in turn is derived from *to auto* (the same), neuters of the definite article and *autos* (same). The suffix *-onym* is from the noun *onoma* (name). We find *taut-* in *tautological, tautophony*, etc. and *-onym* in *homonym, pseudonym*, etc. Thus, a *tautonym* is a "name that repeats itself," as found in certain two-word classification terms (known in zoology and botany as *taxonomic binomials*). Examples: *gorilla gorilla*, the common anthropoid ape of equatorial Africa; *mephitis mephitis*, the common North American skunk. In these *tautonyms* the generic name and specific epithet are identical. They are used in zoology to designate a typical form, but they are prohibited in botanical taxonomy (classification) under the International Code of Botanical Nomenclature. The botanists, poor chaps, have to search for another name for the species, the major subdivision of the genus. Sounds like discrimination to me, but there must be a reason. In a *tautonym*, both words must be nouns. *Foolish fool* or *dopey dope* may be *tautological*, but those aren't *tautonyms* for two reasons: The components aren't identical, and the first element isn't a noun. Identical twins can be concocted, like *sage sage*, but that won't do either, because the first *sage* is an adjective, and in any case, if we go along with the dictionary, the term *tautonym* appears to be restricted to biological taxonomy.

taxiarch (TAKS ee ark) *n.* This word has nothing to do with taxis or arches. It was the Greek title for a commander of a *taxis*, a division of the army. In Athens, a *taxis* was a group of soldiers from a *phyle* (FEYE lee), a tribe or a division of people within a state formed at first on the basis of kinship and later based simply on locality. *Taxis* means "arrangement," related to the verb *tassein* (to arrange); *phyle* was taken intact from the Greek for "tribe." The *-arch* of *taxiarch* has the same effect as the prefix *arch-*, meaning "chief," as in *archbishop*, and is the stem of *arche* (beginning). *Taxiarch* is as good a reason as I can think of for my warning: Don't jump to conclusions in matters of etymology!

taxis   See **taxiarch.**

telegony (tuh LEG uh nee) *n.* There is a belief among some, scientifically unsupported, that a previous mate transmits his genetic influence to the offspring of his former mate and a subsequent mate. For example: Mr. and Mrs. A divorce; the ex-Mrs. A marries Mr. B. According to the theory of *telegony*, Mr A's genes have a serious influence upon the children of the second marriage. Some dictionaries (e.g., *W III*) give the impression that this supposed carrying over of the influence of a former male relates only to quadrupeds, the definition using the terms *sire* and *dam*. Some carry the supposition so far as to include the offspring of all subsequent matings of the female. There is another unsupported theory called *saturation*: the supposed increasing resemblance to the male parent of successive progeny of the same parents. Who dreams these things up? In any event, the term *telegony* is constructed of the familiar Greek prefix *tele-*, the combining form of *tele* (far), and the suffix *-goneia*, from *gonos* (begetting, offspring). The adjective is *telegonic* (tel uh GON ik), which should never be confused with *telegenic* (tel uh JEN ik), meaning "suitable for telecasting; endowed with looks and presence that are attractive on television." If *telegony* were a fact of life, a person whose beautiful mother was formerly wed to a terribly unattractive man and whose father looked like John Barrymore would never qualify for the male lead on a soap opera.

telestic   See **telestich.**

telestich (tel ES tik, TEL es tik) *n.* As opposed to an *acrostic* (from Greek *akros*, extreme or end, plus *stichos*, line or row), a poem or prose composition in which the initial (in a single acrostic), the initial and final (in a double acrostic) or the initial, middle and final (in a triple acrostic) letters of the lines form words, a *telestich* is a type of poem, usually a short one, in which only the consecutive final letters of the lines form one or more words or names. This word is formed of the Greek prefix *tele-* (the combining form of *telos*, end; not that of the other *telos*, far) plus our old friend *stichos*. In the improbable event that you run into the word *telestic* (tuh LES tik), you mustn't think that it's a misprint for *telestich* that dropped the *-h*. *Telestic* is a perfectly good, if rare, word in its own right, from Greek *telestikos*, a verbal of *telein* (to initiate into mysteries or sacred rites) and is an adjective meaning "pertaining to the mysteries," or, more simply, "mystical." If there were any cockneys in ancient Greece, they would have dropped their initial, not their final, aitches.

tenebrae   See **tenebrism.**

tenebrific   See **tenebrism.**

tenebrious   See **tenebrism.**

tenebrism (TEN uh briz'm) *n.* From Latin *tenebrae* (darkness), a noun plural in form but singular in meaning, we get the name, taken intact from the Latin, of certain church services (Matins and Lauds) celebrated in the final part of Holy Week to commemorate the sufferings and death of Christ, with the chanting of psalms and the progressive extinguishing of candles until only one is left burning under or behind the altar—a most impressive and moving ritual that lingers in the memory. Apart from that special use, the Latin word has given rise to a number of terms dealing with darkness: *tenebrific* (ten uh BRIF ik), meaning "gloomy" or "gloom-producing," *tenebrious* (ten EB ree uhs), *tenebrose* (TEN uh brose) and *tenebrous* (TEN uh bruhs), all meaning "dark, murky," and figuratively, "mysterious, obscure" and *tenebrism*, the name given to a school of painting usually associated with the Italian painter Caravaggio (c. 1564–1609?), who submerged most of his forms in shadow and with dramatic effect illuminated the rest by means of a beam of light emanating from a specific identifiable source. The members of the school were known as *tenebrists* (TEN uh brists). Cognoscenti like to use the term *tenebroso* (ten uh BROH soh) as a learned synonym of *tenebrist*, but more modest art historians are satisfied with the latter. W. M. Rossetti, in an article in the *Encyclopedia Britannica* (1886), wrote of the "school of the Tenebrosi, or shadow painters," which seems to me to be something of an oversimplification. An article in the February 1963 issue of *The Burlington Magazine* states: *"The Last Supper* introduces us to a *tenebroso* effect." Your recollection of that masterpiece will tell you much about *tenebrism*: One picture *is* worth a thousand words!

tenebrist   See **tenebrism.**

tenebrose   See **tenebrism.**

tenebroso   See **tenebrism.**

tenebrous   See **tenebrism.**

tenson   See **sirvent(e).**

tenzon   See **sirvent(e).**

thanatism (THAN uh tiz'm) *n. Thanatos* is Greek for "death," and *thanato-* is its combining form. In ancient Greek culture, *Thanatos* was the god and personification of death and the twin brother of *Hypnos*, god of sleep, whence we got *hypnosis* and other *hypno-* words (see **hypnopedia**). According to the eighth-century B.C. Greek poet Hesiod, the twins were born of the goddess *Nox* (Night) by parthenogenesis. *Thanatos* contributed a fair-sized collection of *thanato-* words to our language. *Thanatopsis* (than uh TOP sis) may be familiar to us as the title of the poem of that name by the American poet William Cullen Bryant. *Thanatopsis* means "contemplation of death," from the prefix *thanat-* (omitting the *o* before a vowel) combined with Greek *opsis* (sight, view). *Thanatognomonic* (than uh tog nuh MON ik), "characteristic of death," weds *thanato-* with *gnomon* (indicator). *Thanatography*, an account of a person's death, uses *-graphia*, from *graphein* (to write). *Thanatophobia* should be obvious: "morbid fear of death." *Thanatology* (than uh TOL uh jee), with the familiar *-logy*, from Greek *-logia*, based on *logos* (discourse), is the study of death, its characteristics and causes. To get back to our headword: *Thanatism* is the belief that at death, the soul dies together with the body. Ernst Heinnich P.A. Haeckel, in the McCabe translation of *The Riddle of the Universe*, says: "We give the name of *'thanatism'* ... to the opinion which holds that at a man's death ... his 'soul' also disappears, that is, that sum of cerebral functions which psychic dualism regards as a peculiar entity, independent of the other vital processes in the human body." In the December 1900 issue of *The Academy, a Monthly Record of Literature, Learning, Science and Art*, these words appear: "We prefer to say that even atheism and *thanatism* are speculations." Most things are.

thanatognomic   See **thanatism.**

thanatography   See **thanatism.**

thanatology   See **thanatism.**

thanatophobia   See **thanatism.**

thanatopsis   See **thanatism.**

thank'ee-marm   See **thank-you-ma'am.**

thank-you-ma'am, also **thank'ee-marm** (pronounced as they appear) *n.* Neither of these is an expression of gratitude but simply, in American colloquial usage, a "hollow or rut across a road" that causes the people in a vehicle passing over it to nod involuntarily, the way one might do in acknowledging a favor and expressing thanks. Originally, such ridges were often built as a means of spilling off rain water. Their purpose now is to make drivers slow down as a precaution when they near thickly settled neighborhoods. In *Kavanagh, a Tale* (1849), Henry Wadsworth Longfellow describes a trip in which "We went like the wind over the hollows in the snow;—the driver called them *'thank-you-ma'ams,'* because they made eveybody nod." Oliver Wendell Holmes, in *The Guardian Angel* (1867), quotes a metaphorical use of the term: "Life's a road that's got a good many *thank-you-ma'ams* to go bumpin' over, says he." William Howells uses the alternative term in *The Landlord at Lion's Head* (1897): " ... one of the *'thank-ee-marms* in the road ..." It's a pleasant bit of fanciful usage, like the British road colloquialism "silent policeman," denoting a raised strip across a road put there to slow drivers down as they approach a thickly settled residential or commercial area, a sound device also known as a "rumble strip."

theandric (thee AN drik) *adj. Theandric* is our adaptation of Greek *theandrikos*, from *theandros* (god-man), built on the nouns *theos* (god) and *aner* (man), and means "simultaneously divine and human, partaking of both the divine and human." Edward Irving, in *Sermons* (1828), wrote of "Heretics ... asserting that there was only one operation, *Theandric* or Godmanly." The form *theandrical* is also found. In *A Treatise Concerning the Fulnesse of Christ* (1656), Henry Jeanes gave the following definition of the word: "*theandrical*, that is, divinely human." A closely related adjective is *theanthropic* (thee an THROP ik), with roughly the same meaning: "possessing the nature of both God and man at once divine and human." Here, *theos* is joined with *anthropos* (man) to form the ecclesiastic Greek noun *theanthropos* (god-man), from which our adjective was formed. In *Gleaning of past Years* (1868), the statesman and scholar William Ewart Gladstone pointed out that "the *theanthropic* idea, the idea of God made man without ceasing to be God, was ... familiar ... to the old mythology." The form *theanthropical* (thee an THROP ik uhl) has been used but is rare. *Theanthropism* (thee AN thruh piz'm) is the doctrine of the union of divine and human natures, or God as man, in Jesus Christ. Bishop Lightfoot, in his *Commentary on St. Paul's Epistles to the Colossians, etc.* (1875), made the clear statement that "the monotheism of the Old Testament is supplemented by the *theanthropism* of the New." Apart from that theological meaning, *theanthropism* is used in discussions of mythology. Thus, the same Gladstone, in his *Homer*, a literature primer, speaks of the "*theanthropism* ... of the Olympian system." As you might suppose, there are the forms *theanthropist* (thee AN thruh pist), used both attributively and adjectivally, and *theanthropology* (thee an thruh POL uh jee), synonymous with *theanthropism*. *Theanthropos*, mentioned above, now obsolete, was once a title given to Jesus. One form that I would not have predicted is *theanthropophagy* (thee an thruh POF uh jee), combining *theanthropo-* with -*phagy*, from Greek -*phagia* (-eating), based on *phagein* (to eat). Jeremy Taylor, in *The Real Presence and Spirituall of Christ in the Blessed Sacrament Proved against the Doctrine of Transubstantiation* (1654), spoke of the Catholics who "deny anthropophagy [cannibalism], but did not deny *theanthropophagy*, saying, that they did not eat the flesh or drink the bloud of a meer man, but of Christ who was God and man," a perfectly logical theological distinction, as far as I can see. As opposed to the doctrine of *theanthropism*, *ebionism* (EB ee uhn iz'm), the doctrine of the *ebionites* (EB ee uhn ites), a Christian group of the first century, held that Jesus was only a man and that Christians were subject to the Mosaic law. This group developed into a distinct sect in the succeeding century. To *ebionize* was to follow or imitate the tenets or practices of that sect. In a sermon delivered by the Reverend Robert Gell in 1650, he referred to the "*Ebionites*, who denied the deitie of Christ," and Frederick W.

Farrar, in *The Life and Work of St. Paul* (1879), wrote of the "*Ebionite* hatred still burning against St. Paul in the second century." *Ebionite* came from Latin *ebionita*, based on the Hebrew *ebyon* (poor).

theandrical See **theandric.**

theanthropic See **theandric.**

theanthropism See **theandric.**

theanthropist See **theandric.**

theanthropology See **theandric.**

theanthropophagy See **theandric.**

theotokion (thee oh TOH kee on, thee oh toh KEE on) *n. Theotokos,* in Greek of the Christian period, is an epithet of the Virgin Mary, meaning "Bearer of God" or "Mother of God." That word is formed of Greek *theos* (God) plus *-tokos* (bearing), from *tok-,* the stem of the verb *tiktein* (to bear, bring forth). *Theotokos* has its Latin equivalent in *Deipara,* from *deus* (God) plus *-para* (bearing), from *parere* (to bear). *Deiparous* (dee IP uh ruhs) is an adjective meaning "bearing a god." (The Greeks and Romans were deeply interested in the genealogy of their divinities.) Now, as to *theotokion,* that is a "hymn of the Eastern (i.e., Greek Orthodox) Church in praise of the Virgin Mary as the Mother of God." That hymn forms the final *troparion* (troh PAIR ee uhn) of a canonical ode. And what is a *troparion?* That is the term for a short hymn chanted liturgically in rhythmic prose during services in the Eastern Church, specifically a stanza of one of the nine scriptural canticles forming part of the morning service of the Eastern Church on certain designated days of the year. If you want to hear one, consult the calendar of your friendly neighborhood Eastern Church (Greek, Russian, Ukrainian or whatever) and don't be late.

theotokos See **theotokion.**

Therapeutae (ther uh PYOOH tee) *n. pl. Therapeuein* is a Greek verb with a number of related meanings, starting with "to attend" (generally) and continuing with "to worship" and "to attend medically," which is the basis of our familiar noun *therapy,* meaning "medical treatment" generally but these days commonly taken as a shortened form of *psychotherapy.* It is the senses of *attend* and *worship* that gave rise to the name *Therapeutae,* New Latin from Greek *therapeutai,* the plural of *therapeutes* (attendant, worshiper, medical attendant), denoting a sect of Jewish mystics who lived in Egypt in the first century A.D. The Alexandrian Jewish theologian Philo (c. 20 B.C.–c. A.D. 50) described them as ascetics devoted to meditation and contemplation. The sect resembled the

Essenes, but unlike them, it included women. Their name is sometimes anglicized to *Therapeuts*, by which name they are mentioned in the English translation of David F. Strauss's *New Life of Jesus* (1865). They were taken, says Strauss, as "the Egyptian branch of the Essenes," and Robert A. Vaughan, in *Hours with the Mystics* (1856), called them "a sect similar to the Essenes, [numbering] many ... whose lives are truly exemplary." When I first ran across this word, I mistook it as a term for ancient physicians, but the uppercase *T* made me sufficiently inquisitive to indulge in a little investigation, and the foregoing tells the story.

therianthropic (thair ee an THROP ik) *adj.* This adjective is descriptive of an organism combining human and animal forms, and *therianthropism* (thar ee AN throp iz'm) is the "representation of such forms or the worship of them as gods." *Ther* and *Therion* mean "wild beast" in Greek, and our old friend *anthropos* is "man," as we know from words like *anthropology, anthropoid*, etc. *Theriolatry* (thair ee OL uh tree) is "animal worship," *-latry* being based on Greek *latreia* (worship). *Theriomorphism* (thair ee oh MOR fiz'm) is "belief in gods with the form of beasts." The Egyptians worshiped the deity Anubis in the form of a jackal, Horus in the form of a falcon and other animal gods. The *-morphism* came from Greek *morphe* (form). Getting back to *therianthropism*, the Egyptian goddess Hathor had a woman's body and a cow's head; Anubis was sometimes represented as a man with the head of a jackal; Thoth had the body of a man and the head of an ibis; Medusa had wings, and snakes for hair; and the well-known Sphinx was a winged lion with a human head or at times a ram's or hawk's head. These deities must have made religion quite fascinating (and scary) in the old days and a lot more absorbing than the dry sermons that required the services of a church official who went around waking up little boys by tickling them with a feather in colonial days. See also **manticore** and **theroid**.

theroid (THAIR oid) *adj. Thero-* is the combining form of the Greek noun *ther* (wild beast), which has given us a number of words having to do with the animal form or nature. *Theroid* describes a person brutish in form or nature. The Greek word *theroeides*, combining *thero-* with *eidos* (form), is the immediate ancestor of *theroid*. Henry Maudsley's *Body and Mind* (1870) tells us: "There is a class of idiots which may justly be designated *theroid*, so like brutes are the members of it." Mention has been made in scientific journals of the appearance of animal peculiarities of anatomy in persons exhibiting *theroid* mental characteristics. *Therio-* is the combining form of a related Greek noun, *therion* (wild animal) and has also given us words having to do with animal life and representation. Cf. **therianthropic** and the related words discussed there.

thesis   See **hemiola**.

thirdings   See **heriot**.

thurible (THOOR uh b'l) *n.* A *thurible* is a "censer," a vessel in which incense is burned, as in religious ceremonies. *Thurification* is the "burning of incense," and a *thurifer* is an "acolyte who carries and swings the censer." The Latin source of these words is *t(h)uribulum*, and that is based on the Latin noun *t(h)us* (frankincense—which goes back to Old French *franc encens*, meaning "pure incense"); and there is actually an English noun *thus*, pronounced the way it looks, or *THOOHS*, if you think that this *thus* pronounced *THUS* is confusing. Zarathustra never spake incense, just thus. As Macbeth spake in Act III, Scene 1: "To be thus is nothing;/But to be safely thus." And as Artemus Ward says in *Moses, the Sassy*: "Why is this thus? What is the reason of this thusness?" The reason is that who would have thought that *thus* (incense) could ever have been defined thus? Let us discard this *thus*; a *thus* by any other name would smell as sweet.

tombac (TOM bahk) *n.* This word has appeared in a great variety of forms: *tombaga, tambaycke, tumbeck, tombago, tambaqua, tumbanck* and goodness (or the *O.E.D.*) knows what else. The current form, adopted from French, is *tombac*, equivalent to Italian *tombacco*, Portuguese *tambaca*, Spanish *tumbaga* and, adopted from Malay, *tambâga*. Whatever the form, it is the name of an alloy that originated in the East Indies, of copper and zinc in varying proportions, mostly copper (82 to 99%). It is found in the East in gongs, bells, etc., and in Europe (under different names: Prince's metal, Mannheim gold, etc.) it is used in the manufacture of cheap jewelry. There is *red tombac* (more than 92% copper), *yellow tombac* (82 to 90% copper) and *white tombac*, in which arsenic replaces zinc and the alloy. By its various names, *tombac* is mentioned in travel literature over the years from 1608 to 1872. In some of the words, the *tombac* is a mixture of gold and copper, copper, tin and zinc, etc. Whether it is used today or not, it would make a good (if rather easy) anagram in crossword puzzles.

tragelaph   See **hircine.**

triage (tree AZH, TREE uhj) *n.* *Triage* is French for "sorting, selection," a noun of action from the verb *trier* (to choose, sort, select). Our verb *try* is related in that it comes via Middle English *trien* from Old French *trier* (to pick out, sift). The *O.E.D.* makes short work of *triage*, confining the definition to "the act of assorting according to quality," and quotes examples of its use in sorting fleece and coffee beans. The *Supplement* goes much further, extending the use of the word to the assignment of degrees of urgency to wounds or illnesses so as to determine the order of treatment. A quote from a 1974 issue of *Time* further extends its use as follows: "In the West, there is increasing talk of *triage*, a commonsense if callous concept that teaches that when resources are scarce, they must be used where they will do most good." More specifically, a 1975 issue of the Toronto *Globe and Mail* states: "The concept [of *triage*] should now be applied to countries crippled by food shortages, famine and overpopulation ... ," and a 1979 issue of *The Guardian* (London) carries the use of what by now has become a quite versatile word a step further: "There is (*sc.* in New York) an unofficial '*triage*' system in which teachers and school administrators concentrate their limited resources on helping those students who seem to be capable of succeeding." W III describes "the process of grading marketable produce" as a British sense of the word, and adds the definition "the lowest grade of coffee berries consisting of broken material." Its definition relating to "patients and esp[ecially] battle and disaster victims" specifies the purpose of this type of *triage*: "to maximize the number of survivors." If you run into the word, you will have to use a certain degree of *triage* yourself to determine whether you are dealing with broken coffee beans, famine, teachers and students, hospitals or battle and disaster victims. Quite a word. What next? Dating services, marriage bureaus, harems?

trigamy   See **digamy.**

trim   See **trimmer.**

trimmer (TRIM ur) *n.* This word obviously means "one who *trims*," but the verb *to trim* has an unusually large number of meanings (16 in the *O.E.D.*). One of them is "to modify one's attitude in order to stand well with opposite parties; to move cautiously, or 'balance' between two alternative interests, positions, opinions, etc."; in other words, "to sit on the fence," to maintain neutrality on a controversial issue, to act as a *mugwump,* a term originally applied to Republicans who denied support to James G. Blaine, their party's nominee in the 1884 presidential election. Despite the popular belief that *mugwump* came from the expression "to sit on the fence with one's *mug* on one side and one's *wump* [rump] on the other," it was taken from the Algonquian language, where it meant, literally, "great man," and satirically "big shot." From that sense of *trim,* the word *trimmer* was applied to one who *trimmed* between opposing political parties and came to denote any person who performed a "balancing act" between two parties or opinions so as to stay in favor with both sides. There is another angle on *trimmer.* To *trim* a boat is "to balance it so that it doesn't capsize." In politics, this means balancing between the extremities of rival factions that threaten the "ship of state." Such was the argument used by George Savile, marquis of Halifax, to justify his own policy in the British constitutional troubles of the 1680s. In this sense he wrote a pamphlet entitled *The Character of a Trimmer,* published in 1688, which includes an eloquent passage to the effect that the only thing a *trimmer* is *un*compromising about is his patriotic opposition to foreign designs of invasion and the like. Perhaps he was an early advocate of the "extreme center." Savile described the *trimmer* as follows:

> Our *Trimmer* is far from Idolatry in other things, in one thing only he cometh near it, his Country is in some degree his Idol; he doth not

Worship the Sun, because 'tis not peculiar to us, it rambles about the World, and is less kind to us than others [kindly note the 17th-century observation about the English weather with its "sunny intervals" and "showery spells"; there'll always be an England]; but for the Earth of England, tho perhaps inferior to that of many places abroad, to him there is a Divinity in it, and he would rather dye, than see a spire of *English* grass trampled down by a foreign Trespasser.

Shades of Mrs. Thatcher and her pretty rough speeches these days to those at Brussels who would have England cede some of her sovereignty to the say of a tighter E.C.! In an 1872 issue of his *Journal*, Sir Walter Scott spoke of "an attempt to govern *par bascule* [by see-saw]—by *trimming* betwixt the opposite parties." As to the adoption of *trim* and *trimmer* in that sense, I would incline to credit it to the 14th definition in the long *O.E.D.* list: "*Naut[ical]*. To adjust (the sails or yards) with reference to the direction of the wind and the course of the ship, so as to obtain the greatest advantage." To sum up: A *trimmer* is a "timeserver," and that's the long and short (or middle-sized) of it.

tripody   See **prosodion.**

triptych   See **polyptych.**

triptyque   See **polyptych.**

trochee   See **dolichurus.**

troparion   See **theotokion.**

tuft (TUFT) *n. Tuft*, in its common uses, is a familiar word, but one use in British English may come as a surprise. A *tuft* is a "gold tassel" that formerly adorned the top of a mortarboard (the "cap" that is a part of the uniform known as "cap and gown," also called *academicals* in British English) worn by undergraduates at Oxford and Cambridge. Originally, this distinction in dress was a privilege allowed only to the sons of peers having a vote in the House of Lords. Later, this privilege was granted to all peers and their eldest sons, and in 1870 it was made optional. *Tuft* was university slang for a student with that privilege. Thackeray, in *A Shabby-genteel Story* (1840), tells of a "lad [who] went to Oxford ... frequented the best society [and] followed with a kind of proud obsequiousness all the *tufts* of the university." The term *tuft-hunter* was originally applied to those who obsequiously sought the society of the university *tufts*. Later, it included any person who sought to become a familiar of persons of title or rank generally, and eventually it was applied to any toady or sycophant. Thackeray used the term in *The Newcomes; Members of a Most Respectable Family* (1855), in a passage describing a person who "was accused ... of being a *tuft-hunter* and flatterer of the aristocracy." In his *Personal and Literary*

Memorials (1829), Henry Beste wrote of one who "made no disgraceful *tuft-hunting* distinctions in favour of noblemen ... " *Tuft-hunting* is a special brand of *lion-hunting* in the sense of chasing after celebrities and persons of rank, a strenuous activity of certain party-giving social climbers whose names become all too familiar to readers of gossip columns.

tuft-hunter   See **tuft.**

tychism (TEYE kiz'm) *n. Tyche* is Greek for "chance" and with an uppercase *T* was the name of the goddess of fortune. When the gentleman gambler in Frank Loesser's *Guys and Dolls* sang "Luck, be a lady tonight," he *was* addressing a lady—a goddess. *Tyche*, with an upper- or lowercase initial, lent her (or its) name to *tychism*, the doctrine that the element of chance must be taken into account in reasoning, whether cosmological, philosophical or other. The word was coined by the U.S. mathematician and philosopher C. S. Pierce in 1892, who said: "I endeavored to show what ideas ought to form the warp of a system of philosophy, and particularly emphasised that of absolute chance ... which it will be convenient to christen *tychism* (from *tyche*, chance)." In his *Study in Moral Theory* (1926), J. Laird wrote: "The theory that every event ... *must* occur precisely as it does occur I shall call *determinism* ... The opposite theory I shall call *tychism* ... either general or restricted." A 1978 issue of *Scientific American* carried the statement that " ... Pierce's doctrine of *'tychism* ' maintained that pure chance—events undetermined by prior causes—are basic to the universe." In reference to its *chance* discovery, a rare mineral consisting of carbonate and sulphate of magnesium and sodium was christened *tychite*. (I didn't know mineralogists were that well versed in Greek.) There is a series of *tycho-* scientific terms, among them *tychoparthenogenesis* (teye koh par thuh noh JEN uh sis—exceptional parthenogenesis, that term meaning "egg development without fertilization," from Greek *parthenos*, maiden, hence the Parthenon in Athens, dedicated to the virgin goddes Athene, plus *genesis*, origin) and *tychopotamic* (teye koh POT uh mik—occurring occasionally in or near rivers, *potamos* being Greek for "river"), referring to the floating organisms of pools and overflows from rivers). Probably superfluous caveat: Do not confuse any of those *tycho-* words with *Tychonic* (teye KON ik), which describes anything relating to the Danish astronomer Tycho Brahe (1546–1601) or his system of astronomy, or *Tychonian* (teye KOH nee uhn), a disciple of that system. Ignorant of the term *tychism*, and unsatisfied with *randomness*, I coined *randomism* years ago when asked to define my creed.

Tychonian   See **tychism.**

Tychonic   See **tychism.**

tychoparthenogenesis   See **tychism.**

tychopotamic   See **tychism.**

tyrosemiophile (teye roh SEM ee oh file) *n.* I am going to include a second, entirely unrelated word in this discussion: **misapodysis** (mis uh puh DEYE sis). Both words are borrowed from Philip Howard's instructive and entertaining column "Word-Watching" in *The Times* (London). They are chosen as a demonstration that if you know enough Greek roots, you can string selected ones together and invent interesting words that fill a need and obviate circumlocutions. I say "invent" because my search has revealed no lexicographical inclusion of either word. *Tyrosemiophile* : Take *tyro-*, the combining form of *tyros* (cheese); add *semio-*, the combining form of *semeion* (mark, sign); then add *-phile*, from *philia* (loving), and you have "cheese-mark-fancier," a term applied, according to Mr. Howard, to "collectors of the labels on French cheese boxes." (Whence "French" and whence "boxes," Mr. Howard? What about Edam, Gouda, Emmenthal, Jarlsberg, Muenster, Provolone, Gorgonzola, Cheddar, Double Gloucester, Leicestershire, Liederkranz, boxed or unboxed?) A not very useful word, perhaps, but what else would you call a *cheeseboxlabelfancier*? The word appeared in a work by the American writer Thomas Pynchon, who is never timid about coining neologisms. Now *misapodysis*: Take *mis-*, the combining form of *misein* (to hate) or *misos* (hatred); add *apodysis*, from *apodyesthai* (to undress), formed of the prefix *apo-* (away, off) plus *dyesthai* (to dress), and you get *hatred of undressing* (i.e., in public, before someone). An extreme case of *misapodysis* is found in the practice, in some nunneries, of bathing in one's nightie, even in private, or so I'm told. *Apodysis*: how else avoid the cumbersome circumlocution?

tzedaka(h) (tse DOK uh) *n.* You will have found that the great majority of words discussed in this book are of classical Greek or Latin origin, but words of many other origins have been included as well. After all, we are one world, and the nations are dependent on one another for many aspects of life, including language. The English language has long been internationalist; no isolationism in that department. We borrow these foreign words that can't be quite fully translated in a way that conveys all of their subtle connotations. We speak of *Zeitgeist* (German for the "spirit of the age"); *dolce far niente* (Italian for "pleasant idleness"); *entre nous* (French for "between ourselves"); *mañana* (Spanish for "tomorrow—some time in the future"); and *guru* (Sanskrit for "wise leader"). And we have loaned as well as borrowed, when our foreign cousins have seen fit to adopt an English term not quite translatable into their vocabulary. Here, we have *tzedaka(h)*, taken from Hebrew *sedaqah* (righteousness). *Tzedaka(h)* means "charity," and specifically, the "duty to help fellow Jews." Freemasons, Elks, Rotarians and countless other groups, as well as ethnic or national enclaves of co-nationals in foreign lands, feel that type of obligation, but the Jews, against the background of millennia of persecution, feel it especially strongly. Dagobert David Runes, in his *Concise Dictionary of Judaism* (1959), defines *tzedakah* as "righteousness; charity." The 1962 *New*

Jewish Encyclopedia tells us: "The Jewish concept of 'charity' has ... been refined to mean more than the mere giving of alms; it has been considered as 'Tzedakah,' an act of justice and righteousness." In *The Joys of Yiddish* (1968) Leo Rosten discusses *tzedaka* and its variant *tsadaka* extensively and gives their origin as Hebrew *tzedek* (righteousness). His definition: "The obligation to extablish justice by being righteous, upright, compassionate—and above all, helping one's fellow man." He quotes Josephus (Jewish scholar, first century A.D.): "He who refuses a suppliant the aid which he has the power to give, is accountable to justice." A noble sentiment indeed; and to plunge from the sublime, how about the Yiddish *chutzpah* (unmitigated effrontery, gall, cheek, nerve), *shlemiel* (simpleton, loser), *shlep* (drag, pull), *mavin* (expert, connoisseur), *megillah* (long, prolix account, rigmarole)? These loan words have been naturalized into English and can be found in many an English dictionary. I have occasionally performed an act of *tzedaka(h)* in explaining one of them to an unenlightened *goy*.

Ucalegon (yooh KAL uh gon) *n.* A *Ucalegon* is a "next-door neighbor whose house is on fire." I received a letter from a reader in Lafayette, Louisiana, in which (after words of praise, I am happy to say, about my *1000 Most Challenging Words*), she wrote: "I wonder ... that you could refrain from including the word 'ucalegon.' This is a splendid word that I have had the opportunity to use once in my life, when my husband called me to say that our next-door neighbor's house was on fire. 'Oh,' I said, 'then we have a *ucalegon*.' I think he has been a little in awe of me ever since." That sent me to the dictionaries, and I found only one that listed *Ucalegon*, but that was with an uppercase *U*. The winning dictionary was good old *W II*, and there I read: "*Ucalegon* (u-kal-e-gon) *n.* ... In Trojan legend, one of the ancient counselors who sat with Priam on the wall. Aeneas speaks of the flames reaching *Ucalegon*'s house, next to that of Anchises [father of Aeneas], before he fled from the city. Hence, a next-door neighbor whose house is on fire." In this delightful *W II* item, the pronunciation parenthesis includes a symbol over the *u* giving it a *yooh* sound, as in *unite*, the accent on the *kal*, and a schwa symbol over the *e*, all resulting in *yooh KAL uh gon*. *W II* sent me to the *Aeneid*, where I read, in translation, that in answer to Queen Dido's plea, at the end of Book I, to Aeneas to tell her about "Grecian guile, your people's trials," he commences (start of Book II) his recital of the destruction of Troy. Fire is everywhere. "The spacious palace of Deiphobus has fallen, victim of the towering Vulcan. And now, *Ucalegon*'s his neighbor, burns ... " In the beautiful compressed style of the original, the four significant words are " ... *iam proximus ardet Ucalegon*." (Book II, lines 310/311.) The foregoing translation is that of Allen Mandelbaum (University of California Press, 1971). I find "*Ucalegon*'s, his neighbor, burns" awkward. Such are the demands of prosody, one supposes, but I don't know why this wonderful scholar decided to substitute his iambic pentameter for Virgil's heroic dactylic hexameter in the first place, though who am I to begrudge the excellent man his privilege? So you see there did exist a *Ucalegon*, complete with uppercase *U*, and my correspondent was perfectly correct in her awe-inspiring response to her husband's cry of alarm. I have advised her, however, that she must capitalize the *U* even though the name is used generically, just as we must capitalize the initial in *Sherlock* when we characterize someone as a "regular Sherlock" for having solved a mystery, or the *E* in Einstein when we call someone "an Einstein" because he has an I.Q. of 200+. The generic use of the eponymous original's name doesn't deprive him of his uppercase initial. Getting back to the translation of the Latin, *Bartlett's Familiar Quotations* gives us: "*Ucalegon's* afire next door," while *The Oxford Dictionary of Quotations* presents: "Already neighbor *Ucalegon* burns," which is most faithful to the original; but alas, in a dazzling display of metathesis, the second (1953) edition index misspells *Ucalegon* "*Ucelagon*," and in the third (1979) edition the quotation has disappeared!

ultroneous (ul TROH nee uhs) *adj.* *Ultro* is a Latin adverb with a variety of meanings. It shares with *ultra* the meanings "on the farther side, beyond" and is thought to be derived from *ulter*, a supposititious word, i.e., one not found in Latin literature but assumed to be the basis of a derived form, in this case *ultro*. *Ultro* has many more meanings than the more common *ultra*: "besides, moreover, also" and figuratively, "superfluously, wantonly," but its relationship to *ultroneous* is explained by its additional meanings "spontaneously, voluntarily, of one's own accord, unasked." *Ultroneous*, then, means all those things, but in adjectival use. Sir William Hamilton, in *Discussions on Philosophy and Literature, Education and University Reform* (1852), expressed the opinion that "the exercise of the student in the University classes, should be partly exigible [requirable, non-optional], partly *ultroneous*." A witness who testifies of his own accord without being cited [subpoenaed] is described as *ultroneous* in Scots law; it used to be inadmissible but is now merely considered less credible than that of one who has been required to testify. In *Horae Subsecivae* (Spare Time, Unoccupied Hours—1863), James Brown used *ultroneousness* in a special sense: "The law of personality, of *ultroneousness*, of *free will*, that which in a great measure makes us what we are ... "

upaithric   See **hypaethral.**

usquebaugh (US kwih baw, -bah) *n.* The *O.E.D.* lists 21 variant spellings of this word! It is derived from Irish and Scots Gaelic *uisce* or *uisge* (water) plus *beatha* (life), i.e., "water of life," and in this respect is akin to Latin *aqua* (water) *vitae* (of life—genitive of *vita*). *Aqua vitae*, which today denotes alcoholic liquor, was originally a term in alchemy. The related *aquavit* or *akvavit* is a very dry Scandinavian ginlike liquor flavored with caraway seeds. Well, after all this learned etymology, what do you suppose *usquebaugh* is? Whiskey! Just good old plain old whiskey. In Farquhar's *The Beaux' Stratagem* (1706) we read, "An honest Gentleman that came this way from Ireland made her a Present of a dozen bottles of *Usquebaugh*." In one of his *Waverley Novels, The Legend of Montrose*, Sir Walter Scott wrote of "a flask of *usquebae*, designed for the refreshment of Lord Menteith." I don't think it would do you much good, in an English pub or an American bar, to ask for an *usquebaugh*, whether straight (or as the British say, neat), or with water or soda. You can give it a try, but I'd stick to *whiskey*, or, in the British spelling, *whisky*, though the Irish retain the *e*.

usucapient   See **usucapion.**

usucapion (yooh zooh KAY pee uhn) *n*. In Roman law, this is the term for the acquisition of ownership of property through long uninterrupted and undisputed use. Such use is known in our legal system as "prescription," and the right so acquired is called "prescriptive." The term under Roman law was one year for personal property (chattels) and two years for real property. The term of possession under our law varies from jurisdiction to jurisdiction. Easements, as well as ownership rights, are acquired in this fashion. *Usucaption* (yooh zooh KAP shuhn) is a variant form. To acquire such title is to *usucapt* (yooh zooh KAPT) it, and one claiming such title is a *usucapient* (yooh zooh KAYP ee uhnt) or *usucaptor* (yooh zoo KAP tuhr). All of these words are derived from Latin *usucapere* (to acquire ownership by length of use, to obtain by prescription), formed of *usu* (by use—the ablative of *usus*, use) plus *capere* (to take). Beware of squatters! They could wind up owning what you had fondly gone on believing was yours.

usucapt   See **usucapion.**

usucaptor   See **usucapion.**

vellicate (VEL uh kate) *vb*. In Latin, *villicare* means "to pluck" or "twitch"; it is the frequentative of *vellere*. (A *frequentative*, which I discuss in my *1000 Most Challenging Words*, is a verb that serves to express the frequent repetition of an action expressed by another verb. In other words, *vellere* means "to pluck or twitch," and *vellicare* expresses the frequency or nervous repetition of that action.) From *vellicatus*, its past participle, we get *vellicate*, a word not much used these days but common in medical usage in the 17th and 18th centuries, meaning, as a transitive verb, "to irritate (body tissues)," referring to the action of certain medications. It meant as well "to tickle" or "titillate." It was so used by the poet and naturalist Erasmus Darwin, Charles's grandfather, in

Zoonomia, or the Laws of Organic Life (1801): "So when children expect to be tickled in play … by gently *vellicating* the soles of their feet, laughter is most vehemently excited." Intransitively, *to vellicate* is "to twitch or otherwise move convulsively." *Vellication* can be used to denote the act of twitching or tickling, or the twitching of any part of the body, especially a muscle. And in *Letters to and from the Late Samuel Johnson* (1788), edited by Hester Lynch Piozzi (Mrs. Thrale), we read in one from the great S.J.: "These *vellications* of my breast shorten my breath." He used it figuratively in *Prayers and Meditations* (1781): "At night, I had some mental *vellications*, or revulsions." *Vellicative* is the predictable adjective. John Mason Good, in *The Study of Medicine* (1822), wrote: "They [the teeth] are colloquially said to be set on edge … from jarring noises … [or] from *vellicative* or acrid substances." (Or, in my experience, from fingernails scraping along a slate blackboard.)

vellinch (VEL inch) *n.* This word has a variety of spellings. The *O.E.D.* lists *valinche, valincher, velinche* and *velincher,* but no *vellinch,* which is vouched for by *WIII,* where it is said to be a variant of *valinch,* an alteration of *valentia,* itself a modification of the Spanish noun *venencia,* and that, according to my Spanish dictionary, is a "tube for sampling sherry." As to *valentia,* that is Spanish for "courage, gallantry, exploit, boast, great effort, imagination, and—wait!—a second-hand shoe shop in Madrid." What that has to do with tubes for sampling sherry must remain a mystery. A *vellinch* is a "tube for drawing a sample from a cask through the bung-hole," also known as a *shive hole, shive* being a term for a "thin wooden bung" for a cask or a "thin cork" for a wide-mouthed bottle. (*Shive* has lots of other meanings not relevant here. As Casey Stengel was fond of saying: "You could look it up." And once you start looking …) A *vellinch* is sometimes called a *flincher,* which is an obvious corruption of *valincher* or *velincher.* This whole comment is a good sample of the sort of thing you get into if you own a lot of dictionaries.

vespertilio (ves pur TIL ee oh) *n.* Bats come out in the evening, and *vesper* means "evening" in Latin (hence, *Vespers* for evening prayers and the adjective *vespertine,* describing evening phenomena). In my *1000 Most Challenging Words,* under *acronical,* I discuss *vespertine* and *crepuscular* and say that they "cover things that happen in the early evening, at dusk, just after sunset," whereas *acronical* "applies to phenomena occurring at sunset." It is not surprising that the Romans chose *vespertilio* as their word for "bat," and that is what it means in English. In a book by Sir Thomas Herbert published in 1665 with the lovely title *A relation of Some Yeares Travaile Begunne Anno 1626, into Afrique and the Greater Asia,* the author writes that "These *vespertilios* … hang in swarms upon the boughs of Trees." He doesn't add "upside down," the way I've always seen them, but we can infer it. The *Vespertilionidae* are, according to the *O.E.D.,* "a large family of insectivorous bats, including the common British species." The same dictionary lists the tantalizing nonce word *vespertilionize* with the definition "to convert or turn *into* a bat [emphasis is mine]," as used by Charles D. Badham in an 1854 book entitled *Prose Halieutics. Halieutics*, according to the book from which I quoted above, "is the art and science of fishing ... " This partially explains the following sentence from the Badham book: "Others ... have *vespertilionized* this skate into the Sea-bat." But good for Badham: It takes courage to coin a word like *vespertilionize* !

vespetro (VES puh troh) *n.* Quite a word, *vespetro*. It is distinguished in a number of ways. First, it is not in the *O.E.D.* Second, it is the name of an extraordinary alcoholic drink: a liqueur with a base of brandy, to which are added anise, fennel, coriander and angelica, the whole being sweetened with sugar. Angelica is an umbelliferous plant of the genus *Angelica* (*umbelliferous* denotes a member of the family known as *Umbelliferae*, which includes carrots, celery, etc., as well as angelica, characterized by being topped by a cluster rising from a given point at the top of the stalk, known as *umbels*, from Latin *umbella*, sunshade; the type of angelica used in *vespetro* being *Angelica Archangelica*, cultivated for its scent, medicinal qualities, etc.). Now—last but not least—comes the derivation. It was taken as is from the French *vespétro*, which, according to French dictionaries and at least one English dictionary as far as I have discovered (*W III*), is based on three French words: *vesser* (to break wind noiselessly; Cassell's French-English dictionary lists the noun *vesse*, elegantly translated as "silent evacuation of wind" but marked "indecent!"); *péter* (to break wind—no mention of silence this time; *Cassell* gives *péter* a string of meanings, including "to fart," and marks this one "vulgar and not decent."); and *roter* (to belch; no disapproval by *Cassell* this time). So the *ves-* of *vesser* or *vesse*, plus the *pét-* of *péter*, plus the *ro-* of *roter* add up to our headword *vespetro*! But nobody says what farting noiselessly, farting noisily and belching have to do with *vespetro*, and one is left to imagine that indulgence in that rather elegant-sounding liqueur produces a series of inelegant bodily manifestations. I'll have *Armagnac*, if it's all the same to you.

vilipend (VIL uh pend) *vb.* From Latin *vilis* (paltry, mean, worthless, base), which gave us the adjective *vile*, plus *pendere* (to suspend, consider, weigh, estimate), which, from the meaning "suspend" or "weigh" in the literal sense, gave us *pend, pendant, pendent, pending*, etc., we got *vilipend*, meaning "to consider as of little value, to despise, to treat contemptuously, to disparage, to vilify, to abuse." Sir Walter Scott, in *Waverley; or 'tis Sixty Years Since* (1814), wrote of "a youth devoid of that petulant volatility which ... *vilipends* the conversation and advice of seniors." In *Vanity Fair* (1848), Thackeray condemned one for "*vilipending* the poor innocent girl as the basest and most artful of vixens." As an intransitive verb, to *vilipend* is "to be disparaging or depreciatory." *Vilis* and *pendere* gave the French *vilipender*, the Italians *vilipendere* and the Spanish and Portuguese *vilipendiar*, so it seems that the vile practice is rather widespread.

virelay   See **sirvent(e)**.

virga (VUR guh) *n. Virga* is a Latin noun with a number of meanings: "twig, sprout, slender branch, rod, switch, scourge, wand, staff, cane, streak, stripe (a colored stripe in cloth)." The one we are interested in here is "rod," for at least two reasons. *Virga* is the term for trails or wisps of water, drops or bits of ice falling from a cloud but never reaching the ground because they melt or evaporate before they get there. If they reach the surface of the planet, the technical name is *praecipitatio*, which in common parlance is *precipitation*, familiar from TV weathermen's lingo. I said there were two reasons: first, because the wisps or trails of moisture or ice in the air do sometimes resemble *rods*; next, because of the British idiom "to rain stair-rods" where we would say "rain cats and dogs," (which they say as well). The British use of *rods* in their (to us) peculiar phrase is the opposite of the wispy *rods*, i.e., *virgae* (plural of *virga*), which never get to the ground. Their *rods* do get to the ground, and how! (Cf. The French *pleuvoir* or *tomber des hallebardes*, literally "to rain halberds," the 15th- and 16th-century shafted weapons with axelike cutting blades, beaks and spikes.)

virlai   See **sirvent(e)**.

vomitorium (vom ih TOHR ee uhm) *n.* Since this word is recognizably Latin, and because you have probably read about the ancient Roman custom of resorting to self-induced vomiting during a banquet to make room for the next course (by means of tickling the back of the throat with a feather), you might jump to the conclusion (always dangerous in etymology) that a *vomitorium* was some sort of little room where this rather horrid operation was performed. But no: A *vomitorium* was a "passage in an ancient amphitheater leading to and from the seats." The word was anglicized to *vomitory*, an "opening or passage in a theater allowing the audience to enter and leave." Tobias Smollett's *Travels through France and Italy* (1766), describing the ruins of an ancient amphitheater, speaks of " ... the remains of two galleries, one over another; and two *vomitoria* or great gateways at opposite sides of the arena." In *The History of the Decline and Fall of the Roman Empire* (1776), Gibbon writes: "Sixty-four *vomitories* (for by that name the doors were very aptly distinguished) poured forth the immense multitude." No feathers, no tickling; just entering and leaving the amphitheater with the contents of the tummy intact. Nonetheless, the word is dervied from the Latin *vomitus*, the past participle of *vomere* (to vomit), and the exiting (if not the entering) of the spectators through a *vomitorium* is an understandable if somewhat unpredictable extension of the concept.

vorpal (VOR p'l) *adj.* When Alice, in *Through the Looking-Glass*, held the book "in some language she didn't know" up to the mirror, the words went "the right way again," and she read a poem entitled "Jabberwocky," about that frightful beast, the Jabberwock, and how he (whoever the hero was) "took his *vorpal* sword in hand," and how "the *vorpal* blade went snicker-snack" and "he left it dead." " … It's *rather* hard to understand!" said Alice, " … However, *somebody* killed *something*: that's clear, at any rate." Obviously, the blade was very sharp indeed; "keen, deadly," is the definition of *vorpal* given by the *O.E.D. Supplement*. W. H. Auden saw fit to use the word in *New Year Letter* (1941) when he wrote: "Wave at the mechanized barbarian/The *vorpal* sword of an agrarian … "

water-tath   See **tath.**

woop-woop (WOOP woop) *n*. This is a term heard in Australia and New Zealand (sometimes *woop-woops* or *wop-wop*), thought by some to be sham aboriginal, for a "backwooods town or district." It is sometimes preceded by *the* and sometimes capitalized (as two words). The American equivalent would be "one-horse town" or "whistle stop" for a small town, and "boon-docks" for the backwoods; in Britain, a sleepy little town is a "one-eyed village." *Woop-woop* is said by some to come from the "geelorious town o' Whoop-Up" in E. L. Wheeler's *Deadwood Dick on Deck* (1878), a fictitious American gold-mining town way out in the boondocks. The inventor of *woop-woop* certainly went way out of his way geographically if that theory is to be given credence. Vance Marshall, writing under the pseudonym Jice Doone, in *Timely Tips for New Australians* (1926), defines *Woop-Woop* as "a humorous method of alluding to the country districts used most frequently in New South Wales." Noel Harvey Hilliard's *Maori Girl* (1960) contains this bit of conversation: "'Where do you come from?' 'Up in the wilds, the *woop-woops* … '" The term *woop-woop* is sometimes used as well to denote a denizen of the backwoods, a country bumpkin. *Woop-woop* sounds perfectly plausible to me: I've been in Walla Walla.

xeniatrophobia   See **xenodochiophobia.**

xenodochiophobia (zee noh doh kee oh FOH bee uh) *n*. A concoction from a group of Greek elements, this means "fear of foreign hospitality," i.e., worry about foreign hotels. We start with *xenos* (foreign; cf. *xenophobia*); add *doche* (reception, entertainment, hospitality; akin to *dechomai*, to receive hospitably); and wind up with the familiar *phobia*. Voilà: *xenodochiophobia*, a common American ailment inhibiting travel abroad. ("Should I bring along soap? Toilet paper? Disinfectant?") In his letter to the *New York Times* of Sunday, March 12,

1989, Mr. Louis Jay Herman of New York City adds "a few more suggested contributions to the Hellenizing of travel language," to which I shall add a bit of etymology: *cacohydrophobia* (ka koh heye droh FOH bee uh), built of *kakos* (bad), *hydros* (water) and *phobia*, resulting in "fear of bad water," or, as Mr. Herman puts it in a loose but effective translation: "Can I drink what comes out of the tap in this joint?" He continues, "This can also be Latinized as malaquaterror (which speaks for itself) and, for nonclassicists, turistaphobia will do perfectly well." I would even more freely translate *turistaphobia* as "dread of Gyppy tummy, Delhi belly or Montezuma's revenge," but now we're playing fast and loose (accidental but apposite pun). Next: *xeniatrophobia* (zee nee ah troh FOH bee uh), from our old friend *xenos* plus *iatros* (doctor) plus an even older friend *phobia*, meaning "dread of foreign doctors," who suffer not so much from inadequate medical skills as from inadequate acquaintance with the English language, as far as my experience indicates. Now: *xenonosocomiophobia* (zee noh nos oh ko mee oh FOH bee uh), joining *nosos* (mischief), *komion* (carrying off) and our intimate friend *phobia*, meaning "fear of foreign pickpockets," who, in my travels, have proven more adept than our own pros. Finally: *hypselotimophobia* (hip suh loh tim oh FOH bee uh), from *hypselos* (high), *timos* (price; lo! the cascading dollar!) and the by-now *Ancient Mariner*-type clinging albatross *phobia*, adding up to "fear of astronomical prices" (have you had breakfast in Tokyo lately?). There being no classical Greek for *airplane*, I can't manufacture a classical etymology for "dread of plunging airplane," but the English will suffice, unless you prefer *Icarianism* or *Phaethonianism* (see the former in my *1000 Most Challenging Words*).

xenonosocomiophobia   See **xenodochiophobia.**

yarmulke   See **zucchetto.**

zariba (zah REYE buh) *n*. This is an Arabic word, taken over intact, for "cattle pen" or "enclosure," from the root *zarabu* (to shut in). In parts of Africa, especially the Sudan, a *zariba* is an "enclosure, commonly built of thornbush, to ward off attack from enemies or wild animals," but the term is applied generally to any fortified camp. The transliteration of the Arabic has taken a number of different forms. In O'Reilly's translation of Werne's *Expedition to the Sources of the White Nile* (1849) we find: "A shining *seriba* of reeds, the stalks of which ... perhaps only afford resistance to *tame* animals," a description seemingly at variance with the reference to wild animals in the definition given above. The poet Eliza Dook's *Journal* (1852) notes: "The Sultan has planted a *zeribeh*, or circular inclosure, with two issues." Note *planted*, which must refer to thornbush; the *issues* were outlets. Sir Samuel Baker's *The Nile Tributaries of Abyssinia* (1867) tells us: "We employed ourselves ... in cutting thorn branches, and constructing a *zareeba*." The term has also been applied to a troop formation to resist attack and was used figuratively in an article by A. White in an 1898 issue of the *National Review*: "The ... Tsar ... is ... surrounded by a *zereba* of detail and enticed from affairs of State by organized diversions." The word has also been used as a verb. Intransitively, *to zariba* is "to build a *zariba*." An 1885 issue of *The Nineteenth Century* contains the following: "Orders were given to *zereba* ourselves ... The Brigadier ordered the force to *zereba* on the best position that was near." A year later, the *Contemporary Review* described "a large garden, *zarebaed* in with aloes and henna." I feel *zaribaed* in myself, with many more obscure words to write about. Good word, though.

zarzuela (zar ZWAY luh, -ZWEE-) *n.* This is the name of a traditional type of Spanish operetta with spoken dialogue, often on a topical theme treated satirically. It gets its Spanish name from the *Real Sitio de la Zarzuela* (Royal Residence of the Comic Opera), a palace near Madrid, where the first *zarzuela* was performed in 1629. Joseph Hergesheimer, in *Bright Shawl* (1922), defined the *zarzuelas* as "operettas of one act, largely improvised with local allusions." A 1973 issue of the *Oxford Times* tells us: "The modern *zarzuelas* are really operettas or lyric dramas, which are a kind of Spanish equivalent of Gilbert and Sullivan and the Viennese operetta, full of tunes which have become part of Spain's popular culture." Back in 1888 *Lippincott's Magazine* mentioned " ... the absurd things ... seen in pantomimes by the *zarzuela* companies at the theatres." Pantomimes are an English specialty, dramatic entertainments produced for children and others in the Christmas season, usually based on fairy tales and legends, with songs, dances, lots of clowning, topical jokes and familiar stock roles. The *Lippincott* reference to "pantomimes by the *zarzuela* companies" may give British readers some idea of the nature of this Spanish entertainment.

zetetic (zee TET ik) *n.* As an adjective, *zetetic* means "investigating, inquiring" or "proceeding by investigation or inquiry"; as a noun, in the singular or plural form *zetetics* (but always treated as a singular), it means "inquiry, investigation." It is derived via Modern Latin *zeteticus* from Greek *zetetikos*, based on the verb *zetein* (to seek). In *The History of Philosophy* (1660), Thomas Stanley informs us that the *"Zetetic* Philosophy" was so called "from its continual enquiry after Truth" (a lofty aim, we must agree!). An 1859 book by S. B. Rowbotham entitled *Zetetic Astronomy* had the subtitle: "A description of several experiments which prove that the surface of the sea is a perfect plane and that the Earth is not a Globe!" The exclamation point is part of the subtitle, not mine, apparently stressing the validity of the conclusion in the face of the established belief to the contrary. An 1853 edition of William Thomson's *Outline of the Laws of Thought* tells us: "[Logic] has been called … *Zetetic* or the Art of seeking." *Zetetic* also has the meaning "investigator, inquirer," and the term was used more specifically to denote an adherent of the Greek skeptic school of philosophy. Rowbotham's *Dictionary* (1858) tells us that "the ancient *Pyrrhonists* were called *Zetetics* or seekers." Pyrrho of Elis (c. 300 B.C.) was the founder of the first school of skeptic philosophy, which held that it was impossible to achieve certainty of knowledge. He advocated universal skepticism, and the term *pyrrhonism* came to acquire the meaning of "skepticism" generally or "absolute incredulity." His disciples were known as *pyrrhonists*, and it seems wrong to identify them as *zetetics*. To *Pyrrhonize* is to practice *pyrrhonism*, i.e., "to doubt everything." Wouldn't the good citizens of Missouri be astonished to discover that they were all *pyrrhonists*?

ziggurat (ZIG oo rat), also **zik(k)urat** (ZIK oo rat), *n*. Thus we identify an Assyrian or Babylonian temple tower of pyramidal form in which each ascending story is smaller than the one below, so that a terrace is left all the way around. The January 5, 1898 issue of the *English History Review* mentions the "*ziggurat*, or great tower, of which the Tower of Babel was a famous example." Joining the successive stepped-back stages were outside staircases, and the whole structure was surmounted by a shrine. Its name was taken from the Akkadian word *ziqqurratu* (height, pinnacle), Akkad being the northern division of ancient Babylonia and the Accad mentioned in Gen. 10:10, where we read that "the beginning of his [Nimrod, the mighty hunter's] kingdom was Babel, and Erech, and *Accad* … " Some identify Akkad with Agade, about 18 miles south-southwest of what is now Baghdad, the capital of Iraq, which the Ayatollah would have loved to get his hands on. Ah, history! All the way from the *Ziggurat* of Babel to pal Khomeini.

Zingg (ZING) *adj*. Theodore *Zingg*, born in 1905, was a Swiss meteorologist who specialized in petrology, the study of rocks: their origin, mineral and chemical composition and alteration. He developed a system of classification of pebble shapes (apparently, there's a system for everything) in which two ratios are formed from three mutually perpendicular diameters, and these are used to classify pebbles as belonging to certain fixed shape categories. His system is known to petrologists as the *Zingg system*. Petrologists are concerned about the relation between sphericity and the *Zingg* shape indices. There are four basic *Zingg* shapes: disks, spheres, blades and rods. You and I walk along the beach and admire the pretty colors, and sometimes the shapes, of those millions and millions of pebbles, but I don't think we pay much attention to *Zingg* classification. On coming across a particularly striking little pebble, we might exclaim, "Zing! Isn't that one a beauty!" but that kind of *zing* has nothing to do with friend Theodore.

zizis   See **daven.**

zoanthropy (zoh AN thruh pee) *n. Zoanthropy* is a type of monomania, a form of insanity restricted to one subject, in a person otherwise sane (*monomania*, from the Greek adjective *monos*, single, alone, plus *mania*, madness). The subject in *zoanthropy* is the belief of a human being that he is an animal. The derivation, here too, is elementary: *zoon* (animal) plus *anthropos* (man), both Greek nouns. One form of *zoanthropy* is *lycanthropy*, in which the person imagines himself to be a wolf; from Greek *lykos* (wolf) plus our old friend *anthropos*. We have heard about the werewolf, or wolf-man, a person afflicted with *lycanthropy*, also known as a *lycanthrope* or *lycanthropist*. *Werewolf*, also *werwolf*, is from Old English *werwulf*, formed of *wer* (man—related to Latin *vir*) plus *wulf* (wolf). There are many legends about werewolves, men who could assume the form of wolves, with the appetite of wolves, who roamed about at night devouring infants. The Greek historian Herodotus (fifth century B.C.) tells us about the tribe of Neuri, who could turn themselves into wolves once a year. A member of the family of Antaeus, the giant wrestler slain by Hercules, was selected annually by lot to become a wolf for nine years. Other legends involved other animals: When wolves disappeared in England, witches often "became" cats. And haven't I read somewhere about enchanted princes who became frogs?

zoetrope   See **phenakistoscope.**

zootrope   See **phenakistoscope.**

zucchetto (zooh KET oh, tsooh-) *n. Zucca*, in Italian, means "pumpkin, gourd" and colloquially "head," or, in equivalent slang, "bean, nut, noodle," etc. *Zucchetta* is its diminutive: "small pumpkin," or what the British call "marrow," a vegetable not seen in America, really a large variety of what we call "zucchini," a plural—one never hears of a "zucchino"—and what the British as well as the French call "courgettes." Enough of this botany: Change the *a* to *o* and you have *zucchetto*, meaning "skullcap" in Italian and English (finally!) and particularly the round cap worn by Roman Catholic ecclesiastics, differing in color according to rank: black for priests, violet for bishops, red for cardinals and white for the Pope. Before we get away from the etymology, the Italian *zucca*, in its colloquial sense, has a synonym, *cucuzza*, and that may go back to Latin *cucurbita* (gourd). *Zucchetto* has a synonym, *calotte*, which has a variety of additional meanings in the field of architecture that have nothing to do with ecclesiastical skullcaps: "small dome, upper zone of a dome, inner dome of a double dome, metal cap for a cupola." *Calotte* comes via French from Italian *calotta*, which in turn comes from Greek *kalyptra* (cover), a word that has itself been taken intact into English as a botanical term denoting a hood that covers a number of botanical features and is related to the Greek verb *kaliptein* (to cover). In J. D. H. Dale's translation of Baldeschi's *Ceremonial*

According to the Roman Rite (1853) certain clerics are advised that "They should take off their *zucchettos* in the act of genuflecting," and in M. J. F. McCarthy's *Five Years in Ireland* (1901) there is the tale of how "[Pope] Leo XIII ... took off the *Zucchetta* (sic) he had been wearing and gave it to [one] Father O'Brien." Another type of cap worn by Roman Catholic ecclesiastics is the *biretta*, which is quite different from the small, round *zucchetto*, in that it is square and stiff and has three or four upright projecting pieces that go from the center of the cap to the edges. It is called *berretta* in Italian and sometimes in English and at times is spelled *biretta*. It is derived from Late Latin *birretum* and is akin to *beret*. Another type of religious skullcap is the *yarmulke* (YAR muhl kuh), worn by Orthodox Jewish males most of the time, always during prayer and religious study, and usually by all Jewish males while attending religious rites like Bar Mitzvahs.

zumbooruk (ZUM booh ruk, zum BOO-) *n*. This word, subject to a number of spelling variations like so many words of Hindustani origin, derived from the Hindustani noun *zamburak*, based on the Persian word *zambur* (hornet), is the name of a small cannon mounted on a swivel, especially one fired from a support mounted on the back of a camel. The gunner was known as a *zumboorukchee*. James B. Fraser, in *Travels in Koordistan, Mesopotamia, etc.* (1840) mentions "a large body of *zumboorukchees*," and a 1904 issue of *Blackwell's Magazine* describes "rakish swivel-guns, bell-mouthed *zumbooraks*." From reports in travel books about India in the old days, it appears that the swiftness of camels and the skill of *zumboorukchees* combined to produce a very effective weapon.

zumboorukchee　　See **zumbooruk.**

zyme　　See **zymurgy.**

zymite　　See **zymurgy.**

zymurgy (ZEYE mur jee) *n*. This is a word easy to find in any dictionary, since it's sure to be on the last page. From Greek *zyme* (leaven, ferment) plus *-ourgia*, based on *ergon* (work), *zymurgy* is the "branch of technological chemistry that deals with fermentation processes," as in wine making, brewing and distilling. *Zyme* is itself a word in English, taken intact from the Greek, meaning "ferment" (the chemical reaction, not the psychological kind involving agitation and inner tumult), and its adjective is *zymic*. There is a whole series of *zym*-words having to do with fermentation, but my favorite is *zymite*, designating a priest who uses leavened bread in the Eucharist.